MARKETING AND PUBLIC RELATIONS FOR MUSEUMS, GALLERIES, CULTURAL AND HERITAGE ATTRACTIONS

Visitors to museums, galleries, heritage sites and other not-for-profit attractions receive their information in changing ways. Communications channels are shifting and developing all the time, presenting new challenges to cultural PR and Marketing teams. *Marketing and Public Relations for Museums, Galleries, Cultural and Heritage Attractions*, as well as providing some of the theory of marketing, provides the latest available case studies coupled with comments and advice from professionals inside and outside the cultural sector to describe the possibilities and outline strategies for the future.

A strong theme of change runs through each chapter. The economic climate is already affecting the publicly funded sectors and business and private sponsorship. How will it change over the next few years? The print media is contracting; reading and viewing patterns are changing as online and mobile media grow. What are the trends here, in Europe, the US and elsewhere? Sustainability and global warming are not just buzz words but will have a real impact on public and private institutions and their visitor patterns. Population patterns are also changing, with new immigrants arriving and the proportion of over-60s increasing in Western countries. Cultural tourism has enjoyed a great surge in popularity and huge investments are being made in museums, galleries and events. Marketing and PR play a crucial role in the success of such ventures and are illustrated with case studies from the UK, US, Australia, Middle East and New Zealand.

Marketing and Public Relations for Museums, Galleries, Cultural and Heritage Attractions is aimed at students of marketing, museums, culture and heritage as well as professionals working in a range of cultural organisations from small to large, and at different stages of market development – from new entrants to those offering mature products. This includes museums, galleries, heritage and visitor attractions, and community organisations, as well as organisers of festivals, markets, craft fairs and temporary exhibitions.

Ylva French has over 25 years' experience as a marketing and public relations professional working in the arts, tourism, leisure, museums and heritage. She set up her own marketing communications agency in 1988, and since then has operated as an independent consultant in the arts and museum sectors, as well as running the Campaign for Museums. She wrote the *Blue Guide London* (A&C Black – five editions) and with Sue Runyard has co-authored the *Marketing and Public Relations Handbook* (2000).

Sue Runyard is former Head of PR for the Royal Botanic Gardens, Kew, the Victoria & Albert Museum, the Natural History Museum, and the J. Paul Getty Museum in Los Angeles. She has served as press officer for two cabinet ministers during a secondment to the Cabinet Office, and has administered a national Marketing Grants Scheme, working with hundreds of heritage and tourism organisations throughout the UK. She has published several books and papers and contributed to many overseas projects.

MARKETING AND PUBLIC RELATIONS FOR MUSEUMS, GALLERIES, CULTURAL AND HERITAGE ATTRACTIONS

Ylva French and Sue Runyard

Routledge
Taylor & Francis Group

LONDON AND NEW YORK

Published 2011
by Routledge
2 Park Square, Milton Park, Abingdon, Oxon, OX14 4RN

Simultaneously published in the USA and Canada
by Routledge
270 Madison Avenue, New York, NY 10016

Routledge is an imprint of the Taylor & Francis Group, an informa business

British Library Cataloguing in Publication Data
A catalogue record for this book is available from the British Library

Library of Congress Cataloging in Publication Data
A catalogue record for this book has been requested

ISBN 10: 0–415–61045–1 (hbk)
ISBN 10: 0–415–61046–X (pbk)
ISBN 10: 0–203–81375–8 (ebk)

ISBN 13: 978–0–415–61045–2 (hbk)
ISBN 13: 978–0–415–61046–9 (pbk)
ISBN 13: 978–0–203–81375–1 (ebk)

Typeset in Trade Gothic and Univers by
Keystroke, Station Road, Codsall, Wolverhampton

MIX
Paper from
responsible sources
FSC® C004839
www.fsc.org

Printed and bound in Great Britain by
TJ International Ltd, Padstow, Cornwall

CONTENTS

PREFACE

What is the future for marketing, audience development and public relations in museums and galleries and at heritage attractions? The pressure is on to deliver more visitors within limited budgets and at the same time create favourable conditions for increasing earned income and stimulating sponsorship and donations. Maintaining good relations with hard-pressed local authorities, government departments and other stakeholders remains a priority.

This new book addresses these issues with pithy contributions from leaders in the sector. It aims to spread good practice and inspire creative communications inside and outside organisations of every size.

This is a book for practitioners of marketing, audience development and PR working in the cultural sector. It is also a book for students preparing for a career in museums, galleries or heritage.

We take a practical approach to communications – in all its forms – based on our experience, but we start with strategic planning and analysis. PR and marketing people are often dropped into the middle of a fast-moving scenario that demands instant action. It is possible to stumble through a job – or even a career – on a short-term, direct-reaction basis, but it is not advisable. We hope this book will inspire you to sail through day-to-day challenges while engaging your team and colleagues in longer-term thinking and planning, meeting whatever the next decade will bring.

Ylva French and Sue Runyard
February 2011

QUOTES FROM LEADERS OF THE SECTOR

Marketing and PR have found a role in the management of arts and heritage organisations. They have progressed from being 'bolt-on' activities to being a fundamental tool of management and an essential ingredient of success. Here, some leaders in the field give their thoughts.

Having a great idea is only the start of a journey; executing it is as big a challenge, and then capitalising upon it in marketing and PR terms is essential and may seem easy. It rarely is. A clearly thought-through plan encompassing branding, timetable and manpower is essential for success.

Penelope, Viscountess Cobham, Chairman, VisitEngland and Museum Prize Trust

Museums and galleries cannot simply rely on the world discovering that they are good. It is crucial to think through all the processes – from high-level advocacy work by members of the board, individual public presentations from the director and other senior staff, and a concerted programme of marketing based around exhibitions and activities, to making the most of every possible creative opportunity to gain press coverage. Of course, this must be matched by what visitors discover themselves, whether at the gallery or online – the experience must be engaging and welcoming to all.

Sandy Nairne, Director, National Portrait Gallery

Early on in my time at the Museums Association, the theme of one of the conferences was 'Backing into the Limelight', reflecting the reluctance and diffidence that museums displayed in speaking up for themselves. It is very different now. A wide range of disciplines is part of the armoury of the modern museum professional and there is an acceptance that marketing and PR in all their forms are essential rather than desirable. Much of what the Museums Association does is on a national scale but our recent Love Museums campaign and this book underline that the best and most effective work is done on the ground. There are no better advocates for a museum than those who know it best.

Mark Taylor, Director, Museums Association

Never has there been a more challenging time for cultural organisations. Following on from the global recession, governments and the private sector alike are cutting budgets. Therefore, this new book is especially timely to help cultural professionals sharpen their skills in marketing and public relations. Often it is said that the USA is the best place to be for arts marketing and fundraising. However, the mixed economy model of the UK, with money coming from both the public and private sector, appears now to be the best of both worlds, but only time will tell who is right.

Colin Tweedy, Chief Executive, Arts & Business

The steady ascent of the importance of public relations for museums and galleries matches exactly their increasing dependence on the private sector for both their vigour and survival. In the twenty-first century this dialogue with both benefactors and the wider public will become central in defining both an institution's role and its long-term aspirations.

Sir Roy Strong FRSL

Firstly, I'm not an expert on PR/marketing but I have learnt a huge amount about both subjects over the last 15 years since building the Alnwick Garden. Most importantly, I strongly believe that there has to be substance behind your claims and your marketing. The only times I've felt uncomfortable with what I'm selling is when I've realised that what I'm selling isn't being delivered. Never underestimate people's intelligence; they know and can see through the 'hard-sell' and none of us likes to be sold short. Having said that, if you build something as big as the Alnwick Garden you can't sit and wait for people to visit unless they're aware of its existence and the story and values behind it.

Jane, Duchess of Northumberland

This is the age of difference. We've all had to get used to new cultures at home and when we travel abroad. In this new world, everyone is clamouring for recognition on the basis of their age, gender, race, sexuality, disability and faith. People want to see their differences acknowledged and not be trapped in other people's ideas of who they should be and how they should behave. For example, women don't want to behave like men to get ahead; Muslims don't want to have to sink a few beers to be considered sociable; gay men and women don't want to stay in the closet; and those with disabilities don't want to be 'invisible'. Meeting all these needs is a challenge for any organisation, but properly managed it can open untapped customer and visitor demographics. How can people of very different and not so different cultures, backgrounds and traditions share and enjoy the same space?

Colleen Harris, Diversity Consultant and Executive Life Coach

What I object to is using social media 'simply' as a marketing tool – as another set of platforms from which to broadcast traditional marketing campaigns – as digital billboards. Social media is fundamentally about having a conversation with the museum's audiences; to misunderstand that is not only to miss an incredible opportunity to connect with audiences in new and powerful ways, but also potentially to damage the museum's brand by coming across as a social media spammer.

Nancy Proctor, PhD, Head of Mobile Strategy & Initiatives, Smithsonian Institution, Washington, DC

Far from being autonomous functions, marketing and education are interdependent elements of every museum's strategy for audience development, if it wishes to be successful. Each can articulate (with a light touch) the museum's philosophy, purpose and intellectual agenda. Each should work together to reach the same target audiences. Education can promote the museum to its public, and marketing can educate the public in the museum's collection and disciplines.

In practice such cohesion is hard to achieve – museums often set their marketing teams short-term targets, whereas education staff may work to longer-term goals. The theories on which they base their professional activities can differ radically. Yet, when a museum overcomes these differences, the results can be astonishing.

David Anderson, former Director of Education, V&A London

ACKNOWLEDGEMENTS

We would like to thank all the professionals who have contributed to this book – a truly international cast at every phase of their careers. Enjoy their pertinent quotes and be inspired by their case studies:

- David Anderson, OBE, Director General, National Museum of Wales
- Maria B. Andersson, Information Director, Swedish National Maritime Museums
- Adrian Babbidge, Consultant
- Richard Bagnall, Managing Director, Metrica
- Janet Barnes, Chief Executive, York Museum Trust
- David Barrie, CBE, Former Director of the Art Fund, Chair of Make Justice
- Graham W.J. Beal, Director, Detroit Institute of Arts
- Adrian Bevan, Consultant, formerly of VisitBritain
- Bob Bloomfield, Head of Innovation and Special Projects, Natural History Museum
- Rebecca Burton, Deputy Head of Commercial and Customer Services, Bristol Museum and Art Gallery
- Seb Chan, Head of Digital, Social and Emerging Technologies, Powerhouse Museum, Australia
- Ruth Clarke, Community Projects Manager London, Sutton House National Trust
- Viscountess Penelope Cobham, Chairman, VisitEngland and Museum Prize Trust
- Arthur Cohen, Chief Executive Officer, LaPlaca Cohen, New York
- Ina Cole, Freelance Arts Professional

- Alec Coles, OBE, Chief Executive Officer, Western Australian Museum, Perth
- Sandie Dawe, MBE, Chief Executive, VisitBritain
- Ivo Dawnay, Communications Director, National Trust
- David Dombrovsky, Executive Director, Centre for Arts Management and Technology, Carnegie Mellon University
- Richard Doughty, Chief Executive, Cutty Sark Trust
- Harvey Edgington, Broadcast and Media Manager, National Trust
- Dr Pamela Erskine-Loftus, Qatar Museums Authority
- Selina Fellows, Independent Retail and Commercial Adviser
- Susie Fisher, Director, the Susie Fisher Group
- Dr David Fleming, OBE, Director, National Museums Liverpool
- Fiona Fox, Director, Science Media Centre
- Jennifer Francis, Head of Press and Marketing, Royal Academy of Arts
- Peter and Iona Frost-Pennington, Muncaster Castle
- Carmel Girling, Deputy Head of Marketing and Communications, Birmingham Museum and Art Gallery
- Pete Gomori, Marketing Manager, Tate
- Will Gompertz, Arts Editor, BBC
- Dr Patrick Greene, OBE, Chief Executive Officer, Museum of Victoria, Melbourne
- Loyd Grossman, OBE, FSA, President, British Association of Friends of Museums
- Colleen Harris, OBE, Diversity Consultant and Life Coach
- Laura Haynes, Chairman, Appetite
- Erin Hogan, Director of Public Affairs, Art Institute of Chicago
- Michael Houlihan, Chief Executive Officer, Te Papa Museum, NZ
- Tina Houlton, Head of Marketing, Royal Botanic Gardens, Kew
- Ashley Jones, Commercial Manager, Wimbledon Lawn Tennis Museum
- Robert Jones, Strategist, Wolff Olins
- Kate Knowles, former Head of Communications, Dulwich Picture Gallery
- Louise Lane, Director of Communications, Heritage Lottery Fund

- Richard Linington, Planning Solutions, National Museum of Brewing

- Gail Dexter Lord, Co-President, Lord Cultural Resources

- Alan Love, Research Director, BDRC Continental

- Joanna Mackle, Director of Public Engagement, British Museum

- Tracey McGeagh, Director of Marketing and Communications, National Museums Liverpool

- Gillian McLean, Director of Marketing, Communications & Trading, National Museums Northern Ireland

- Steve McLean, Senior Manager, Great North Museum

- Anna Mighetto, Marketing Manager, Världkulturmuseet (World Cultures Museum), Gothenburg

- Tom Morgan, Head of Rights and Reproductions, National Portrait Gallery

- Baroness Estelle Morris of Yardley, former Arts Minister

- Gerri Morris, Director, Morris Hargreaves McIntyre

- Gillian Morris, Head of Human Resources, Ashmolean Museum of Art and Archaeology

- Jane Morris, Editor, *Art Newspaper*

- Sandy Nairne, Director, National Portrait Gallery

- Sally Osman, Communications Consultant

- Helen Palmer, Consultant, Palmer Squared

- Dr Vassily Pankratov, Director, Gatchina Palace and Estate

- Jane Percy, Duchess of Northumberland, Alnwick Castle

- Barbara Pflaumer, Associate Vice President Communications and Marketing, LACMA

- Jon Pratty, Online Publishing Consultant

- Nancy Proctor, Head of Mobile Strategy & Initiatives, Smithsonian Institution, Washington, DC

- Gillian Rankin, Marketing Manager, Scottish Mining Museum

- Jesse Ringham, Digital Communications Manager, Tate

- Marylyn Scott, Director, The Lightbox

- Lynn Scrivener, Consultant, LSM Marketing

- Truda Spruyt, Associate Director, Colman Getty

- Karin Stahel, Communications Manager, Canterbury Museum, NZ

- Carole Stone, Managing Director, YouGoveStone

- Sir Roy Strong, FRSL

- Susie Stubbs, Communications Consultant

- Mark Suggitt, Consultant

- Mark Taylor, Director, Museums Association

- Dr Delma Tomlin, Director, the National Centre for Early Music

- Vanessa Trevelyan, Head, Norfolk Museums & Archaeology Service

- Susan Turner-Lowe, Vice President for Communications, The Huntington Library, Art Collections, and Botanical Gardens, San Marino, California

- Colin Tweedy, OBE, Chief Executive, Arts and Business

- Sheryl Twigg, Press and PR Manager, National Maritime Museum

- Sue Underwood, OBE, Qatar Museums Authority

- Jose Villarreal, Editor, Art Daily

- Hilary Wade, Director, Tullie House Museum, Carlisle

- Iain Watson, Acting Director, Tyne and Wear Museums

- Katrina Whenham, Media and PR Manager, Historic Royal Palaces

- Kate White, Marketing and Visitor Services Officer, Pitt Rivers Museum

- Kate Winsall, Marketing Manager, National Maritime Museum

- Barbara Woroncow, OBE, Deputy Chair, Leeds Cultural Partnership

- Sally Wrampling, Head of Policy and Strategy, The Art Fund

CASE STUDIES

FIGURES

PART 1

MARKETING AND PR PRINCIPLES FOR THE TWENTY-FIRST CENTURY

CHAPTER 1

MARKETING IN
A NEW DIMENSION

An introduction to marketing

Marketing and its history

Marketing in the new dimension

Cultural organisations in the digital age

Museums and the brand promise

The marketing process

Organisation

AN INTRODUCTION TO MARKETING

Having a great idea is only the start of a journey, executing it is as big a challenge and then capitalising upon it in marketing and PR terms is essential and may seem easy. It rarely is. A clearly thought-through plan encompassing branding, timetable and manpower is essential for success.

(Penelope, Viscountess Cobham, Chairman,
VisitEngland and the Museum Prize Trust)

The role of marketing in museums, galleries and other not-for-profit cultural organisations is no longer an ad hoc activity but a discipline central to the organisation's functions both in terms of developing 'the product', i.e. what it has to offer and in terms of 'sales' – promoting and making accessible its displays, collections and services to the public.

With the inevitable decline of public sector funding, museums and galleries need effective marketing and PR now more than ever before. Getting the message across both to members of the public and opinion formers is vital to ensure the future health of these institutions. If the study and care of collections are at the heart of museum practice, communicating the value of those pursuits has to be embedded in the museum as well.

(Loyd Grossman, OBE, FSA, President, British Association of Friends of Museums)

Cultural institutions have come a long way from a time when they were led mainly by specialists producing events and exhibitions based primarily on their own collections and curatorial interests, to the twenty-first century – responding to the consumer-led society, aiming to provide more of what visitors may want as well as challenging established ideas and tastes, and breaking new ground in terms of contents and interpretation.

From here it is a short step to the interactive, value-added, personalised experiences that today's visitors increasingly demand. Museums and heritage attractions around the world are also conscious of the need to raise additional income from commercial activities as public funding and subsidies have been reduced. This trend has accelerated in the aftermath of the 2008 credit crunch. As a result of this new consumer-led approach and increased commercialism, museums and galleries have been accused of 'dumbing down'. They are mounting exhibitions on popular subjects – from Grace Kelly's and Madonna's dresses to James Bond and *Star Trek*. They stock their shops with branded merchandise and serve cappuccinos in elegant cafés in order to attract visitors with greater disposable income.

At the same time, a commitment to audience development has emerged in response to influences and public funders. No longer can museums and galleries justify their existence by catering to a narrow, well-educated audience – the traditional museum-visitor. The last twenty years has seen a transformation in audiences in many countries, thanks partly to the more populist approach and partly to the application of audience development and niche marketing. Free entry to the UK's national museums and galleries has undoubtedly played a part in transforming the profile of visitors. (There will be more on charging later on.) But other countries which charge for entry have also experienced a surge in visitor numbers. Museums and the arts are popular!

Stunning architecture has provided a new, dynamic dimension to museums and galleries. The building itself has become an exhibit; it started with the iconic Guggenheim in New York (Frank Lloyd Wright 1959) but the opening of the striking Guggenheim Museum in Bilbao (Frank Gehry 1997) marked a new era in creating outstanding architecture for cultural buildings as well as using culture to regenerate the local economy through tourism. In countries where new museums are opening on a significant scale, the architecture is now almost more important than the content. The 2010 shortlist for the Royal Institute of British Architects' Stirling Prize featured three museums: the revamped Ashmolean Museum, Oxford; the transformed Neues Museum, Berlin; and Rome's brand new MAXXI – National Museum of 21st Century

Figure 1.1 MAXXI – National Museum of 21st Century Art (Architect: Zaha Hadid; Photo: Helene Binet)

Art, designed by Zaha Hadid and ultimately the winner. The challenge for so-called 'parachute' museums anywhere is to make them relevant to local people and not just national status symbols designed to attract international tourists, or outposts of American or European cultural institutions.

In the spirit of populism – and the need for revenues to sustain ongoing restoration – historic houses and heritage sites have also transformed themselves to widen their appeal; this applies equally to the stunning rise of the privately owned Alnwick Castle, or any of the 350 historic houses, gardens and ancient monuments for which the National Trust – a membership organisation – is responsible. There is a heavy price to pay for enthusiastic cultural tourists exploring ancient sites and cathedrals when this is not matched by care and conservation, as the Italian authorities have discovered at Pompeii.

This chapter will set out how the basic principles of marketing developed in the commercial sector and how they were adopted and developed in the not-for-profit sector.

> **Early on in my time at the Museums Association, the theme of one of the conferences was 'Backing into the Limelight' reflecting the reluctance and diffidence that museums displayed in speaking up for themselves. It is very different now. A wide range of disciplines is part of the armoury of the modern museum professional and there is an acceptance that marketing and PR in all their forms are essential rather than desirable. Much of what the Museums Association does is on a national scale but our recent Love Museums campaign and this book underline that the best and most effective work is done on the ground. There are no better advocates for a museum than those who know it best.**
>
> **(Mark Taylor, Director, Museums Association)**

MARKETING AND ITS HISTORY

As marketing developed in the nineteenth century in response to industrialisation and large-scale manufacturing it was mostly about sales. Earlier producers and retailers had been mainly involved in supplying their local markets but now they looked further afield. The development of printing enabled pioneers to introduce some of the techniques still popular today, including brand names and prominent messages, displaying these on billboards and posters, and through advertising in newspapers and magazines. 1788 had marked the launch of *The Times* newspaper (then the *Universal Register*) in the UK, following in the footsteps of earlier newsletters and publications. Although there were more than 300 newspapers published in the United States in the early nineteenth century, they had tiny circulations. It was the arrival of high-speed printing presses which created a mass market for newspapers. By the 1890s, the first circulation figures of over one million readers for one title were recorded in the United States. (Source: Frank Mott; Newspaper Society – see Resources).

Many more titles followed, and with the invention of the electric telegraph, the era of press agencies dawned. In the United States, Associated Press was formed in 1846 by a group of newspapers sharing the cost of covering the Mexican wars. Paul Julius Reuter realised the importance of the telegraph, and inspired by the laying of the first undersea telegraph cable between Britain and France in 1851 and the subsequent trans-Atlantic cable, he seized the opportunity and founded what was to become the Reuter's Telegram Company in 1865. The Press Association followed in 1868. The first trans-Atlantic telegraph cable made the communication of news between continents possible within hours, rather than days or weeks. The world continued to shrink as telegraphic cables linked continents and made fast news coverage of two world wars a reality. The next dramatic development in world communications was the satellite. The first was Sputnik, launched by the Russians in 1957, followed by the American Telstar five years later. Britain's first satellite communications dish was installed at Goonhilly in Cornwall in 1962. (Source: Connected Earth – see Resources).

The accurate measurement of readership of the printed media, vital to the advertising industry, started with the foundation of the Audit Bureau of Circulation in the UK in 1931. The monitoring of television viewers followed as the medium took off after the Second World War, although no wholly satisfactory system for accurately measuring television viewing has yet been devised. Traditionally, television viewing has been measured through diaries kept by a random sample of the public. Meters have also been used but are expensive to install. Nielsen Media Research (US) is working on a system which will combine measurement of television broadcast and internet use. In addition, a Coalition for Innovative Media Measurement has been set up by major advertisers and broadcasters in the United States to promote new techniques for measuring audiences including online, launching the UK system, TouchPoints, in the US. Here is a sample of what is now available:

In 2009/10, people in the UK watched 3.7 hours of television per day, listened to the radio for 2.1 hours, and accessed the internet for 1.8 hours a day. Internet use has increased by 38% in two years. 37% of adults use social network each week. Of the time they spend communicating, adults spend 75% talking or chatting face-to-face. This percentage share has fallen from 77% in 2008 and 81% in 2006. The share spent on the phone – landline or mobile – has stayed relatively constant at 11%, whilst SMS texting and picture messaging has grown to a 4% share; for 15–24 year olds this figure is now 9% and growing.

(TouchPoints – see Resources)

This range of communications media inspired manufacturers to use a growing range of sales techniques developed by marketing professionals. After the Second World War, marketing became synonymous with advertising, as the recently produced American television series *Mad Men* illustrates. It is set in a New York advertising agency in the 1950s and 1960s and conveys the excitement and creativity of a new industry targeting an increasingly sophisticated consumer, and gradually recognising that many of the buying decisions were now being made by women.

The Museum of Brands, Packaging and Advertising in London's Notting Hill brings this history of consumer culture to life through household products and shopping-basket favourites in a nostalgic journey from Victorian times to the present day. (Kansas City is opening a Museum of Advertising Icons in 2011.)

Post-war development of marketing was also influenced by the developing science of psychology. The simple process of supply and demand took on a new dimension as advertising agencies and marketers delved into the mind and motivation of the consumer. This was the beginning of consumer-focused marketing which still dominates today, based on increasingly sophisticated market research, including focus groups and other probing techniques. In his revealing study of advertising, *The Hidden Persuaders*, first published in 1957, Vance Packard questioned the morality of using motivational research and subliminal messages. But the new techniques were widely adopted and are still used today.

Marketing as a separate discipline had been first recognised in the UK in 1911 when the Sales Managers' Association was founded to improve sales techniques. This later became the UK's Chartered Institute of Marketing. In 1976 the Institute confirmed its definition of marketing, still valid today:

> **The management process responsible for identifying, anticipating and satisfying customer requirements profitably.**
>
> **(Chartered Institute of Marketing)**

The American Marketing Association, founded in1937, developed from the Association of Teachers in Advertising, which started in 1915. AMA published the first *Journal of Marketing* in 1936. Its definition of marketing was revised in 2007 and is as follows:

> **Marketing is the activity, set of institutions, and processes for creating, communicating, delivering and exchanging offerings that have value for customers, clients, partners and society at large.**
>
> **(AMA)**

From the 1970s onward the growth of public services and not-for-profit organisations led to the development of a new kind of marketing based on society's values and the consumer's needs and wants. Social marketing is now practised by a range of enterprises including national governments promoting health and anti-crime measures, and a host of charitable organisations promoting their own causes. This development also influenced the allied discipline of public relations which came to play a growing role in social marketing. The ethos of social marketing was embraced more readily by museums and galleries for whom the 'profit' aspect of commercial marketing was not relevant or was uncomfortable.

The era of big brands started in the 1980s, increasingly targeting the youth market, and expanding beyond their products as they endorsed through sponsorship services, fashion and sport across the world. This globalisation of products included brands such as Coca Cola, Lego and Nike – now some of the most recognised names and logos in the world. In reaction to this, a new anti-advertising, anti-globalisation movement took off, influenced among others by Naomi Klein's book *No Logo*, published in 2000. The use of brands in conjunction with sponsorship of cultural attractions and exhibitions continues to be controversial and is debated further in Chapter 6 on brands and branding. Meanwhile, many cultural organisations have developed their own names into powerful brands, with Tate being one of the most successful in the UK, the Louvre in Paris and MOMA in New York, just to mention a few.

While globalisation and mass-market brands seemed at first to simplify marketing techniques, limiting consumer choice, the development of new technology and social media has created greater opportunities for niche products and niche marketing, as illustrated by the concept of 'the long tail', first identified in 2004 by Chris Anderson writing in *Wired* magazine and using Amazon, the book retailer, as an example of a supplier able to provide small quantities to more and more people. The title of his subsequent book encapsulates the theory: *The Long Tail: Why the Future of Business is Selling Less of More.*

MARKETING IN THE NEW DIMENSION

So where are we now in the cultural sector? In 1999/2000, the authors defined the guiding principle for cultural marketing as:

> **Marketing is simply the strategic and systematic approach to audience development which meets the overall objectives of the museum and galleries.**
> **(French and Runyard 1999)**

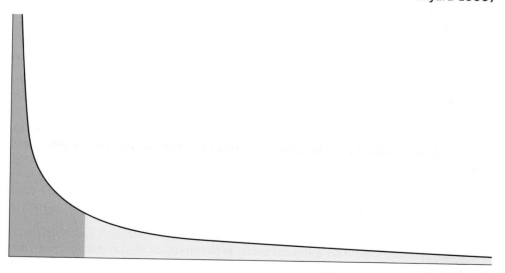

Figure 1.2 'The long tail'– popular demand to the left and products to the right

Writing this in 2011 against a background of public sector cuts there is a greater emphasis than before on income generation as well as maintaining traditional cultural objectives; we suggest a new definition for cultural, not-for-profit attractions:

> **Marketing is the strategic and systematic approach to audience and brand development which meets the overall objectives of the cultural organisation and maximises income streams without sacrificing the mission.**
>
> **(French and Runyard 2011)**

The late Peter Drucker, a leading management guru who wrote many books on marketing, was able to reduce the concept to just a few words which are more than appropriate in the context of cultural marketing. These words of wisdom have been repeated (and claimed) by many who have followed in his footsteps:

> **Marketing is looking at the business through the customers' eyes.**

Marketing continues to evolve, reframing its role, and refreshing processes and talent in order to deliver greater value. This is particularly important at a time when Western economies are emerging from recession into a somewhat uncertain future in terms of the overall size of the public and not-for-profit sectors.

> **Across the commercial world chief executives recognize the importance of the marketing function while questioning whether they have the right skills at a time of rapid technological change in all areas of communications, distribution and delivery.**
>
> **(Source: The Marketing Transformation Leadership Forum, Chartered Institute of Marketing)**

CULTURAL ORGANISATIONS IN THE DIGITAL AGE

Museums and galleries cautiously embraced new technologies from the 1970s onward, seeing the benefits in terms of creating computer-based records, organising data, and storing digital images of objects. The arrival of the Internet and the World Wide Web in the 1980s marked a step-change in communications. As venues, museums were initially defensive about adopting internet technologies for public-facing purposes, according to Ross Parry in *Museums in the Digital Age*. Initially there was a fear that virtual visits would replace the physical experience. When the Campaign for Museums launched the 24 Hour Museum website in 2000 (now Culture24), the media envisaged virtual walk-through galleries or a portal where you could search across the world for objects. Instead they saw a new promotional gateway, providing information, news and links to all the UK's museums, galleries and heritage attractions.

> **Today, the contemporary museum sector is one in which digital culture is actively collected, where computer-based interpretive media allows exhibitions to support experiences in more flexible, creative and empowering ways, and where institutions**

are tuning their modes of delivery and audience engagement to the emerging channels of our evolving digital society.

(Ross Parry, *Museums in the Digital Age*, 2010)

Computerisation of data and the development of platforms that distribute the information to visitors and involve them in the story and interpretation is the model most museums and galleries are now aiming for (popularly referred to as Web 2.0). As outlined by Jon Pratty (in *Museums in the Digital Age*) we are moving from the Miss Havisham model to the Fagin model. No longer is the museum like Miss Havisham, sitting amongst the cobwebs waiting for people to turn up at the party. Now it is like Fagin, running around the city, slipping into all sorts of places, being discovered, moving things around, being exciting and of course being prepared to review the situation. When the first mobile phones arrived some 25 years ago (the size of bricks), no one envisaged how they would transform into mobile platforms which visitors now use to access information on their cultural visits. The iPad adds another dimension.

> But here with the iPad (and whatever follows as a result of it changing the tablet marketplace), we finally have a light, portable, and easy to use device that allows museum tours to be enjoyed collectively – even as a family group. In fact, the development work needed to convert an existing iPhone-optimised web content into one that suits the iPad is relatively minimal.

> Consider the options for visitors stopping by a showcase or a set of objects wanting to know more about them. They pull out the iPad (their own or one they have hired at the front desk) and flick through to the collection information about those objects, pull up the videos in which the makers are interviewed, and pass the device between family members to show each other. Better yet, if they so wish, all this content is still available online for reference when they get home or back to school.

> (Seb Chan, Head of Digital Technologies, Powerhouse Museum, Sydney)

Culture Mondo was created in 2005 as an open network of digital cultural specialists working together to facilitate strategic and relevant knowledge exchange. It links cultural portals around the world and brings together participants once a year at a Roundtable to share and discuss developments.

MUSEUMS AND THE BRAND PROMISE

Museums, galleries and cultural attractions increasingly understand the importance of investing in their 'brand' – a set of values. (The details are discussed further in Chapter 6.) This brand promise needs to be delivered, not just through communications but through visitor services and the visitor experience. Cultural attractions have moved with the times and mostly put the customer at the heart of management thinking. In many organisations, the delivery of the brand promise is in the hands of marketing and visitor services, but not always integrated with the curatorial and product development functions.

Sir Roy Strong, former Director of the National Portrait Gallery (NPG) and the Victoria and Albert Museum (V&A), was the first UK director to understand and to use the media and 'brand image' with aplomb. He says that he learned a lot from staging an exhibition at the National Gallery in Ottawa in the 1960s where 'PR was taken for granted', and from the Frick Collection which depended on the private sector for funding. He was appointed as Director of the NPG in London in 1959. At that time, any contact by staff with the press was expressly discouraged. Everything changed with a series of sparkling exhibitions, a great deal of social networking, and plenty of media coverage.

Arriving at the V&A in 1973 as its youngest-ever Director, he found an organisation that was little known among the general public, and lacked focus and identity. He says:

> **When I went there the Director never even saw posters or any printed matter. I had a terrific battle to establish that every piece of paper which went out passed across my desk. What goes up as a poster or through the letter box is how people will conceive the place.**

A top-notch advertising agency was appointed; the press office was supported and encouraged; gifted designers were used; and the programme of exhibitions was revitalised and made relevant to a broader audience. The UK museum scene would never be the same again, and suddenly museums were hot stuff. The V&A became known by its initials to a wide public, and gained a reputation for always having something 'going on'.

It is easy for the public to be cynical about brand values which put customer services at the heart of their offer, when many privatised public services such as banks and energy providers continually renege on their promises and some airlines do not conform to minimum levels of standards of service set by their trade association, or even by law. (After the suspension of flights for several days in 2010 because of the Icelandic volcanic ash clouds, some airlines refused at first to reimburse stranded passengers.)

So how do marketers in the cultural sector maintain and develop the customer-focused approach, and how do they both champion the visitor and influence operational activities? Faced potentially with shrinking resources, maintaining standards will be a challenge, and customer service is one area which will be under considerable pressure.

Accountability is central to more credible, influential marketing. Measuring and proving marketing's value in the language of the organisation – visitor numbers, revenue, margin and satisfaction rates – is essential. Integration is equally important. Museums in particular have been notorious for operating in silos. This is no longer efficient, credible or sensible. While clear lines of responsibilities (for the collections and conservation, for example) are part of the organisation's systems, the role of marketing and PR as guardians of the brand and all it stands for, gives them a seat at the boardroom table in this rapidly changing world.

Today cultural institutions face the challenges of new technology, sustainability and reduced public funding, while the expectations of politicians and public are greater than ever. Museums, galleries and heritage sites are expected not only to preserve their collections and buildings for future generations, while educating and entertaining today's public, but also to create an environment in which multiculturalism and social cohesion thrive. The extent to which they can cope with these demands over the next decade is a matter for speculation.

THE MARKETING PROCESS

In this book we set out principles and techniques to achieve this new integrated marketing, using the increasing range of tools available to the marketer and public relations practitioner. Marketing is a continuous process which we aim to cover in greater depth in the chapters that follow. Marketing involves several elements:

Market research means examining both past and current visitor patterns and profiles to identify trends. It should also include non-visitors, to discover who they are and why they don't visit.

Forecasting based on these trends is essential in order to plan ahead. This includes analysing population changes within the catchment area as well as tourism patterns.

Product development is a continuous process for all cultural attractions with changing programmes of temporary exhibitions and events. It also means reviewing the permanent exhibitions and visitor services and facilities. In the UK, the National Lottery has allowed museums and galleries to participate in a development bonanza over the past 16 years, resulting in much improved and enhanced visitor experiences. Others, such as privately owned historic houses, have not been able to benefit from this, making renewal and maintenance even more of a challenge. The product life cycle (see Chapter 4) applies just as much to exhibitions and displays as it does to cars or other fast-moving consumer goods. It is important to get this right in order to attract new as well as returning visitors.

Price is the key ingredient in the commercial marketing process and may appear less so for those museums providing free entry. However, they all charge for something, such as temporary exhibitions, the shop, the café and parking, and for many organisations charging is essential for survival. Setting the right price for a service or admission is key to successful marketing. It is also important to bear in mind that visitors may well perceive the time and cost of travel to a destination as part of the price, and they will include it in their concept of value for money.

Promotion is the visible part of the marketing process and today it is not just about advertising. New technology has not replaced traditional methods of promotion, just added new layers, calling for greater skills and adaptability from marketers and PR professionals.

The last stage of promotion is selling – closing the deal – which may be an online transaction to buy a book or an image, an advance timed ticket for a blockbuster exhibition (bypassing the queue at the venue), a ticket for a concert or event, or a general admission ticket, or membership.

Distribution, the final element of the marketing process, would seem to have less relevance to geographically fixed attractions. But this is no longer the case. Museums and galleries are now available online anywhere in the world – round the clock. And they also use outreach – popping up in libraries, schools and shopping centres and in other cities and countries through touring exhibitions or 'branch' museums.

ORGANISATION

Museums, galleries and heritage attractions vary enormously in size, and will handle their marketing and PR requirements accordingly. Some will have large curatorial or research functions, and some, because of their scale, will have large teams of visitor services staff. These factors – and historical accident – can affect how they position their marketing and PR within the organisation, and how well they staff and fund them. Whether a large team or one person juggling lots of different functions, we believe that success and effectiveness is dependent on giving the Marketing/PR manager/officer access within the organisation. If it is important to drive visitor numbers, raise the profile and develop audiences, marketing and PR must be integrated with policymaking and management, and be seen to be so by the whole staff.

Techniques available have widened dramatically in recent years, to include websites, email communications, electronic newsletters, and social media such as Facebook, Twitter, Flickr – and others yet to come. As described in the section on *Museums in the Digital Age* above, the development of computerised services within the museum including the first websites were undertaken by IT professionals. Museums prone to departmentalism soon found that the internal barriers created to some extent by the level of skills and knowledge required had to be broken down, and that curators as well as communications professionals within the organisation had to be part of driving the new technology. While curators have increasingly become involved with data and digitisation, communications professionals are now mainly responsible for external digital communications, as an integrated part of the overall marketing and PR function.

The ideal set-up for the future is an integrated marketing and PR team with IT capability, where areas of responsibilities are clear but everyone has signed up to the marketing and PR strategy. Read more about this in 'Equipped to be effective' in Chapter 2.

Consultants with special skills in marketing, research and PR provide an invaluable resource for cultural attractions with limited budgets. This can be an opportunity to tap into cutting-edge advice, develop a long-term strategy, or to deal with a short-term crisis, using the experience of others. Briefing and managing consultants to maximise results is part of this process and will be covered later.

CHAPTER 2

PUBLIC RELATIONS IS MORE THAN PR

An introduction to public relations

Fundamental characteristics of public relations

Every member of the organisation contributes to PR

Accuracy

Consistency

Creativity

Timing

Learning from others

Professionalism

Equipped to be effective: integrated and organised

AN INTRODUCTION TO PUBLIC RELATIONS

PR: The determined, planned and sustained effort to establish and maintain mutual understanding between an organisation and its publics. Also understood as reputation management.

(Chartered Institute of Public Relations)

Everyone thinks that they know what Public Relations is about, and sometimes PR is used as a derogatory term linked to 'spin', sound-bites, and attempts to put gloss on bad news. There is much more to Public Relations than this, as this book will demonstrate. Even where the function is not necessarily specified, public relations activities are carried out on a day-to-day basis by every member of the organisation's team. Engaging the public and expanding the public's perception of the organisation is core to most museums, galleries and cultural institutions. This task applies equally to education teams, curators and all public-facing departments of the organisation.

> **Museums and galleries cannot simply rely on the world discovering that they are good. It is crucial to think through all the processes from high level advocacy work by members of the board, individual public presentations from the director and other senior staff and a concerted programme of marketing based around exhibitions and activities, to making the most of every possible creative opportunity to gain press coverage. Of course this must be matched by what visitors discover themselves, whether at the gallery or online; the experience must be engaging and welcoming to all.**
>
> **(Sandy Nairne, Director, National Portrait Gallery)**

Within cultural institutions, public relations should be at its most integrated, flowing directly from the mission. The first task of the PR manager is to ensure a good understanding of public relations within management and across the organisation, right up to board level. Success in this area comes with integration at policymaking level, so that the PR manager rarely has to be briefed from scratch, but is immersed in the mission and ethos of the organisation.

There are good practical reasons for this to do with time and effectiveness, the most obvious of which is that when talking to a journalist – who represents thousands, if not millions of people – the PR person represents his or her organisation by being informed, accurate, enthusiastic and plausible. It works best where there is trust between the PR person and management, and worst where the PR person is lacking in information or confidence.

There is nothing accidental about good public relations. Luck may play a part, but careful analysis and forward planning is essential. The reputation of a cultural institution is made by its academic staff, the nature and status of its collections, and by the quality of the visitor experience. The role of public relations is to communicate and enhance this internally and externally.

All aspects of the PR manager's job have become more challenging within the past decade. Fragmentation of the media has complicated the task of reaching out with news and messages. The public have become more demanding as consumers. Competition for people's leisure time has increased dramatically. Stakeholder relationships have also become more fraught as society changes, with increasing opportunities for conflict. Within this tower of Babel, public relations professionals distribute the organisation's messages, while simultaneously attempting to maintain harmonious relationships, internally and externally. The messages flow from the mission and reinforce the organisation's brand values.

Generally PR is more noticeable when it fails than when it works smoothly! There are numerous examples across the world of how a reputation challenged by a disaster can be effectively ruined by the way the company or organisation handles the bad news – in 2010 the disastrous BP oil spillage in the Gulf of Mexico was made much worse when the PR aspects were badly handled from the top. Cultural organisations on the whole rarely encounter that level of public disapproval or national or international crisis.

The way PR works best is at an invisible level. The organisation should shine, not the PR team. Public relations should be constantly active in the background, making and maintaining relationships for now and for the future. Here are some of the areas of operation – there will be more in Chapter 5:

- Media relations: getting to know journalists; familiarising them with the organisation and its purposes; maintaining useful records; and acting as and preparing spokespeople.

- Public information and social media: preparing a host of online and printed material for public consumption, working closely with IT and the marketing team.

- Internal communications: participating in the policymaking and planning cycle of the organisation, and assisting in the flow of information around the staff and trustees.

- External stakeholder relations: establishing and maintaining channels of communication with various groups, opinion-formers and segments of the public, as identified in the corporate plan.

- Issue management: looking to the future, identifying issues, potential crises and developing strategies to meet them.

So public relations has several jobs to do within and outside the organisation. It is the channel as well as the means of communications, and how it is done is just as important as what it does; it is the process of maintaining harmonious and understanding relationships between the various internal parts and with stakeholders and others externally.

FUNDAMENTAL CHARACTERISTICS OF PUBLIC RELATIONS

Here are some fundamental characteristics of all types of well-managed public relations: every member of the organisation contributes; accuracy; consistency; creativity; timing; learning from others; and professionalism.

Every member of the organisation contributes to PR

Directors and the Board know and understand that the organisation's reputation and relationships are formed at many different levels. It is not just the responsibility of the PR team. All members of staff make a contribution, whether consciously or unconsciously. It is helpful for the PR team to make this relationship more explicit and, through information-giving and training, ensure that everyone is giving out broadly similar messages.

It should be obvious that front-of-house staff have an important public relations role to fulfil. The way that visitors are greeted, received, directed and serviced reflects immediately upon the organisation's reputation, and the PR manager will want to have input into staff training and briefing. But all staff, members and trustees are communicating something about the organisation, its principles and its mission. They will also have contact with stakeholders and influencers, and need to be well versed in the organisation's purpose and aspirations. Getting an accurate and sustained message across is a team effort.

The cultural institution needs to think carefully about the messages it wants to convey to the world at large, ensuring that they are used frequently and that they are amplified and explained in all internal communications. The rationale behind policy and the brand needs to be understood so that staff feel both informed and enthusiastic about the organisation's objectives. It will be helpful if they have had an opportunity to contribute towards the thinking that frames policymaking, and confident managers will create structures that allow this to happen. (See Chapter 13 Internal communications.)

The importance of relationship management within the organisation is reflected in the role and position of the PR function. Staff are quick to pick up if the PR manager seems remote from central management.

Here are just a few negative signs of poor or ineffectual public relations:

- The public relations manager never or rarely participates in board meetings.
- The chair and/or members of the board have a direct line to the media, expressing their own agenda.
- The marketing or PR manager has no authority or involvement with consultants retained by the Director or Chairman.
- Curators or other staff are exchanging behind-the-scenes gossip with friendly journalists.
- External agencies report only to marketing or PR officers and never see the Director or Chairman (or vice versa).
- Constant voicemail is on in the press office.

In other words, frequent and open contact at senior levels with an appropriate degree of transparency throughout the organisation will add strength to the organisation's communications.

Accuracy

Written and spoken messages must be true to the organisation's mission and reflect accurately what it stands for and what it delivers to the public. Public relations cannot be a substitute for a failing product or programmes. PR consultants are sometimes brought in by cultural organisations in crisis and asked to perform magic by: creating a smokescreen of half-truths; initiating positive media stories out of nothing; inventing a public profile for an organisation that needs to change but has no intention of making changes; or simply 'making the media go away' rather than confronting an uncomfortable situation.

A seasoned PR practitioner with established media contacts can sometimes use their relationships to win attention and be persuasive in the face of damaging accusations or negative opinion, but the moment they are discovered in a lie, their reputation is lost, and harm is done to their organisation or client. It could be tempting to keep the PR manager in the dark in a financial crisis, for example. This is a dangerous and counter-productive move. It is exactly at moments of crisis that the well-briefed PR manager will prove his or her worth.

Consider a hypothetical case of a museum that has just discovered an accidental release of laboratory pathogens into the water supply. Managers might feel that having the story denied by the press office is a good idea, for a host of reasons. However, there is no such thing as a watertight lie, and ultimately the museum will look not only guilty of the crime, but dishonest and socially irresponsible. An informed PR manager can make holding statements while the situation is clarified, releasing sufficient information to show the risk but also how well the internal detection systems worked, and how swiftly the museum has acted to contain matters.

This is an example of how vital it is for the PR team to be embedded within the communications network of the organisation, and how seriously we need to take transparency. Anyone who has dealt with an enquiry under the Freedom of Information Act will know how important it is to be clear, honest and responsible in all our work. Problems that stem from poor information exchange should be identified in the communications audit and PR strategy, and need to be addressed, before external communications can play a proactive and positive role. (There is more in Chapter 14 Communicating with stakeholders).

Consistency

It goes without saying that consistency is part of accuracy in the sense that frequent message changes make the organisation look confused. Another aspect of consistency is the courage and determination to continue with a considered line over and over again. In the early days of advertising it was quickly realised, and remains true today, that repetition of a product name works. Repeated exposure of a simple message will eventually find its mark. This can be a source of frustration in academic or intellectual circles, where boredom sets in long before the public have registered a corporate message. In fact, changes to logos, slogans and corporate messages are often initiated before they have done their work – simply because someone in the organisation feels they are old and stale.

Frequent changes at the management level – in the directorate, the board or the PR team – make the organisation look weak and inconsistent. Sometimes messages to the media appear to dry up during a hiatus, or to keep changing as each new incumbent takes stock, reviews and adjusts the messages. It is very easy to drop out of the media's consciousness, especially if they are no longer sure what you stand for. Nothing beats the drip-feed of news generated consistently by a determined PR team.

So, consistency of messaging and consistency of effort are both important. Only sustained public relations activities over a period of time can be successful in the hubbub of information which now bombards the public – from the printed, broadcasting and online media, with editorial matter as well as advertising – a veritable onslaught of messages. Only a fraction of these messages get through and are interpreted correctly, so we have to be both consistent and persistent. Part of the routine of PR work is to keep the lines of communication open at all times; to demonstrate that the organisation is constantly active, and that there is always something of interest going on.

Creativity

Part of the challenge of public relations is to be creative as well as clear-thinking and analytical. It is important not to be overwhelmed by routine work. PR people are appointed because of intelligence, tact and technical know-how, but are often judged on their performance by their flair. If flair is a combination of inspiration and originality, there must be an opportunity for these qualities to develop. This means stepping out of the daily deadlines for occasional brainstorming, re-engineering, and problem-solving sessions with the marketing and other teams. Early involvement in inter-departmental planning of programmes and events starts the information and gestation period, and sparks new ideas and new thinking and is good for both senior and junior staff. Fresh thinking can be bought in from outside consultancies and agencies, but it is good to generate your own as well.

Figure 2.1 Couple in Nature Discovery Zone, Ulster Museum (courtesy of National Museums, Northern Ireland)

Making space for creative thinking also means living with the consequences. New ideas need to be tested against corporate objectives and the marketing and PR strategies, not pursued for their own sake. True originality also implies a level of risk, so sometimes people have to be allowed to fail, as long as lessons are learned. Totally risk-averse organisations soon stagnate.

A good PR person is a valuable resource, someone who keeps in touch with new ideas and developments through contact with other institutions and a wider world. They should suggest useful ideas and different insights. By their nature, museums, galleries, and cultural organisations become immersed in their own subjects, while knowing that they have to be outward-facing and engage the public. Part of the PR person's role is to notice trends and be aware of public opinion, helping colleagues to connect with a wider public.

When a public relations officer or consultant stops providing creative input, it is time to assess the reasons. Are they bored, incompetent, or simply being deprived of opportunity?

Timing

Is good timing a matter of luck or judgement – or a combination of both? Life is littered with great stories released at a bad moments, and tiny stories that hit the headlines accidentally. Many PR practitioners would put a gift for good timing at the top of their wish list. Get it right – and amazing rewards are possible. Get it wrong – and even the best story will fail to attract attention.

Let us take luck out of the equation and say that experience can teach us a great deal about timing. Observation of how the media operates can show us what works and what does not. Choosing to release a story on a day when there is known competition – such as the opening of a new garden on the press day for the Chelsea Flower Show is probably not a good idea. Emailing a press release at 5 p.m. on a Friday is not good; neither is holding a press launch on a Monday morning. These are things that can usually be avoided as part of the planning process. Equally, if you are obliged to issue news about poor performance or some other institutional failure, choosing a day when a major event is going on might be considered sneaky – but worth a shot – 'a good day to bury bad news'. While August is the silly season for some, for others it is a golden opportunity. One thing about timing that is always true is that it is never too early to start promoting a major exhibition or launch of a new attraction. Journalists might tell you that it's too soon for them to act, but it is never too soon to start creating awareness.

Timing is also about being on the ball and connected with the world, as discussed above. We need to be alert to what is going in other institutions, and we need to develop an instinct for what is newsworthy by reading, watching and listening to a wide range of media. It's about catching a public mood at the right time, and recognising when prevailing conditions are favourable.

There are times when bad luck plays its part and plans go wrong because of major unscheduled events. Big disasters can divert journalists into covering topics outside their usual beat, sometimes for many days. This temporarily renders all efforts useless, and the skill is in quickly inventing a strategy for recovery.

Learning from others

Public relations professionals are never allowed to rest on their laurels and it is a big mistake to think that we know it all. We can decide that we are going to avoid repeating past mistakes, but we should also learn from other people's mistakes and triumphs. Good ideas are worth adopting and adapting, and a great deal of that goes on in PR. Imitation of others does, however, need to sit alongside our own original ideas – an innovation quickly begins to look like yet another stunt if it is overplayed. This book is full of original ideas from our case study contributors – see Appendix.

It is a good idea to watch what other organisations do. Networking, PR seminars, and the trade press are all good sources of information for finding out what others are doing. When something is a resounding success, don't be afraid to ask why. People are often very willing to share experiences and make recommendations. It can sometimes be interesting to ask a journalist why they covered a particular story.

Professionalism

Standards in public relations are laid down by professional associations in European countries, most of which are members of the Confédération Européen des Relations Publiques (CERP). In the United States, standards are set by the Public Relations Society of America .

Membership of a professional association, such as the Chartered Institute of Public Relations (CIPR) or the Chartered Institute of Marketing in the UK is a good idea for several reasons, but in particular for practitioners in the museum and galleries sector, who may feel remote from more usual, commercial areas of public relations and benefit from networking, seminars and website resources. Membership is also an accreditation for the employer when taking on new in-house PRs and employing consultants. See the Resources section for website addresses.

In every industry there are practitioners who describe themselves as professionals without the training or accreditation which professional institute membership implies. This does not necessarily make them worse at their job, because membership cannot guarantee an effective PR delivery. Professionalism, however – whether as a member or non-member – is important and means observing the principles described above inside and outside the organisation. The principles of practice contained within the CIPR code are shown below.

FUNDAMENTAL TO GOOD PUBLIC RELATIONS PRACTICE ARE:

INTEGRITY

- Honest and responsible regard for the public interest;

- Checking the reliability and accuracy of information before dissemination;

- Never knowingly misleading clients, employers, employees, colleagues and fellow professionals about the nature of representation or what can be competently delivered and achieved;

- Supporting the CIPR principles by bringing to the attention of the CIPR examples of malpractice and unprofessional conduct.

COMPETENCE

▪ Being aware of the limitations of professional competence: without limiting realistic scope for development, being willing to accept or delegate only that work for which practitioners are suitably skilled and experienced;

▪ Where appropriate, collaborating on projects to ensure the necessary skill base.

TRANSPARENCY AND AVOIDING CONFLICTS OF INTEREST

▪ Disclosing to employers, clients or potential clients any financial interest in a supplier being recommended or engaged;

▪ Declaring conflicts of interest (or circumstances which may give rise to them) in writing to clients, potential clients and employers as soon as they arise;

▪ Ensuring that services provided are costed and accounted for in a manner that conforms to accepted business practice and ethics.

CONFIDENTIALITY

▪ Safeguarding the confidences of present and former clients and employers;

▪ Being careful to avoid using confidential and 'insider' information to the disadvantage or prejudice of clients and employers, or to self-advantage of any kind;

▪ Not disclosing confidential information unless specific permission has been granted or the public interest is at stake or if required by law.

(Guidance reproduced by kind permission of the Chartered Institute of Public Relations December 2010)

EQUIPPED TO BE EFFECTIVE: INTEGRATED AND ORGANISED

Too often in cultural organisations the marketing and PR function is seen as some kind of add-on to the 'core business'. You will know the scenario: the vision is articulated, the strategic plan published, the programme set and then someone suddenly remembers about the audience, or, more specifically, that they need someone to do some promotion! The marketers and PR professionals are summoned, usually too late in the day, to give a voice to our product and to dig us out of a hole. This is convenient because if it all goes wrong, we can then blame them for being ineffective without needing to consider any possible inadequacy in our product, or in the planning process.

This is of course both counterintuitive and unhelpful. The needs and nature of the market are critical drivers of any successful organisation. It sounds obvious, but is surprisingly often overlooked, especially in the not-for-profit cultural sector, where the temptation is always to be driven by our own, rather than the public's interests.

To be fair, marketing specialists do not always help their own cause. There is a temptation, particularly when there are limited strategic opportunities within an organisation, for them to revert to a merely promotional role, producing endless runs of formulaic print and web content.

The truth is that marketing and, where they are available, marketing specialists, should be at the centre of the generation of organisational mission and vision. They should be fully integrated into the strategic planning process and must be central to the creation of our programmes. They, more than anyone, should be able to understand the brand, positioning and potential of any organisation and how it relates to its audiences; and, of course, how to reach those audiences.

In short, an organisation that fails to value or fully utilise its marketing resource, does so at its peril, not least because there will be many competitors in the market who use them better. So to any CEO or Director, I say: keep your marketers close to you; listen to them, encourage them – even trust them(!). That way, your vision will be clear, planning will be more effective, programmes better focused and audiences larger . . . and if it still all goes wrong, at least you can blame them with some justification.

(Alec Coles, Chief Executive Officer, Western Australian Museum, Perth, former Director of Tyne and Wear Museums)

In this era of new technology, the model of integration which the comments above emphasise should be planned into the organisation of your marketing and PR functions, with the added ingredient of IT to take advantage of social media developments. Here is one suggestion from Seb Chan at Powerhouse, Sydney on how that can be achieved:

The purpose of this diagram [overleaf] is to show how to get the most out of your 'online strategy'; here the web team is independent of both IT and marketing. It also shows the existing areas from which resources will need to be (re)deployed to deliver a holistic online strategy and a distinct social media strategy.

Every organisation has well-developed IT strategies, and their main impact on web strategy tends to be around hosting environments, backup, and security, as well as in the interconnection of web applications between internal and external environments – ecommerce, collection database access, etc. Increasingly we will find that organisations begin to move more of their hosting, backup and security, as well as some corporate applications out to cloud-computing environments. Whilst many in the cultural sector already have their websites externally hosted, many more functions will move external as utility computing takes over. Obviously each organisation will also have a well-developed marketing strategy that overlaps with web strategy in the online space, usually in terms of brand consistency and continuity and offline/online campaigns, targeted email marketing, etc.

Social media overlap with all three areas – web, marketing and IT. The size of these overlaps will vary from organisation to organisation but it is critical to understand that social media strategy is *not* just marketing or web.

Let's take a look at the overlaps with reference to some of the work of the Powerhouse. Social media overlaps with marketing at the Powerhouse most significantly for the Sydney Observatory blog. The Observatory blog exists to engage new audiences, build an online community, but also to operate as a significant part of the online marketing and promotion of the physical world site as well. The blog is also a key part of the Museum's web strategy for the Observatory – content

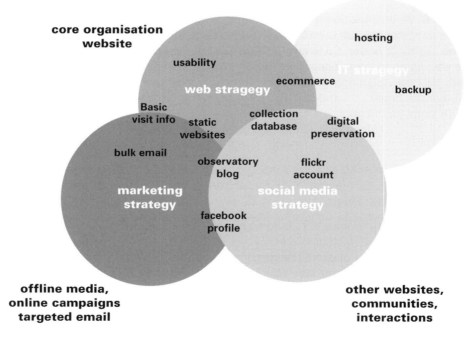

Figure 2.2 Intersecting strategies (adapted from Seb Chan, Powerhouse Museum). You could add your 'PR function' into this diagram between the 'marketing strategy' circle and the 'social media strategy' circle, overlapping both.

production has been decentralised and the blog operates as a de facto content management system. In other organisations a Facebook profile or group, or a MySpace page/persona would also be good examples of where marketing and social media strategy clearly intersect with resource implications.

Social media overlaps with IT strategy in two key areas. The first of these is hosting and security. Once museum content begins to be decentralised to third-party sites such as Flickr and YouTube there are very real issues that need to be dealt with around ownership and control. The second is around digital preservation. Once content is decentralised how is it to be 'preserved'? And, more importantly, how are community interactions on these and the museum's own social media projects preserved? Does it even make sense to preserve 'the conversation'? What happens to a project blog once the project is completed – how is it 'archived'?

(Seb Chan, Powerhouse Museum)

There is no magic formula for the optimum size or staffing of a public relations office, press office or marketing department, but it is certain that rewards are only won by effort. Most public relations work consists of time spent on the telephone, on email, and in face-to-face meetings, so it stands to reason that the number of staff hours available will directly affect results. It is a labour-intensive occupation. New technology enables us to be more efficient in our handling of information, but also requires time to be spent on record keeping and data maintenance. In council offices and other organisations, departments 'contract' PR time although no funds necessarily pass between them. This will only work with forward planning and flexibility allowing for new developments and crises.

Public relations work is a professional specialism, so senior staff should have both appropriate qualifications and experience. More junior staff can learn on the job if they have the right personal qualities and training time is available. They should be articulate, intelligent, and tactful, as well as computer-literate and, ideally, good writers. The new arrival whose experience has been gained in the private sector will face something of a 'culture shock', being possibly used to more generous budgets, larger staff and quicker decision-making processes. The job satisfaction that comes with the mission of the organisation has to compensate for the shortfall.

If there ever was a time when PR could be handled on a part-time basis, with a desk, a telephone, and a card index – it is long gone. An investment in staff, technology and centrally located office space is needed for effective PR, and the serious-minded organisation will make those investments despite the difficult economic environment in which we operate.

There are dozens of different structures for a PR department. Sometimes it is combined with marketing and sometimes quite separate operationally, but as we are demonstrating in this book, new media are increasingly bringing the two together, simply as 'communications'. The PR manager should report to the director; if the PR manager is remote from the director by one or two links in the chain of command, it will be very difficult to establish the understanding, confidence and trust that make for swift, effective decisions. In addition, because of the challenges of the work and the level of performance required, the PR manager will need to be a senior appointment if the size of the organisation makes this possible. The range of PR work is extreme, from high policymaking and sophisticated advisory work to day-to-day press relations and administration, so junior assistants will be needed.

Geographically, the PR team needs to be central and within easy reach of most parts of the museum or institution or heritage site; there may be any number of events at the same time in different locations such as a press tour, a visiting film crew, or a training seminar – and telephones still need to be answered in the office (although mobile communications has made this part of the job easier). Also, there may be a need for troubleshooting at any moment in any direction, and time is very precious.

The workload of PR and marketing teams will typically fluctuate throughout the year, and from year to year, depending on the activities of the organisation. While a museum or gallery should 'own' its ongoing PR effort, in the form of permanent or long-contract staff, there is a place for the independent public relations consultant or agency in smaller seasonal venues. They are useful when the larger organisation is handling a major launch, such as a new building or important exhibition, and trying to reach out to new markets or wider audiences. They can also be helpful when a sponsor or donor is involved, requiring additional layers of PR work.

How do you know how Facebook works if you don't have your own page? If you don't have the time or interest yourself, ask around and you will find a younger colleague who is right up to date on the latest social media. Specialist marketing, PR and media magazines can now be accessed easily online for free or for a subscription. Watching TV, listening to the radio, reading newspapers and magazines is of course vital. And don't forget to network, talk to others, go to conferences and seminars, and share experiences.

With so much going on in the world of communications, it is vital to keep up to date and in touch with threats and opportunities. This is where PR and marketing professionals can add real value to their organisation.

CHAPTER 3

THE MARKETING STRATEGY – STAGE 1: THE INTERNAL AUDIT

The marketing strategy and the business or corporate plan

The internal review: Part 1 of the marketing audit

When, who and how?

Visitor numbers to the venue, the website, subsidiary facilities

Income from admission, the shop, café, online sales

Visitor profile

The visitor experience – in the building and online

Location

Marketing activities now and in the recent past

Audience development initiatives and special projects

The next stage

THE MARKETING STRATEGY AND THE BUSINESS OR CORPORATE PLAN

The marketing strategy is for the long term. It provides the backbone to all marketing and communications activities and to tactical marketing plans. It has a number of different elements – audience development, online and social media and public relations. It may be the overall communications strategy for the organisation, in which case it will also include internal communications, stakeholder partnership and customer relations as well as advocacy – in fact everything covered in this book.

In this chapter we will look specifically at 'stage one' of putting the marketing strategy together or reviewing it, starting by examining internal factors. This process may overlap to some extent with a brand review explored in Chapter 6.

A 'master plan' may look 20–30 years into the future. It should be about a vision for the future and how to get there. A 'strategic plan' is about setting the direction, and looking ahead 3–5 years, usually delivered through the business plan. The marketing strategy will be part of all these, but its form and details will vary. It may be tempting in times of financial hardship to put the master plan on hold and limit the vision for the future. But without a master plan the museum or attraction has nothing to aim for and nothing up its sleeve when the opportunity arises. When the National Lottery was first launched in the UK in 1994 with its defined pots of capital funding for arts and heritage, it was the cultural institutions with their master plans already in place who were first off the block and who won sizeable grants in the early years.

The marketing strategy will also form an integral part (possibly adapted and in a less detailed form) of any approach for funding, sponsorship, lottery application and other grant applications. Even a planning application may require sight of the marketing strategy.

It may seem a simpler option to start the marketing strategy from a blank piece of paper – set up a brainstorm and initiate some blue-sky thinking. After all, this will be much more fun and creative than plodding through a lot of data from the past. But the audit of internal and external factors will provide invaluable information on past, present and future activities. It will show up shortfalls in performance targets and suggest better ways of measuring success and setting benchmarks for future reviews. It will throw up internal obstacles and external challenges, as well as opportunities for the future (see the External review and the SWOT analysis in the next chapter). This will ensure that the marketing strategy is rooted not just in ambitious plans for the future but in the realities of past achievements, with their mistakes as well as successes.

These are some of the objectives of the marketing strategy:

- Overall strategic direction and how to achieve those aims
- Marketing objectives relating to those aims based on the mission
- Tactics – detailed activities and plans to meet targets and monitor achievements
- Demands/funders/sponsors and others
- Political expectations
- Academic ambitions
- Financial/resource considerations.

The marketing review and audit will present a picture of the organisation; the scope of its collections and/or display; and its historical and present-day purpose, including any additional major services or programmes. It will describe how the museum or cultural centre is set out, and how it presents itself. It will paraphrase the mission statement and explain who the intended audience or audiences are. The funding base will be described – sufficient to explain how growth and change can or cannot take place. Achievements and opportunities will be outlined, as well as constraints and limitations. The tone of the report will be as if written for a reader who comes to the subject afresh. This allows everyone to remind themselves of the purpose of the institution and the key objectives in the mission statement.

In the twenty-first-century audience-focused museum, a critical role of the marketing function is to feed deep insight into the organisation: insight into the needs, wants and motivations of audiences; insight into how effective the organisation is in achieving its social and financial objectives; insight into the effectiveness of displays, facilities and services at engaging audiences; and insight into the success of the exhibition programme.

This insight needs to inform the corporate plan. The responsibility for shaping the proposition, reaching and communicating with audiences, engaging with them, meeting their needs, making meaning for them, generating outcomes and, most importantly, getting them to return, is shared equally by each and every department within the organisation and rooted in a philosophical commitment to the audience.

(Gerri Morris, Director, Morris Hargreaves McIntyre)

THE INTERNAL REVIEW: PART 1 OF THE MARKETING AUDIT

The internal review is a systematic, critical and unbiased appraisal of the internal factors that have affected the performance of the museum/gallery over a defined period, and includes: visitor numbers; income; visitor profile; visitor experience; location; marketing activities; audience development initiatives and special projects; results; and next steps.

When, who and how?

Reviewing the marketing strategy is normally part of the annual updating of the strategic plan and/or business plan. Bids for funding, plans for a new attraction, venue or service are also good reasons for initiating a new marketing strategy or reviewing the old. The arrival of a new chief executive, a new marketing team, the challenge of a funding crisis may also generate an overhaul of the marketing strategy.

Who is the best person to lead the review? A new marketing director or manager in any cultural organisation should be able to carry out such a review within six months while still fresh and able to look at the organisation almost as an outsider. A marketing consultant with experience in the cultural sector is a good alternative, bringing detachment and experience, which may not be available in-house. Also, if information may be disclosed which reveals inefficiencies and past mistakes, management can distance itself from the process, while still implementing changes.

The process will vary depending on the size of the organisation and the time available. The pressure may be on to meet a grant application deadline or shortfall in funding. So, set a timetable for the review. A marketing consultant would start by reviewing all available data (see below) mainly through desk research; possibly initiate a survey or further research to meet any obvious gaps; then move on to interviews with the marketing, PR, and visitor services teams in order to review past and present marketing activities as well as providing an independent view of the visitor experience. Senior management and board members should also be included, as appropriate.

It is important for the person leading the review to take a pragmatic approach to the data and information available; and to use the data to draw marketing-related conclusions.

Visitor numbers to the venue, the website, subsidiary facilities

The crudest measurement of the museum or attraction's success or failure is the number of visitors. Most museums, galleries and heritage attractions, whether free or charging, produce monthly visitors figures and publish them on an annual basis showing growth or decline. But visitor figures reveal much more if carefully analysed. As part of the audit, the monthly pattern should be examined and related to the peaks and troughs of the year – short school holidays in the autumn and winter; the moving feast of Easter; and the longer summer holidays.

It would be useful to look back at three years or so to pick up any variations. The appeal of the attraction or its location will influence these peaks and troughs. The impact of marketing campaigns, special events and new exhibitions should be identified on the month-by-month graph. Campaigns or launches which do not show up in the admission figures for the museum should be investigated further. Do not forget to examine your website statistics in the same way. You may also relate your social media activities to this annual month-by-month flow.

Admission-charging museums and attractions have the advantage of ticketing, which through current technology and differentiated pricing can provide not just crude visitor numbers, but peaks and troughs during the day and week, as well as basic visitor profiles, breaking down the visitor figures into children, adults, families, students and retired.

Figure 3.1
Standing in line
for art: Banksy
exhibition
(courtesy of
Bristol Museum,
Gallery &
Archive)

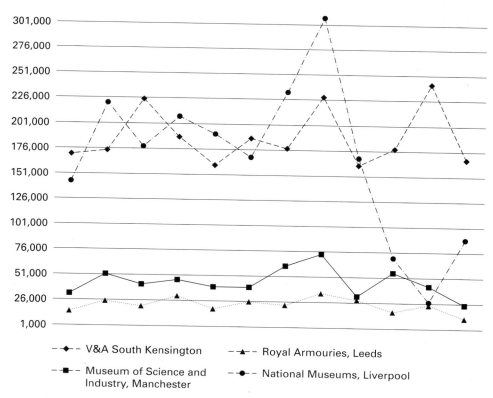

Figure 3.2 Attendances at a selection of national museums shown month-by-month throughout a year (DCMS, 2010)

The website is part of the museum or attraction's experience, and amplifies its themes and purpose. While it provides essential information for those planning a visit, it is also used to follow up on a visit, researching additional information on objects and experiences. It is also becoming a stand-alone experience – not a virtual museum (an idea that died in the 1990s) but a rich resource offering services and information not necessarily available within the gallery, such as research, learning and socialising. This makes measuring website use and its associated social media more important than ever; maintaining comparable data is the biggest challenge as you update your metrics.

Website visitor flows should reflect the overall visitor pattern but may have different peaks and troughs related to social media activities, news items or presence and links to other major websites. (See Chapter 17 Research) for how to measure visitor flow, website visits and social media.)

The audit of visitor figures should also look separately at those areas which can be accessed without necessarily entering the museum. Many attractions in town centres have popular cafés where parents may gather between delivering and picking up children, or tourists rest their weary feet – and use the toilets. It is important to get a handle on these numbers and how these users can become museum or gallery visitors if they aren't already.

Some attractions also have gardens; historic houses often have a lower admission charge for the gardens than for the property as a whole. What are the trends here? Are more people bypassing the house and opting for the gardens? If so, why? If outside areas are used for major events during the summer, this should also be measured and be part of the audit. Don't forget to include any impact by weather – good or bad.

Income from admission, the shop, café, online sales

Fluctuations in the monthly visitor pattern will be reflected in the income figures. Is the shop and/or café meeting its income targets? Are online sales an opportunity missed or are there other ways of reaching this growing shopping market? Any discrepancies or missed opportunities should be investigated. It may be a change in prices or staffing in any of these areas which has impacted on the income figures.

At a time when free museums and galleries may be considering introducing charges it is important to carry out the competitive review to see what others are charging (see Chapter 4) but also to introduce admission systems that will deliver the maximum benefits in terms of information about visitors. Comparisons with other attractions in the area are important and form part of the competitive review in the external audit.

Visitor profile

So who are these visitors? What lies behind the peaks and troughs, and how can we maximise our knowledge and use it to best purpose? Visitor surveys are of course part of the answer. During the process of the audit it might be possible to fill any gaps in knowledge by carrying out a quick visitor survey over a short period of time. However, it works best when surveys are carried out on a rolling basis, in order to get a more complete picture of visitors through the year. If this is not possible, twice a year over a two-week period would be a good alternative.

The list of additional topics to be covered in visitor surveys could be large but keep it manageable for the best response. Ideally surveys should be carried out by a specialist organisation through interviews. Some venues use self-completion questionnaires which can work if properly constructed and analysed and if there is a good response. It is also possible to use computer terminals and ask visitors to sit down for five minutes before they leave to record their answers. Website visitors should also be surveyed perhaps once a year using a pop-up questionnaire and perhaps offering some incentive for completing it. (More in Chapter 17 Research.)

Use a standard format for the basic questions about age etc. to make year-by-year comparisons easier and also to provide a benchmark for comparing your visitors with those in other organisations. Don't forget to include the home postcode or zip code because it will provide information on the geographical spread of your audience and also about the status and average household income of each residential district identified, using segmentation programmes. (More in Chapters 7 and 17.)

Your annual visitor figures measure visits; you also need to know the proportion of repeat visitors. Depending on your venue, its local popularity, the frequency of changing exhibitions, your repeat-visitor rate within one year may be as high as 30–40%. This is a good thing, as it shows your popularity, but it could hide a problem in attracting new visitors.

The visitor experience – in the building and online

The visitor research may also provide some information for the marketing audit on the satisfaction levels with the current offer. In addition, the leader of the audit should examine every aspect of the visitor experience onsite and online through staff interviews and direct observation.

The visitor experience starts online. It includes: the journey and parking or access from public transport; the nature of the arrival and welcome; orientation; information on the exhibition such as audio-guides; tours; labels, guided tours; toilet facilities; the café and shop. Visitor services are now taken seriously by most cultural attractions with professional staff, supported in many places by volunteers. Good customer care cannot be taken for granted – training is essential. Today's public is much more demanding than in the past and likely to voice even the smallest complaints, which if not properly handled can snowball into a major incident.

A review of complaints over a period will form a useful part of the audit as it will show up any shortcomings in facilities or customer care and in the visitor experience as a whole. Will the visitor return or recommend a visit to a friend – always the crucial question?

In summary, the visitor services audit will look at the following:

- Does the organisation conduct regular, consistent visitor surveys?
- What do such surveys tell us?
- Do all members of staff share the customer care mission?
- How wholeheartedly does the management support good customer care?
- Have physical access issues been addressed? (In the UK, public venues are subject to the Disability Discrimination Act – see Resources.)
- Are cultural and intellectual differences between visitors being catered for? (See Equality Act 2010.)
- Have access issues been considered in relation to the website as well as print? (As above.)
- Are safety and security procedures being followed?
- Is staff training proving effective?
- Are front-of-house staff and volunteers properly supported by others?
- Are good lines of communication in place for complaints, suggestions and information-sharing?
- What systems are in place to monitor quality of care?
- Does information material serve the public well?
- Does directional signage work in terms of circulation and finding your way around?
- Do the exhibitions, displays and the museum/attraction as a whole deliver a 'satisfactory' experience – or preferably more ('I would recommend it to a friend')?
- Has the 'experience' reached its peak in the product life cycle? How much longer before it will need to be 'tweaked' or completely remodelled?
- And are the toilets of an acceptable standard? Are they regularly monitored?

Any perceived shortcomings in the visitor experience in terms of displays, interpretation or temporary exhibitions may need a radical and more long-term approach, involving exhibition and attractions consultants as well as re-training in-house staff.

It is a public expectation that museums and cultural attractions should meet the green agenda. The internal audit should consider how far your attraction has achieved its sustainability targets and whether the public is aware of your efforts. There may be positive elements to publicise or threats to address.

Location

Location is as much about perception as reality. People will make inordinate efforts to get to something they really want to see – Alnwick Castle in the North of England; Auschwitz-Birkenau Memorial and State Museum outside Kracow; Cadillac Ranch in Amarillo, Texas; or the Apartheid Museum on the outskirts of Johannesburg – these are unique places but not exactly on the beaten track. So location does not always matter. But when your offer is just one of many similar museums, galleries or historic houses, location becomes crucial. The wonderful Dulwich Picture Gallery in South London, Aston Hall just outside Birmingham, the Culinary Archives and Museum in Rhode Island, and Plymouth Plantation outside Boston, even the Getty in Los Angeles, are not in the middle of anywhere, nor well served by public transport. They have to work that much harder to overcome the location handicap.

So consider your location in terms of your venue's uniqueness in relation to its location. Often this is a question of perception as much as reality. Your internal audit will of course review your signage inside and outside the attraction. Ask any newcomers to your museum as they arrive how easy they found it to get there, whether they came by car, by public transport or on foot. Send out staff members to check on old signposts and see whether new ones have been put in place. The audit should enumerate and describe the signage as it exists, and make recommendations for improvements.

And what about your opening hours, are they clearly displayed outside and also on the website? Are the current opening hours relevant to the local community or are they a barrier – are you closed on Saturdays or Sundays, for example?

Historic houses and smaller museums in the countryside and seaside resorts tend to close during the winter months, reopening at Easter and closing again in October. Some of the UK's historic houses have successfully broken this pattern by opening their doors just before or just after Christmas for a few days, recreating the ambience of a country house Christmas with a welcoming log fire in the entrance hall.

Adjusting working hours and days can be a sensitive business for the management to address. It impacts on contracts of employment and any union agreements, licensed activities and shop trading hours, and on volunteers.

Marketing activities now and in the recent past

The review should consider current and past marketing activities and the resources devoted to these, their success and failures, whether measured or just anecdotal. This would include campaigns, print and distribution, advertising, website, social media and public relations, and internal communications. Start by analysing events and launches held during the previous year, including campaigns aimed at particular periods or exhibitions. Also include campaigns to attract additional school visitors and niche audiences, or to promote alternative use of facilities – for events and conferences, for example. Measurements include additional visitors to the attraction and the website; additional spend in the shop and café, media coverage, visitor comments; and return on investment (campaign costs measured against additional income).

The Metropolitan Museum of Art in New York carried out an economic impact survey for their Summer exhibitions in 2008, demonstrating the generation of $610 million in spending by tourists from all over the world. The average spend was $718 on hotels, eating out and local transportation, plus $426 on shopping while in New York (Metropolitan Museum of Arts Summer Exhibitions Survey November 2008). This kind of survey can play an important part in an advocacy programme.

The internal review is a good opportunity to consider the impact of printed material and other forms of communication (such as the website) with groups of staff and visitors to see how they perceive the messages, the visual images and the overall impact of the museum's or gallery's brand. PR activities should be reviewed at the same time.

Marketing spend is frequently spread over several budget headings, including exhibitions and events as well as the ubiquitous 'publicity'. For the purpose of the marketing audit, and ideally for the future, it is very important to bring these marketing spends together under one heading. Sensible decisions about allocating resources and boosting marketing cannot be taken if management does not have a clear understanding of actual total spend in this area. Museums and galleries supported from public funds are accountable either to a government department, the intermediary or to the local authority or council supporting the museum. Non-charging museums are expected to raise up to one-third of their annual income from admission charges to special exhibitions, events, shops and cafés, and other sources, and must be as vigilant and financially savvy as independent museums, private historic houses and cultural attractions, whether commercial or run by a not-for-profit trust.

The internal audit is an opportunity to establish how lines of communications work, or do not work, and what ideas the staff have for how they can be improved. This is probably the most sensitive part of the review and could best be carried out by an outsider. When our nineteenth-century cultural edifices were constructed, little consideration was given to staff and service areas, except perhaps for a grand office for the director. Curators and others have traditionally had to find an office in any remote corners of a sometimes huge building, cut off not just by distances but by the flow of visitors. Modern offices are usually open-planned, encouraging management by walking around and communication.

Audience development initiatives and special projects

Audience development projects frequently fall outside the overall marketing objectives of the organisation. The marketing audit is an opportunity to integrate such projects into the marketing process and to evaluate the results on the same basis as outlined above, deciding whether they could be a valuable part of the overall marketing strategy. An audience development project may have been driven by the education department or inspired by a special exhibition, and may have been financed separately through a grant process.

THE NEXT STAGE

The final stage of the internal review is an analysis of the results and a checklist of activities and services that work well and those that do not. This will form part of the Strengths and Weaknesses in the SWOT analysis (Chapter 4).

While the internal audit is the starting point for the audit and for the development of the marketing strategy, it can also provide useful information for all kinds of activities. It is advisable for the director and key managers to have a chance to comment at draft stage and to discuss any curious or controversial features with the person or team who carried out the audit. Serious shortcomings should not just be accepted but be included on an immediate action list for improvements. Ideally this list should identify a person responsible for each improvement suggested, and include a schedule for the work.

When feedback has been collected and absorbed, the scene is set for the preparation of the external review (see next chapter). You may choose not to tackle all of the issues simultaneously or immediately. Resources and workload may be a factor. The most useful thing that an audit can provide is a clear sense of priorities, so that both long- and short-term strategies can be designed, ideally with a chance for every department to contribute towards it, and to move in the same general direction.

CHAPTER 4

THE MARKETING STRATEGY – STAGE 2: THE EXTERNAL AUDIT

THE EXTERNAL ENVIRONMENT IS CHANGING

The most innovative products with huge launch budgets fail if they haven't taken the external environment into account. Some factors can be predicted and some cannot – 'the unknown unknowns' – as a famous American defence secretary called them a few years ago. But we can be prepared by analysing the external environment systematically as part of the marketing review, draw conclusions from the results and develop our marketing strategy to be flexible in the face of uncertainties ahead.

These external factors include economic and social factors such as population growth or decline, as well as political changes which have a bearing on government, local council or sponsorship funding. As we have seen in Chapter 1, technological developments have had a massive impact on institutions as they digitise their collections and adapt their marketing to new media opportunities. The green agenda is creating demands for sustainability and is linked to a 'go local' drive.

The mature markets in Western Europe and the US, where almost half the population regularly visits cultural attractions, cannot rest on their laurels as migration changes the population patterns and political aims shift. In cultural centres across the Middle East, India and China, the challenge is just as great, as cultural institutions aim to instil a sense of heritage and wonder in a population which stretches from the very rich to those on or below subsistence levels. Marketing is a discipline which needs to be in tune with both internal and external politics, developing strategies which aid the institution's long-term goals and which are built on a thorough understanding of the existing and the available markets.

POPULATION AND DEMOGRAPHIC TRENDS

As part of the external audit, you will need to analyse demographic trends as they may affect your attraction in the near future. Start by identifying the main areas that your visitors come from, using your visitor profile and any postcode research (mentioned in the previous chapter). Using a segmentation programme, such as ACORN, will give you a map of your catchment area. Further desk research will reveal more information on the population within your reach and their profiles; as well as an indication of population trends over the next 5–10 years. The last published Census in the UK was in 2001 and another took place in March 2011. European countries gather similar statistics. In the United States, the US Census Bureau holds a variety of information on communities, income, and population growth. The last full census was carried out in 2010. (See website addresses in Resources.)

Publishers of regional newspapers and advertising agencies collect detailed information about demographics and behaviour patterns of their local population. When it comes to test-marketing new products, regions will be chosen because of their characteristics: age ranges; income levels; car ownership; disposable income; and leisure habits. Looking at your region through the eyes of an advertiser can provide a remarkable insight. (See Chapter 17 Research.)

The sort of information that you need about your area is as follows:

- Breakdown of age groups
- Projected trends of these age groups
- Numbers of schoolchildren and schools, and projected trends
- Numbers of retired people, estimated and projected
- Income level breakdown
- Occupational breakdown/trends
- Educational attainment levels
- Ethnic mix/breakdown and trends
- Growth trends – potential new arrivals or departures
- People with disabilities.

Once you have a clear picture of your potential audiences across your catchment area, compare it with your visitor profile (Chapter 3) and see where the gaps are. Which are the missing segments and which audiences are already well represented?

CULTURAL PARTICIPATION

Participation in cultural activities in Europe and the US is growing, not just in line with population growth but as a percentage of the population as a whole. This should not be a surprise, because it is strongly linked to educational achievement standards, and these are rising. Surveys such as the UK's *Taking Part* also show that there is a 'hard-core' of committed cultural audiences, as well as a large number of people who dip in and out of cultural activities, including crafts and choirs.

Taking Part is a major participation study undertaken on a rolling basis by the Department for Culture, Media and Sport. It is based on face-to-face interviews with a sample of the population, and includes children. In 2009/10 it showed that 47% of adults had visited a museum, gallery or archive in the last year – a small increase on the previous year. Visits by children aged 11–15 also increased to 55%. These figures are broken down regionally and vary across the country, with London showing the highest levels of participation at 56%, and the East Midlands the lowest at 40%. Nationwide, 70% of adults had visited a heritage site. This rose to 81% in the South East.

Similar figures are currently not available from the EU. The Euro Barometer measures cultural activities across the EU rather than by country, but more information may be available in individual countries.

THE LEISURE AND TOURISM ENVIRONMENT

Culture is now recognised as a major driver of tourism. Its impact has been recognised across the world; from the Middle East, with new museums and cultural quarters; to China, with an ambitious programme of investment in new museums; and to Cairo, where the Grand Egyptian Museum at the Pyramids is due to open in 2012. Festivals of arts and literature thrive not just where you expect them in Salzburg or Glyndebourne, but in large city centres and small towns across Europe.

Speaking in 2010, David Cameron, UK Prime Minister, said:

> **People sometimes characterise culture as a choice between old and new; between classical or pop, great heritage or modern art. But in Britain it's not one or the**

Figure 4.1 Steaming water, ancient stone, new museum (courtesy of Roman Baths, Bath and North East Somerset Council)

other, it's both. It's Glyndebourne and Glastonbury. The Bristol Old Vic and the Edinburgh Fringe. The Bodleian Library and the Hay literary festival. Ascot and the Millennium Stadium; Nelson's column and the Olympic Park's Orbit.

We have so much to be proud of, so much to share with each other and so much to show off to the rest of the world.

Tourism presents a huge economic opportunity. Not just bringing business to Britain but right across Britain, driving new growth in the regions and helping to deliver the rebalancing of our national economy that is so desperately needed.

(Source www.number10.gov.uk September 2010)

VisitBritain estimates that cultural tourism is worth £4.5 billion to the UK's economy. Chapter 9 considers the practical aspects of taking advantage of cultural tourism. Here, we will consider the external audit and how to assess the potential market for your particular museum or heritage attraction.

In the UK, VisitBritain provides the overseas marketing strategy and implements promotional programmes across the world. Local councils play an important part in tourism directly, through destination marketing organisations (DMOs) and tourist agencies. Most European countries have their own tourism organisations, whereas in the United States it is the individual states which take the lead.

From your own visitor profile you will already have an idea of how far your catchment area stretches and how big your tourist (staying visitors) and day-visitor market is. Can this be expanded? What is the picture for the town or region as a whole? Are there local tour operators you could work with? Is there a conference centre which attracts national and international conferences? And how unique is your collection or exhibitions or cultural attraction when considered on a national scale?

At one time forecasters predicted a huge growth in leisure time – and certainly the number of people enjoying a long and relatively prosperous retirement has increased. However, a significant proportion of the population work longer hours than ever, sometimes with more than one job to augment their income; or alternatively in professions where 12-hour days are the norm. At the same time, sections of the local community don't work at all, but don't have the resources or interest to pursue a cultural activity. Your competition review will identify competing leisure activities as well as places people visit. For more long-term leisure trends you need to consult others; possibly your local council, but more likely one of the forecasting institutes. Their work is usually reserved for paying clients but they share some of the headline information through conferences and leisure publications.

COMPETITORS – THE COMPETITION REVIEW

Provided there is sufficient time, the competition review is possibly the most enjoyable part of the external audit. This is an opportunity for the marketing manager or the consultant to go and see what others are doing within the catchment area. Or if time is not available, recruit some of your more experienced volunteers to go 'mystery shopping', comparing facilities at rival attractions.

The competition review should list all actual and potential competitors for your main markets. Also consider your various niche audiences – schools, other learners, venue-hirers, specialist exhibitions, etc. Who are your competitors here? Competition is not always obvious. Today it could just as well be the local garden centre with its café and playground, or the brand new shopping centre, open seven days a week and into the evenings. And the major growth in how people spend their leisure time has been in online activities and electronic games; before that it was television.

For each identified attraction or leisure venue, consider some of these factors:

- What is special (distinctive – the USP) about the venue or attraction?
- How do visitor services compare with yours?
- Current visitor figures (if available) and profile of visitors
- Admission charges (or not); ease of access (free parking, for example); good signage
- Future plans for new features or a new venue at these attractions, as well as for your area as a whole; what will the impact be of a huge new shopping centre, a multiplex cinema, or a new art gallery?
- Are there opportunities for partnership and cooperation?

Identifying your neighbouring cultural attractions as competitors does not mean that you cannot work with them as partners. Together you can extend the cultural offer in your area and create partnerships to attract new audiences, including tourists. Of course, you are still in competition on any given day when people are choosing their leisure activity. Here is the experience from York, one of the UK's leading cultural destinations:

> York is a competitive environment as there are many museums and attractions competing for the time and attention of the 7.1 million visitors who come every year. However, we have always seen our role as helping to attract visitors to the city as well as attracting those visitors to our museums. The importance of the city as a brand led us to expand our activity into the city itself in 2008 with 'The Grand Tour in York', in association with the National Gallery, which saw over fifty high-quality replicas of paintings from the national collection plus some from York's collection being exhibited in the streets across the historic heart of the

city. It was incredibly successful as a marketing campaign, reaching a worldwide audience.

We are currently leading on a regional project 'Art in Yorkshire' – supported by Tate, which brings together nineteen public galleries in a year-long festival of exhibitions and events happening across Yorkshire. Working with Welcome to Yorkshire, the tourism agency for Yorkshire, will enable us to reach a greater number of people within the county and beyond to raise the profile of our galleries.

The future success of museums and cultural institutions must lie in co-operation. We need to take a wider approach to cultural provision by institutions reinforcing each other in the public's mind. In York we are seeking to work together with the other cultural institutions to create a framework where we can all flourish.

(Janet Barnes, Chief Executive, York Museums Trust)

PEEST

The liveliest session at any marketing seminar is usually the PEEST workshop. This is a good way of involving your colleagues from different departments in the external audit; everyone will have something to contribute. The elements that make up PEEST are:

Figure 4.2 Grand refurbishment of York Museum (courtesy of York Museums Trust)

- Politics – funding environment and policy changes
- Environment – city and rural planning
- Economic environment
- Social factors (not covered above)
- Technology.

Politics and the funding environment

Politicians are getting more involved in culture. They see it as: an image booster for the city or the region; an industry contributing to the local or national economy; and as a social force, nurturing the national identity while recognising diversity. So changes in the political makeup of government, whether at national or local level, will have ramifications on every cultural organisation. It is important to keep up to date with the political timetable and the cultural agenda of political parties. As part of your PEEST review consider the local political environment and how it might change in the future.

Whether you receive grants or subsidies from central or local government, or from an intermediary body such as the Arts Council, political changes may have a dramatic impact upon your funding, as in the UK during 2011. The marketing audit should consider how cutbacks in funding may affect visitor numbers and income.

Environment – city and rural planning

Major new developments in your area may have an impact on the future of your organisation, and should be assessed in your external audit. A simple change in the road layout could affect access or 'passing trade'. A new block of apartments with no parking spaces might put pressure on parking slots that your visitors use. A change in public transport routes may damage or enhance your ability to attract visitors. Such issues can also cause a great deal of local controversy. In Chapter 14 (Communicating with stakeholders) there is more information on building your relationship with local government.

New and existing attractions are subject to pressures to improve their sustainability. One of the immediate impacts may be in the distances that people are prepared to travel if they are conscious of their carbon footprint. The National Trust, for example, with responsibility for hundreds of historic properties throughout the UK, has addressed this issue in a variety of ways in its future strategy called 'Going Local – Fresh tracks down old roads'. This means shifting power from the National Trust central office to individual properties, empowering them to focus on their immediate neighbourhood in terms of partnerships and supplies, such as sourcing local food for cafés and restaurants. It also includes using local suppliers and workers for restoration projects wherever possible.

The economic environment

The economic environment, including trends in tourism, will affect not just visitor numbers but all forms of income generation. Pricing structures and programming should be influenced by the economic wellbeing or otherwise of the surrounding community. As Western economies recover from the 2008/10 credit crunch and recession, make sure that your marketing strategy is ready to take advantage of the opportunities that this will bring.

Social factors

Population changes and their impact on the cultural sector have been discussed already but the external audit should also address any social factors which are likely to impact on the marketing strategy. Assumptions based on the past need to be challenged – age, for example. Traditionally, museums and galleries have grouped 'old' visitors into one segment that includes everyone over 60 – or even everyone over 50. A much more segmented approach must now be taken to this age group which makes up 30–40% of the population in Western economies. It includes the 'young' retired (so-called baby-boomers) who behave very much as they did when they were in their 40s – enjoying a good lifestyle and making demands on quality and entertainment. At the same time the over-75 age group is growing, some will be less mobile but still active culturally. At the other end of the age spectrum there is a whole generation of young people who are dependent on social networks and mobiles and need to be communicated with in bite-sized pieces.

It is useful to understand the nature, behaviour and motivations of your local population and how it is related to social class (see Chapter 17 Research) for information on different segmentation approaches). *Taking Part* reveals that the level of education is still a strong indicator of museum or gallery visiting.

But the characteristics of your catchment area can hold surprises. Regardless of income, first-generation immigrants can be highly ambitious for their children, and although they may not be keen on visiting museums and galleries themselves, they will see benefits for their offspring. Areas of high unemployment might re-position your attraction as a social meeting place without any action on your part. We need to understand these trends and to accommodate our socially mobile population.

Technology

The impact of new technology on museums and cultural attraction has already been referred to in Chapters 1 and 2. In the area of marketing and public relations the new media technology has revolutionised the delivery of messages and promotional campaigning. The question here is – What will happen in the future? Your external review will attempt to look 5 years ahead and you will find some predictions in other parts of this book.

One school of thought is that technology will consolidate – internet, mobile phones, social media – and concentrate on improvements and interoperability. But there are some – the doom merchants – who predict that the internet or mobile phone network will collapse and fragment from overload or cyber crime. The majority of forecasters are much more positive and see the internet gradually moving towards the 'semantic web' – an idea that has been around for the past decade (Ross Parry, *Museums in a Digital Age*) where the emphasis shifts from information to meaning. The semantic web would enable users to search across specialist silos, i.e. online databases, for research, writing and other creative activities. So how far your cultural institution has digitised its collections and created searchable databases should be considered as part of the external review. The institution may get left behind and be less able to take advantage of income-generating opportunities in the future if digitisation is lagging behind. Similarly, your website should now be Web 2.0 interactive and ready to handle the next phase of innovation, including new platforms, social media and gadgets.

This part of PEEST will need to be reviewed at regular intervals as technology is constantly changing. The marketing strategy and marketing plans will reflect the world as it is today and what might happen in the next few years. However, few could have predicted even in 1990 that the internet would have become such a huge part of everyone's lives or that the mobile phone would be an everyday and essential part of the lives of people around the globe, reminding us that the future – for planning purposes – is at best a guess.

At this stage in the planning process, a great deal of information will have been collected and now needs to be sifted and graded for importance. If your marketing strategy is also acting as the communications and/or PR strategy for the organisation, you will also need to read the next chapter (Public Relations) before progressing to SWOT.

ANALYSING THE RESULTS OF THE INTERNAL AND EXTERNAL AUDITS

The SWOT analysis

The external audit is an important piece of research, designed not to gather dust on the shelves, but to form the basis for both your marketing and PR strategy. It will also need regular input as situations change.

The SWOT analysis (TOSW is another term for it – with the headings in a different order) is a well-established formula which brings together the results of your audit in a convenient and easily understood format. SWOT is there to guide the marketing strategy and it should include those factors which are likely to have a bearing on marketing. This can be developed into an interactive session and is another way of involving colleagues – as long as it is guided by the results of the work which has taken place during the internal and external audits.

Strengths

- Aspects of product, programme, collections, staff, building which are competitively strong
- Successes in the past and currently
- Activities/events and resources over which you have control.

Weaknesses/unsuccessful activities

- Aspects of product, programme, collections, staff, building which are competitively weak
- Activities/events over which the institution has not exercised control and has no resources to manage.

Opportunities

- Positive events/trends over which the attraction has no direct control but from which it can benefit.

Threats

- Negative factors/trends in the environment, now and in the future.

Setting the marketing objectives – the Ansoff Matrix

From here, it should be possible to set the overall marketing objectives; these should be 'SMART' – specific, measurable, achievable, realistic and timed. Consider the different options for expanding visitor numbers and income, based on the SWOT analysis, using another useful formula – the Ansoff Matrix.

There are four to six different ways of growing the market, not mutually exclusive, based on the Ansoff Matrix, first published in the 1950s by Igor Ansoff in the *Harvard*

Business Review as a framework for analysing and expanding business activities. It remains a useful tool for analysing the best options for growing visitor numbers, use and income in the not-for-profit sector. These are the options based on the matrix shown in Figure 4.3.

- Increasing your share of the existing market – concentrating on selected segments, developing the offer, and differentiating the product.

- Expanding the existing market by increasing the frequency of visits, renewing the product through exhibitions and events.

- Developing new markets for the existing offer, exhibitions and events by direct marketing activities aimed at new market segments – through audience development.

- Developing new exhibitions and services aimed at existing visitors and users by revising old products and introducing new ones.

- Creating new products and services aimed at new markets through technology, value offers and new marketing tactics.

- Increasing the profitability/spend of existing visitors by adding value, adjusting the price and promotional activities.

Product Market	Present	New
Present	Market Penetration	Product Development
New	Market Development	Diversification

Figure 4.3 An Ansoff Matrix

The product life cycle

The product life cycle is the third tool which is useful in analysing the results of the audit before proceeding to the full marketing strategy. Does this graph (see Figure 4.4) apply to your attraction? It identifies the progress of a product – say a new attraction, gallery, café, or exhibition, from the launch to its decline.

The curve for cultural and heritage attractions – traditionally considered less susceptible to fashion and trends – is likely to show an initial peak when a new museum or gallery opens its doors or a major investment takes place; as seen in the example of the Great North Museum (see case study in the Appendix). After the opening, a levelling-off occurs, as the initial launch campaign wears off and most of the immediate market segments have been satisfied. There may even be a drop in visitor numbers as marketing activities are limited by available budgets.

Further peaks will then develop when a new product is launched – a touring exhibition, for example, or when new segments of the market targeted, or marketing and PR efforts increased. Over time, without any changes in the venue's facilities, exhibitions or the attraction's offer, visitor numbers are likely to decline through lack of interest, tired exhibitions and out-of-date facilities, and/or in response to new competing attractions.

With the help of the internal and external audits you should be in a position to identify those elements of your offer which have reached the end of their life cycle and make recommendations to senior management on future investment.

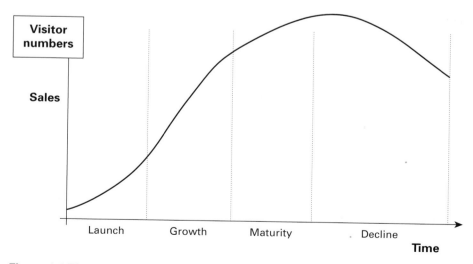

Figure 4.4 The product life cycle

FINALISING THE MARKETING STRATEGY

The marketing strategy, as outlined earlier, is based on the long-term mission and the objectives for the organisation as a whole. It will set the strategic direction for the organisation's communications and deliver visitor numbers and income. The marketing objectives should be developed in as much detail as possible (with review dates).

Key messages may be developed here and in conjunction with the public relations strategy. They will guide the tone and thrust of communications across all media platforms and will need to be further refined as part of audience segmentation. Outline the tactics to be undertaken to achieve these objectives within the budget and timescale set, including monitoring and evaluation.

These are the key points to be covered by the strategy:

- Mission – why are we here and what/who is the museum/gallery for?
- Objectives – overall organisational objectives/aims for the future
- Strategies/strategic direction – what we plan to do to achieve those aims
- Marketing objectives
- Key messages
- Budget and timescale
- Tactics – detailed activities and plans to meet targets and monitor achievements
- Monitoring and evaluation.

To create the detailed marketing plan, go to Chapter 7. See also that chapter's case studies in the Appendix.

CHAPTER 5

A PUBLIC RELATIONS STRATEGY FOR EVERY OCCASION

The communications audit

Research and planning

Analysis leading to strategy and overall objectives

Identifying key audiences and key messages

Implementation, setting the timescale, and evaluation

Public relations strategies

Media relations

Social media and public information

Internal communications

External stakeholder relations

Issues and crisis communications plans

Advocacy and lobbying

Building a sustainability strategy – green issues

Building networks

Entering for awards – is it worth it?

The annual report – has it had its day?

Freedom of Information requests

THE COMMUNICATIONS AUDIT

The communications audit is the first step in developing the overall public relations strategy for the organisation. Taking time to do this at the start of a new phase of the organisation or in the face of a major challenge will pay off in the long run by providing a framework for a range of activities. In many ways the process is similar to that for developing the marketing strategy, and the marketing strategy forms a good starting point if it is already available. However, it will have very specific, more limited objectives, while the PR strategy will be wide-ranging, aimed at creating a strong profile for the organisation with all its audiences, and at protecting the organisation's reputation universally.

Research and planning

Research for the PR strategy starts with an internal and external communications audit which follows the same lines as the marketing audit (see Chapters 2 and 3), but is looking essentially at what messages are communicated and how they are interpreted. Internal communications are discussed in greater detail in Chapter 13, but their importance in successfully implementing a comprehensive PR strategy cannot be overstated.

The internal audit may be led by a director or chief executive, especially if they are newly arrived and seeking new directions. It should examine the following:

- How staff perceive the organisation
- What they consider the organisation is essentially about
- Who they see as the competition
- How they receive their internal messages
- How and when they communicate these messages to the public and other users
- Where they think the organisation will be in 5 years' time
- How they perceive change and opportunities for the future
- Comments by the public.

The most interesting answers will no doubt come from the first question. It is unlikely that the chief executive, chairman, the curators and the public services staff will come up with the same answer. The challenge will be to define in simple terms what the organisation is about and to get internal stakeholders lined up behind this definition. They should also be able to agree and buy into a similar view of the organisation's future. Where will we be in 5 years' time, bearing in mind the external forces to which the organisation will be subject?

The external audit should seek the views of a variety of people, including those reviewed in the marketing audit; those whose views influence others; and those who actively or passively have an influence on the way in which the institution is perceived.

Start with the media's perception of the museum through a media evaluation exercise which over a period of time measures the organisation's media coverage and evaluates the contents of articles and broadcasts against agreed messages. You might follow this with a survey among journalists undertaken by a research or PR agency. Aside from the media, how is your museum or attraction perceived by different segments of your public? In addition to visitor surveys, it may be useful to undertake non-visitor surveys and/or focus group research among the general public and opinion-formers.

There are other ways of testing public awareness and perception if the above methods are outside the budget. It is possible to purchase single questions on omnibus surveys – regular surveys which the commercial sector conducts to test product awareness and buying habits. However, this will only work for organisations with an established 'brand' which already has some public awareness. Or you could work with a local business college looking for a real-life project to cut their teeth on. A few weekend afternoons with a simple survey form down at the shopping centre should reveal some interesting findings. (See Chapter 17 Research.)

A consultancy working on a new business plan for the organisation to underpin a major bid for funding, for example, may incorporate awareness research in their work. They can ask questions which it is difficult for an in-house PR manager to raise and they will sometimes be given a more candid response than would ever be given directly to the organisation. This has real value, and can help you to identify key public relations messages for the future.

The results of this research will have identified the strengths and weaknesses of the organisation's current communications strategy and form the starting point for the next stage, which will allow new ideas and new thinking to emerge in identifying future opportunities, threats, and new directions. Think-tanks or brainstorming sessions are nothing new, but this does not stop them from being useful when the museum, gallery or attraction is faced with a major change, such as a changed funding situation, or the threat of increased competition from new attractions in the area. The objectives should be clearly stated: How do we survive with our grant cut in half? How do we build our reputation as a museum of natural history or fashion or film? What will our audiences want in the year 2020 and what can we deliver?

Setting up a successful brainstorm can greatly benefit from some outside assistance to ensure that it is productive and stimulating. Here are some practical ideas.

- The facilitator should be well briefed about the organisation

- He or she should be assisted by a note-taker (although parts of the discussion may be free-wheeling)

- The director or chief executive may choose only to take part in the later part of the event to ensure a free-flowing discussion

- The participants should include a cross-section from all departments (ideally not more than twelve); or a mixture of trustees and staff

- Hold the event away from the offices if possible – and somewhere fairly isolated – no phones or even mobiles, although laptops are standard

- Some staff or trustees may be asked to prepare short scenarios in advance.

The process may start with the facilitator asking the participants to work through a traditional SWOT analysis based on the information collected so far. This will throw up a number of useful starting points for a free-ranging discussion. This is where a well-briefed facilitator is important in order to keep the session on track and add other pertinent questions to stimulate further discussions, similar to those covered in the internal audit, and to reach some conclusions.

When a step-change in the way the organisation operates is required, it is useful to have a structured discussion focusing on three or four possible scenarios and future directions. Towards the end of the day or session, allow sufficient time for the discussion to be properly summarised, and then finish with an action plan. The brainstorm may have provided some ideas which need further exploration and research, perhaps among users, to gauge their relevance and practicality. A working party may be required to take forward ideas and turn them into something more tangible. Further research among visitors or the competition may be required. It could be that your colleagues perceive one particular feature or quality of the collection as the defining element in the museum or attraction, but visitors actually come for some other feature, or just to enjoy the building and its facilities.

It is easy to become paralysed at this stage and continue the search for more information. This desire to dwell on research and delay action is a growing phenomenon because we have access to more and more information and are faced by challenging technological, economic and political changes.

Analysis leading to strategy and overall objectives

The PR manager or consultant should draft the objectives for the future, based on the information and any new thinking generated by the audit process. The board of trustees, the management committee and those who have participated in the discussions may wish to have further input at this stage.

The agreed public relations objectives should relate to the existing mission statement – the rather bland statement now standard in most corporate plans – and may well update it, but will need to be more detailed for the public relations strategy. The PR strategy should have clear objectives and targets with measurements. These should relate to the organisation's brand, audiences and communications processes.

Identifying key audiences and key messages

The next stage is to identify key audiences and key messages. These will vary for the individual strategies and plans but the core audiences and core messages should be covered in the overall PR strategy. This becomes a working checklist for various campaigns outlined in the next section (Public relations strategies). Key audiences include stakeholders now and in the future, as well as visitors and non-visitors, i.e. *potential* visitors.

Messages need to be fashioned, not just for these key audiences but for the media through which you are communicating. Your research, planning and analysis should have identified the main elements in the visitor experience which already appeal and which are likely to appeal in the future. It is important that the main message about the attraction is clear and distinct and aligned to the marketing strategy and vice versa, enabling the PR team to develop subsidiary messages for particular events or programmes.

The attraction's many audiences will need to be segmented. There are different ways of approaching segmentation of visitors outlined in greater detail in Chapter 7 (Creating the marketing plan) and Chapter 17 (Research). In addition, the PR strategy should include those audiences who are not necessarily part of the marketing strategy – trustees, key stakeholders, funders, etc.

Implementation, setting the timescale, and evaluation

There is now a plethora of communication tools available in both public relations and in marketing. It is important that the right tools are chosen for a particular strategy or campaign and for the targeted audiences. Some of these tools communicate directly with the target groups; others use the media as an intermediary. Here is a list of PR tools, in no particular order:

- Press releases
- E-newsletters
- Social media
- Your website
- Public and private events
- Conferences

- Exhibitions
- Sponsorship – Corporate Social Responsibility
- Newspapers and broadcasting
- Photography
- Stunts and other media events.

Getting the mix right is crucial for success. It is easy to put too much emphasis on media relations and ignore the importance of direct communications through personal presentations and newsletters, your website, and the way you deliver your own events. It is also easy to get carried away with social media activities, which seem cost-effective but do not necessarily influence all the relevant audiences.

The public relations strategy should include an action plan and timetable, as well as a section setting out the evaluation process by audience and in terms of overall impact. It is useful to set targets for communicating which can be measured, and if a survey has been carried out as part of the public relations audit, to set targets for awareness and then run the survey again in one or two years' time. (More in Chapter 17 Research.)

Remember that the PR strategy is not set in concrete and needs to be reviewed regularly. At the same time it is there for a reason – to achieve the agreed objectives and to maximise limited budgets. It is easy to be thrown off course, sometimes by necessity when a sudden crisis occurs, but more often through lack of discipline. Someone has a good idea – perhaps it is the chairman – wanting to invest in a flashy annual report, eating up most of the publication budget, or a stagey event for a dubious charity. Or it may be a creative PR idea which takes up an enormous amount of time and energy and delivers none of the key audiences. So go back to the PR strategy every time someone says 'Why don't we do that?' and see whether it fits into the framework.

PUBLIC RELATIONS STRATEGIES

The overall public relations strategy divides into a number of different programmes, each with their own plans and targets. Some will be part of the PR manager's responsibilities; others will be carried out by visitor services, marketing, the director and his/her team, or finance and HR. The inter-disciplinary nature of delivery underlines the need to collaborate closely with other departments during the planning stage. It also demonstrates the special qualities needed by any PR manager to engage the support of colleagues in other departments.

PR strategies in operation are outlined below – and some are covered in greater detail in subsequent chapters.

Media relations

This is the cornerstone of public relations, with potentially the greatest influence on awareness-raising and reputation. It includes: having an overview of the media appropriate for your many different audiences; familiarising them with the organisation and its purposes; maintaining useful records; and acting as and preparing spokes-people. (See Chapters 9 and 10.)

Social media and public information

A large chunk of communications is focused directly on the public. This means that key messages should pervade all online communications including websites, e-newsletters and social media, as well as any printed material for public consumption. All of this should be done in close conjunction with the marketing and IT teams – there are suggestions at the end of Chapter 2 about how this can be organised. Managing your presence on social media is a vital part of your brand.

Internal communications

This may well be part of the HR department in a large organisation, or it may sit in the director's or manager's office in a smaller organisation. Regardless of who holds final responsibility, the PR team should have an input into policymaking and the planning cycle for the organisation's internal communications, and should assist in the flow of information among the staff and trustees. (See Chapter 13.)

External stakeholder relations

The stakeholder relations plan is shared by the director's office and public relations and includes maintaining channels of communication with various groups, opinion-formers and segments of the public, as identified in the corporate plan and public relations strategy. (See Chapter 14.)

Issues and crisis communications plans

Issue management is about looking to the future, identifying issues and potential crises, and developing strategies to meet them. This is not just about working with the current concerns of the organisation. It is about the issues that affect the audiences with whom the organisation needs to have good working relationships, now and in the future. These could be existing stakeholders but they may be individuals or organisations with whom the organisation has not yet developed a relationship.

From here could flow both the crisis communications plan (see Chapter 16) and a Corporate Social Responsibility (CSR) programme. CSR is more commonly associated with major corporations but is just as appropriate for cultural organisations building networks for the future. There is more about Corporate Social Responsibility in Chapter 14 (Communicating with stakeholders).

Advocacy and lobbying

Advocacy and lobbying should be built into the public relations strategy as an ongoing activity. Everything we have covered so far will enable the organisation to take an informed and strategic approach to advocacy and lobbying in the longer term, as well as devising short-term strategies when the need arises. There are times when immediate action or reaction is required. That is when the 'crisis communications' plan kicks in (see Chapter 16).

The communications audit will have identified key audiences who influence the future of the museum or attraction, and also where communications are working well and where there are shortfalls. The development of key messages will provide the bedrock for the ongoing advocacy strategy, with additional research informing short-term strategies in challenging situations. Access the latest research on the value of culture to the economy through your government or local government department, museums association, or tourism organisation. All board members, the senior management team, and the staff should be advocates and, when the pressure is on, they need to be briefed and encouraged. Your key targets are those who influence your funding directly and indirectly, and include national and regional politicians, civil servants, local councillors and public servants. Others will come to the fore as part of issue management. Joining forces with others is important when a whole sector or region is under threat from cutbacks or redevelopment.

The tools are those outlined in Chapter 14 (Communicating with stakeholders) and include:

■ E-news and printed news to selected individuals

■ Invitations to private views as well as meetings with senior management and the board, informal lunches and PR launches

■ Meetings at their office or venue

■ Attending conferences, seminars and networking events where politicians are speaking

■ Contributing to 'hot' issues – sustainability, for example.

When political issues are at stake and when you are building a long-term relationship with government departments, it is useful sometimes to look at it from their perspective. In 2007, Estelle Morris, Baroness Morris of Yardley, a former Minister of the Arts in the UK, gave some useful advice to delegates at a Campaign for Museums conference. Here is a summary of what she said:

> **Every single minister is different in how they perceive the organisations and area they are responsible for. When responsible for the arts, Estelle Morris saw them as a 'squabbling family' but she was always 'on their side', after all she couldn't do her job without them.**
>
> **When a minister is new, particularly in a new government, they make their mark, change things, and leave a footprint, even if things are OK. Within the DCMS it was important to know where the power lay – was it sports or was it arts? 'What do the others think? And what am I going to change first?'**
>
> **Those on the outside have to understand the political dividing lines as well – Labour v Conservative. And that the minister's most important relationship is with the public – they are accountable to the electorate – and must win the next election.**
>
> **The department, when faced with a new minister, inevitably brings in the great and the good, and the leaders of the sector. It's sometimes difficult for ministers to meet those doing the work. So Estelle Morris set up a small group of curators as a sounding board. The cultural sector should involve ministers (and civil servants) along the way, inviting them to exhibitions and events, and not just get in touch when decisions are being made.**
>
> **The sector should understand the financial framework and where the decisions are really being made. They should think carefully about going public – politicians can easily get upset at a premature announcement. The sector should also give credit when ministers have done their best.**

When building a political campaign, the gloves are off and the tactics are different. Here are some pertinent comments from David Barrie, Director of The Art Fund from 1992 to 2009. He was an active lobbyist for the arts and organised the campaign to restore free admission to all national museums. He is now a consultant as well as Chair of the campaigning organisation, Make Justice Work.

> **Getting the Government to do what you want is pretty much like any other kind of persuasion: you need to see things from the relevant Minister's point of view, and then to find ways of making it easy (or at least less difficult) for him or her to help you. The first step is to develop your case as thoroughly as possible, and to try to anticipate every possible objection. Don't ask for the impossible, and take full account of the wider policy context – above all whatever the Government (and Opposition) have said on the subject. Civil servants and Special Advisers are crucial – especially in warning you of technical problems, though of course they**

won't help if they don't like what you're proposing. Listen to them, and try to get them on your side. If they actively oppose you, you will be in trouble. Ministers, especially weak ones, will usually follow official advice unless they have very good reasons to overturn it (remember *Yes Minister*?). Work out the cost implications (savings are especially appealing) and line up your supporters – preferably people the Minister will trust, or at least respect. Think-tanks that are close to the Government can be very useful allies.

The process often starts with a formal letter, but don't kid yourself that Ministers read every letter that's sent to them, still less that they draft the replies. Unless it's something simple and uncontroversial, you'll probably need to see the Minister in person to make your case. Famous or powerful allies can be very helpful. It's much harder for the Private Office to turn down a meeting with someone the Minister knows well or can't afford to offend. Sometimes Ministers want to help, but think they can't; more often they either don't want to help or just don't care. But they may not tell you directly, preferring to make soothing noises in the hope that you'll get tired and lose heart. This is when patience and determination count.

Whatever you do, don't succumb to flattery – it can be beguiling to be told by a Minister that he or she really values your opinion and takes it very seriously. But once it's clear that quiet persuasion isn't helping, you may need to exert a bit of public pressure. There are many ways of doing this, ranging from petitions and Parliamentary Questions, through to a full-blown public campaign. The goal in every case is the same: to make life sufficiently uncomfortable for the Minister that he or she will eventually decide it's less painful to do what you want than to go on resisting. Politicians need to be popular and hate to be publicly criticised. Bad headlines make them change their minds more quickly than anything else. If it becomes clear that public opinion is swinging behind your proposal, you're probably close to victory.

Organising a campaign, however, is not easy. It depends on developing political and media contacts and being able to react very quickly to events. Journalists can't afford to be patient: if they want a quote, you have to give it, and fast. A long-running campaign can be very demanding, and should not be undertaken lightly. This is the stage at which you may well need to consider hiring professional help.

Building a sustainability strategy – green issues

Museums and cultural attractions in receipt of public funding will usually have sustainability targets set as part of their funding agreements. Many will find that in some areas they are already ahead, saving on heating and air-conditioning makes economic as well as 'green' sense. However, museums and art galleries have responsibilities that sometimes cut across normal targets; for example preserving artefacts and heritage sites in proper conditions, and managing Victorian buildings.

Figure 5.1 Green issues covered in the 'Your Ocean' Gallery (© National Maritime Museum, London)

How does this impact on public relations? It can be difficult for the public to understand the constraints that cultural and heritage sites operate within. So it is important to be clear in communications and in the displays themselves that decisions have been made about lighting and temperature to protect artefacts or buildings.

In addition, museums and heritage sites have a duty to explain the impact of global warming to the public as it is relevant to their collections or buildings. The case study from the National Maritime Museum, Greenwich (introduced below and included in the Appendix) illustrates how museum staff became involved as 'green champions'. Also in London, the Science Museum is involving the public in the debate around climate change through its new exhibition (2010) *Atmosphere*, and has its own think-tank – the Dana Centre – which invites the public to join curators and scientists in debate and discussion, creating awareness on and offline. The museum is committed to using its long-established expertise in science communication to provide information on climate science for everyone, no matter their level of prior knowledge.

Building networks

In public relations and marketing the gathering and understanding of information is critical to success. So how does one keep in the swim on all the potential issues affecting the cultural sector? Building networks is a good way to pick up developing news, and reading selectively but widely is crucial.

The internal network is of fundamental importance. Colleagues should be sharing information in formal and informal meetings. External networks need a more strategic approach. When new in post, it is highly recommended for a marketing or PR officer to spend some time getting around the local community and introducing themselves. You can segment your networking constituency in exactly the same way as you segment your audience. Contacts will be needed in the main funding bodies; the key leisure and tourism attractions; the tourist board or convention and visitors' bureau; service agencies, and local press and broadcasting media.

Inboxes now overflow with e-newsletters, so be selective in subscribing to those that are relevant and which you have time to read, sharing relevant information with your colleagues. Check local newspapers or online local media for community matters and key players. This will be helpful with any local issues.

American neighbourhood associations are on the whole more outspoken and more demanding than their UK (or other European) counterparts, and it can take a great deal more work and dedicated teams to handle local relationships. Planning applications are the catalysts for local disputes in all countries, and need to be carefully presented on well-prepared ground. Knowing what the hot topics are beforehand can help considerably in devising schemes that take into account local requirements – or at least having your arguments prepared. Developing trust and mutual understanding are the highest goals here, and need time and commitment to achieve. When things get confrontational, you may need a good lawyer on the team! (More in Chapter 14.)

Entering for awards – is it worth it?

Entering for (and winning) awards should be part of the public relations or marketing strategy. Museum of the Year awards, specific interpretation or audience development awards, marketing and PR awards, and architectural awards are all useful in PR terms. They are also excellent for morale within the organisation. Build the timetable for regular awards into your PR strategy, and in good time explore what you could submit. Some entries can be quite time-consuming but many are now online. When opening a new building, it is quite likely that the architects and exhibition designers will be well prepared and ready to share in any glory. Make sure you use your accolades in all your communications, as illustrated in the case study from the Wimbledon Lawn Tennis Museum (introduced below and included in the Appendix). See Resources for details of some award schemes.

Sally Osman, Communications Consultant, served two terms as a judge for the prestigious Art Fund's Museum Prize where the winner (the Ulster Museum in 2010) takes away £100,000. Here are her impressions as a non-museum professional:

Judging the Museum Prize for the last two years has been a revelation. As a trustee of the prize's key sponsor, the Art Fund, I see some of the incredible energy, ambition and intelligence emerging from galleries and museums across the UK through the applications we consider.

But travelling round the country as a judge, listening and questioning teams about how and why they do what they do, has transformed my view of what success looks like, not just for the organisation, but for the community it serves.

Success is defined not just by the charm, splendour or newness of facilities, or by the integrity and appeal of the collection/exhibition, or, perhaps most importantly, by public impact and value. Success means all three working in harmony. What this means in practical terms is that everyone involved in the process – from curators to educators to volunteers – is a communicator, a marketer. Integrated thinking about creating something of true value for audiences is everyone's responsibility.

The best are doing this brilliantly. It defines the good from the great and, combined with intellectual and academic rigour, will distinguish the next generation of curators and leaders. Every museum we visited – from the largest to the smallest – was doing something inventive and inspiring to engage people at very different levels.

Storytelling is key. Setting collections in broader narratives, judicious use of digital and interactive to enhance not detract, breathing colour and life in to objects, never patronising – to children or adults.

Strong leadership, collaboration and teamwork also distinguish the good from the excellent. We saw inspiring examples of taking a museum or gallery beyond its walls and into a community, using its assets to build connections, engage, intrigue and change the nature of relationships with the public.

The best are textbook case studies that commercial businesses, let alone other cultural organisations, can learn from. Sharing ideas, insights and lessons from the best with the rest is imperative in challenging times.

The annual report – has it had its day?

Annual reports are a legal requirement for many organisations: national museums, trusts, charitable organisations and private companies all have to give an annual statement that includes the previous year's financial accounts. These, once glossy publications, have shrunk and are increasingly converted into a short legal document, printed in-house. They are sometimes augmented by a smart online pdf document and/or a magazine-style printed report. The magazine approach is an attractive and accessible way of telling a wider audience about your achievements and plans for the future. While the website is the first point of access for those who want to know more about your organisation, a well-produced report of some kind is a useful tool for your stakeholders, potential funders and politicians.

A tip here is to make sure that any publication produced primarily as a pdf should be based on an online format so that it can be read easily, and include a summary and a limited number of illustrations (so that there are not too many pages to print out), plus a search facility.

Freedom of Information requests

The accounts and annual reports of cultural organisations are available online as part of a general requirement for transparency. In addition, publicly funded organisations in the UK are subject to the Freedom of Information Act 2000. The Information Commissioners' Office (ICO) has introduced a model publication scheme that all public sector organisations should have adopted from January 2009. This sets out in detail how public bodies should make the appropriate information available and easily accessible to the public (through their website in most cases). Here is a typical statement on the 'About Us' pages of a website of a national museum:

> **In general, the museum is required to respond to [Freedom of Information] requests within 20 working days. Some information held by the museum, such as personal or commercially sensitive data, or information provided to the museum in confidence, may be exempt from disclosure under the terms of the Act. In some cases where information is exempt from disclosure, the museum is nevertheless required to consider if there is any overriding public interest in disclosing the information in spite of the exemption. If the museum is unable to disclose some or all of the information which an applicant has requested, the reasons for non-disclosure will be explained to the applicant.**

So the PR Manager should be informed about all Freedom of Information requests, whether they are from the media or not, even if he or she doesn't deal with them personally. They will be in the firing line if an issue raised under the Act has not been dealt with inside the period required, or full information has not been provided for any of the reasons raised above. This may be because the enquiry is spurious; for example, from someone who was not successful in bidding for a contract and was subsequently refused details of other bidders. However, the media's instinctive sympathies tend to be on the side of the enquirer.

Freedom of information as a concept was of course imported into the UK from the United States where it has operated for many years. Similar legislation applies in Australia and many other countries. However, there are significant differences in national legislation. In the US it only applies to cultural organisations that receive State or Federal funding. Guidance can be sought from individual state governments, central government, and professional organisations.

Here are some guidelines for dealing with such requests:

1 Depending on the extent and seriousness of the request, the director or other responsible officer sets up a team meeting which may include a senior admini-strator, the PR manager, and anyone directly involved – with legal advice available as required.

2 In that meeting, consider the following points:

   ▪ Exactly what information is being requested?

   ▪ Is it too broad to be accomplished, i.e. should a more specific request be sought?

   ▪ Does the organisation hold this information?

   ▪ In what form? (paper records, card files, e-mails, electronic archives)

   ▪ Where is it held – in one department or across departments? (Find the right person with the relevant institutional memory.)

   ▪ Who is best-placed to lead the effort? Probably a senior administrator. This is probably not a PR function.

   ▪ Is it possible to anticipate any implications of releasing this information into the public domain? (This gives the PR team a chance to prepare.)

3 The leader should schedule a further meeting within the time frame in order to consider and discuss the assembled information.

4 Either the lawyer or the Chief Executive should vet the information for complete-ness; non-inclusion of data-protected material; non-inclusion of private com-mercial information.

5 Prepare for follow up questions or press impact.

CASE STUDIES IN THE APPENDIX

Case Study 5A: The National Maritime Museum and sustainability

Kate Winsall, Marketing Manager, and Sheryl Twigg, Press and PR Manager, National Maritime Museum, write:

> **In 2007 the National Maritime Museum received the Visit London Award for Sustainable Tourism. The Museum, which incorporates the Queen's House and Royal Observatory, Greenwich, is exceptionally proud of this accolade and strives for environmental excellence to act as an example of good practice within the leisure and heritage sector.**

Case Study 5B: Taking awards seriously at Wimbledon

Ashley Jones, Commercial Manager, Wimbledon Lawn Tennis Museum, writes:

> We at Wimbledon Lawn Tennis Museum have always taken awards very seriously. Our reasons are twofold: first, that Wimbledon prides itself on being the best tennis tournament in the world so it is important that the Museum is seen to be delivering to the same standard, and secondly, as a Museum we have a quite small marketing budget and the positive PR produced by awards judged by independent third parties is extremely useful.

Figure 5.2
Rafael Nadal at the
Wimbledon Lawn
Tennis Museum

CHAPTER 6

EVERYTHING YOU WANT TO KNOW ABOUT BRANDS AND BRANDING

WHAT IS BRANDING?

When did brands and branding become so powerful (and so threatening) that they generated a whole counter-movement inspired by Naomi Klein's book, *No Logo*, published in 2000? Well, it didn't happen overnight, in fact it took more than a hundred years before brands got something of a bad name.

The evolution of mass marketing and the growth of choice marked the beginning of brands. When there was only one kind of soap in the shops, the name and the look of the packaging didn't matter much. But once there was choice, Pear's soap (and others) realised they had to stand out from the crowd by differentiating themselves. An emotional relationship between the product and the consumer was created in the first Pear's soap advertisements in the 1890s, evoking childhood and goodness, using the painting 'Bubbles' by Sir John Everett Millais. This was the beginning of something new and different – the brand. Many others were joining in at around the same time. Pears continued to reinforce its brand messages through its popular annuals as well as the Miss Pears competition, a masterclass in branding and how to sustain it.

Figure 6.1 Pears soap advertisement (courtesy of the Museum of Brands, Packaging & Advertising)

So what is brand all about? Well, much more than the logo. As the Pears example shows, while creating a strong graphic for the name was important, it was the choice of image and underlying emotional messages which chimed with Victorian values – this was the brand. In addition, Pears had developed a unique product: a transparent, concave soap with an identifiable scent associated with cleanliness. From this example, still relevant today, emerges one of the most important elements of branding – authenticity. The product or organisation should measure up to the brand, the promise and its values.

It was in the late twentieth century that brands became global and 'king'. The longevity of well-established brands such as Heinz, Coca Cola, McDonald's, Nike, Volkswagen and Lego is a testament to their quality and consumer acceptance. The brand counter-movement is perhaps more of an attack on the globalisation of large companies and their products than a critique of 'brands' per se. Global businesses are seen to market their products across borders using the brand as a tool, creating a perceived loss of local culture and delivering sameness and less choice. The French continue to resist McDonald's (while devouring them secretly); the British resent Tesco opening on every High Street (but have made them the biggest supermarket chain in the country); while, in the US, Japanese cars were a no-no until people realised they were more economical. And everyone everywhere wears branded jeans.

So the notion of packaging consumer goods in brown paper bags has been left behind by generations of consumers. It seems that we like our products to have an identity. Even Muji (the retailer who rejects brands) has become a brand in itself with a clearly emotional message. Brand consultants have transformed the way we see the world. Here is a comment from one of the pioneering companies:

> Cultural organisations need constantly to answer the question 'why?' Why should I visit you? Why should I support you? Why should I become a member? Why should I work for you? As government funding around the world becomes tighter, answering these questions becomes more urgent. That's where marketing, and particularly branding, comes in. It's something every cultural organisation needs to get right – and get right quickly.

> (Robert Jones, Strategist, Wolff Olins)

The development of the 'branded' museum, gallery or visitor attraction was influenced by the growth of global branding as well as a more competitive environment both for people's leisure time and for funding. The Victoria and Albert Museum in London became the V&A (see Roy Strong's comments in Chapter 1). The Museum of Modern Art in New York became MoMA. The Louvre built a pyramid, and is spreading its brand not just in France but in the Middle East. The Guggenheim, named after its founder Peggy Guggenheim, re-invented its image – and brand – through exciting new architecture, first in New York, then in Bilbao and other places.

The Tate Gallery started life in 1897 as the National Gallery of British Art; it was in 1932 that it formally took the name of its founder – the sugar manufacturer Sir Henry Tate. 'Tate' was re-developed as a global brand by design agency Wolff Olins, when

Tate Modern opened in 2000. Tate incorporates four venues – two in London, one in St Ives, and one in Liverpool. Tate has consistently lived up to its brand messages, which imply quality as well as innovation and excitement by constantly renewing its offer. In 2010, it is about to embark on an additional building at Tate Modern. It also leads the sector in new media development.

Branding and managing the brand is crucial to the success of the institution's investment in the brand:

- Branding is the strategic, proactive management of communications issues

- If the brand isn't managed, the external world will do it for you – inaccurately

- Negative branding will harm your ability to build or sustain audiences, and to raise financial support from public and private sources.

Your brand is about your museum, gallery and visitor attraction and what you stand for. A sustainable brand should meet three criteria:

- Authenticity – as the Pears' example illustrates, the product should live up to the brand message. It cannot just be a sticking plaster on a failing business or attraction. So the museum, gallery or visitor attraction claiming uniqueness of contents or portraying themselves as especially family-friendly, must be able to live up to these claims.

- Emotion and engagement – a great brand should appeal to the emotional self as well as to the rational visitor looking for a day out.

- Differentiation is about identifying what is genuinely different in the collection – but mostly in the experience. The uniqueness of the offer can be hard to define but the brand audit process is one way forward.

So it's not just about the logo!

THE RELATIONSHIP WITH MARKETING AND PUBLIC RELATIONS

The public relations strategy (as outlined in the previous chapter) plays a central role in safeguarding and building the brand. This includes protecting the value of the museum or attraction's name (which may be recognised for accountancy purposes as

Figure 6.2 The V&A logo, originally designed by Ivor Heal in the 1970s, and modified over the years

Figure 6.3 The Museum Victoria logo. A delicately coloured logo must also work in black and white

Figure 6.4 Logo, the Museum of Modern Art, New York

an asset) as well as its intellectual property rights. Whether it is possible to register the name as a trademark will depend on the uniqueness of the name and other factors. It may be worth investigating, but it is not necessary in terms of the success or failure of the brand. The success of the brand will depend on investment, on strengthening its visual impact, and on reinforcing its use throughout the organisation and all published material internally and externally. It is these actions, sustained through time, that will add value to the brand and protect it from infringement.

Ideally, the process of creating a new brand or reviewing an existing brand should be developed alongside the marketing and public relations strategies. As a separate process undertaken by a brand consultant, its conclusions and recommendations will inform the marketing and public relations strategies and plans – these are the tools for implementing brand changes and sustaining brand values. The corporate identity or logo is designed to strengthen the profile of the organisation and build recognition value. This final stage of the branding process has become increasingly important as we have all become more visual in how we perceive the world around us. Consider the logos or visual images which identify the hundreds of 'apps' in the Apple Store. Very few words are needed to differentiate or identify one from the other. Users are expected to choose almost instinctively the right one, once they are downloaded on their own smartphones.

So it follows that the museum, gallery or attraction investing in a corporate identity needs to consider its communication strategies as a whole. The identity should work comfortably with a range of subsidiary means of communications relating to exhibitions, the website, education services, the library, the events programme, and so on. Corporate identities need to be reviewed at perhaps 5-yearly intervals to ensure that they are fresh and relevant.

CREATING A NEW BRAND

In developing the brand for the Great North Museum, a complex set of relationships were negotiated, from building and collection owners with strong historical associations, to funders with performance-led targets including the development of new and out-of-region audiences. The new visual identity developed for the launch of the project was created to reflect the new brand and to be instantly recognisable. It was designed to work on all communications material and to be suitable for a broad range of merchandise.

(Steve McLean, Senior Manager and Iain Watson, Acting Director, Tyne & Wear Museums – read the full case study in the Appendix)

In the museums and heritage sector the opportunity to create a completely new brand arises infrequently. Most brand processes concern existing venues with a long history and an established awareness among its audiences.

When starting from scratch, the collection or the location may have already determined the name before the brand process starts. A new museum in Scotland celebrating the life of the poet Robert Burns is called the Robert Burns Birthplace Museum – no surprise there. The Grand Egyptian Museum opening in 2012 is called 'grand' because it is the largest museum in Egypt and has a stunning view over the pyramids at Giza. The proposed museum dedicated to the second largest ethnic group in the US is already known as the National Museum of the American Latino. The museum in Washington dedicated to the media is called the Newseum – perhaps not so obvious. In all these cases, even when the name itself was given rather than chosen, some sort of branding process will be required to develop the identity, messages, profile and visuals of the new venue.

The process

■ The process of reaching a successful brand solution starts with a commitment by the project team, management, existing staff; trustees and directors. This commitment should include an understanding of what the branding process is

Figure 6.5 The Great North Museum logo, in this case, for the Hancock Museum

about – not just developing a name and a logo – but also identifying values and messages. One person should be appointed to take the lead internally.

- The creative brief should be as specific as possible and include objectives, target audiences, timeframe and, most importantly, the approval structure and budget.

- The shortlist of appropriate companies and consultants may be drawn from recommendations from other museums and attractions, prior knowledge, and a search of professional associations' membership lists. It is crucial to appoint a brand consultant with relevant experience in the sector, who embraces the full brand ethos, and is not just a visual designer. Anyone who brings their first drafts of what they think your logo should be to the interview is probably only interested in the design work and may have no real understanding of the branding process.

- For a new venture the branding process may include brainstorms and sessions with the project team, the key funders, and any staff already on board, and then with stakeholders in the wider community.

- Market research may also be carried out among target audiences to test the acceptance and expectations of the offer as formulated by the project team. At the second stage, when names and identities are beginning to be formulated, conducting focus group research with potential visitors may be helpful.

Outcomes and conclusion

Towards the end of this process, the brand consultancy will present their findings, ideally in a discussion session with members of the key team. Soundings with a wider group may follow before defining key messages and progressing to the name and visual identity. Several options may be on the cards. Generally, the smaller the group making the final decision on this, the better. Presenting a range of identity options to a large group of people is likely to generate few clear favourites.

The practicalities and impact of the final choice should be carefully considered. Does it infringe upon any existing names or visual identities? Does it work in other cultures or languages and outside the cultural or heritage sector? Is it adaptable for all marketing and PR purposes? Does it work in black and white as well as colour? Is the regular-print or online size clear, and is any subtext or strapline legible in these sizes? Does it meet current disability discrimination legislation?

A note on pro bono work

This is an area where designers sometimes offer to develop the brand or logo without charge. It may be a friend of the chairman, someone trying to break into the cultural field, or a design company seeking your name on their client list. The experienced PR or Marketing Manager will know the pitfalls of seeking and accepting such work. Here are some of them:

■ It is unlikely that the full branding process will be followed – the designers are likely to move straight to the visuals

■ It is difficult to reject designs which are inappropriate or unacceptable.

■ Designs that are accepted may not be sufficiently worked-through to ensure flexibility for all scenarios, thus incurring further costs down the line.

■ And in the past most of this kind of work has been undertaken on the basis that a large print order will follow, where the designers can recoup their costs. This is not always a good option for the client or such a good idea for the designers either because the amount of print commissioned by marketing departments in the online world is rapidly shrinking.

So think carefully before accepting such offers and make sure that there is a written agreement which sets out exactly what the designers are offering and what you are expecting.

REVIEWING AN EXISTING BRAND

Introduction to rebranding

> **Even the best brands get tired over time, both in terms of what they stand for and visually. I think the best judge is often your audiences and it is worth asking them questions about what they think of your brand every few years to see if this matches the impression you are trying to convey.**
>
> **(Jim Richardson, Sumo Design)**

Most museums and cultural attractions are more likely to be involved in a review of an existing brand than developing one from scratch. The triggers are many and might include:

■ A decline in visitor numbers – a need to target new audiences – move into new markets

■ Cuts in funding and the need to maintain and raise awareness with political as well as private funders

■ A major redevelopment which shifts your appeal into a new market and raises the expectations of visitors

■ New competitors on the block – another family attraction opening just around the corner

■ Academic credibility – your curators feel that their work is not recognised

- Developing a group name – you are a group of museums, all with different names – you need a brand that recognises them as a family

- A very tired, and visually out-of-date logo and/or every department doing their own thing stylistically, thus creating a visual 'jungle'

- A marketing campaign targeting new audiences; a major event or exhibition.

Reviewing the brand with a consultant

Reviewing the brand of a large organisation or family of museums or attractions is a major undertaking and will usually require a substantial budget. It will be important to involve staff in the initial stages to ensure buy-in once the new identity is launched. A brand process that aims to unite disparate museums or attractions under one umbrella is particularly challenging where each venue has an established history and their own name. The various members of the 'family' may not share values, aims or mission. In this situation, a brand consultancy provides useful distance and neutrality.

This process will take time and should start with working groups within and across the various member venues, establishing common aims and objectives. The extensive review will involve stakeholders, some of whom may have allegiance to only one of the museums or attractions.

The internal leader for this process will need a great deal of commitment, goodwill and energy, to bring such a process to a successful conclusion. There are several models for how individual venues can thrive under one identity – the Tate was mentioned earlier. The visual solution in this situation is very important. The Great North Museum case study illustrates how a parent body, in this case Tyne & Wear Archives and Museums, can use its own logo as 'marque of quality' which allows each of the (twelve) venues in the group to promote their own names and also convey their individual brand appeal.

Here is another approach from Norfolk by Vanessa Trevelyan, Head of Norfolk Museums & Archaeology Service:

> **Marketing, and the communicating and audience development function that it implies, is an integral part of how Norfolk Museums & Archaeology Service operates, and is represented on the Senior Management Team in order to help shape the museum 'product'. Although we have developed an overarching brand for the service, each of our eleven museums is different, and appeals to different audiences, as can be seen from our audience research.**

> **Each museum, therefore, has its own local brand which has been developed with different marketing consultants, and takes into account the collections, the stories being told in that museum, the target audience and local sensibilities. With so**

Figure 6.6 The Great North Museum (Photo: One North East)

much potential for independence it is essential that these all operate within clear style guidelines and contribute to the overall concept of 'Bringing history to life', which is our current mission statement.

We are not the National Trust and I feel that to impose a universal brand style in our case would run the risk of suppressing the uniqueness of the individual museums. Consistency is provided through high standards of design and presentation. I hope that the overall result of our strategy is to communicate the existence of a network of lively and responsive museums.

The review process (without a brand consultant)

In a smaller organisation it may be up to the manager responsible for marketing and/or PR to undertake the initial review before appointing a creative consultancy to develop new visuals or re-jig existing ones. Here are a few guidelines:

- Gather together examples of all printed material and print-outs of online material produced by your organisation – right down to the last staff notice and education flyer. Make up a display board of the various images, straplines and different names, which are used within the organisation.

- From here, move on to external references in the media, online and anywhere else where your attraction may be included – guidebooks, for example. Again assemble and note all differences (and use of old logos you have abandoned years before).

- Create a list of all the things your museum or attraction wants to stand for, based on your marketing and/or PR strategy, or business plan, including the mission.

- Set up a brainstorm with representatives of your staff and volunteers to consider the existing visuals and messages. Use a SWOT analysis to help to stimulate the discussion aimed at identifying new ideas and new opportunities.

- Discuss your findings with your director and trustees and then put together the creative brief with clear guidelines and budget as outlined above.

Once agreed, implementation of the proposals will follow the various stages described above. Maintenance of the new regime will be critical. One member of staff will need to 'own' the brand strategy – it could be the marketing or PR manager – and make sure that even those producing their own notices stick to the brand elements agreed (see below).

This process works well for a new campaign or a big event, too. Here you need to consider your existing brand and how it will sit with any new visuals. Any temporary campaign brand should not dominate or overshadow the existing brand but work with it. There may also be sponsors and funders to be considered (see the note on this below).

Rebranding – reaching new markets

You may be quite happy with your brand – in terms of graphics – but need to adjust your image in order to reflect a change in your offer and/or a campaign to attract a new audience. You may want to convey a more family-friendly welcome, or an appeal to a younger, singles market. You may have adjusted your programmes accordingly and launched an intensive promotional campaign, but the right people still don't come. Maybe there is nothing in your overall brand image that speaks directly to them.

Here is an example from Alton Towers in the UK, a major visitor attraction that is popular with younger visitors:

> We wanted to reposition the park so that it would attract more families. At the time that I joined the company only 35% of the park's visitors were families, with the majority being young adults and thrill-seekers, said Morwenna Angove, Director of Sales and Marketing, Alton Towers Resort. We readjusted our brand positioning so that it was all around 'fantastical escapism'. But while it's all very well to do that from a marketing perspective, we realised we needed to make sure it infiltrated into the real guest experience, whether they're here for a day or a week.

Every employee of Alton Towers was involved in checking the visitor experience and highlighting any hotspot that might need something done about it. Family-focused facilities were introduced: baby-changing rooms were upgraded, smoking was banned across the whole resort (apart from in designated areas), hotel rooms were themed to appeal to children, and the monorail trains that deliver visitors to the park were wrapped in brightly coloured new designs based on park characters. All employees were trained in dealing with families.

Morwenna Angove concluded that the family-friendly moves paid off, rebalancing the visitor mix to the current figure of 50% families and 50% young adults.

Branding pitfalls – dos and don'ts

- Remember that everyone has a brand. Even the smallest museum, gallery or attraction has developed a persona and some level of awareness among its audiences

- In this fast-moving consumer-led culture your brand needs to be reviewed and readjusted at regular intervals

- It is not just about your logo but your internal and external messages and overall presentation

- Lead any branding process from the front with support from senior management and clearly defined responsibilities

- Involve all staff at the beginning of such a process through workshops and questionnaires – everyone has to be on board

- Do test awareness among your key audiences through simple research or focus groups

- Use an experienced (in your sector) brand consultant if the budget allows

- Don't throw the baby out with bathwater – if you have a well-established name stick to it – remember Royal Mail (changed to Consignia at vast expense for six months and then changed back to the old name)

- This isn't just about an advertising campaign or a one-off event – it's your identity. Your advertising should reflect that – not the other way round

- Don't go straight to visuals without research and consultation – use the brand process

- Use pro bono services cautiously

- Stay in control of the creative team, whose ideas may go off in the wrong direction

- Involve only the smallest number of people possible in making the final decision

- Make sure that messages and visuals are acceptable culturally with your staff and audiences, and flexible enough to work in all your different areas of activity

- Negotiate with your sponsors and funders to achieve a successful balance of credits on your printed and online material

- Don't make a news story out of a brand change unless there is something else to say – a new development, new programmes, or a new partnership. Media coverage can make any brand story look like a waste of money

- Maintain and grow the brand (see below).

A note on working with sponsors and funders

A requirement to acknowledge all of your funders and sponsors on all your printed and online material is a challenge, but one that often has to be faced without causing a design disaster. Accommodating a plethora of logos and endorsements alongside your own hard-fought-for brand is a tightrope act and, as in everything to do with branding, it can be a contentious situation. But here are a few tips:

- On posters and flyers, try to group the supporting organisations' logos into one line – all the same size

- Differentiate this line clearly from your brand and the name of the event or campaign

- On websites, use the same approach on the home page and then include lines of endorsement at the bottom of each page if required.

Laura Haynes, Chairman of branding group Appetite, has some advice (see also Chapter 15 (Commercial and fundraising activities) for further advice on avoiding 'logo soup'):

> **Be proud of your brand and the benefits that a well-designed, well-presented brand mark can offer. Don't be bullied by the funders; understand that they have brand guidelines, but so do you and while everyone should stick to their own guidelines, sometimes compromises have to be made. But, these compromises should be done to benefit all of the organisations involved. The arts organisation, at centre stage, and the funders and sponsors aligning themselves to the arts brand.**

Developing the logo and maintaining the brand

Your final choice of visual identity should be flexible and simple. Choose widely available typefaces, single colours which can be achieved with four-colour printing (less important than it used to be as printing develops), large and small type-size choices which work online and offline, clear outlines which reproduce well in black and white, and so on. And do remember any disability discrimination rules – people with visual impairments must be considered.

The creative team will have provided guidelines for implementation of the final visuals. This should be a practical document – not a rod for everyone's back, creating headaches for every department. Horror stories are legion about guidelines which require a graphic designer to interpret them correctly.

So your guidelines for how to use the typeface, logo, name, strapline and visuals, in colour or black and white, should be as simple as you and the creative team can make them, and then circulated to all. Where departments have been used to making up their own flyers and notices, create simple templates to which they can add their information, in the agreed typeface, or by hand. Liaise with IT to recreate the branding on the website and other online material.

Go back to the research stage to identify all the different areas where your name and logo was used (or misused) internally or externally and ensure that there is a mechanism for introducing the new logo. Also ensure that entries in guidebooks and online and offline listings are updated. This can be tedious work and you may need some temporary help to track down and eradicate as much of the previous logo as is possible.

Having achieved your brand new look across all platforms, it is a question of maintaining it within reason. A certain amount of adaptation will inevitably take place internally and externally, leading to the occasional re-appearance of old names or logos. But persevere!

Once a year, or more frequently in a large organisation, pull together as much available material as possible and see how the brand is being used and where adjustments need to be made – or where your colleagues need encouragement to toe the line. Take every opportunity to reinforce the new brand image around the museum, gallery or attraction, on signage and on notice boards.

Give the staff uniforms an overhaul if you haven't already. At the new Ulster Museum, gallery attendants wear attractive sweatshirts with the museum's name and logo, as part of the redevelopment of the old museum. Produce smart name badges with logos for staff. Use PR events, such as launches and private views to show off the logo at the welcome desk, the podium, or as a backdrop on the screen during any presentation. Include the logo on PowerPoint slides or other visual materials used by your colleagues or by you in external presentations.

CASE STUDY IN THE APPENDIX

Case Study 6A: A new brand for the Great North Museum

In April 2006, the Hancock Museum in Newcastle upon Tyne closed its doors to embark on an exciting £27 million development, involving its merger with two university museums (the Museum of Antiquities and the Shefton Museum) and Newcastle University's Hatton Gallery. The result, the 'Great North Museum', was launched on 23 May 2009 and since opening has become the most visited attraction in north east England and one of the top 10 most visited museums in the UK. Steve McLean, Senior Manager, and Iain Watson, Acting Director of Tyne & Wear Archives & Museums describe the process of developing a new brand for these long-established organisations.

PART 2

FROM THEORY INTO PRACTICE

CHAPTER 7

CREATING THE MARKETING PLAN

Planning and people

Audience/market segmentation

Budget, evaluation and monitoring

The 'tipping point'

INTRODUCTION TO THE MARKETING MIX AND THE FOUR PS PLUS

Everyone who knows anything about marketing will be familiar with the four Ps which make up the marketing mix. But they may not be very sure how they apply to cultural marketing because the terminology is based on the commercial marketing tradition. And where do the new media fit, you will probably ask. After all, marketing is now less about advertising and more about social media – or is it? In any case Figure 7.1 may be interesting.

From this diagram (produced by a social media expert) it is clear that marketing spend is moving away from paid-for advertising, print, and even direct mail, into new media marketing tools. These may at first glance appear 'free' but there is a cost both in terms of design, hosting, editorial, technical support, and so on which has to be considered in the marketing budget.

So do the four Ps still work in this new media world? Of course they do, but with adaptations. They are simply a memory board to help you to formulate your tactical plan. Already, some are using six Ps and possibly more. This chapter will explore the full range of Ps as part of the marketing mix and how they might fit into your marketing plan.

PRODUCT

While marketing terminology such as *offer* and *product* may still alienate some people in the cultural world, they are useful shorthand in developing your marketing tactics. The product is your museum, gallery, historic house or heritage site. You need to focus on the exceptional features – the USP (unique selling proposition) of your product. What makes it special to the visitor? Is it the design and interpretation of your award-winning exhibitions? Is it the fun that can be had using the interactive exhibits, or your sophisticated audio or new media guides? Is it a great meeting place, with a good shop and restaurant? Is it a learning experience with great facilities? Is it one thing or several? Could it be the whole experience or the general ambience?

The digital model 2010

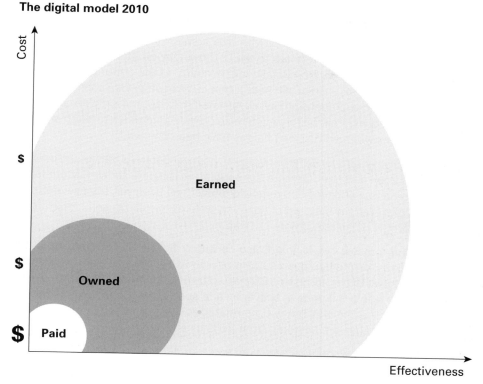

Figure 7.1 The digital model 2010 (after Vijay Solanki): 'paid' is bought media – e.g. a banner ad or poster site; 'owned' is your website or Facebook page; 'earned' is where you are recommended or where your brand's content is shared – e.g. someone shares a great museum experience with a friend via Facebook or Twitter. 'Earned' is cheaper and more credible!

So there may be more than one product – ranking them in order of importance and relevance to different audiences will help to prioritise your marketing activities in line with your overall brand and key messages.

PRICE

- Admission charges
- Special exhibitions rates
- Free admission
- Discounting (or added value?)
- Season tickets; 'Friends' etc.

Price both influences demand and determines income. It is therefore an essential ingredient of the marketing mix, and your marketing plan should consider the structure of your pricing very carefully. Museums with free admission still charge for special exhibitions and so this applies to them as well. There may be hidden costs such as travelling to your venue and parking to take into account. In the cultural sector, price is usually based on 'what the market will bear' – that is, what others are charging, rather than a cost analysis. The competition review outlined in Chapter 4 provides essential input in pricing decisions. Past history might also provide guidelines through analysis of peaks and troughs when admission charges have been changed.

Consider the price structure for different types of visitors – families, seniors, students, groups, etc. In Europe and the US where the population is aging, senior discounts are becoming less generous or have been removed altogether. However, the use of differential pricing allows even the simplest of ticketing systems to collect useful information on the general profile of visitors. (More in Chapter 17 Research.)

During the pricing process, you should also consider the additional costs of audio guides or downloads, printed guides and catalogues. The audio and a simple printed guide may be included in the admission charge, softening the impact of charging (and simplifying the process). The price of souvenirs and special menus in the café should be determined in the same way but will be related to the cost of production. Mark-ups in commercial venues are anything from 30% to 100%.

The overall marketing plan should also set out some guidelines on discounting as part of targeted promotional activities. Paying attractions are regularly approached to be part of local campaigns run by tourist boards and marketing consortia through radio, TV or other media. You may have a general policy not to discount, in which case you may prefer 'added value' – providing, for example, to give away a free guide. It sometimes pays to join in a simple two-for-one promotion where everyone is doing the same thing and high-profile marketing is involved. Don't forget to limit any offer to a set period with a clear closing date and set up ways of monitoring the results.

Historic houses and those with garden attractions find season tickets a good way of bringing people through the spring, summer and autumn to enjoy the different seasons; measure how often people use their season ticket, either through the admissions system or through a visitor survey at the end of the season. This will help in assessing next year's price, based on the value-for-money received by the customer.

Friends and members schemes have grown steadily, forming an important part of the museum's or gallery's fundraising activities. The benefits they enjoy such as free entry can distort the price structure when it is extended to special events, for example. It is important to apply the same rigorous pricing analysis to membership benefits as you would apply to admission ticketing.

Dynamic pricing (also known as yield management) simply means changing prices to reflect levels of demand. Airlines are the most familiar users of dynamic pricing. But the whole concept of increasing prices when demand grows is taking root in other sectors too: car rental companies, hotels, utilities, online retailers – and now theatres, according to the American Association of Arts Marketing. Could this work for museums and galleries? It means offering lower admission charges at the end of the day, for example. It could mean offering a discount to those who booked well in advance for a blockbuster exhibition. Dynamic pricing also offers the opportunity to re-set pricing to react to unpredictable changes in the marketplace.

PLACE

- Location, building
- Frontage on street
- Signage and opening hours
- Disabled access
- Transportation

Place is not so much about your building (except for the standard and quality of its facilities) as it is about the location. You may not be able to do very much about this, although it has been known for museums and cultural attractions to move. The Design Museum near Tower Bridge in London since 1989 is heading for a new location at the old Commonwealth Institute in Kensington. The rationale behind such a move must be very clear: more space and easier public access. Only time will tell if it works.

For the majority of museums and galleries it is a question of working with the existing location. Issues relating to this will already have been flagged up in the internal audit (Chapter 3). It is now a question of addressing these in constructive ways, for example, maximising on any street frontage and being creative about signage and banners.

Signage is a word that will be found engraved on many a marketing consultant's heart! In a crowded city environment it can be difficult to achieve the kind of access signs that you see for major tourist attractions on Britain's motorways – large brown signs. Many environmental improvement schemes in city centres favour the 'finger' signpost, preferably black with gold lettering, on the basis that a discreet sign looks good – but it is invisible! The purpose of a sign is to be seen. Planning regulations may prohibit permanent signs outside the building or on the railings. Get round this with colourful banners or using window space that faces the road – as seen at the Wellcome Collection in London's busy Euston Road.

The arrival of interactive map technology (GPS) makes access so much easier; visitors will know exactly how to reach you either by car or public transport. Those with handheld wi-fi devices will carry the information with them and update as they go along; others will need to print out the directions.

If you are tucked away and not easy to find, do make sure that the name of the organisation is prominent and that something signals that you are open and welcoming – the lights on and the door open? A glass front door (with a solid outer door when the museum or gallery is closed) is a perfect arrangement. In the UK, the new Equality Act (2010) incorporates previous legal disability requirements which are now standard for all public buildings, including self-opening and closing doors as well as ramps wherever required. These will also assist families with pushchairs. Provision of a bicycle rack outside, and pushchair parking space inside are useful and welcoming additions.

Some historic buildings have difficulties in meeting all access requirements (and are therefore exempt in some areas). If this is the case, make it very clear in your promotional material and on the web. See whether you can offer some compensation in the form of a ground-floor display that contains videos or an AV display of areas that are out of reach for people with disabilities.

Opening hours and days are crucial for access and will have a major impact on the marketing plan if too restrictive. We are already in a 7-day-a-week, 24-hour society and attractions need to keep pace. Comparisons will have been made with others in the area as part of the competition review, and comments from visitors should be taken into account. During the 1990s, the UK's national museums and galleries became admission-free. At the same time, those that had been closed one day a week opened all week. With reduced public funding from 2011 museums and galleries are likely to find themselves closing one or maybe two days a week, which is the norm in many other European countries (usually Mondays). In the United States it varies, but many also close on Mondays.

Late-night openings work well in metropolitan centres. Friday evenings are the most popular, but sometimes Saturdays as well, when public openings don't interfere with potentially more lucrative activities such as corporate and private dinners and receptions during week-nights. 'Lates', as they are now popularly known (at least at the National Portrait Gallery) are a good way of targeting a young, more sophisticated crowd, with bars on every floor, talks and music.

What can you do about transportation if you are in an inaccessible location? It should be part of your PR strategy to review and lobby for improvements in transport to your venue as required. Parking is limited in city centres, and in response to the green agenda the attractions sector does not want to be seen as stimulating more car usage. Some attractions have been able to introduce their own minibus services to link to a station, but this is a big commitment which works best at weekends. Even when your site is close to a station or bus stop, it provides confirmation and a sense of arrival if you can display your brand there. At West Dulwich Station in south London, for example, there is a large sign for the Dulwich Picture Gallery, and at Kew Gardens underground station visitors arriving from central London are greeted by a large illuminated poster for the gardens themselves.

Distribution (which is traditionally part of 'Place') means making sure that all those who provide information to visitors and residents in the area know about you. This will be part of your public relations strategy or stakeholder policy but it is just as important for your marketing plan. Ensure that shopkeepers and the business community in your locality are kept informed about your activities, because they are the people who will be giving information and directions to first-time visitors.

PROMOTION

Promotion is the meat of the marketing plan. Starting with your brand (Chapter 6) from which everything flows, choose from the growing list of marketing tools now available to help you meet your objectives – developing your audiences and income. Consider your audiences (see below) and the budget available. Go back to your internal review and check what worked in the past and what did not. But remember also that audiences move on, changing their behaviour in response to fashionable trends as well as new technology.

The website

Most visitors now plan their day out on the internet. Those who already know of you may go straight to your website, while others may search, using the main search engines (Google, Yahoo, MSN) or cultural portals such as Culture24 in the UK, regional or local tourist information tourist websites, or commercial enterprises such as TripAdvisor. Each of these should have information about you and lead to your website.

The website is the beating heart of your communications programme; the design of this and any additional ones for specific exhibitions, mobile website or apps should reflect and endorse the brand. On the home page or just one click away is the all-important visitor information – opening hours, how to get to you, and the facilities available. In addition, the website is your major communications tool, building awareness and promoting your events and activities. Here is an opportunity for interaction, in-depth information on exhibitions, and resources for schools and adult learning, as well as your corporate information. The all-important 'About Us' information should include your mission, names of trustees, directors, and senior staff, as well as your corporate status. The media section should be easy to find from the home page and include up-to-date press releases, downloadable pictures, and named contact points. (Treat with caution any company or organisation which does not disclose this kind of corporate information on their website.)

In addition, to keep up with the expansion of mobile media on phones, iPads and similar platforms you will need a 'mobile' version of your website, designed to fit a smaller screen and load fast. What will happen when the internet is available over people's televisions? Most individual websites will be unsuitable for the television screen as they are set up to be read at a short distance. So future development may include aggregated information websites – broadcasters taking the lead in providing how-to and where-to information as well as themed information on a particular subject – using contents from museums, galleries and historic houses.

How do you move from a simple brochure site to something more sophisticated? Here is some advice from Jon Pratty, Online Publishing Consultant:

> Better websites increase engagement with your virtual visitors. They can learn more about key objects and collections with a session on your website. The website can also be a tool to build the digital skills of staff, and to engage and open up their involvement in the working of the institution. The website can be a great way to increase business for museums too. Lecture or event tickets can be sold online, as can publications and entry offers. Being part of the digital heritage world might mean learning new ways to write, think and promote your site, but it's also about keeping those skills in the museum and making sure the educative effect reaches all in the institution. Make sure there's always someone being trained to update the website and keep it fresh. Here are my suggestions for starting a new website or refreshing an old one – a staged approach:
>
> 1 Who will do the work and who can help? Set up a small internal working group; involve others – local colleges may have a marketing course, or find a business sector secondee.
>
> 2 What's wrong with it right now? You need to be clear about what your site is doing, and where it fails, and where it succeeds. Look at other sites – what is it that they do well?
>
> 3 What does the venue or museum really need and what is the budget? The objectives will be defined in the marketing plan and it need not be expensive.
>
> 4 Make a project plan and timeline. Have a simple set of goals in deliverable stages to show your progress.
>
> 5 Are you tied to a council or someone else's website? What can you do to move onwards? Find good examples of independent sites in the sector and make your case for your own web presence.
>
> 6 Won't this mean lots of training? Some, but there's help at hand. The Collections Trust (in the UK) and other agencies offer online training.
>
> 7 Make it sustainable, part of your volunteer effort, have sub-groups who just do the web work.
>
> 8 Keep tabs on traffic and use it to make a case for more help and investment [see Chapter 17 Research].

9 **Keep up the effort. The website is a permanently open door to your gallery or museum and you need to be present to welcome people whenever they turn up and look at the site.**

10 **Plan ahead – what's new in the gallery? Plan in videos, audio-tours, favourite objects, curator's tours and regular news stories.**

And here is some more advice from Seb Chan, Head of Digital, Social and Emerging Technologies, Powerhouse Museum, Sydney:

1 **Know your audience and their expectations**

2 **Find out what they want to know to engage with you after the visit. Is it e-news, contributing themselves, coming to talks, uploading on Flickr, Twitter feed? Ask your visitors!**

3 **You can now use a simple hosted platform which contains everything for your data, photos and video, and auto-generates a mobile site.**

How do you make sure that online visitors find their way to your website and that your special objects, events and facilities come up high on search engines? This is part of Search Engine Optimisation (SEO) – another emerging science. It starts with the design of the website. Your designer should know how to format pages to achieve a good ranking on search pages. But there are hundreds of millions of pieces of information out there competing for space on Google and other search engines. You can pay for a paid listing slot (see more under advertising) or you may consider employing an SEO specialist consultancy to maximise visibility. Here are a few ideas that you might try yourself:

1 What are the keywords and phrases that people will use when they search for your information? These should appear throughout the website.

2 Use title and description metatags effectively on each page.

3 Changing content frequently is crucial; it makes your site not just more popular with visitors but also with search engines.

4 Build in links to other relevant websites, creating 'link popularity' through reciprocal links, enhancing your search-engine ranking and creating traffic from other websites.

5 Don't use spam to improve your ranking as your site might be blacklisted by search engines.

Apps or applications are mini-websites with limited content (usually not connected to the web), conforming to a set format as specified by Apple or Android, which can be downloaded free or for a price from these providers. They are a way of making money for the publishers (and providers).

If you have an app already, make sure you promote it actively. If you are considering one, check out what's available already and what you might add to the mix. What will be more useful if your budget is limited, an app or making your website suitable for mobiles (that is, a small screen)? Consider the following comments on this subject from a US expert, David Dombrosky, Executive Director of the Center for Arts Management and Technology at Carnegie Mellon University (2010):

1   **User base: While 93% of US residents have mobile phones, the US market penetration for smartphones is 31%. (This means that 62% of the US population uses mobile phones for which they cannot download mobile applications.)**

2   **Connectivity: Whereas mobile websites require users to be connected to the internet, many mobile applications do not require an internet connection once they have been downloaded to your smartphone. This may be important for patrons who are trying to engage with your organization but are in an area where wireless service is not available.**

3   **Platforms: Mobile websites are accessible from all types of mobile devices. Mobile apps, however, are tied to specific types of devices. For example, a patron with an Android smartphone cannot use a mobile app designed for an iPhone. Now, you may be saying to yourself, 'Yes, but iPhones are the most popular smartphones on the market, so we should just design apps for iPhones.' If so, then you will be surprised to learn that Blackberry has 31% of the US smartphone market share compared to the iPhone's 28% and Android's 19% according to the Nielsen Company.**

4   **Price: Mobile websites are less expensive than mobile apps, because they usually lack the design elements and functionality that make mobile apps interactive and appealing.**

5   **Expectations: What do your patrons want from their mobile experience? Have you asked them? If your patrons simply want information (hours, directions, descriptions of work, etc.) then a mobile website is entirely sufficient. If you are looking to provide your patrons with an interactive, one-of-a-kind mobile experience, then you'll need an app for that. In a recent *New York Times* article, Edward Rothstein took a look at a number of mobile apps developed by museums and concluded: 'I have used museum apps to help me navigate museums. But I have generally felt used along the way, forced into rigid paths, looking at minimalist text bites, glimpsing possibilities while being thwarted by realities . . . It is best to consider all these apps flawed works in progress.'**

Most museum websites follow the same predictable, conservative template. So we would like to refer you to some splendid websites for inspiration. However, they change, so what was lively and dynamic at the time of writing may have become turgid and dull by the time you read these words. All we can do is to tell you that in 2010 the following sites were looking good, well-organised and engaging, and highly rated by the Times Online:

1 The Louvre Paris, http://www.louvre.fr

2 The Hermitage St Petersburg, http://www.hermitagemuseum.org/

3 V&A London, http://www.vam.ac.uk/

4 The Rijksmuseum Amsterdam, http://www.rijksmuseum.nl/

5 Museum of the History of Science Oxford, http://www.mhs.ox.ac.uk/

6 Culture24, http://www.culture24.org.uk/home

7 Smithsonian Education, http://www.si.edu/

8 National Archives, http://www.nationalarchives.gov.uk/

9 MuseumStuff, http://www.museumstuff.com/

10 Science Museum London, http://www.sciencemuseum.org.uk/

E-news and social media

E-newsletters are replacing printed material at a fast rate. They are easy to create on a pre-designed template and cheap to distribute through a specialist distribution company that is set up to send out large numbers of emails, and handle the returns and deletions. E-newsletters either have most of the content on the email or contain headlines and links to your website for the full story. They should be regular, at least once a month and, as you will see below, be pithy with not too much information.

Collect email addresses from visitors to the building, the website, and social media sites to add to your databases, and from your professional and media contacts. To comply with the Data Protection regulations – see Resources (which vary from country to country and even within the EU) – you need to offer those on your mailing list the opportunity to opt in or out of regular mailings. Here are some excellent e-newsletters which might inspire you (as at 2010).

- National Archives – monthly, well-designed, no more than three or four stories with links to website for more information. www.nationalarchives.gov.uk

- Art Daily – brilliant daily worldwide art newsletter – always one lead story with excellent photo, followed by ten to fifteen short stories, all with good photos and links to websites. www.artdaily.org

- Watts Gallery (Guildford) – simple and effective regular newsletter keeping readers in touch with the redevelopment of the gallery and flagging up special events. www.wattsgallery.org.uk

Social media is just that – mainly about social networking. It now embraces millions of people, including the older generation who use it to communicate with children and grandchildren. It is not primarily a marketing tool but can be used effectively in niche and targeted campaigns, and there are good examples in the case studies in the Appendix. This is one part of your overall marketing plan which should be light on detail as it is a constantly changing scenario. Plans should be developed for each tactical campaign (see Chapter 8) as well as for your public relations mix. Integration of the aims of marketing, public relations and IT is essential to make successful inroads in this area and to monitor results (see Chapters 2 and 17). But social media should not be treated as just another marketing platform, as this comment illustrates:

> **What I object to is using Social Media 'simply' as a marketing tool – as another set of platforms from which to broadcast traditional marketing campaigns – as digital billboards. SM is fundamentally about having a conversation with the museum's audiences; to misunderstand that is not only to miss an incredible opportunity to connect with audiences in new and powerful ways, but also potentially to damage the museum's brand by coming across as a social media spammer.**
> **(Nancy Proctor, PhD, Head of Mobile Strategy & Initiatives, Smithsonian Institution, Washington, DC)**

Advertising

Advertising in print and on air, traditionally at the heart of every marketing campaign, is now relegated to the sidelines – or is it? The latest viewing figures in the UK show that the majority of the population still get their information and entertainment from television, and from radio.

The biggest decline is in newspaper readership, which continues to shrink. There is more information on this in Chapter 10 (The media overview). Advertising in guidebooks, listings magazines, and local arts and cultural magazines may be good for profile but is less likely to influence the markets you wish to reach. However, it always pays to research current readership and consider whether it fits your overall marketing objectives.

Advertising in national and regional newspapers, special supplements and the cultural pages of Saturday or Sunday papers should be considered for short-term propositions such as major temporary exhibitions or events, when budgets allow. Choose the appropriate newspaper with a readership profile which matches your target audience.

Here is some useful advice from Richard Linington at the National Brewery Centre (see case study introduced below and in the Appendix):

> **As the marketing manager, make sure you research and target the publications you want to be in, thereby ensuring that your budget is used carefully. Don't react to calls from all and sundry, just because they offer you a discount!**

Television advertising may be appropriate for major exhibitions or large-scale events; radio advertising is more likely to be within the budget of most museums, galleries and cultural attractions. Local and specialist radio stations are on the whole thriving and offer cost-effective ways of reaching both wide and niche audiences. Online opportunities should also be investigated and include paying for a placed listing on Google.

> **At the Detroit Institute of Arts [writes Graham W.J. Beal in the case study introduced in Chapter 8 and in the Appendix] the lynchpin of the rebranding campaign was a series of 30-second, mainly black and white, animated spots based around the theme, 'The New DIA: Let Yourself Go' and rooted in the notion of transformation . . . The transformation of the DIA itself is complete and has been successful beyond our expectations. Earlier this year we engaged a company to carry out focus groups and formal polling. To the question 'Who do you think goes to the DIA?' the answer was invariably a version of 'Oh, everyone goes to the DIA!'**

An ongoing, integrated advertising campaign is best developed by an advertising agency with a media-buying department who can negotiate favourable rates. They will also develop the design of ads, whether in print, on radio or on TV. Make sure they work within your brand guidelines as well as your messages. The advertising should not take on a separate life of its own.

Print/distribution

The leaflet was once the central marketing tool for visitor attractions. Have we reached the point when we can stop producing and distributing expensive print and rely mainly on online marketing tools? What are the trends? Most attractions in the UK still produce print, and those targeting day visitors still rely on distribution companies to get their leaflets to key outlets – tourist information centres, libraries, hotels, supermarkets, etc. – at the start of the season (more on this in Chapter 9).

At the National Brewery Centre the leaflet was central to their marketing mix:

> **With the re-opening of the attraction, a full colour, distinctively branded leaflet was designed to give visitors a glimpse of the visitor experience at the National Brewery Centre and encourage them to visit. The leaflet, which folds out, concertina-style, used strong photographic images to help get the core messages across. In the leaflet, it was important to emphasise the free car parking and children's play areas – which are particularly important for the general family days out market.**

> **Liaising with the distributor, we decided on the key locations where the brochure would be distributed. The leaflet has been distributed via a media company to key outlets – motorway service stations, libraries, accommodation providers, for example – and the onsite team of live interpreters have also helped to distribute the leaflet locally. The leaflet is particularly effective in reaching the tourist market. [More in the Appendix.]**

Figure 7.2 Costumed performers with banner at the National Brewery Centre (Photo courtesy of Planning Solutions Consulting Limited)

Posters/outdoor

Posters are only useful if you have somewhere effective to display them. Outdoor advertising remains powerful but expensive; posters in stations, on underground trains, escalators and buses are popular and effective, because they have a captive audience. For a major exhibition, or event, or at the start of the season, posters are a useful way of reaching a wide audience while on their way to work or school, shopping or leisure. Key messages have to be few, short, and readable, and the website address simple and easy to remember.

Incorporating a specially designed barcode will enable people to point their mobile phone or device at the code and the website will come up on the screen. This new technique can be applied in many different situations including interpretation inside the attraction.

Direct selling (mail, telephone, text)

It is still appropriate to send a letter, individually addressed, when you want to reach a particular person with an invitation or fundraising request, but as a general rule avoid direct mail and telephone cold-calling. Both are likely to generate more negative than positive responses. The exception might be use of a local leafleting company to tell your very local community about a special event planned with a local flavour. Unsolicited text messages may have the same impact as cold-calling for some people but is used effectively to remind people who have already booked for something, or to tell them about another event. If you use your e-news or a shorter e-bulletin in email marketing, make sure it is adapted for your target audience and that it conforms to the Data Protection Act. See above and in Resources.

Display/merchandising (windows, front of house)

Urban museums are sometimes restricted by planning regulations as to how they use banners and signs on the exterior of buildings, but the windows should not be forgotten. In many museums these are blocked up from the inside by the backs of displays, showing a blank space or – even worse – dusty installations to those passing in the street. Think of creative ways to use such spaces – maybe you could use a showroom or window dresser to get inspiration.

In addition to the shop (see Chapter 15), people may want something to take away as a reminder or to give as a recommendation to a friend. Make sure you have a stock of leaflets, or plenty of free postcards – branded of course – at the reception or on the shop counter, showing one or more of your most popular exhibits, and including the website address.

'Word of mouth' recommendation

What is the main reason people give for visiting your attraction? Because someone has recommended it. So the visitor experience, from the welcome to the departure, is more important than anything else you do. Visitor services was once about keeping people at a safe distance from the objects. It is now about welcoming people and enhancing the visitor experience. So make sure your attraction delivers on all these points.

Public relations and press relations

In a small organisation, PR and marketing will be integrated by default, as the same person or team are delivering both. In a larger organisation they may be separate, operating in different time frames and to slightly different objectives. In terms of the marketing plan, the PR content should include both the targeting of traditional media, and make a contribution to the management of social media. (See Chapters 2, 9 and 10 for more about public relations and the media.)

Trade fairs, exhibitions, group travel

Some of your targets for new markets – tourists, schools – can be reached through exhibiting (as part of your region or a group of attractions) at trade shows, which bring together buyers and sellers. There are many variations on these, such as the Education Show, British Travel show, or one of the many coach and travel trade fairs that take place around the world. You could also use a recognised mailing house to reach schools, societies and specialist groups or one of the online website resources aimed at teachers. Design some appropriate information material for these markets in conjunction with your colleagues.

Merchandising

Your shop is not just about making money, important as this is (see Chapter 15). It is about visitor satisfaction and raising awareness of your brand. As part of your marketing plan, take a look at the shop and see how far it reflects the brand. It should seem unique to your organisation. You may need professional help in rescuing a tired shop full of old merchandise. Even the smallest museum can do better, but from the marketing point of view it should include souvenirs which reflect the collection, tell the story of the museum or attraction and promote your special events. This is a good place for your art posters. In the USA there is a legal/taxation requirement for shop items to have direct relevance to the collection. Even the bags are part of your promotional arsenal, and should display your brand. (You won't be using plastic bags, of course!)

PLANNING AND PEOPLE

The two additional Ps are Planning and People. The importance of planning has been emphasised in Part I of this book. People, as we have seen, are essential to your success. The attitude of staff will set the tone for the organisation. People are the vital ingredient for the marketing mix in our sector – so pay as much attention to staff and volunteer training, and welcome and visitor services, as to the rest of your campaigns.

AUDIENCE/MARKET SEGMENTATION

So why do some people – possibly half the population – not visit museums, galleries or cultural and heritage attractions? Much research has been carried out to find out why people are not visiting. There are real barriers to participating in cultural activities and visiting museums and galleries, such as no time, no money, or lack of interest. But what do those reasons tell us? Here are some suggestions that provide useful leads for your key messages as well as the visitor experience:

Why audiences don't come

'It's too expensive.'	*means*	'I don't see the value.'
'I don't have the time.'	*means*	'I can't commit to doing it all.'
'It's boring.'	*means*	'It makes me feel stupid.'
'My kids don't like art.'	*means*	'It doesn't engage my kids. If they suffer, I suffer.'
'I just don't think about it.'	*means*	'It's not relevant to my life.'
'It's difficult to find parking.'	*means*	'I don't need one more complication in my life.'

(Arthur Cohen, LaPlaca Cohen, New York)

Using one of the many available segmentation tools, you can analyse your existing audience and match it against your target market to see where your marketing efforts should be directed. The St Paul's case study (introduced below and in the Appendix) features a textbook segmentation of visitors to the cathedral, and there is more about segmentation in Chapter 17 (Research). Whichever segmentation approach you decide to use, it will guide you to the best mix of media for advertising, print and social media, and will also influence the PR department's media plan.

BUDGET, EVALUATION AND MONITORING

What proportion of the overall museum budget should be spent on marketing? No accurate figures exist but most UK museums probably spend less than 5% of their turnover on marketing. This would be laughable in the commercial sector. Attitudes in museums are changing, but only slowly. Few museums and galleries can afford to sit back, even in straitened times, and wait for visitors to arrive – as this book clearly illustrates. It is not simply a question of increasing attendances; it is just as much about raising profile.

Cultural attractions do not always show all their 'publicity' or 'promotions' expenditure under one heading. Various departments or sections of the venue will be spending resources on activities that fall under marketing. Special exhibition budgets frequently have a separate promotional budget. A grant application or funding application will need a marketing strategy with a defined marketing budget. Sponsors of special exhibitions and events will also take a close interest in the marketing and PR plans right from the start of the relationship, and will expect a budget commitment to deliver the agreed marketing and PR objectives.

Monitoring and evaluation should be built into the marketing plan and its importance cannot be overstated. The marketing plan may not be delivering according to short-term targets, but you need to know why – and to take action as necessary. Evaluation is expected not just by individual institutions but by funders, including local government and grant-giving bodies (more about this in Chapter 17).

The 'tipping point'

Finally – how do you know when your marketing and PR has worked and you have reached the tipping point, when the graph goes off the page? Malcolm Gladwell's book *The Tipping Point* illustrates the process in its tale of Hush Puppies quadrupling its sales in one year in New York. According to Gladwell, the success or otherwise of your message getting through in this age of information overload is based on its 'stickiness'. It is also a question of reaching the right groups – the early adopters, and then crossing the chasm to the great majority. It could be down to viral marketing, where your visitors do the work by transmitting their impressions of your messages through Twitter, Facebook and YouTube.

This is still a bit of a dark science, but you will know when you have succeeded. As the Chapter 15 case study from the Pitt Rivers Museum shows, they will be queuing around the block:

> **Some queued for 45 minutes to get in as numbers quickly reached capacity, so inevitably there were a few disappointed visitors, and the tickets for the Pitt Rivers**

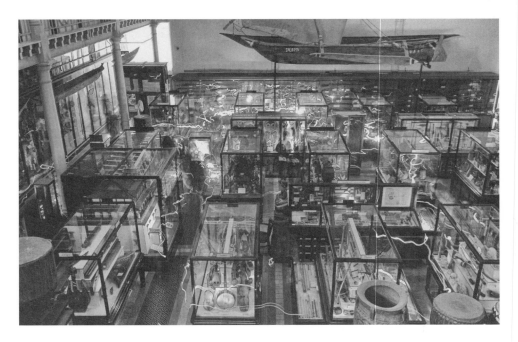

Figure 7.3 Pitt Rivers Museum at night with torchlight (Photo: Rob Judges)

ran out very quickly. However, the wide choice, the repeating programme, and the general ambience ensured that most visitors felt they were witnessing something special.

(Kate White, Marketing and Visitor Services Officer, Pitt Rivers Museum)

CASE STUDIES IN THE APPENDIX

Case Study 7A: The National Brewery Centre – creating a marketing plan

The Bass Museum (as it was formerly known) represented a major heritage attraction in Burton upon Trent, based on the history and world-influencing techniques of brewing that were developed in the town. It was renamed the 'Coors Visitor Centre' in 2002, and subsequently closed in 2008. At its peak, the Bass Museum was generating over 100,000 visits per annum.

Planning Solutions recognised that there was a demand for a major heritage visitor experience in Burton upon Trent and, given the historic buildings and vast array of artefacts housed in the existing site, it seemed logical to explore this opportunity. Discussions with the site's owner, Molson Coors, to reopen the museum as the 'National Brewery Centre', culminated in the relaunch of the Centre in May 2010. Read the marketing plan in the Appendix.

Case Study 7B: Marketing and development at St Paul's Cathedral, the nation's church

As an iconic London visitor attraction and a landmark within the Square Mile, St Paul's consistently welcomes over 800,000 visitors a year – twice that number when including those coming to worship. To ease visitor overcrowding on the Cathedral floor and to introduce new experiences to attract and engage the ever-demanding international tourism market, plans were well underway by 2008 to extend visitor access. Even more of the Cathedral's historical and unique spaces were due to be opened in the next two to three years, namely the Triforium floor up in the Dome and an interpretation hub down in the Crypt.

A marketing strategy was commissioned at the end of 2008 to concentrate on marketing and communications for the period 2009–2011. This needed to take into account the current visitor attraction and audience profile, as well as the planned improvements to the visitor experience and opportunities for new audience development.

Case Study 7C: In a different light – a series of evening events at two Oxford museums

The Pitt Rivers Museum and the Oxford University Museum of Natural History share a single front door, one being accessed through the other. A series of evening events were held at the museums, in association with 'Museums and Galleries Month' and Nuits des Musées in 2005, 2006, 2007 and 2008. The objective for these collaborative events was to encourage visitors to re-engage with the collections by changing the context in which they are viewed, and to draw in new visitors who may find this approach more to their taste. The events were free, and marketed through email networks rather than traditional posters and leaflets, to reach a wider number of young adults and other non-traditional museum visitors.

CHAPTER 8

TACTICAL MARKETING AND AUDIENCE DEVELOPMENT

Promoting courses and special events

Evaluate and monitor

Marketing to minority ethnic audiences

Examining your organisation and developing your programming

Linking with special promotions and events

Taking a consistent approach

Partnerships and collaborative marketing

Strong leadership

Buy-in at every level

Sharing the budget

Implementation and evaluation

Pitfalls

Some inspiring examples

The long tail – developing the niche

Engaging with teenagers

Building return audiences and customer loyalty

Who are your repeat visitors?

Friends and members

AUDIENCE DEVELOPMENT AND THE ROLE OF MARKETING

Audience development involves the whole organisation in reaching out to new and return visitors. It means curators, educators, visitor services, designers, marketing and PR working together to create exhibitions, events, the public welcome, the interpretation and access which appeal to potential new visitors. Publicly funded institutions have a responsibility to attract the widest possible audience from their local community and further afield.

Audience development starts with research and visitor studies. You need to know not only who your current visitors are but also how they are stimulated by what they see

– and if not, why not. Every non-visitor survey shows that there is a section of the population who don't visit cultural attractions because they are 'not interested' or 'it's not for them'. Look again at Arthur Cohen's interpretation of such replies in Chapter 7. The challenge of audience development is to find ways of breaking down these barriers and growing the audience. The role of marketing and PR is to provide the communications support for audience development activities and also for research, monitoring and evaluation. Audience development programmes are sometimes one-offs, based on one exhibition, event or grant-funded project. The long-term aim should be to integrate 'new' audiences and turn them into regular visitors, part of the overall marketing strategy. This requires both developing the product and rethinking the marketing strategy, as this comment from Detroit Institute of Arts illustrates:

> Our big decision was to abandon the specialist-based framework (art history and connoisseurship) of the past hundred years or so and present works of art in the context of shared human experience. We attempted to build on the knowledge that general visitors brought with them, rather than trying to equip them with the terminology of a particular intellectual discipline. This effort was accompanied by two distinct, successive marketing and PR campaigns designed to take the public by surprise and humanize the art museum.
>
> (Graham W.J. Beal, Director, Detroit Institute of Arts, speaking of the transformation of the galleries – see case study introduced below and in the Appendix)

THE IMPORTANCE OF PRODUCT DEVELOPMENT

Renewing and refreshing your exhibitions and events are crucial to audience development in attracting repeat visits as well as new visitors. In the commercial sector, this is imperative; without investment attractions stagnate and visitor numbers drop (see the product life cycle in Chapter 4). How this works in a large-scale commercial attraction is described here by Jane Percy, Duchess of Northumberland:

> Firstly, I'm not an expert on PR/marketing but I have learnt a huge amount about both subjects over the last 15 years since building the Alnwick Garden. Most importantly, I strongly believe that there has to be substance behind your claims and your marketing. The only times I've felt uncomfortable with what I'm selling is when I've realised that what I'm selling isn't being delivered. Never underestimate people's intelligence; they know and can see through the 'hard-sell' and none of us likes to be sold short. Having said that, if you build something as big as the Alnwick Garden you can't sit and wait for people to visit unless they're aware of its existence and the story and values behind it.
>
> In the early days particularly, I experienced bad press, mostly due to misunderstanding, misconceptions and preconceptions, and it would have been easy to have backed down and to have refused to give any more interviews, but if you truly believe in what you're doing and you know that your story is the truthful one then

you need to be prepared to stand up for your beliefs and to fight back. You're not fighting for your own benefit but for the project and the people who will benefit from what you're doing. I always consider, before agreeing to any personal interviews, what my reasons are for agreeing to the interview. What am I selling? What's in it for the Alnwick Garden or for Northumberland?

A few bits of advice about refreshing the product, the impact on our region, working in partnership, and providing good visitor services:

(1) It's important to keep offering a new product if you want repeat visits. You also need to update your product, particularly if it's using state-of-the-art technology such as the Cascade. Technology moves fast and people can see when something starts to look 'tired'. Children are more demanding in the twenty-first century and need to be amused and entertained.

(2) Marketing is even more important if your venue is remote. You need to actively target visitors to divert them on their travels. I don't believe that you can 'put something on the map' purely by PR/marketing. It goes back to my point about substance behind the product. You may get one-off visitors but you need repeat visits, and people need to have enjoyed a good experience to want to return. The Treehouse, for example, is great in the winter. It has a wonderful roaring fire and is cosy and perfect for lunch on a cold wet day. However, the garden at that time of the year is quiet and we need to actively target visitors to come to Alnwick to dine in the Treehouse. The product is good enough to bring parties from Edinburgh, Cumbria and Newcastle – but that needs targeted marketing.

(3) Working in partnership with others in the region is helpful in marketing terms. However, I'm cautious about working too closely with others as I've learnt that everyone wants to copy an original idea and many people have written to me asking if I'd consider helping to develop other Alnwick Gardens – in Cumbria, Devon, etc. I know that Tim Smit has been similarly approached, and by doing that you diminish the value of the original product. There can only be one Alnwick Garden and one Eden Project. I particularly dislike the standardisation of visitor attractions. People need something different to visit, not six gardens with similar water features, treehouses, biomes, etc. However, where I'd love to see standardisation is in a high standard of customer service across the board (something I really care about and which, in general, we're not good at providing in the UK).

(4) Front-of-house organisation is very important. We're in the visitor-attraction business, meaning we care about visitors. If you don't work to treat your visitors as you would wish to be treated yourself then you are in the wrong business. The award I was most proud of winning was 'Loo of the Year' award in 2008. If you care about your visitors enough to provide them with beautiful loos which are clean and attractive it shows that thought has gone into the product and the visitors. (It also prevents visitors from leaving your attraction and increases the dwell time.)

(Jane Percy, Duchess of Northumberland, Alnwick Castle and Garden)

Figure 8.1 Alnwick Garden, looking down the Great Cascade towards the Atrium arrival area (Photo: Peter Atkinson)

A TACTICAL PLAN FOR EVERY OCCASION

The overall marketing plan is about your long-term marketing, your key markets, and how you are going to grow visitor numbers and income. In addition, you will need to develop short-term tactical plans for any number of individual projects involving audience development, individual exhibitions, special events, or new features such as a café or a restored artwork. Below is a step-by-step approach that works well for both PR and marketing and can easily be adapted to many different situations. Don't forget to refer back to your overall marketing and PR plans to ensure that you are in line with the overall marketing objectives and key target groups.

Assemble the information

For a new project or exhibition, a thorough briefing is needed from those involved: planners, curators, designer/architect, collaborating scholars, and sponsors. You need to know what they are doing and what they are expecting from you. If you are receiving a touring exhibition from another museum or gallery, it is useful to hear from their marketing team how things went and what worked most successfully for them. All this information is needed as early as possible. Major projects need one- to two-year lead times in order to capitalise on every marketing and PR opportunity. The information that the marketing officer and PR team needs first is often the last to be decided, including the exhibition title, running dates and confirmed contents. Experience and persistence are your best allies in convincing your colleagues that this basic information is urgent.

The briefing stage is also an opportunity for management to consider and express their expectations. The project may have a high priority within the institution's mission in terms of cementing its academic reputation. It may have been conceived as a way of stimulating new audiences without necessarily thinking through who they are and why they might be interested. It could be first and foremost an income-generating exhibition or programme. This will influence your objectives – and budget.

Describe the product

The background information should be broken down into headed sections for easy reference, adding facts, names and contacts as they become available. Share the information with all your communications colleagues, so that you are working from the same reference material. This foundation document becomes a vital reference document – it saves time later, and helps to ensure consistency.

Analyse the environment

This is where previous research into the external environment will be useful in positioning the product. You could say that it is where the dreams and aspirations of the organisations for this particular project meet the realities of the outside world. There are a number of additional questions to be asked by the marketing and PR team:

- Is there anything about this project that is unique or new?
- When was something similar last done, and with what success?
- Is the news value local, national or international?
- Who would travel for two hours or just thirty minutes to see this?
- Will the product deliver on the promise?
- Is the timing good or bad? What else is going on internally?
- What is the competition – what are other venues doing around the same time?
- Are the opening hours competitive?
- What is the quality of the experience?

- Is the pricing right for the intended market (still being defined)?

- Is there enough time to deliver the audience?

- Does the venue need to adjust other services in order to enhance the visitor experience?

- Are overall expectations realistic?

Define the potential market

The answers to some of the questions will be crucial in defining the audience for this project. Use your overall marketing plan to check through your existing target audiences. Are there other groups who may be interested in this event or project? Every exhibition or programme will be slightly different and potentially open the door to new audiences or help to bring back previous visitors. Organise the list of potential markets in rational clusters. At this stage you may decide to drop some less promising targets but, on the whole, keep most in at this stage.

Brainstorm with colleagues

From here, in developing the brand for this exhibition or event and the details of the marketing plan, it may be useful to go back to the project team, and anyone else who should be involved, for a brainstorm. Share your thinking with colleagues and ask them, 'What am I overlooking – and what ideas do you have?' The human resources locked inside cultural organisations are phenomenal! There will be all sorts of creative ideas available. The key question is always, 'How would you reach that group?' Colleagues may have ideas for innovative promotional activities, and they may have unexpected connections with niche markets (see more about niche marketing below).

By this stage the 'look' and 'feel' of the project should be defined – its name and brand (and how it connects with the overall brand).

Agree the objectives and strategy

The objectives should be precise and form criteria for evaluating your marketing activities at a later stage. Constraints and challenges beyond your control which may affect the outcome of the marketing plan should be flagged up here, as well as strategies to deal with them. Define the overall positioning statement based on your analysis and then summarise the key messages, broken down by key targets. The overall message should be consistent, but there may be different angles which will be more attractive to individual segments.

From your 'wish-list' of potential markets, you must focus on the achievable, within the available budget. Now it is time to design the tactics and look at the most effective ways to reach each of these target markets.

Decide on your marketing mix and finalise the plan

The previous chapter set out the growing range of tools available to marketers and PR professionals. It is a question of judgement, experience and budget to put together the final action plan. Clear thinking is needed at this point. Time, resources and cash may be limited, so they need to be used where they will get best results. This is the true value of the strategic approach. You may give up trying to reach some small segment of the potential market, for example, or decide to do no paid advertising at all and concentrate on PR and social media.

Numerical visitor targets should be set, broken into key audience groups (if these can be measured). There should also be agreed targets for increased turnover in the shop and café. Media and social media coverage targets should be set. Also, if it is part of the objectives, increased awareness of the cultural organisation and its activities as a whole should be measured (see Chapter 17 Research).

Finalise the plan by agreeing the budget and the action timetable with your colleagues. Build in an early review date when, if you are not meeting targets, you can boost one or more elements of the plan. This now becomes your day-by-day, week-by-week action plan which is shared with all those involved. From this point on, it is plain sailing – all that you and your team have to do is perform the thousand-and-one tasks you have identified!

REACHING SCHOOLS AND ADULT LEARNERS

Far from being autonomous functions, marketing and education are inter-dependent elements of every museum's strategy for audience development, if it wishes to be successful. Each can articulate (with a light touch) the museum's philosophy, purpose and intellectual agenda. They should work together to reach the same target audiences. Education can promote the museum to its public, and marketing can educate the public in the museum's collection and disciplines.

In practice, such cohesion is hard to achieve – museums often set their marketing teams short-term targets, whereas education staff may work to longer-term goals. The theories on which they base their professional activities can differ radically. Yet, when a museum overcomes these differences, the results can be astonishing.
(David Anderson, OBE, former Director of Education, V&A, now Director General of National Museum Wales)

Museums, galleries and cultural attractions are in most cases committed to education programmes aimed at local schools and colleges, as well as informal educational activities in the galleries and possibly an adult education programme. Those with public funding may have no choice, but all realise the value of stimulating museum and gallery visiting by children in growing future audiences. School visits in England have grown as part of the 'Renaissance in the Regions' programme which increased visits by up 22% in some regions between 2002 and 2008 (source: MLA).

How does marketing and education close the gap hinted at in David Anderson's comment and make sure that efforts are coordinated for everyone's benefit? While the education staff are best equipped to handle the day-to-day communications with schools, the strategic direction of marketing the educational resources of the museum or attraction should be part of the overall marketing strategy and corporate plan. Marketing input is particularly important when education embraces adult learning with courses and special events. These should cover their cost, unless separately subsidised, and contribute to earned income. Here marketing can analyse the potential audience and create the marketing plan to deliver the objectives.

When problems or new challenges arise, education and marketing can work together to review programmes along the lines suggested below.

Competition review

Undertake some fresh research among competing museums/attractions in your schools' catchment areas (see the competition review in Chapter 3). Are there similar collections elsewhere already producing special curriculum-linked programmes? Is your programme sufficiently different – or complementary? What about courses and events aimed at adults? Liaise with local colleges and see whether there are opportunities for cooperation in areas where you have strengths.

Research your existing school visits

The education department should have records of school visits over time, already analysed by school, age, subject, etc. Look at the trends. Are they up or down? Discuss available data with those delivering the programme, who should be a mine of information about their own particular audience.

What are the trends?

- School visits in the UK have been on the increase for several years – will it continue? Cutbacks in funding for schools and museums will have an impact – and the trend could be reversed.

- Successful education programmes meet current curriculum demands. The National Curriculum in the UK is likely to be much more open-ended in the future, encouraging more flexible schools programmes.

- Independent schools, academies and 'free' schools have more opportunities and budgets for out-of-school visits. This sector is expanding.

- For many museums, demand exceeds supply, so school visits have to be carefully programmed, and unplanned school or student group visits discouraged.

- Child protection legislation and the cost of transport are barriers to educational visits and it is unclear how this might change in the future.

Promoting to schools

Most museums and galleries use direct mail, email and their website to promote their educational programmes to schools. Local authorities regularly mail and email schools and will include information on new programmes in museums in their area. Specialist mailing houses have databases of a whole range of schools, broken down geographically and by type, useful as more schools move out of local authority control. Exhibiting with other attractions at an Education Trade Fair is a good way of meeting teachers and getting some feedback on programmes and facilities, as well as seeing what others are doing. Use training days for teachers (INSET) on particular subjects and themes to introduce a new programme to schools in your area.

Make sure you have an up-to-date database of teachers and others in the local catchment area and send regular e-news on educational activities. Check out the numerous websites for teachers that help them to research the curriculum (see Resources). Don't forget the education press and online news bulletins.

Promoting courses and special events

Courses and special events at your attraction aimed at adults add to your appeal and can be a great way of welcoming new audiences. Friends and regular visitors on e-news mailing lists are the obvious targets but there will be other targets dependent on the subject. Use an appropriate range of targeted marketing and PR tools to reach them.

Evaluate and monitor

Many schools programmes depend on part-time educators and volunteers, but evaluation and monitoring should not be haphazard. Work with the education team to introduce standard measurements for numbers of schools, frequency of visits, size of groups, subjects, etc. so that the programme can be consistently evaluated over time.

MARKETING TO MINORITY ETHNIC AUDIENCES

This is the age of difference. We've all had to get used to new cultures at home and when we travel abroad. In this new world, everyone is clamouring for recognition on the basis of their age, gender, race, sexuality, disability and faith. People want to see their differences acknowledged and not be trapped in other people's ideas of who they should be and how they should behave. For example, women don't want to behave like men to get ahead; Muslims don't want to have to sink a few beers to be considered sociable; gay men and women don't want to stay in the closet; and those with disabilities don't want to be 'invisible'. Meeting all these needs is a challenge for any organisation, but properly managed it can open untapped customer and visitor demographics. How can people of very different and not so different cultures, backgrounds and traditions share and enjoy the same space?

(Colleen Harris, OBE, Diversity Consultant and Executive Life Coach)

As part of your overall audience development programme, you and your colleagues will be addressing the issues raised in the extract above, starting with research. Your overall marketing plan will have identified target audiences, and your visitor profile research may have established the socio-economic and possibly lifestyle profiles of your existing visitors. It is not always easy to measure how far you are already attracting minority ethnic visitors to your venue or which particular groups they come from, except by visitor research (but sometimes this question is considered intrusive) or through observation, although many institutions publish such breakdowns. You can compare your audience profile with that of each region in England using the latest *Taking Part* survey which provides ethnic breakdowns (see Chapter 17 Research).

What is a fact, is that in any major conurbation in Europe or the United States there will be a huge range of immigrants. Some will be second- or third-generation, well-integrated, accessing general media and likely to respond to marketing tactics aimed at their economic or lifestyle group. However, the global nature of media such as broadcasting means that some of your target audiences may hardly ever watch national or regional television, but via satellite may be plugged into their own language news and TV programmes from their countries of origin. Large communities of immigrants also produce their own language newspapers. Different tactics are therefore required to reach these 'closed' audiences, which will involve dedicated outreach, partnerships and a long-term approach.

The London Hub (lead organisation for London's non-national museums) conducted a phone survey of visitors and non-visitors in 2010. 3,500 adults were interviewed; a representative sample of London's population of 7.5 million, some 30% of whom are from minority ethnic groups. The results across London varied considerably in terms of museum-visiting. The motivational factors were summarised as shown below.

MOTIVATIONAL FACTORS

FAMILY VISITORS ARE DRIVEN BY CHILDREN'S NEEDS

People who would consider taking children to museums and galleries are more likely to be intellectually motivated than people visiting without children. Many of these visitors have a strong desire to encourage children's interest in the world around them, or to stay one step ahead of their children by improving their own knowledge on a topic.

ENCOURAGING FAMILY VISITS MAY ALSO HELP TO REACH MORE DIVERSE AUDIENCES

Overall, there are few significant differences in motivation according to ethnic background. Those from black and minority ethnic backgrounds are twice as likely to name 'a nice place to spend time with friends and family' as the main motivation for visiting. Visitors from black and minority ethnic backgrounds are also more likely to visit with children, and so are more likely to cite self-improvement as their main motivation (as are all family visitors).

MOTIVATIONS ALSO VARY BY LIFE STAGE

People aged 16–24 tend to be more intellectually motivated than other age groups: they are more likely to be motivated by learning, often connected to school, college or university.

Those aged 25–44 are more likely to be focused on the needs of children when visiting a museum or gallery.

People aged 45–64 are more likely to name a personal interest in the subject as the main motivation for visiting. These visitors are also more likely to want to engage emotionally with collections – through time travel, nostalgia and appreciating aesthetic beauty.

Those aged 65 and over are more likely to see visiting museums and galleries as simply a pleasant pastime: 23% in this age group name 'an enjoyable way to pass time' as their main motivation.

The results show that intellectual and social motivations are the most significant drivers for visits.

(Source: 2 Insight: a survey of the London museums market www.mla.gov.uk/renaissance london)

Examining your organisation and developing your programming

As part of the audience development programme aimed at achieving greater minority ethnic participation in your activities, the institution needs to examine its offer and how it might appeal to people from different backgrounds. The staff should also be considered – do they reflect the local population in your town or city? The Museums Association in the UK has set up a training scheme, 'Diversify', to assist minority ethnic candidates into work in the cultural sector.

Your schools programme will probably be the most influential in the long run, not just in stimulating future audiences but possibly encouraging parents and grandparents across the threshold in family groups, as the research above shows.

Linking with special promotions and events

Museums and cultural attractions explore religious and traditional festivals and promotions as a useful gateway to ethnic minority communities in their neighbourhood. From Chinese New Year in January/February, to Diwali celebrated by Hindus and Sikhs in October/November, there are opportunities for special events and activities, bringing different groups together to explore each other's traditions and culture.

In the US and Canada, Black History Month happens early in the year whereas in the UK, this celebration of Black and Afro-Caribbean traditions and history takes place in October. Museums, galleries and cultural attractions are invited to join in an umbrella promotion, creating special events and bringing in new audiences.

The 200th anniversary of the Abolition of Slavery celebrated in the UK in 2007 involved hundreds of organisations in staging events and exhibitions. While it might not at the time have generated huge numbers of visitors to individual events, the anniversary raised consciousness and stimulated organisations to consider their collections and programming in relation to ethnic audiences. The media attention created a greater awareness among the general public with new angles on historic events and buildings. The case study introduced below tells the story of a surprising house in South London which is being restored by the National Trust and will open in 2012:

> **Khadambi Asalache, the Kenyan-born poet, architect and mathematician left his house to the National Trust. An intimate home on a busy south London street, the house has an extraordinary interior. Every surface within has been decorated (by Khadambi) with hand-carved wooden fretwork, paintings and collections of objects – a twenty-year journey of creativity that began as a solution to a damp problem in the cellar. [See the Appendix for the full story.]**

Taking a consistent approach

Changing your audience profile to embrace 'new' audiences should be part of a sustained programme in order to be successful. It means establishing a brand which appeals to different groups, and possibly excludes others. When the Världskulturmuseet (World Cultures Museum) opened in Gothenburg, Sweden, in 2006, its remit was to connect with immigrants of different ethnic backgrounds living in the suburbs of the city. Anna Mighetto, the museum's Communications and Marketing Manager, explained their approach:

> *What has been more important in attracting new audiences – programming or promotions?*
>
> **I believe it is the combination of a strategic approach to marketing directed at a broader audience in our target groups with a closer direction and dialogue with niche audiences in the target group. You need to do both.**

Figure 8.2 Public tour at the Khadambi Asalache house (courtesy of the National Trust)

What areas of marketing did you develop to attract hard-to-reach audiences?

We cannot reach them with marketing in the form of advertising. These people come because they have a personal relationship with us in some way – directly with one person or through a peer, friend or relative. These relationships have developed through the museum's programme and educational activities.

Not so much new niche channels as strategic marketing (working with branding, positioning, the offer, target group definition) have been important. We now need to develop this work through social media.

Market research gives us a vital, broader perspective (to compare ourselves with organisations which are familiar to our target group rather than with other museums for example). Be brave and choose. The most effective tools to reach hard-to-reach groups – young adults not used to visiting museums – was to define them as the primary target group for the museum, so that the whole organisation worked in the same direction. This is not always the case in the cultural sector where we try to be 'everything to all people, all the time'.

What have you learnt from past promotional activities which you would be happy to share with others?

- Find out what is really relevant for your target group. Start from their needs, not the organisation's own understanding, prejudices and limits.

- Synchronise the promise and the product (don't communicate coca cola when it is actually milk).

- Connect everything to the values of the brand, rather than just communicating each exhibition.

(Anna Mighetto, World Cultures Museum, Gothenburg)

In 2003/4 Arts Council England invested in a 'New Audiences' programme which encouraged arts and cultural organisations to develop hundreds of projects to attract visitors from all sorts of backgrounds. The results were measured and the report is available on the ACE website (see Resources). Support for black and minority ethnic organisations was a significant achievement of New Audiences. Here is a summary of some of the barriers identified by the research:

- Barriers include lack of relevant product, price, timing, access to promotional material, and lack of peer group representation across staff, artists and audiences.

- Challenges faced by organisations included imbalance of experience and expertise in new partnerships, setting up equitable relationships, and a lack of engagement by the 'mainstream'.

- Partnership working enables mainstream and community organisations to build capacity through the exchange of expertise and experience.

- Successful partnerships require long-term commitment, firm leadership from senior management, time/resources, a willingness to challenge preconceptions, strategic planning, clarity about partners' aims, a skills audit/training, support from mentors, advisers or coordinators, and a dedicated project champion.

- Venues need to review their programming, presentation, physical space, communications, staff training and customer care.

- It is crucial that the links between communities and organisations are able to be maintained beyond the employment of any one key individual.

- There are ethical difficulties around monitoring the ethnicity of audiences, and an effective methodology is needed.

(Arts Council England, *New Audiences Report*, 2004)

PARTNERSHIPS AND COLLABORATIVE MARKETING

Joining forces with others to deliver ongoing marketing activities and one-off campaigns is a cost-effective way for museums, galleries and cultural attractions to increase their marketing and PR spend and deliver a greater return on investment. There are numerous examples across the UK of city attractions getting together, sometimes with their tourist board, in a joint campaign under a common umbrella. And there are several useful case studies in this book (see the Appendix).

Here, from experience, are some of the conditions for success for ongoing marketing through a marketing consortium: strong leadership; an agreed budget; fair contributions from all involved; agreed objectives, regularly reviewed at meetings; independent delivery through an in-house manager or marketing or PR consultant or agency; ongoing evaluation of success.

The conditions for success for a one-off campaign would include: strong leadership; buy-in at every level of the museum or attraction; project funding from an outside source; delivery through one or two partners or agency, but reviewed at regular meetings; evaluation.

Strong leadership

Partnerships and collaboration thrive under strong leadership. Usually it is the largest attraction or museum that takes the lead. See the case study in the Appendix on the Darwin Anniversary in 2008 – an inspiration for anyone involved in a major campaign over several years. The leader is often the person who had the original idea, and while this can produce problems in the longer run, as they lose interest or move on to other things, it is the one thing that will bring the team together and deliver the project. For ongoing consortia it is important that the person in the leadership position grooms one or more others to take his or her place in the future.

Buy-in at every level

The collaboration may have developed as an idea among marketing officers or among chief executives, but to succeed it should have support at every level of the organisation. During 'Museums and Galleries Month' 2006, Birmingham museums and attractions came together to produce a major festival. While the impetus for this was initially at the marketing level, key people from all the attractions involved, including curators and directors, were brought together at an early stage to take part in the shaping of the festival. They were then kept informed of progress as the action group took the event forward.

Sharing the budget

Marketing consortia may work on a contribution model, with a set fee for all once an overall budget has been agreed. Alternatively, the lead organisation may provide some seed money or resources for their team to raise sponsorship or obtain a grant for the event, campaign or programme. To overcome the problem of not having a confirmed budget at the outset, compile an initial working budget which can be augmented with additional marketing and PR spend as more funds may become available.

Implementation and evaluation

The action group should have clear responsibilities for implementing the programme, or hand over the delivery to a marketing or PR consultant. Lines of communication and responsibilities should be agreed for either process to be successful. Build in measurement and evaluation of the project from the beginning, whether through additional visitors with vouchers or from increased press coverage.

Pitfalls

The pitfalls in delivering a partnership or collaborative project are manifold. When the conditions for success (outlined above) fail – particularly leadership and control of expenditure – the project is in trouble and unlikely to continue or be renewed.

Working with different kinds of organisations may also bring problems. You may join a promotion led mainly by commercial partners, such as hotels, restaurants, or non-cultural commercial attractions. Unless you are making a budgetary contribution to the campaign you may have little influence over its direction. Timescales are also likely to be short. On the whole, not-for-profit organisations take longer to make decisions.

Some inspiring examples

'Museums Alive' – a major tourism promotion run on a collaborative basis – was a great success but finally outlived its usefulness. See the case study introduced below and in the Appendix.

'Bath Tourism Plus' (www.visitbath.co.uk) is an ongoing marketing consortium on a large scale – a mini tourist board. It was started in 2004 by Bath and North East Somerset Council as a membership scheme for tourism businesses in Bath. There are now 420 members, including retailers, hotels, attractions, museums and galleries. Established as a destination marketing company, with offices in Bath, it runs the tourist information centre and handles all tourism promotion, including hotel and conference bookings on behalf of the council. It is also responsible for visitor research and campaign valuation.

'Cultureline' (www.cultureline.org.uk) was a one-off promotion coinciding with the opening of the redeveloped London Overground line in 2010. It brought together ten mostly small museums joined by the new service, from Hackney Museum in the north to Croydon Museum in the south. This initiative was funded by a grant from the MLA (Renaissance London) and was promoted through a website, posters along the line, PR activity and social media. All the museums reported an increase in visitors. The leadership in delivering this promotion was provided by a PR company, Colman Getty PR.

THE LONG TAIL – DEVELOPING THE NICHE

The 'long tail' idea illustrated in Chapter 1 encapsulated what many already knew – that there is a large audience, when you aggregate it, for less obvious and less popular experiences, objects and displays.

A special exhibition outside your general collections programme may generate a niche marketing campaign – it could be about stamps, mushrooms, railways, coins, hats or buttons. Each of these is likely to have at least one specialist society which it is relatively easy to reach through direct mail and/or a group travel organiser. Collectors or enthusiasts are not always the 'early adopters' and are more likely to respond to traditional marketing. But check – there may well be a Facebook group for your niche group and they may well be trading on eBay. Every museum and gallery will know from enquiries received about the most obscure objects or facts, that there are people out there looking for the unusual.

There are several questions to deal with before you enter into a concerted campaign to reach any particular niche audience:

▪ Will they reach you anyway? If you have a unique feature, it is likely that enthusiasts will find you. But you need to make your importance and uniqueness clear and accessible in your marketing and on your website (see Chapter 7 on tagging and search engine optimisation).

▪ How much effort and resources should be invested in a niche audience campaign? You have to weigh up the cost in money and resources against the likelihood of converting this particular audience into return visitors. Also, do you ever intend to return to this topic, or was it a one-off?

▪ Don't confuse niche with gaps in your visitor profile. Minority ethnic groups, older people, women, children – these are not niche audiences but part of your mainstream and should be included in your overall audience development plan and marketing strategy.

ENGAGING WITH TEENAGERS

Engaging the attention and involvement of teenagers is perhaps the toughest challenge for any cultural organisation. There is so much competition for their time and energy. In 2010 the Historical Museum of Southern Florida launched an initiative aimed at getting local teenagers not only to enter the museum, but to become involved in museum work. Twenty teenagers participate in the programme via a 3-year museum internship and exhibition development project. They receive a modest payment, they are given basic training, and they work on a 'Teen Miami' exhibition for 2012. Florida has a large minority of immigrants mainly from Caribbean islands. The project should be seen as a long-term social-responsibility contribution to the community, but it will also help the museum to make its interpretation more relevant – it bridges the generation gap and provides lots of material for positive public relations.

In the UK, Stour Valley Arts, Turner Contemporary and the Canterbury City Council Museums and Galleries Service have been working in partnership for more than 3 years on the 'enquire' research project, run by Engage, the national organisation for gallery education. Children aged 9–18 were recruited from out-of-hours school clubs and invited to participate in training and sharing creative activities. Outcomes have included a project film called 'Inspiring Spaces' and the production of teachers' resources including 'Maths Through Pattern', which has been hugely popular with teachers. The most recent resource is on architecture and is called 'A Place to Be' (source: Stour Valley Arts/Engage).

BUILDING RETURN AUDIENCES AND CUSTOMER LOYALTY

Who are your repeat visitors?

In museum visitor statistics, a repeat visitor is someone who comes back to the museum or gallery within a year. They may constitute up to 30% of your visitors. What do you have to do to keep your repeat visitors happy? A changing exhibition programme and a lively events programme will bring people back again and again, encouraged by your e-news and other communication channels. Consider also the shop or café – are you refreshing your displays and products at regular intervals to entice your repeat visitors to browse and to spend money?

Visitor research shows that museum-visiting cycles are often longer than 12 months. What is more, from qualitative research by Morris Hargreaves McIntyre, we now know that these longer-cycle visitors still consider themselves 'regulars'.

The 12-month approach to audience profiling can produce a skew in the opposite direction. Large 'blockbuster' events or exhibitions held in the past 12 months and in receipt of great publicity – causing a bump in the number of visitors – will give an inflated number of 'regular visitors', if measured year-by-year. A long-term approach, combined with qualitative surveying, irons out these inflated periods and gives a much more accurate audience profile.

Does it matter? From a marketing and PR point of view, it means that people who have signed up for your e-news but not visited in the last year still consider themselves as 'regular' visitors to your attraction. They may be using your website regularly. And they will visit again when your programme offers them something fresh – an incentive to attend, or when they have friends and relatives to entertain (source: Morris Hargreaves McIntyre www.lateralthinkers.com).

Creating loyalty across five museums is a challenge. Here Diane Lees outlines the Imperial War Museum's approach.

> The Imperial War Museum's overall aim is to enrich people's understanding of the causes, course and consequences of modern war by encouraging engagement with our collections and visits to our five sites – Imperial War Museum London, Churchill War Rooms, HMS *Belfast*, Imperial War Museum Duxford and Imperial War Museum North.
>
> Whilst each site attracts slightly different audiences – for example, HMS *Belfast* and Imperial War Museum Duxford are more family orientated, whereas Churchill War Rooms' visitors are predominantly from overseas – the marketing challenges for each site are similar. The imperative is to understand your target audience, build awareness and to communicate what makes your venue special within the market place. For the Imperial War Museum, the personal and emotive stories that

can be told through our collections and historic sites are key to encouraging visits, and in future we aim to maximise on this through more co-ordinated and consistent messaging across the whole IWM family. We are also seeking to generate loyalty across all our sites by optimising promotional opportunities both cross site and with other promotional partners as well as capturing visitor data so we can be more targeted in our communications.

(Diane Lees, Director-General, Imperial War Museum London)

Friends and members

Museums, galleries and cultural attractions run major membership schemes developed over the years from 'Friends' societies. They play a huge role in fundraising and stakeholder relations (see Chapters 13 and 14), but they are also visitors, and bring other visitors.

Work with your Friends and members to develop your membership as a branded 'gift', offering not just a commitment to the institution but also benefits. Communications should start from the day they join, with a summary of the benefits they now stand to enjoy, from free entry to invitations for members' private views.

Rolling membership years keeps a handle on the turnover rate. Most membership schemes have a lapse rate of around one-third, so continual promotion of membership is essential. Listen to what lapsed Friends have to say, particularly to those who leave after just one year. Was there a failure of delivery against expectations, and how can it be corrected? Even if your Friends organisation operates independently, work closely with them to integrate their marketing into your overall marketing plan to make it more dynamic, benefiting both you and the Friends.

CASE STUDIES IN THE APPENDIX

Case Study 8A: Visitor-centred transformation of the Detroit Institute of Arts

Under the directorship of Graham W.J. Beal, the Detroit Institute of Arts has undergone a major overhaul of the way in which the collections are displayed, guided at every stage by knowledge of the visitors' reactions. Beal describes it as the DIA's contribution to a global debate about the role of museums in a democratic society. The re-think of the presentation enabled a re-think of marketing and PR. Here Graham Beal tells more of this major transformation.

Case Study 8B: A journey to diversify audiences for the National Trust

Ruth Clarke, Community Projects Manager London, gives a personal account of three consecutive projects that she was involved with over a ten-year period that helped the National Trust in London to extend its audiences.

Case Study 8C: Museums Alive! A long-term regional marketing initiative in Yorkshire

Great partnerships can last for years. Barbara Woroncow, past President of the Museums Association, and Deputy Chair of the Leeds Cultural Partnership, describes a collaboration that brought in new visitors and proved the enduring power of print.

In 1988, the then regional development agency for museums, the Yorkshire & Humberside Museums Council (YHMC), initiated a joint marketing project on behalf of its 200 or so diverse member museums. There was a specific hook on which to hang this new activity as 1989 was designated 'Museums Year' in the UK in celebration of the centenary of the national Museums Association.

CHAPTER 9

MAKING THE MOST OF YOUR TOURISM POTENTIAL

INTRODUCTION TO CULTURAL TOURISM

Tourism is a growth industry across the world. The number of international arrivals shows an increase from 25 million in 1950 to an estimated 806 million in 2005, corresponding to an average annual growth rate of 6.5% (World Tourism Organisation). An increasing proportion are 'cultural' tourists, and they fall into two categories – those who travel because they are mainly inspired by the culture of the country they are visiting, and those who enjoy cultural pursuits as part of a holiday. 57% of overseas visitors give cultural attractions as an important reason for visiting Britain. Overseas visitors generate a spend of more than £1billion in museums and galleries alone.

Sandie Dawe, Chief Executive, VisitBritain sums up what cultural tourism means to Britain:

> It could be said that tourism provides the revenue that keeps our museums and cultural attractions open to everyone. The good news is that one of the main reasons why people spend money coming to Britain is to experience our fascinating history and heritage, and that looks like continuing. The facts are compelling. A Nation Brands Index Survey showed that 65% of potential visitors to the UK would be very likely to go to museums. Out of the 30 million overseas visitors who actually came here in 2009, no fewer than 7.7 million visited a museum and 4.2 million visited an art gallery. Eight of the UK's top ten visitor attractions are museums, and three UK museums are among the top ten most visited museums worldwide. The pull of Britain's diverse museums and art galleries helped secure £1billion spending by foreign tourists in that year.

European countries are at the forefront of cultural tourism with a long tradition of cultural travel, from the pilgrims to the Grand Tour, and a rich cultural heritage. Other countries are investing in their heritage and creating new cultural facilities to tap into this growth market.

The European Capital of Culture programme introduced by the European Union in 1985 is just one opportunity for cities to transform their cultural assets. It can act as a catalyst for cultural development and tourism, illustrated by the case study from National Museums Liverpool on the impact on the museums of Liverpool, European Capital of Culture in 2008. Here is an extract – read all of it in the Appendix:

> During 2008/9, our visitor numbers grew from 2.2m to 2.7m. At the Walker Art Gallery, numbers grew 32% to 353,000, with 56% of visitors coming from outside Merseyside. What we planned and hoped for – a long-term effect with audiences – seems to have been achieved. We didn't expect 2009 visit numbers to exceed 2008, but we were encouraged to find they were 5% higher than in 2007. In 2009, Liverpool was named in the top three UK city break destinations by readers of *Condé Nast Traveller*. In our own profiling survey, 58% told us that one of our

Figure 9.1 Music workshop at the International Slavery Museum, National Museums Liverpool (Photo: Simon Webb)

venues was their main reason for visiting the city that day. And even more amazing, we welcomed more visitors from overseas to our museums and galleries during 2009/10 than we did in 2008/9.

(Tracey McGeagh, Director of Marketing and Communications, National Museums Liverpool)

ASSESS YOUR TOURISM POTENTIAL

So how do you go about increasing your museum's or attraction's tourism potential? Below is a step-by-step plan that you can adapt, depending on where you are in the tourism market at the moment.

Your marketing strategy should have already identified the extent to which your museum, gallery, heritage attraction, special exhibition or event appeals to tourists, and your visitor research should give you an indication of whether you are already welcoming overseas and domestic visitors on day trips – and where they come from. For newcomers to this market, and for those who want to target visitors generally, it is a good idea to carry out an internal and external review and a SWOT analysis to examine your full tourism potential, as set out in Chapters 3 and 4.

In order to assess the tourism appeal of your attraction and how it might become more successful with visitors, you may want to involve a specialist right at the start of the process. Your regional tourist agency, local authority tourism officer or national tourist board might be able to help you here. Or go to a professional tourism association, such as the Tourism Society in the UK and appoint a tourism consultant (see Resources).

Here are some key criteria (based on the Ansoff matrix) for taking forward an active tourism marketing strategy:

- You are located in an already popular or up-and-coming tourism destination.

- Your local council is developing a tourism strategy and investing in the infra-structure.

- Your museum, gallery or cultural attraction has something unique to offer – see comment below.

- You are prepared to invest time and resources in developing the product – for example special tours, private events, supporting material, including foreign language guides if appropriate.

- You are also investing in promotion in collaboration with other attractions, with your tourist board or local authority.

Starting from scratch with a great piece of heritage is a challenge for the director of this palace outside Leningrad:

> **Gatchina was once a great Imperial palace, with unique architecture, a huge art collection and a remarkable garden. It was damaged and emptied during the Second World War, and today only 15% of the 30,000 square metres has been restored. Since I was appointed 9 months ago, marketing and PR have been the key element in our new strategy – basically not to trade on past glories, but to promote the dramatic twentieth-century history of the Palace, and to show the damaged areas as well as the restored ones. It is working, because we have already increased attendance by 15% and income by 25%. Our big challenge for the future is to develop our visitor services, to attract new audiences, such as tourists – who know nothing about the place – and to interpret the story and conservation issues to the public.**
>
> **(Dr Vassily Pankratov, Director, Gatchina Palace and Estate, Leningrad region)**

WORK WITH LOCAL TOURISM DEPARTMENTS, BOARDS AND OTHERS

Developing your tourism market will be a long-term commitment. Start by making contact with your local tourism department or agency. It is also useful to make contact with your national tourist board. They all have a great deal of useful information on their websites (see Resources).

Initially look for some marketing input and advice and establish which trade fairs and promotions the regional tourist board or marketing consortia is actively involved in, with a view to participating yourself.

Further down the line, you also need to establish good contacts with the local tourist information centres as well as local libraries, and arrange for your printed material to be distributed through their displays. Make sure you invite the staff on familiarisation visits. You also need to get your information included on local authority and national tourist board websites with links to your website.

Here are some tips from Adrian Bevan, formerly product development manager at VisitBritain, now a tourism consultant:

WORKING WITH TOURISM PARTNERS

1. Develop your relationship by working with tourism partners. If you're working in isolation you're unlikely to achieve as much. Think about what the regional and national tourism bodies are doing and look at how you can sit alongside them. Working with these organisations can help you understand what their needs are and how your product and brand can support their goals.

2. Make sure your tourism partners know about any imagery you have and make it readily available (royalty-free). There will always be journalists, tourist boards and travel operators who will need to have access to imagery. Don't forget to let your tourism partners know about new products and events in good time. If you're promoting an event or new exhibition to international visitors make sure you are talking to your tourism partners up to three months in advance of your event's launch. Tell your tourism partners that you're happy to welcome visiting journalists. This could be an opportunity to obtain some free publicity.

3. 'Short breaks' – what can you offer this important visitor who may have no more than a few days but will want to experience something educational, creative and rewarding? Visitors now want to achieve something during their short break. Can your product be combined with local accommodation and activity partners to maximise the opportunity? A short break should be action-packed. By working with other partners you could find yourself creating a new 'experience/product' or new event that could help give you an edge.

4. Don't forget the importance of working through and with the travel trade – both on the domestic front and to attract international visitors. Get along to British

Travel Trade Fair or World Travel Market to see how you might do this. Remember when approaching the travel trade to present your information simply and concisely (in their language). You don't want the travel trade to struggle understanding what you want to offer them.

5. One of the emerging opportunities is that of 'local distinctiveness'. Domestic and international visitors are asking more and more for experiences that give them an opportunity to connect with local places and local people. Think about what makes you stand out and makes you distinct. Think about cross-promotional opportunities where you can work with other locally distinctive experiences, such as local eateries and suppliers that can help you to develop a more distinctive offer.

Throughout this book there are great examples of collaboration. In the tourism field, the online magazine 'Creative Tourist' offers something new and different, using digital media to create an exciting buzz about Manchester and eight museums and galleries. It is an inspiration. The full case study by Susie Stubbs is in the Appendix, but here is an extract:

So does Creative Tourist work? As an online magazine, it is editorially independent and attracts around 22,000 unique users every month, with high dwell times on the site and low bounce rates. 80% of readers are from outside the North West – exactly its target audience. The site has won two digital awards, and publishes original features, news, podcasts and audio from some of the UK's best-known writers and artists. Running alongside, and timed to coincide with the three peak tourism seasons in the city, are its city guides. Pegged to these guides are parallel marketing campaigns that use a combination of on and offline media to boost web traffic and encourage downloads of the city guides (and thus visits to Manchester).

PREPARE THE APPROPRIATE INFORMATION

Travel trade and tour operators putting together specialist tours tend to work up to two years in advance. Your background information pack – online and in print – therefore has to include essential visitor information as well as details of upcoming exhibitions and events. This includes the prices for special events for groups and individuals (bearing in mind that tour operators and travel trade will expect a commission). Well-organised information and a professional approach to marketing will give tourism organisations and partners the confidence to go out and market your product for you, knowing that you are doing all you can to make it a successful, quality experience.

For up-to-date information on group travel companies, cultural tourism companies and other specialists in the travel market, contact your local tourism officer or tourist board. You need these for your direct mail and e-news updates. There will be advertising opportunities with the tourist board or local authority as part of their local, national or international campaigns. Sometimes the expense of appearing in tourism brochures and handouts is beyond the means of the cultural attraction. Remember that your cultural product is a valuable ingredient for any such campaign, and that you have the opportunity to develop stories for the editorial content of any promotion. The same applies to images, as outlined in the tips above.

In many cities there are museum or leisure cards aimed at residents and visitors, giving free access to museums and galleries and sometimes linked to transport cards. There are also commercially operated schemes, promoting your venue in return for discounts on admission charges or free entry. Participants get a return based on the number of visitors generated. The use of smartcard technology means that traffic can be accurately measured and it also provides useful information on visitors for participants.

One of the well-established schemes is run by the Leisure Pass Group in many cities throughout the world. In Philadelphia for example, the scheme provides entry to some 30 attractions in the city, including the Philadelphia Museum of Art, the National Liberty Museum and the Franklin Institute.

WORKING WITH HOTELS, BED & BREAKFAST ESTABLISHMENTS AND OTHERS

Your city may already have several tourism networks, including the chamber of commerce, where you can meet others, learn from them and tell them about your product. Invite them to hold meetings at your museum.

In order to reach visitors who have already arrived in your area, make contact with hotels and accommodation providers to display your leaflets and to participate in weekend break promotions. Sometimes such marketing initiatives can be negotiated directly with the manager on the spot, but many hotel groups centralise marketing, so it will mean finding the right contact at head office.

Head porters, concierges, head waiters and desk staff are useful contacts in hotels. They have direct contact with customers, and make recommendations on what to see and do. It is useful to include them as well as tourist information centre staff in familiarisation visits and previews of exhibitions.

Bed & breakfast providers may well have a local association. They are also good places to distribute your printed literature. Increasingly visitors are staying in cottages and self-catering flats; this makes them more difficult to reach. Local shops may be useful as well as the local tourist information centre.

WORKING WITH TOUR AND COACH OPERATORS

Tour and coach operators put together tour packages and market them directly in the UK and overseas. Into this group fall most of the heritage or cultural tour operators plus ground handling agents who specialise in this sector. Ground handling agents are the people who look after travellers on package tours from other countries. They may have an input into programmes, but the overseas operators will have the final say on the content and how it is marketed in their own country. In the UK, tour operators are members of UKInbound, a trade association representing all UK's inbound tourism businesses.

Ground handling agents and tour operators make their plans and price their services one or two years in advance. They are interested in group discounts, but they also need to know that you are geared up to look after their customers. Coach operators have shorter lead times – particularly for day trips. Specialist group travel organisers devise themes for their tours, or follow particular geographical routes. They may well approach

Figure 9.2 Group visitors put an additional strain on facilities, including parking (Photo: Paul Bigland)

you with an idea for including you on one of their one-off programmes to coincide with an upcoming anniversary or a major exhibition happening elsewhere, but which also has connections across the country.

For every type of group – from the older generation day-trip to the connoisseurs on a special programme – make sure you can deliver a quality experience, from arrival right through to departure. This means providing information on parking in advance, a warm welcome at reception, clean and plentiful toilets, an appropriate tour or special event, quality refreshments, and a selection of gifts and souvenirs. As well as looking after the tour leader and/or guide it is well worthwhile paying some attention to the coach driver – large attractions offer special facilities, including an opportunity to wash down the coach! And do contact the tour leader afterwards for feedback on the visit.

TOURIST GUIDES, GUIDING AND LANGUAGES

The tour leader and the tourist guide are extremely influential in terms of whether your museum or attraction will be visited again, as some of them also set up their own tours for small groups and individuals. In the UK and other European countries there are standards for professional guides, and associations that you can contact with updates on your attraction and forthcoming exhibitions.

A large group arriving at your museum or attraction can cause major disruption for your individual visitors, particularly if the group is having a guided tour. It is up to you to organise this through a pre-booking system and by limiting guiding in the galleries or congested spots. You may decide to have certain days or times for groups only, or to arrange for pre-talks to take place in an education suite or lecture theatre.

Overseas groups may come with a guide from their own country whose knowledge of your attraction is limited. So try and make sure that they have information in advance. For individual visitors, analyse current and future visitor trends to see which countries your visitors are coming from before producing foreign-language audio guides.

WORKING WITH TRANSPORT PROVIDERS AND TAXI DRIVERS

In many cities taxi drivers are a good source of information. Yet how many times do you visit a town and discover that the taxi drivers do not know where the local museum or gallery is situated? You can reach cab drivers with literature through their local association, or through the cab companies themselves. Why not include them in your tourism familiarisation events?

You also need to stay in touch with transport providers generally. Your local tourism network might be a good starting point.

MORE ABOUT YOUR WEBSITE AND TOURIST MAGAZINES

Your website should be geared up with information, especially for visitors from further afield as most of your individual visitors will check out their route online. As well as information on events and exhibitions, provide a practical section for group, coach and tour operators. Your region will probably have its own tourism website for you to link to. There are also cultural portals in many countries. In the UK make sure that your data is on Culture24.

Printed material is still important for visitors on the move, although many will be updating themselves daily on their mobile device using apps and mobile websites. Listings magazines, such as *What's On*, exist in print and online everywhere, and should be included in your press mailing.

Individual visitors holidaying in the area, or staying with friends and relatives, may not know about your attraction before they arrive. Foreign students on English language courses have lots of free time. Will their host families recommend you – have they been to your attraction? Organise an Open Day for host families and bed & breakfast owners once a year to build closer links for the future and familiarity with your attraction. A solid local visitor base is a good start for the visiting friends and relatives (VFR) and student markets.

ARE YOU IN A CONFERENCE DESTINATION?

Is your city already an established conference destination, or are there new hotels or a conference centre at the planning stage? If so, consider what you can offer in terms of daytime experiences for accompanying partners, and in terms of evening events for delegates and their partners. Make contact with the conference centre and local conference organisers and show them around your attraction. Museums with good hospitality and event facilities may be used as part of a conference. See Chapter 15 on how to maximise on this business for your own museum.

DEVELOPING A NEW CULTURAL DESTINATION

Patronage provided by tourists and the tourism industry can be a spark for cultural development. However, sustained cultural change requires commitment to excellence, creativity and the development of human potential from within society itself – this requires patronage from the public sector. Ultimately, as our work at Bilbao demonstrates, the success of cultural tourism depends on the involvement of the creative resident population.

(Barry Lord and Gail Dexter Lord, *Artists, Patrons and the Public: Why Culture Changes*, 2010)

Across the UK and the world, exciting plans are under way to develop new cultural destinations. In the Gulf there are major plans to introduce new museums with famous partners, such as the Louvre, the Guggenheim and the Smithsonian Institution. The case study Notes from the Gulf (introduced below and in the Appendix) shows that the growth in museums started before these grand projects and was based on the home market.

SOME TIPS ON BEING DIFFERENT

The point has already been made by Adrian Bevan above that, in this age of mass tourism, people are increasingly looking for individual experiences. Differentiating your destination and its attractions is more important than trying to appeal to everyone. Here is a pertinent comment from Wales:

> **The basic point [of the tourism promotion] was being missed – the singular, sometimes unsophisticated, sometimes contemporary but always authentic expression of a small nation's culture can be far more attractive and engaging to the outsider than the marketing messages that make it look indistinguishable from any other western, industrialised complex.**
>
> **(Michael Houlihan, former Director General, National Museum Wales, now Chief Executive Officer, Te Papa Museum, Wellington, NZ)**

The box below shows some more comments on this subject from participants in a VisitBritain cultural tourism workshop, attended both by providers and producers, which echo this quote. These ideas apply just as well to your niche marketing.

WHAT ARE THE KEY MESSAGES FOR CULTURAL ATTRACTIONS VENTURING INTO THE TOURISM MARKET?

- Authentic, local, sustainable

- People-focused side of history – stories

- Quality, value for money

- Delivering on promise

- Consistent over time and between organisations

- Unique (needs an honest comparison of self v competitors – is it genuinely unique, or is it similar but still special?)

WHAT MAKES THE DIFFERENCE?

- Genuinely meaningful to the market segments one is pursuing

- Authentic experiences and artefacts and locations deliver what the web cannot

- Experimental – experiences with a difference, e.g. out of hours, segmentation, give choice but not too much

- Invest in staff so they make places come alive, are confident in offering additional information and adding value to customer service.

(VisitBritain Cultural Tourism Conference 2008)

MEASURE THE RESULTS

Set annual targets for your tourism marketing and measure the results as part of your overall marketing monitoring and evaluation. Look separately at casual overseas and domestic visitors and the group market and see where you have been most successful and how you can develop further.

CASE STUDIES IN THE APPENDIX

Case Study 9A: Notes from the Gulf; marketing in a different dimension

Throughout this book we have been describing how to operate in a Western cultural tradition, using its behaviour patterns and attitudes. Marketing and PR need to work within different environments. This case study looks at a part of the world that has seen dramatic new developments in the cultural sector. Sue Underwood and Pamela Erskine-Loftus, who work for the Qatar Museums Authority, describe what they have learned from their experiences.

Over the last five years the face of Persian Gulf museums has changed dramatically. For many in the West, the arrival of the Gulf States in the museum world has been caused by the announcements of international agreements with existing Western museums, such as the Louvre and Guggenheim projects in Abu Dhabi in the United Arab Emirates (UAE), for the creation of satellite branches, although this term is not often used to describe them. These projects have received considerable coverage in mainstream media as well as museum and arts press, both positive and less so. Other new museum projects in the Gulf States have taken an internal collaborative approach to development, such as that between the Zayed National Museum and the British Museum, London, and the development of a museum of Bedouin life with the Smithsonian Institution, Washington, DC, both also projects in Abu Dhabi.

Case Study 9B: Making the most of Liverpool, European Capital of Culture 2008

Tracey McGeagh writes: In 2005 when I joined National Museums Liverpool (NML), the buzz about 2008 Capital of Culture was already audible and growing day by day. It gave us an unprecedented opportunity to showcase Liverpool's museums and galleries, and a chance not just to grow our audience numbers but to attract new visitors who would come back time and again.

Case Study 9C: Manchester Museums Consortium's Creative Tourist – a new collaborative model for museums marketing?

Two years ago, Manchester Museums Consortium faced a dilemma. It had secured funding – from the Northwest Regional Development Agency and Renaissance in the Regions – to stage an ambitious programme of international exhibitions and events. Part of this funding was to be used to promote the programme to 'cultural tourists', those national and international visitors who may be persuaded to visit Manchester on the strength of its cultural offer. The dilemma the Consortium faced was this: how could it make marketing work for the Consortium as a whole, for the eight very different museums and galleries that formed its membership, and for a programme that was both disparate and lengthy (it would run for two years and include everything from performance art to historic collections displays)? How, in other words, could it keep its members happy while satisfying the needs of a highly discerning and dispersed audience?

CHAPTER 10

THE MEDIA OVERVIEW – THE FUTURE IS . . . ?

The future – has it already arrived?

National newspapers on and offline

Broadcasting goes from strength to strength

What is happening to local news?

Magazines and their future

Who's who in social media?

Bloggers, freelancers, photographers and the public

THE FUTURE – HAS IT ALREADY ARRIVED?

Has the future already arrived? From your bed in the morning, you stretch out your hand for the ready-made cup of tea (old technology), grab your iPad or similar and within seconds you are reading your favourite newspaper (new technology). In the background your digital radio alarm clock is giving you the news round-up or some wake-up music. At the bottom of the bed the integrated TV/computer springs into life with the breakfast show, but you switch to your email inbox – sharing interesting titbits with friends or colleagues on Facebook or LinkedIn – or you read them on your hand-held device while jogging. You check the opening share prices via apps as you sweat it out on the underground, with your free newspaper in one hand (or has that already gone?) and your iPod plugged in, playing your favourite download list from Spotify. Feel the overload already? Oh I forgot, your mother just phoned . . . now where is the mobile?

In this chapter we will consider how the media (traditional and new) is changing, and how that impacts on your marketing and PR activities – now and over the next few years. We have gathered together information from people 'in the thick of it' to give us a perspective of how communications media are developing.

This is Len Downie, former editor of the *Washington Post*, speaking about the future of journalism in the autumn of 2010 (James Cameron Memorial lecture, City University, London):

> **American journalism is at a transformational moment – in which a long era of dominant newspapers and influential network television news programmes is rapidly giving way to a new journalistic era in which both the gathering and distribution of news is more widely dispersed.**

So what is the future for newspapers in Europe and United States? Len Downie continued:

> **The most aggressive of the older American news organizations are changing fast. Like the *Guardian* and the *Financial Times* here in Britain, the *Washington Post* is no longer just a newspaper. It is now a multi-platform news and information provider.**

What underpins newspapers and online media is of course advertising. Here opinions are divided. Some agencies are moving a greater proportion of their advertising online while others continue to rely mainly on traditional media which appear to have more impact:

> **More than half (52%) of respondents said television was more memorable than any other form of advertising medium, followed by 10% who said newspapers, and just 2% for online video adverts and 1% for online banner ads and on iPhones and iPads.**
>
> **(YouGov for Deloitte for the *Media Guardian*, Edinburgh International Television Festival 2010)**

So what happens to journalism? This is Alan Rusbridger, former editor of the *Guardian* speaking in January 2010 (Hugh Cudlipp Lecture, London College of Communications):

> **This, journalistically, is immensely challenging and rich. Journalists have never before been able to tell stories so effectively, bouncing off each other, linking to each other (as the most generous and open-minded do), linking out, citing sources, allowing response – harnessing the best qualities of text, print, data, sound and visual media. If ever there was a route to building audience, trust and relevance, it is by embracing all the capabilities of this new world, not walling yourself away from them.**

The individual has access to more information than ever before as data from government, archives, museums, galleries and universities become available online. Take Google, with its ambition to digitise and organise all human knowledge! Traditional media will continue to gather, analyse, write and edit before broadcasting or printing news and opinion, while everyone can have their say on new media. It is chaotic and individualistic – a minefield for the marketer and PR officer – tailored to the means of delivery and the ever-shortening attention span of its participants. Any individual can join in, and start a demonstration or just peaceful queues at exhibitions. One morning in 2010, a message sent out on Twitter and Facebook by a 17-year-old student encouraged 10,000 people to gather in a Stockholm square to protest about the election of far-right candidates to Parliament – proof positive of the power of social networks. Popular uprisings in Middle Eastern and North African countries in 2011 were fuelled by the web and social media.

As Alan Rusbridger said: 'In the digital world, the distance between impulse and action is shorter than ever before.'

Museums and galleries are already part of this revolution. The Tate, the Smithsonian Institution, the British Museum and others are leading the way. They design and produce their own programmes, broadcasting them through their own website or YouTube and offer them to one of the established online media outlets. There are online cultural news services such as Art Daily – a 7-day-a-week international update on art around the world. In the UK, Culture24 updates its home page daily with news stories from around the UK. A whole host of publicly supported and independent cultural websites, portals and e-newsletters keep those working in the sector and the potential visitors informed.

So in the face of this technological and journalistic revolution, how are traditional and social media likely to develop over the next few years? It's a brave person to predict in 2010 where we might be in 2015 – let alone 2020 – but this chapter outlines some of the trends.

NATIONAL NEWSPAPERS ON AND OFFLINE

While the readership and print-run of national and major regional newspapers in Europe and the US are slowly decreasing, some are building new audiences online, and transforming themselves (as described above) into multi-media platforms. Here is Len Downie's description of the *Washington Post* newsroom in 2010:

The *Washington Post* . . . operates out of a completely reconstructed newsroom in downtown Washington, DC – with a digital universal news desk for all of its print and digital outlets, several television and radio studios, and state-of-art multi-media production facilities . . . reporters all produce both digital and print journalism. They blog regularly on their subject beats – from politics, economics and national security to education, sports and religion. They produce audio and video podcasts. They converse with their audiences through online chats and social networks. They discuss their journalism on television and radio. And their work is digitally tagged and manipulated to maximize its exposure via search engines, online aggregators and social networks.

Yes, that's a lot of work, especially in newsrooms, including ours, where there are fewer journalists than there were just a few years ago.

These new conglomerates provide a huge range of opportunities for cultural news, features and advertising. News stories may appear in print as well as online. In-depth cultural coverage may feature online or in printed weekend supplements or magazines. Journalists may blog about it and send a tweet to support it. All will work to different deadlines and need different approaches. However, the same story – the opening of one exhibition for example – can be covered in a multitude of ways.

Advertising online is spreading from the early banner ads to sponsored features, and click-through blocks in the middle of news and feature columns. Multi-media journalists gather their information not just from PR officers in cultural institutions but from social networks, bloggers and comments on their own website.

So are people still reading newspapers? In 2010 the UK's top national titles were slowly losing circulation but still maintaining relatively healthy figures, compared with the United States. The popular newspapers such as the *Sun*, the *Daily Mail* and the *News of the World* still have circulations above 2 million, while only the *Sunday Times* amongst the 'broadsheets' sells more than 1 million copies. The *Daily Telegraph* at about 680,000 outsells *The Times* at 500,000, with the *Guardian* at 290,00 and *Independent* at 190,000 (ABC UK, April 2010).

Experienced PR professionals know the difference between a feature in *The Times* and one in the *Daily Mail*. One will impress the influencers – but the other will turn out the visitors.

Compare this with the readership of the largest newspapers in the United States (with five times the population of the UK), and the regional fragmentation as well as decline in readership of printed newspapers in the US becomes clear. Only the *Wall Street Journal* and *USA Today* get anywhere near 2 million, with the *New York Times* at just over 1 million, and the *Los Angeles Times* and *Washington Post* at around 600,000 (Audit Bureau of Circulations, March 2010).

BROADCASTING GOES FROM STRENGTH TO STRENGTH

The time people spend watching TV [in the UK] remains stable alongside internet growth, with the average person watching 3 hours and 45 minutes of TV per day. Despite the growing choice in technology and services available, watching TV remains the activity that most adults would miss the most. Compared to 2007, a growing number of 16–24s (up 8 percentage points) and over 55s (up 7 percentage points) say that watching TV is the activity they would miss the most. It's not just scheduled live television which continues to be popular. Ofcom's consumer research from the first quarter of 2010 shows that almost a third (31%) of households with internet access used it to watch online catch-up TV – up 8 percentage points over the year.

(Source: Ofcom, August 2010)

Detailed statistics on television viewing by channels and programmes in the UK are available to subscribers of BARB (Broadcasters' Audience Research Board). 2010 channel statistics showed that terrestrial TV channels capture 55% of the audience, with a growing proportion of viewers on digital channels. The BBC with seven channels attracts around a third of the total TV audience; ITV with four channels is just behind. So far, BSkyB with ten channels, attracts around one-tenth of the audience. Top programmes such as *EastEnders* and *Coronation Street* attract around 5 million viewers. The General Election debates in 2010 attracted around 10 million viewers.

In the US and across the world, Nielsen provides rankings and information to the advertising industry on broadcasting, online, mobile and social media.

So the impact of television continues unabated, as the figures above show, despite the growth of the internet and social media. Digital, satellite and cable television offer a huge range of programmes on a multiplicity of channels with great PR as well as advertising and sponsorship opportunities. More and more material is being bought in or commissioned from independent producers. The decision-makers are the commissioning editors who receive a constant stream of proposals. Careful research and preparation is needed before putting forward your programme ideas, and it has to be way ahead of the opening of any major exhibition or venue. 24-hour news channels in the UK, the rest of Europe and the US all welcome topical short cultural news and features to lighten the mix of hard news.

The demand for low-budget programmes is partly responsible for the growth in reality shows and fly-on-the-wall documentaries. Should you participate in this trend and give your staff the chance to become household names? There are successes and failures among the various series that have been made in UK cultural institutions. *Behind the Scenes at the Museum*, broadcast in the UK in 2010 showed smaller museums coping with both triumph and disaster. The National Trust did well with the series focused on Sissinghurst, despite obvious personal conflicts, while there were some cringingly awkward moments in an English Heritage fly-on-the wall series. A well-crafted programme on the many different aspects of the Natural History Museum took the public into the stores and laboratories of one of the UK's largest museums, and the museum emerged with flying colours. The BBC filmed three series of *A Year at Kew* without problems, despite some tricky episodes which were resolved by agreement. The results increased attendance, and book and DVD sales, as well as awareness of the role of the Royal Botanic Gardens.

So what makes it safe to proceed with this kind of 'all-access' TV? Most organisations have learnt from others that it can work as long as the objectives of the programme and those of the organisation are in harmony, and a proper contract of agreement is in place, as well as day-to-day liaison on minor issues.

WHAT IS HAPPENING TO LOCAL NEWS?

Throughout the US and Europe, local newspapers and local radio and television stations are under pressure to secure funding support and/or advertising revenues. Despite this, in the UK in 2010 local newspapers remain the second most important advertising medium after television, and they are making successful transitions to multi-media platforms. Local media reach around 40 million print readers a week and 37 million web users a month, with some 1,200 core newspapers and 1,500 websites (Newspaper Society).

The Newspaper Society of the UK produces a range of statistical information sources for registered users. These include the 'Media Portfolio' database which provides access to details on a wide range of local multi-media platforms linked to regional newspapers, including websites, niche magazines, specialist sections and supplements, and radio and TV stations. It also publishes the 'New Society Database' and 'JICREG' (the Joint Industry Committee for Regional Media Research). These can be searched by various criteria for media opportunities covering any area and they include a demographic local/regional profile.

For UK museums and attractions, the influence of the national media and its London bias can be frustrating for those outside the capital. The Welsh Assembly and the Scottish Parliament have created competing news centres in Cardiff and Edinburgh. At the same time, the BBC has split its operation and set up a major broadcasting centre at Salford, in Greater Manchester. This will strengthen the influence of the North of England, adding to the national and regional centres in Cardiff, Bristol, Birmingham, Glasgow and Manchester, as well as its 59 local radio stations. This can only be of benefit to cultural attractions around the country.

Liverpool's year as European Cultural Capital (see the Chapter 9 case study) put Merseyside on the map as a source for cultural news. The 'Liverpool Biennial' was covered by all national newspapers. Bristol hit the headlines with its Banksy exhibition (see below and in the Appendix) and Edinburgh demonstrates its cultural credentials each August with the hugely important and widely reported International Edinburgh Festival.

London, with its concentration of cultural attractions, continues to dominate the news agenda. The UK is not alone in this bias. In France, Paris is in the same position, despite the Louvre opening a new museum in Lens, in the Nord Pas de Calais region. Countries such as Germany, with strong regional governments and media, do not have the same problem. In the United States the East Coast continues its cultural dominance while the West Coast basks in the sun – and film and television industries. As this book illustrates, however, there are significant cultural attractions in Chicago, Detroit and Philadelphia, and of course Los Angeles, challenging New York and Washington. The difficulties include the immensely fragmented media, the vast distances and the different time zones. National campaigns only succeed with complex traditional and new media strategies. (The Chapter 11 case study from LACMA shows how to plan and execute a successful media campaign in Los Angeles.)

MAGAZINES AND THEIR FUTURE

According to the Periodicals Publishers Association (PPA) magazines are thriving in the UK. Over 3,000 consumer titles were published in 2010, reaching 87% of the adult population. Surprisingly, perhaps, 15–24 year olds are the most likely age group to read magazines. Magazines drive 'word of mouth' and bring a 'halo' effect to advertising, according to the PPA.

Women's, lifestyle, news and current affairs, business and finance magazines are still growing in terms of circulation. Men's lifestyle magazines are also doing well. TV titles, together with stalwarts such as *Take a Break*, *Saga Magazine* and *OK!* are among the top sellers. However, overall circulation of magazines is declining – they are fighting to hold on to readers as well as advertisers. Magazine publishers are launching into the unknown with e-magazines online designed for iPad and other hand-held devices (ABC UK, August 2010).

WHO'S WHO IN SOCIAL MEDIA?

The social web is a twenty-first-century phenomenon created by young entrepreneurs – mainly for themselves and their friends – which has grown into many multi-million pound businesses. What was fun and innovative has become serious competition for established media, not just in terms of readership but also advertising. Social networking sites developed mainly from online dating sites and discussion forums set up in the 1990s. The huge social media sites now popular (2010) were only established in the last decade, and will continue to change over the next few years.

The popularity of individual networking sites varies from country to country. So before launching a campaign using one or more of these social media, do some research among your own visitors, asking them which sites they use regularly.

Myspace, set up in 2003, is still one of the largest networks, with members' profiles, music and videos, as well as instant messaging and real-time updates for your friends. It has some 300 million members, one-third of whom are active. It has been owned by News Corporation since 2005 (Myspace).

Facebook was set up at Harvard in 2004. The network is still owned by its founders and has 500 million active users, half of whom log on every day. An estimated 150 million people access Facebook on mobiles, customising their profiles, posting and sharing messages and taking part in discussions. Privacy settings have been enhanced to protect younger people from predators.

LinkedIn is the oldest professional network for business people sharing information and comments. It is independent and has 60 million users.

There are a number of other social networks with many millions of participants but they are not as well known as the ones above (at the time of writing).

Photo-sharing sites started with Photobucket which was soon overtaken by Flickr, now hosting some 3.6 billion photographs. It is part of Yahoo.

YouTube, the video-sharing site, followed in 2005 and is now owned by Google. Members can upload videos up to 10 minutes long.

Social news sites followed, and Twitter, founded in 2006, has cornered the market with its 'tweets' – short messages. It is still independent. Twitter has over 100 million users, and in 2010 some 50 million tweets were created each day.

Wikipedia is an information website, published by the Wikipedia Foundation, and was created in 2001. It relies on volunteers for its comprehensive encyclopaedic information. It is in the interest of institutions to ensure that any information on the site referring to your museum, collection, facilities and history, are correct. In 2010, the British Museum entered into an arrangement with Wikipedia to update and provide information on a huge range of subjects where they have expertise. It has 78 million visits per month, 90,000 contributors, and 3.5 million articles in English (Wikipedia, 2011).

TripAdvisor (part of Expedia) is the world's largest travel site, enabling travellers to plan and comment on their trips, including visits to attractions. It pays to keep an eye on this site (and others) so that you can refute any wrong information. (More in Chapter 16 Communicating in a crisis.)

BLOGGERS, FREELANCERS, PHOTOGRAPHERS AND THE PUBLIC

The public has always had a role to play in news gathering, by phoning their local newspaper with titbits or participating in late-night phone-ins on talk radio. This participation has, thanks to new media, grown phenomenally as discussed above. Everyone can now be a journalist or news photographer in the making, whether we like it or not. The stream of information which flows from the public is further enhanced by blogs. There are millions of them already – individuals letting off steam on numerous

Figure 10.1 Young visitors arriving for the Banksy exhibition (courtesy of Bristol Museum, Gallery & Archive)

subjects. Journalists themselves are joining the blogosphere and 'tweeting' their latest offering to their followers. The Banksy exhibition in Bristol is a brilliant example of how social media created a huge success (see the case study introduced below and in the Appendix).

News desks have recognised the power of the public and now actively ask for first-hand reports – 'Were you one of the people trapped on Eurostar?' or 'Did you see the Cutty Sark go up in smoke?' Via mobile phones, people are sending in photos and videos, and texting their own views of what is going on. This is a challenge for the PR manager in a crisis, as we will see in Chapter 16 (Communicating in a crisis), but it is also a challenge for news organisations. How are they handling the flood of information?

How can they ensure it is accurate, and how can they translate it into interesting and informative news and features? 'With difficulty' is probably the answer. Nick Davies in his book *Flat Earth News* (see Resources) found that only a small percentage of news stories were properly checked. It is up to PR professionals to play their part in this revolution by providing balanced, accurate and reliable information in their media communications which can be easily translated to the web or printed page for those with shrinking editorial resources.

CASE STUDY IN THE APPENDIX

Case Study 10A: Banksy at Bristol – the unexpected impact of social media

In June 2009 an exhibition called 'Banksy versus Bristol Museum' hit world headlines. Banksy – a graffiti artist from Bristol – had 'taken over' Bristol Museum and Art Gallery in secret to curate his first ever museum exhibition. After this stunning success, the museum had to consider how to prolong the effect and maintain their profile. Rebecca Burton, Deputy Head of Commercial and Customer Services, Bristol Museum and Art Gallery talks about the exhibition and its aftermath.

With over 100 pieces of Banksy art, many created for the show and referencing Bristol's collections, the exhibition was a huge popular success. Over 300,000 people visited in 12 weeks, making 'Banksy versus Bristol Museum' one the year's most visited exhibitions globally.

CHAPTER 11

ENGAGING WITH THE MEDIA THROUGH PR

Relationship with the media

The press office in action

Audience segmentation and targeting the media

Timing

Website, social media and podcasts

Press events

Press trips

Press views

Private views

Press conferences

Embargoes

Photo and film opportunities

Media interviews and appearances

Awareness campaigns

Bloggers, freelancers, etc.

The electronic press office – databases

Working with PR consultants

RELATIONSHIP WITH THE MEDIA

Are the traditional PR activities of contacting journalists and sending out press releases breaking down as the media changes? On the one hand there is a multitude of TV channels, online platforms, print and blogs, and on the other huge media platforms consolidated by established newspapers. Does this mean more opportunities through many more channels, as in marketing? Some remain targeted at journalists and mediated through online news, newspapers, broadcasting, local media and magazines, while others are aimed directly at consumers.

The answer must be yes to both. We are all absorbing information from a growing range of sources, including word of mouth. What has not changed is the competitive world in which we as marketing and PR professionals operate. The cultural map has expanded everywhere. We take a trip to Paris from London or Berlin for special exhibitions; visitors from Scandinavia or Spain head for London's range of galleries once or twice a year; Middle Eastern destinations are raising their cultural profile with new architecture (see Chapter 9 Your tourism potential); American cities offer world-class art galleries, not just to those on their doorstep but for visitors from across the United States or Canada.

So how do you get your messages across to the right media against such competition and with so many choices? One cultural online news editor receives up to 500 emails a day. The media-savvy PR manager or consultant has to segment, choose and target. You can of course use email releases to hundreds of journalists at a touch of button. Just as easily, the person at the other end can delete your missive. Creating a good story, choosing the media, and building relationships with those who are important to your institution are just as relevant today as before. You just have to do more of it and back it up with your direct marketing and PR through social media.

The relationship between public relations practitioners and journalists in business and politics will always remain tense, but in the world of culture it is different. Cultural and heritage organisations usually get a friendly reception. But arts journalists are hard-pressed – they are frequently the first to go when budgets are cut – and then they turn freelance. This has an impact on what they can cover and where they can go. It means that we have to provide easy and accessible information with an individual angle for those who can deliver good coverage.

In the cultural sector, tensions between journalists and PR officers are most likely to flare up when the organisation is under pressure financially or through some other crisis. This is when the press officer comes into her or his own, taking charge and handling the communications in the best interest of the organisation, while managing access to senior staff and chairmen. (More on this in Chapter 16 Communicating in a crisis.)

Investment in good relations with your local or regional newspaper, radio and TV stations, and with key national journalists, will pay off all the year round, but particularly in a crisis. This doesn't necessarily mean wining and dining – not many people have time or budgets for that – but including them in your special events; meeting for a cup of coffee; organising interviews with key people to keep them well-briefed; and getting out of the office to network at events with other PRs and journalists.

In addition to the growth of social media we are seeing a boom in celebrity culture. Celebrities invade every part of our daily lives – writing columns, appearing as pundits on chat shows, and sharing their travel experiences in the feature pages. Should a celebrity be part of your PR campaign? Maybe – but tread with caution (see more about this in Chapter 12 Events).

Just a few years ago, travel writers in particular used to complain about the mass of mail waiting inside the front door after a trip, and newsrooms constantly ran out of fax paper. Today, they and other journalists are bombarded with emails, tweets and texts from electronic press offices (including yours). A whole new industry of 'free' press-release distribution services has developed, sending thousands of untargeted press releases to the world's media. This has inspired the CIPR (Chartered Institute of Public Relations) and PRCA (Public Relations Consultants Association) to get together with the NUJ (National Union of Journalists) to draw up a few very sensible rules of engagement (see box).

EXTRACT FROM THE 'MEDIA SPAMMING CHARTER'

- Practitioners should invest time in researching the editorial scope and interests of a journalist/blogger before approaching them, to ensure their area of responsibility is relevant to the communications programme.

- Confusing, misleading, inaccurate or non-targeted emails may damage the reputations of the practitioner, the employer and the client.

- Practitioners should be aware that journalists/bloggers may block individuals or companies if they believe they are being sent emails and other content that they perceive to be irrelevant to their work.

(www.cipr.org.uk)

So has the cultural sector got better at media relations? Here are some comments from Jane Morris, formerly editor of *Museums Journal*, and now editor of the *Art Newspaper*:

> In general there is much greater awareness of PR/media among all types of museums, and it is much easier to get information, organise interviews and source images than it was, say, 10 years ago. But the ability of museums to deal really effectively with the media is still very variable. This is, for many, mainly a resourcing issue, but I think the majority still don't realise how much good quality

(and high value, if you considered it in terms of advertising space) coverage can be achieved.

The cuts in the numbers of arts journalist posts across the media, the reductions in freelance rates and so on, means that the media is more dependent than ever before on PRs 'placing' stories/packages etc. with very specific, targeted media. That's not going to work so much with a news-driven, investigative-type publication like the *Art Newspaper*, but in the more consumer-focused publications and broadcast outlets, there is increasing reliance on their relationships with the PRs. However, that means that the PRs have to think about individual publications/ sections, since this is more about creating something exclusive for a journalist or editor than sending out a heap of identikit press releases.

THE PRESS OFFICE IN ACTION

Cultural organisations vary in their structure and practices. There may be institutions where press enquiries are still handled 'off-the-cuff'. Establishing a new press office regime in that environment is a challenge. It means getting those colleagues with special contacts in the media on board, assuring them that you are not a barrier but a means of ensuring accuracy and continuity in the communication with the media.

The Dulwich Picture Gallery case study (introduced below and in the Appendix) provides a valuable insight into how an incoming press and PR manager can help to turn around a small gallery on the brink of disaster.

With limited resources and a competitive media environment it is easy to lurch from one media campaign to another without standing back and reviewing your longer-term strategy. How do you avoid this and get back on track? Planning is the key word. Your day-to-day PR and press activities should be part of your public relations and/or marketing strategy, designed to raise the profile of the organisation (see Chapter 5). Media relations is at the heart of this strategy and will include a number of separate campaigns through the year for upcoming exhibitions, new features and facilities.

Putting a tactical PR plan together at short notice with the arrival of a new object or chairman requires some clear thinking and a short-term plan. With major exhibitions or the opening of a new attraction, the longer the lead-in, the more successful it will be. The stages outlined in Chapter 8 (Tactical marketing) work well for your short-term and long-term PR plan:

- Assemble the information about the gallery, artist or exhibition.
- Describe the product – outline the key features – what's different, unique.
- Describe the environment – what else is going on at the same time.
- Define the potential market and segment the audience – who will come especially for this, who will come anyway.

- Brainstorm with colleagues – with input from the architects, curators, exhibition designers.

- Develop the objectives and align the PR strategy with the marketing campaign (images, key messages, timing, etc.).

- Create the PR plan with key targets, images, and timing – finalise.

More than ever, marketing and PR have to work together – new technologies and the competitive environment are creating a much stronger relationship and dependency. This is Helen Palmer of Palmer Squared, writing about the Manchester International Festival 2007, of which she was Marketing Director:

It's all in the preparation!

For any major event, festival, or launch, such as the inaugural biennial Manchester International Festival in 2007 (MIF), you have to spend time developing a robust and meticulous plan that will become your daily bible. Our approach to planning had to reflect and respond to the innovative nature of the festival – an ambitious, demanding and innovative new model – yet be realistic and flexible enough to be deliverable. The strategy was supported by a carefully scheduled and costed action plan that also in effect became an advocacy tool, generating buy-in from the team, board, key funders and numerous partners, firstly as it was presented and then as it was (seen to be) delivered.

While marketing and PR are often treated as two complementary but quite different disciplines, it was vital that marketing and PR fed off each other, working from a single timeline and a single set of objectives. With such an ambitious festival concept – a programme created entirely from new commissions – media interest was sparked very early. In fact this started over two years before the festival, and well before any of the programme could be confirmed, let alone publicised. So we had to focus on managing information and expectations internally and externally, as well as making sure that the PR campaign created the right buzz at the right time, without peaking too early, and delivering secure benefits for our media partners.

But when festival fever takes hold – and it did – it would have been easy to slip into being reactive and making impulse decisions that could easily have wasted valuable resources. This is when the strength of the plan really kicked in. Whilst there are always great ideas that never come to fruition and opportunities that come along at unexpected times to mess up the carefully crafted schedule, MIF's marketing planning delivered real punch. We welcomed over 200,000 visitors and secured over £11m worth of media coverage.

So I lied a little. Preparation isn't everything. Creativity, energy and blood, sweat and tears are also essential, but they'll count for little without 'the plan'.

AUDIENCE SEGMENTATION AND TARGETING THE MEDIA

Having established your target audience for a particular event or exhibition, consider how this fits in with your overarching institutional aims and objectives. Will this project present an opportunity to attract new audiences and different markets? If so, will there be additional activities – events and outreach, for example – to support such a campaign? Is it more about bringing back your regular visitors? If so, how can you inspire them to visit for this particular event or exhibition?

From here, decide on the groups of media to be targeted and, within each group, identify the key publications or programmes. Timing is crucial (see below) as are the messages. Competing titles may require different approaches. Finding key messages, hooks and angles requires a creative approach to media relations and is much more challenging and rewarding than just producing the standard press release.

At this stage, it may be useful to highlight within each list those whose coverage will be essential to success, both in terms of attracting visitors and in satisfying the expectations of your trustees, directors and curators. Think hard about the messages – and develop the unique or quirky points that will attract journalists to read further than the first line of your release. The messages you choose to emphasise may be different to the curatorial interpretation. There's nothing wrong with this (but see Will Gompertz's comment below), as long as you remain within the content and spirit of the project and can defend your position.

Here is some advice from Will Gompertz, BBC Arts Editor and previously Head of Media at Tate:

> **My advice to someone who is responsible for communicating the activities of a museum or gallery to the general public is quite plain: Tell your target audience what is happening and invite them to attend. For this you have myriad communication channels from which to choose; select the most appropriate one for the audience you wish to engage. Do not suggest programme ideas to the curators or keepers with whom you work, under the auspice that you think they would help attract your intended audience. To do so is to put your organisation at risk. The audience does not know what it wants and will trust the specialists to present the most suitable programme; so should you.**

TIMING

Timing is everything in media work, which is why you need a well-organised office with efficient systems to handle the complexities of proper scheduling. Lead times (the period needed between placing a story and its publication or broadcast) are different for different sections of the media. Even today, when online news can be flashed around the world in a moment, it still takes up to five months to plan, lay-out and publish a high-quality glossy magazine. But that might change as online versions appear.

Similarly, broadcasters may take months to consider and decide on a proposal, unless it is for a news programme, and production can sometimes take years. The idea for the magical 'A History of the World in 100 Objects' series was first discussed at the British Museum 'over a cup of coffee' with the BBC in 2005, and the series was launched on BBC Radio 4 in 2010. By then it had grown into a major production, including 500 museums, TV, children's TV, mechanisms for public participation, and a dedicated website:

> **A History of the World has been a unique public service partnership between the British Museum and the BBC. The essence of the project was to present a world view of history to the widest audience, using the British Museum's collection as a starting point, through the Radio 4 series 'A History of the World in a 100 Objects' presented by Neil MacGregor, Director of the British Museum, with contributions from a wide range of public voices. As a result, the collection has been brought into people's homes through popular media channels including children's TV, regional, national and international radio channels and online. Press and advocacy contacts were engaged from an early stage in collaboration with the BBC and specific stories on the wider project as well as individual objects were generated throughout the course of the year.**
>
> **(Joanna Mackle, Director of Public Engagement, British Museum)**

So plan well ahead whenever possible. It is never too early to start telling the media about your major opening or major exhibition. The news desks may tell you that it's too soon, but you are 'lobbying' them by trailing your event, and will follow up with other releases as the date gets nearer. The box below shows an example of an outline schedule for a major exhibition or event, ready to implement the moment it becomes a certainty.

PR TIMETABLE FOR MAJOR LAUNCH OR EXHIBITION OPENING

From two years ahead

Initial short press release and introductory email letter, with suggestions for potential collaborations, to TV commissioning editors (producers), appropriate programme editors and production companies (features, not current affairs) with any available images. Follow up with telephone calls, meetings and briefings. Add information to advance press section on your website.

One year ahead

Short press release to wider array of media, depending on your target audience, including specialist magazines and specialist correspondents (women's, lifestyle, art and antiques, etc.).

Six months ahead

Prepare separate in-depth approaches for different sectors of the long-term press – mostly magazines and TV programmes with shorter deadlines than the production teams identified above. Create an early image bank for the website and set up special advance briefings to individual journalists on your key target list.

Six weeks ahead

Email press release to complete target list, with links to image bank and further information. Follow up with your key contacts.

Three weeks ahead

Issue invitation to press view (and follow up nearer the time).

One or two weeks ahead

Create photo opportunities for different media and set up any advance broadcasting interviews. Follow up with local radio and local press.

Day before event

Issue short (brief) news statement to press associations and news desks.

On press view day

Distribute a launch day release (printed and on CD with images).

After opening

Follow up on all requests, and email opening kits to all key press who did not attend.

WEBSITE, SOCIAL MEDIA AND PODCASTS

The website is in many cases the first port of call for journalists seeking information about your institution. Look at it regularly from the user's point of view. How many clicks does it take to find your press information and how up to date is it? What about general information about your organisation? Is your 'About Us' section comprehensive, including the names of senior staff, directors and trustees? And is your governance and funding clearly set out, with copies of your annual reports? The more information you can appropriately disclose online the less time you will have to spend informing the media and the public, and the more open you will appear as an organisation.

The press pages should have: a 'look ahead' section with upcoming exhibitions and events (bear in mind that some magazines and programmes are planning up to a year ahead); access to current and past press releases; an image bank (either available to all or by registering); and named contacts with email addresses. It may not be ideal to put mobile phone numbers on the site, but do make sure that your answerphone includes out-of-hours contact information – and be meticulous about responding to messages quickly. Also include a section on filming, photography and media visits (more below).

'Social media cannot be done in 10 minutes a day!' says Dr Nancy Proctor, Head of Mobile Strategy & Initiatives, Smithsonian Institution, Washington, DC:

> **Like anything, doing social media well requires commitment, resources and experience. The start-up cost is low and the learning curve fast, but a quality social media effort requires more support from the organization than just 10 minutes a day (which I think many of us hoped would be enough at the beginning of the phenomenon) and it needs to be an integral part of other marketing, education, interpretation and outreach efforts in order to support the museum's mission fully.**

Work with IT and marketing colleagues to develop a social media programme alongside the traditional press campaign, aimed at journalists as well as visitors. The case studies linked to this chapter provide good examples. The use of Twitter to promote National Poetry Day shows how it can be done on a small scale. The hugely successful Banksy exhibition at Bristol Museum and Art Gallery was featured on YouTube and continued through to Facebook and other social media sites. LACMA, the Los Angeles County Museum of Art, which operates in a very competitive, multi-cultural market, has used social media effectively alongside traditional approaches, including blogs, podcasts, Flickr, iTunes, Twitter, etc. These options, which continue to grow and develop, have made it possible for attractions to communicate efficiently and cost-effectively with a wide range of publics with news of exhibitions and events.

The 'blog' is a way of generating stories in other media outlets, as journalists are avid readers of blogs. It is also a good way of involving one or two of your more creative colleagues in developing stories and writing directly for the public. It can appear on your website, be trailed on Twitter and get quite a following if you find the right tone of voice. Podcasts have been around for some time but have staying power as useful promotional and outreach tools. The podcasts of 'A History of the World in a 100 Objects' from the British Museum and available on the BBC website have been downloaded 10 million times around the world in less than a year. It is a medium that adapts easily to providing information in different languages. The RAF Museum at Hendon, London produces a series of podcasts, and in 2010 added one in Polish, celebrating the contribution of Polish Airmen to the Battle of Britain.

Some social media successes are the result of serendipity (and 'viral' marketing). The Barbican Art Gallery hosted an art exhibition of live birds in a sound landscape. Several people filmed this on their phones and uploaded the snippets on YouTube (downloaded some 600,000 times to date). This inspired tweeting and subsequent Facebook activity, and created queues for the otherwise rather low-key exhibition. The Guggenheim in New York set up a competition with YouTube to find new video talent. More than 23,000 submissions from over 90 countries were received and whittled down to 125 shortlisted videos, and presented to the YouTube Play jury for consideration.

Twitter was imaginatively used for a one-off European-wide promotion – 'Ask a Curator'. This involved curators in some 300 institutions in answering questions from the public. It was organised by Sumo Design company (based in Newcastle on Tyne) and promoted on Culture24 and other networks.

Social media is in constant flux and development but is now an integral part of the lives of half of the adult population – anyone under 35 or 40 will be using social media daily. So consider your target audience for every campaign and decide which of the huge array of media tools will be most effective in reaching them. Bear in mind that social media is primarily about networking and directed by the users. Don't try to impose yourself in this network but work out ways to stimulate interest and awareness for your events and exhibitions, as shown in the case studies.

The rise of online and social media has created great challenges for the modern PR professional and their media relations strategies. Not long ago journalists were the gatekeepers of access to – and influence over – an organisation's target audiences. Well-connected PR professionals could leverage their relationships with journalists to seek to achieve positive coverage in the publications that their target audiences read. Ways of measuring success are still being developed. See advice from Metrica in the case study introduced below, and from the Tate in the case study in Chapter 17.

PRESS EVENTS

Chapter 10 made it clear that journalists are finding it harder to get out from behind their desks. This means that your press events have to be relevant, informative and well organised. Once you have established that your plans for a media event meet all these criteria, it will be easier to attract press and/or to get national journalists to come out of the capital to attend regional events. (See Ina Cole's comments in Chapter 12 on how to attract journalists and VIPs to regional events and press views.)

Press trips

Through your local network, tourist board or local authority, work with others to create an attractive itinerary for a press trip introducing a number of smaller attractions and galleries. The national tourist board may bring a group of overseas journalists to your region. Take their advice on what to include to gain their attention. Working with an experienced PR consultant or agency will take some of the challenges out of an organised press trip, such as the travel and accommodation arrangements, time-keeping and entertaining.

Press views

Timing is crucial. Use local and national sources (such as the Arts Council anti-clash diary in the UK) to ensure that you are not competing with another major exhibition press day or big launch. Divide up the time between photographers and TV crews on the one hand, and journalists on the other. Make sure that your key colleagues – architects, designers, curators and artists – are on hand at specific times for interviews.

It is also a good idea to invite press office colleagues from other museums, galleries, and the local and national tourist boards to the press view, or to one of the private views. They should all know what you are doing – it is part of networking.

Private views

For major openings, you might plan several private views in succession – for Friends, for museum and gallery colleagues, and for VIPs and patrons or sponsors. See Chapter 12 for more nitty-gritty information about organising your events.

Press conferences

Press conferences are only occasionally relevant in the cultural sector. As part of a campaign to 'save' the institution or a specific object, they have a place, particularly if it is newsworthy. The launch of the 'Staffordshire Hoard' appeal is a good example of this – see Chapter 15. The chairman or chief executive should be introduced by the press officer, outline the subject and then introduce any others involved, and finally take questions. Make sure that there is a written statement, available online and in print on the day, and access to images on disc or online. Allow for TV and radio interviews, in an adjoining room, before or after, depending on the timing. Press conferences are generally held in the morning, so coffee, biscuits, etc. is quite adequate refreshment. If the news you want to announce is highly specialised or low key, you may be better advised to host a press lunch and arrange a more informal briefing.

Embargoes

To prevent the story from being used in advance of a press conference, you may decide to use an embargo, if it is sufficiently important. Embargoes are often applied to speeches made at an event or major opening, because they may change in delivery. The embargo is a request printed on the front of the release or invitation, or emphasised in any telephone conversation, asking journalists not to publish or broadcast the information before a fixed time on a fixed day. Such a request is usually honoured, and should only be used where circumstances make it essential.

PHOTO AND FILM OPPORTUNITIES

We live in a visual age and there are thousands of photo opportunities out there in the printed and online media – and not just for still photos. Increasingly online media feature short videos – and so should your website. The international daily online e-news 'Art Daily' has taken photography to new heights, featuring a selection of stunning photographs from around the world every day.

Here is the Editor of Art Daily, Jose Villarreal, explaining how this daily online news magazine is produced:

> **Some museums, galleries and auction houses have me on their press mailing lists. So I get an email and, if interested, I email them back asking for pictures. Other museums, I trace with a robot that alerts me when their press page changes. That way, I get a 'head start' on the competition.**

> **We only use pictures that have been authorised by the museum, gallery or auction house. We also buy pictures from Associated Press, Reuters and EPA. All photos are official photos. We are very strict on this. We never 'surf the web' to see where we can get an image from another website. We like to respect the artist´s or photographer´s rights just as we expect other to do unto us.**

> **The team basically consists of me, and just me. I run this ship alone. I have a part-time systems administrator who does programming and a part-time graphic designer, who helps out with the layout. I receive over 500 emails each day. I sort them out and publish what I believe to be the best. I think that all these years**

have given me the experience needed to sort things out and offer our readers the best news of the day.

We get almost a million page views per month and about 400,000 unique visitors. These numbers have doubled this year (2010) due to the fact that I have been analysing what people like to read and what not. I stop publishing what does not interest people.

Photo opportunities are an essential tool in your press campaign. Sometimes you will know well in advance – for example, when a huge object is going to be moved, or something amusing or particularly precious is about to be put on display. These opportunities are best offered to one or possibly two non-competing titles or one agency. For a major press view, all picture desks, broadcasters and agencies should be invited. Invitations to photocalls should be emailed and followed up by a phone call to make sure they have gone into the diary. The picture editor will decide each day what is worth covering.

When setting up your photo opportunity, plan for both still and moving pictures wherever possible, so that printed media and broadcasters will be equally happy. Make sure that you record your own version and add it to your website. Sometimes, the photo opportunity presents itself without much warning. Use your quick list to get as much press there as you can. Always have a back-up photographer, particularly if your chairman or director is involved, so that you have the right picture for your own purposes.

MEDIA INTERVIEWS AND APPEARANCES

It may be the visual age but sound-bites remain very important. In their quest for interesting and sometimes juicy stories, journalists will be listening out for the quotable quotes – pithy sayings and controversial or challenging statements. It is easy for the most experienced interviewee to put his or her foot in it by saying the wrong thing. Politicians and captains of industry are held to account daily for any slip of the tongue. Fortunately in the cultural sector, the media are not usually trying to trip up the unwary. However, that does not mean that spokespeople don't need training or preparation – they do.

Media training is highly recommended for the director and possibly the chairman and other senior staff in high-profile organisations. Several companies offer this kind of training in small groups or individually. Press interviews can be unnerving, except to the most seasoned spokespeople. Media training gives confidence to the interviewee in sometimes difficult situations, and helps to develop a smoother, jargon-free approach with popular media.

In smaller organisations, the PR officer – who has ideally had media interview experience themselves – can prepare museum staff for interviews by giving them a dry run. Question-and-answer sheets should be prepared for major launches and press events.

They can be useful in setting out a form of words to any particularly tricky questions, and in recording important details such as costs and sponsorship support. They can then be used by all the staff involved, ensuring consistency in the way things are described.

It is always a mistake to go into any radio or TV interview without a clear objective and a set of key messages. Recorded interviews are particularly risky for the unprepared interviewee, because they may be tempted to talk at length. Once the interview is edited for broadcast, key points might be edited out. It is sometimes difficult to persuade others of this fact, but live interviews give the interviewee much more control of the situation. The well-organised, confident interviewee can get their messages across, almost regardless of what they are asked.

Occasionally issues arise which are potentially of great embarrassment to the organisation. These could be questions of provenance, an accident on the premises, or professional malpractice (more about this in Chapter 16). Generally it is best to issue an 'on the record' statement as quickly as possible in response to tricky questions, whether written or oral – even if it is only a holding statement. Any off-the-record comment or statement can easily backfire in the hands of certain media. Flat denials and lies are equally dangerous as they have a way of coming back to haunt the organisation when the truth seeps out. Say nothing which you would not wish to see as headlines the next day!

PR people have to work in close conjunction with specialist staff who may have reservations about contact with the media, usually based on fears of being misreported. Here are some tips from the Science Media Centre:

> Scientists often worry about whether everything they say is absolutely accurate, but to get the message across to the general public through the media you have to simplify your science. It is important to concentrate on the overall message instead of worrying about the finer details.
>
> (Jenny Gimpel, Media Manager, UCL)

> Journalists try very hard to get what you say right, but that is not to say you won't have the odd bad experience. Despite this, remember that engaging with the media is one of the best ways of preventing the scare stories of the future.
>
> (Adam Finn, vaccine scientist)

> Remember that news interviews are your chance to share your expertise with the wider British public. It's heart-breaking how often scientists waste this opportunity to get the best information out there in the public domain because they go into the interview obsessed with impressing their peers, or John Humphries, or the man from the protest group sitting next to them. The best rule of thumb is to ignore all these people and target your main messages at the tens of thousands of people watching or listening at home, many of whom are concerned about the subject and need to hear from the real experts.
>
> (Fiona Fox, Director, Science Media Centre)

AWARENESS CAMPAIGNS

There is a proliferation of awareness campaigns which museums, galleries and cultural attractions can choose to join – everything from 'Science Week' to 'Black History Month'. And there is no doubt that they appeal to the media as they focus attention on a particular topic and create opportunities for features, listings and sometimes news.

Social media has added a new dimension to such campaigns, as the case study on National Poetry Day shows. 'Museums at Night', which takes place in European countries in the middle of May is organised by the French Department for Culture with support from ICOM. In the UK it is promoted by Culture24 and the national campaign in 2010 used Twitter and Facebook, inviting visitors to upload their photos on Flickr.

Based on the fact that most of these umbrella promotions provide a free publicity vehicle for attractions, they are of course worth supporting. However, there is a cost in staff time for those who want to get really involved by creating special events. To help decide whether you should take part, try this checklist:

- Is there time to plan ahead – ideally 4–6 months?
- Can one member of staff spearhead the events initiative and another drive through PR?
- Is joining with others an option – an existing local network or setting one up?
- Could your Friends help to get some of the events off the ground?
- Can you create some newsworthy activities, events and photo opportunities for local and regional media?
- Can you produce supporting material on your website, e-news and print using the appropriate logo?

If the answer is yes to most of these – go for it!

BLOGGERS, FREELANCERS, ETC.

As newspapers and broadcasters reduce their permanent staff, the number of arts and cultural journalists working freelance is increasing. Most press officers already have a list of reliable freelancers whom they email regularly and who frequently come up with the goods. Don't hesitate to add new names that appear promising or delete those no longer active.

Anyone can be a blogger now. Many are journalists producing authoritative and amusing comments on the issues of the day. Some appear on online newspaper or broadcasting sites, or just in the blogosphere. There are a couple of issues here to consider.

First, what is said about your institution in blogs could be important, depending on where and when it appears. It is useful to set up systems for monitoring the internet, including blogs.

Secondly, bloggers may approach you as journalists seeking information and facilities such as access to press views, interviews, etc. You will have to deal with these on a case-by-case basis. If it is an already established journalist operating as a blogger there is no problem. But if you are inundated with over-eager student bloggers and amateur journalists you should feel justified in saying no.

Many museums have set up their own blogs with RSS and Twitter feeds, as in the LACMA case study introduced below. It can work very well if you strike the right note. It can allow those with a real flair and niche following to develop their own followers, enhancing the museum or attraction's reputation. Seb Chan at Powerhouse Museum, Sydney sets the standard for this.

THE ELECTRONIC PRESS OFFICE – DATABASES

The electronic press office now common in most arts organisations involves standardising databases, making them searchable by type of publication and journalists'

Figure 11.1 Visitors looking at sculpture in the Lynda and Stewart Resnick Exhibition Pavilion (copyright 2010 Museum Associates/LACMA)

special interests, so that press releases and photographs can be emailed to journalists and media outlets as efficiently as possible. It also includes a press centre on your website with up-to-date information and downloadable pictures. In smaller organisations this transition may still be under way and a variety of mailing lists may still be in use, involving posting out hard copy to some journalists and emails to others.

Subscribing to a media service is one way of short-circuiting this transition by accessing up-to-date databases and the media service handling your email alerts, news releases and even pictures. Arts Media Contacts (see Resources) is one such service in the UK which specialises in cultural press contacts. Press release and image distribution is also available as an out-sourced service by many different companies, nationally and internationally, but see the caveat at the start of this chapter about media spamming.

In addition you will need your own media database of local and regional contacts and those subject-specialist freelancers and magazines who you are most in contact with. If you are in the UK, make sure that you conform to the Data Protection Act (or any other similar legislation in other countries). You should not share your database with others except by agreement from the recipients and you should make it easy for your recipients to delete themselves from your mailings. This applies also to your e-news where the unsubscribe link should always be working! In addition:

> **If an organisation intends to send emails to groups of individuals, then the organisation should use the 'bcc' facility rather than the 'cc' facility to ensure that the recipient of the email is not able to see details of other members to whom the email has been sent. Failure to do so is likely to constitute a breach of the 7th principle of the Data Protection Act.**
>
> (Information Commissioner's Office – see Resources)

WORKING WITH PR CONSULTANTS

Ambitious occasions call for a huge input of PR time as well as expertise. Now is the time to bring in a PR agency or PR consultant to give you that extra muscle to achieve your targets. At first glance it could be a bewildering choice but by speaking to others in the sector you will soon have a shortlist of agencies or consultants with the right experience and a good reputation for delivering the goods.

Prepare a short brief, along the lines of the PR plan above, and make it clear which tasks you expect the agency to fulfil and the targets by which you will measure success. You don't need to spell everything out. It is for them to take a creative approach to the brief. Include a budget or range of budgets, because this will determine the time committed by their senior staff, and enable them to offer a tailored service. It is important to meet a few of the shortlisted contenders just to make sure that their proposals stand up to scrutiny, and so that you can choose the one that you and your colleagues feel comfortable with. Try to get them on board as early as possible in order to get maximum value from their input.

Make sure that you monitor the PR consultant or agency's performance on a regular basis, with frequent meetings and updates (rather than formal reports). Don't let the timetable which you have all committed to slip. And make sure that you review the project and their input at the end. And thank them when they have done a good job!

> I've worked with and am now a consultant myself and it's rather like an extension of the diversity discussion. How do we as consultants accommodate difference in a single culture? As a consultant I am a stranger in a new land and I learn the language of that land, but I hold on to my roots – my values and my purpose.
>
> I adjust my identity to each organisation so they can relate to me, but still retain the true me to bring my specialism, advice and skills to meet their objectives and goals. Good consultants resist the temptation to get drawn into the organisation's politics and staffing issues and retain a professional distance. Sometimes this means the consultant becomes the 'whipping' boy for all that's wrong, but often it means your impartiality is valued.
>
> (Colleen Harris, Diversity Consultant and Executive Life Coach)

CASE STUDIES IN THE APPENDIX

Case Study 11A Marketing and PR at a small, underfunded gallery

Today, Dulwich Picture Gallery enjoys an international reputation. This has not always been the case. Kate Knowles, now retired Head of Communications, was only able to be employed for two days a week when she first started at the gallery, and everything had to be done on small resources.

Case Study 11B: Reaching an ethnic mix from an electronic press office at LACMA, Los Angeles

Barbara Pflaumer, Associate Vice-President for Communications and Marketing, Los Angeles County Museum of Art, describes how a great Los Angeles collection moved its press office into the electronic age, and now reaches out across language barriers to its local communities with inventiveness and a sense of immediacy.

The Los Angeles County Museum of Art (LACMA) is located in one of the most culturally diverse cities in the world. It is said that over a hundred languages are spoken in the public schools here. Connecting with the various ethnicities and diverse cultures that populate this megalopolis is a challenge for anyone, but for the non-profit environment with its limited resources this is especially true.

Case Study 11C: Twitter campaign for National Poetry Day

National Poetry Day was established sixteen years ago to celebrate the reading, writing and performing of poetry. It takes place on the first Thursday of October each year. An umbrella campaign with lots of grassroots involvement from poets and educators, National Poetry Day has always relied on PR to communicate and maximise its impact. Colman Getty has worked on the PR campaign for National Poetry Day since its inception.

As part of an ongoing strategy to grow National Poetry Day's visibility in the digital sphere, it was decided in 2009 to establish a presence on the social networking website Twitter, which, with its emphasis on writing with economy and wit, was already becoming a firm favourite in the poetic community.

Case Study 11D: Measuring social media in PR

Trying to measure the results of a social media campaign might be a fool's errand, but here, Richard Bagnall, Managing Director of Metrica, comments on the role of such campaigns and gives sensible advice.

The rise of online and social media has created great challenges for modern PR professionals and their media relations strategies. Not long ago journalists were the gatekeepers of access to – and influence over – an organisation's target audiences. Well-connected PR professionals could leverage their relationships with journalists to seek to achieve positive coverage in the publications that their target audiences read.

CHAPTER 12

EVENTS AS PART OF PUBLIC RELATIONS

Setting objectives

Getting the organisation right from the start

Budgeting and sponsorship

Consider the target audience

The guest celebrity and VIPs

The invitation list and the invitation

The format of the event

Welcome, catering and entertainment

Briefing your colleagues

Dos and don'ts

On departure and the review

Staging or attending an event away from your own venue

SETTING OBJECTIVES

As part of your public relations strategy, events are a great way of showing off your collection or refurbishment and bringing influential people to your venue. Nothing can beat direct communications with target groups for impact, and nothing can communicate your brand values more strongly than a well-organised event on your own premises and on your own terms. And yet, so often events we go to as professionals are disappointing in some way, when from the moment of arrival to the point of departure no one seems to have thought through the objectives of the event and the messages which you as the guest or audience should be taking away with you. (There is more about public events in Chapter 15 Commercial and fundraising activities.)

Clear objectives, good organisation and quality in delivery should be the goal for every type of event at your museum, gallery or attraction, and for other events which you or your colleagues organise or contribute to outside the organisation. From trustees' meetings to Friends' events, from press views to workshops or seminars – you should apply the same planning and evaluation process.

The inspiration for a special event may fall into one or more of the following categories:

- To ensure continuing and secure funding; to attract new funding from sponsors; or to prepare the ground for a lottery application by bringing influencers to your site.

- To create media coverage to raise the profile of the museum for funding purposes; or to attract visitors to a new gallery or exhibition through press views or briefings in relation to a new development or existing virtues, or by highlighting special events.

- To generate funding or engage interest in educational activities and the educational programmes.

- To raise the academic standing of the institution through seminars, workshops, lectures, conservation demonstrations or 'behind the scenes' tours.

- To create goodwill and interest among tourist information staff, hotels and guest houses, guides, tour operators and others who influence this market – as part of your cultural tourism strategy (see Chapter 9).

- To prepare the ground for a new development, leading to a planning application.

In each of these cases and others, the organising team should define: the desired outcome; the number and standing of guests to be targeted; opportunities to communicate an overall message as well as one-to-one conversations; networking; photo opportunities; demonstrations of activities; viewing of new facilities; and, if needed, feedback and comments on proposals for the future. There should also be some follow-up built into the overall plan. The opening of the new Wing at the Chicago Art Institute was carefully planned with a series of events over two years (see the full case study introduced below and in the Appendix). Here is a short extract:

> **Thus, in New York, about 18 months before the Modern Wing opened, the Art Institute hosted a luncheon event for art, architecture, and cultural critics. In late 2008, approximately six months before the opening of the Modern Wing, the**

museum hosted further similar events in Berlin, Frankfurt, London, and Paris for international art and architecture critics as well as travel writers and industry professionals. These events were designed not only to introduce attendees to the museum but to Chicago in general as well. Appearing at each of the events in other cities was the director of the museum, Jim Cuno.

GETTING THE ORGANISATION RIGHT FROM THE START

It is never too early to start – the longer the lead-in time to a major event the greater the success (as illustrated above). Planning may be in the hands of a small group or formal committee but it is essential that one person is in charge of co-ordinating and implementing all the details. It is very easy for something quite obvious to be forgotten (the microphone for example) if there is too much delegation or too many people involved.

Prepare a critical path or simple checklist with key dates when the various elements have to be completed, and circulate this to everyone involved. Make sure that the staff who will have a role to play are informed as early as possible. Everyone should be briefed about the nature of the event. Consider any health and safety issues. You may be required to carry out a Risk Assessment; if so, you need basic training and the appropriate form from your Human Resources department. Also check whether up-to-date licensing arrangements for your venue and type of event are in place to avoid a crisis on the day.

Carole Stone is one of London's most experienced networkers. She is Managing Director of YouGovStone. Here are her tips for a successful event:

1 However grand and exciting the venue, people come to events to be welcomed and looked after.

2 Invite those you don't think would come – you never know.

3 Attention to detail is vital – names spelt correctly, with title where necessary. Keep the badges in a box. No one wants to see badges not collected on the table.

4 Over-book – a third do not turn up. Be brave.

5 Keep to time – don't keep people waiting for the official start and keep any speeches short and snappy.

6 Keep glasses full. No one should be heard saying: 'What do I have to do to get a drink around here?'

7 Keep a look out for anyone who looks lost and introduce them to someone immediately.

8 Deliver on promises next day – send that information or email address you promised, or a thank you note.

9 Add everyone who attended to your database, and send an email to 'no shows' saying you hope all is well with them.

10 Enjoy the event yourself – otherwise no one will enjoy it.

BUDGETING AND SPONSORSHIP

Start with an outline budget and see where additional resources can be obtained. The sponsor of the exhibition you are launching may be able to provide some additional cash sponsorship to cover the costs. The architect of your new wing may chip in. Can you persuade your chosen caterer to sponsor part of the cost? (Catering is usually the largest part of the budget, and caterers will sometimes provide wine or a discount in return for being able to display publicity material.) You may be able to obtain the wine at wholesale prices for a large event, and ask your caterer to cover or reduce the corkage. It may be possible to save on the cost of printing invitations (see more below) by allowing a credit line for the printer. Remember, however, that you are aiming to influence people one way or another through this event, so don't cut too many corners, even when times are tough, and remember that it is your brand that should come across most strongly.

Here are some of the costs involved in any event:

- Printing and mailing (although emailing invitations will save on this budget)
- Catering and extra tables, chairs, etc.
- Flowers and any special displays
- Backdrops, stage, sound-system
- Film, AV or PowerPoint presentation (out-of-house production)
- Staff costs, such as cloakroom, security and car-parking, and your own additional staff costs
- Photography
- Guest celebrity
- Entertainment and music
- Give-aways and PR follow-up
- Litter picking and cleaning.

CONSIDER THE TARGET AUDIENCE

The objectives for the event will define the target audience. Think carefully about the mix of different groups. The launch of a new exhibition is an excellent opportunity for creating interest and profile, and the traditional approach is to have a press view and separate private views. This certainly works well for major museums and galleries who can attract a good press attendance for the press view and can separate their key audiences for the private views, so that influencers and other VIPs can enjoy a more exclusive event. Friends and others may have their own events, but probably pay for their own wine.

Museums and galleries outside the capital, or with smaller events and exhibitions to launch, may decide to combine several audiences into one event to ensure a good attendance and to save on costs. When audiences are mixed in this way, careful briefing of staff (see below) becomes even more important, so that any 'special' guests who need nurturing are identified and looked after.

At least once a year, all those on whom the museum or attraction depends for its existing and future funding should be invited to a special briefing, with breakfast or lunch, as a group, or individually. For such stakeholder events (see Chapter 14) look critically at your existing contacts and then at the wider community. Where are the gaps? Who are the community leaders who you should be in touch with? Are there other movers and shakers in your local area who it would be useful to invite? If you occasionally need to renew your licence for entertainment and alcohol, don't forget your local councillors and licensing officers. If you have battles ahead on the planning front, don't forget members of the planning committee, the head of planning, your local MP and possibly MEP, senator or member of the Congress.

Attracting the media and other influencers to events outside London is a challenge. Here Ina Cole outlines how she set about it, first at Tate St Ives, Cornwall and then at Compton Verney in Warwickshire.

I was appointed for the inauguration of Tate St Ives and Compton Verney, and their geographic remoteness – on the beach and in the open countryside respectively – provided a challenge. A key area of my work was profile-raising, and I adopted a global approach from the onset, simultaneously inviting groups of regional, national and international press to all exhibition launches. The support of train operators and regional tourist boards was secured to cover travel and accommodation, as cost implications would otherwise have been prohibitive.

When developing media campaigns for far-flung attractions it is important to establish momentum, secure a ring-fenced budget for launch activity, and remember that it can take time to foster relationships. A sound affiliation with exhibition curators needs to be maintained, as mutual reliance will escalate as a launch approaches. Seamless delivery in terms of scheduling, travel and hospitality is imperative, particularly when journalists are travelling from afar. A convivial atmosphere on the day is crucial, but a keen eye must be kept on the order of events and journalists' individual time constraints.

In the 1990s, St Ives became something of a mini Cannes of the art world, activated by the pulling power of heritage. Much effort went into sustaining critical acclaim

and high visitor numbers for the gallery, with exhibitions such as 'Barbara Hepworth: Centenary' breaking all attendance records. Compton Verney launched with bravado in 2004, with the astonishing 'Luper at Compton Verney', an installation by film maker Peter Greenaway. Although markedly different from each other, the two attractions did share a certain 'X-factor'. Remoteness can become an asset, seen as intriguing, energizing, and an escape from the city-centric existence. Identifying a venue's 'difference' and using it as a thread that entwines all external messaging has, for me, always been the necessary ingredient for success.

(Ina Cole, Freelance Arts Professional)

THE GUEST CELEBRITY AND VIPs

We live in a celebrity culture, so the pressure may be on you to come up with an appropriate well-known or even famous person to add that touch of glamour or gravitas, and help to build excitement and media coverage for your event.

Is this the right occasion for that once-in-a-lifetime royal visit to your museum, gallery or heritage attraction? Your request will be helped if your venue has been substantially redeveloped, or received public funding or lottery money, or connects to a passion or interest of the royal guest you are targeting. You should think a year ahead and get support from the Lord Lieutenant in your region in the UK, or anyone particularly influential on your board. Make your approach in a straightforward way with a letter from your chairman to the Private Secretary (by name) of your chosen royal. In the UK it is easy to find out correct names and titles by contacting Buckingham Palace. Follow your letter with a telephone call after three weeks or so, if you have heard nothing, to make sure that the invitation has been received and to get some idea of when your invitation will be considered – the royal diaries are usually made up in batches of six months in Autumn and Spring.

Your invitation to a member of the royal family should highlight what is special and different about your venue and your project, and say why a royal visit would be of benefit to the local community, visitors, and schoolchildren who use the attraction. Mention all those who support the visit, but make it clear that the royal personage would meet some 'real' people – not just a line-up of councillors or trustees. Do give a range of alternative dates. Remember that it is not correct to invite royalty in the wrong order, so work your way down rather than up if you are turned down by one. Invitations are not passed on.

If successful, your programme for the day will be compiled in conjunction with the Private Secretary's office and will, depending on who it is, involve quite a lot of preparation and security. The intention is to cover every detail and formality beforehand in order to achieve a relaxed visit on the day. So, be guided by the Private Secretary, but offer additions involving children, or a glimpse behind the scenes, as well as the more formal tour. (If photographs are to be taken, establish whether the event will be on the Royal Rota, whereby the number of photographers is limited and photographs pooled.)

Is it appropriate to invite a Minister, the local MP, the Mayor or other political figure to this or other events? In the case of a royal acceptance, seek advice from the Private Secretary. For other events, bear in mind that politicians are notoriously unreliable and frequently retained at the last moment for an important debate or vote, so consider some kind of fallback, particularly for events more than half an hour from Westminster or the relevant seat of government.

Make sure that a preliminary email letter with a date is sent as early as possible to the diary secretary of any VIPs. Make it clear if you wish them to speak and do follow up with a phone call to their PA. Act likewise with the 'great and the good', such as members of boards, trusts and foundations. The earlier they know, the more likely that they will accept.

When considering a celebrity, ask yourself what is he or she going to do? Will they add credibility to the event – or are they there simply to help obtain media coverage? The latter can never be guaranteed, so paying large sums for someone in the news may not be the answer. Evening events are particularly challenging because this is a time when the media are simply not going to turn up unless your guest is a mega-star. Sometimes you will be lucky enough to find a celebrity who will make an appearance for a nominal fee, perhaps because they are a local resident or visitor.

If you decide to pay for a celebrity, make sure that the terms are clearly agreed in writing, including your expectations about photocalls and press interviews. Provide a good, short briefing to help them get their facts straight. One way of getting celebrities 'on the cheap' is to link up with a charity. You and the charity could share proceeds from such events as a Friends' summer fete or music festival in the museum garden, or a lecture.

THE INVITATION LIST AND THE INVITATION

For a large event, such as an opening, the invitation list can be a nightmare. It is easy to fall back on the 'old list' compiled over time, with no clear idea of who the people are and why they were put on there in the first place (or whether they are still alive!). Simply sending all the people on the list a letter asking them if they want to go on receiving invitations from you is likely to have a very haphazard response!

Tackle this problem with a group of helpers and break the list into categories, asking those of your colleagues in regular contact with the separate groups to check and update. Maintaining and updating a series of key lists (councillors, local business leaders, local museum and arts contacts, etc.) is much easier than trying to keep your big list up to date. The lists should be on Excel or a similar format, searchable by category of guest, and include full address and email address. Correct spelling and any official titles or decorations should be added for formal invitations. Be sure to do effective cross-checking (which Excel will make possible) as some people will be duplicated on different lists.

For formal and large-scale events we will no doubt go on producing printed and mailed invitations for some time. Send a 'save-the-date' email in advance and follow up with email reminders. For private and press views, email invitations are fine. There are technical options for adding names into embedded or attached invitations which can be printed out and kept as a reminder.

For a formal event, use Debrett's Online, or another etiquette guide, to help you get the wording right. It will also help with order of precedence, forms of address, and so on.

Although people are increasingly slack about responding, the RSVP element of the invitation is important because it allows you to chase those who have not responded. This can be particularly important for 'cultivation events' where you are aiming to influence potential funders and politicians. Use a dedicated email address for responses and, if you are using a telephone number, make sure that it is answered by a person or a dedicated answerphone. There are now a number of event companies which will handle all the responses online and provide you with regularly updated information.

If responses are slow and you want a good turnout, start a phone-round, a week or so ahead of the event. A well-organised response list (alphabetical by surname and by organisation) should be compiled from the replies and, if appropriate, badges should be made up in advance. Name badges are essential when you don't know all the guests and when networking is important. Make sure that staff members from your own organisation are badged as well as your guests.

THE FORMAT OF THE EVENT

There are standard formats for most hospitality events in the cultural sector. For early evening events, guests arrive to find a drinks service of both wine and soft drinks with canapés. A speech or speeches are made; there is a viewing of the gallery or building being celebrated – or presentation of awards; followed by more drinks and then departure. Daytime events, such a morning press preview, might offer coffee/tea service, pastries and sandwiches. A boardroom lunch may include a break after the main course to allow for a proper discussion around the table. Celebratory dinners may feature an outside speaker introduced by the chairman or director.

Anything that you can do to add a memorable element to this formula is welcomed – for example, a performance of some kind, whether music, dance or spoken word, performed by professionals or children.

The question of speeches is always difficult. If people are standing, try to keep them to a maximum of 15–20 minutes by restricting the number and length of speeches

Figure 12.1 Setting for a grand dinner at Dulwich Picture Gallery (Photo: Stuart Leech)

(sometimes hard to enforce). Make sure that the microphone works, that it is adjusted for the speaker (women have softer voices than men), that everyone can hear by testing in advance, and that you or someone else knows how the system works – in case one of your speakers turns the microphone off instead of on (which happens all the time!). If guests are sitting down, 30–45 minutes for speeches should be sufficient as part of a more general event. For a seminar or workshop it is of course different. VIP guests will need to be briefed so that they can say the right things in their opening remarks.

PR managers may be asked to write speeches for an event at their museum or attraction. A straightforward welcome speech highlighting any new features and the programme for the event is something most PRs are happy to tackle. Set out the full text or key points in large type on cards which your director or chairman can use as an aid. Not everyone in the cultural sector has the ability to present complex ideas in a way which engages their audience. Directors usually do it pretty well, but they or other specialists on the staff may need some help to keep it lively. See comments in Chapter 10 (Engaging with the media).

WELCOME, CATERING AND ENTERTAINMENT

Nothing can spoil a special occasion more than having to stand in a long line for the reception desk, cloakroom, or bar. Make sure that your welcome arrangements work – no queuing outside, quick registration at the reception desk, efficient cloakroom – all these things matter. At a large event, you will want to know afterwards who came. Make sure that returned badges are put in a separate box to the 'no show' badges.

In your advance survey of the areas to be used for the event you will have identified what will be required in terms of additional branding, decorations and backdrop. Anything extraneous – staff notices, graffiti in the toilets, badly stored items – will detract from the overall impression you want to create, so they need to be dealt with. Flower arrangements may not always be popular with curators inside the galleries but they can do wonders in the reception and help to mask areas which are unsightly or closed off to visitors. Additional signage can no doubt be produced internally, but for a major event invest in a professionally produced backdrop and screen for your speakers.

There are professional companies which specialise in setting up sound-systems in sensitive and difficult environments, such as cavernous galleries. For an important occasion don't be tempted to make do with something your in-house team puts together – there is nothing worse than a failing microphone at a major event. Check that the sound levels throughout the gallery or room to be used are good. Have a technician on duty at the event, if possible, or make sure that you or someone else is stationed near the microphone to assist the speaker if needed. Make sure that your director and other speakers are visible to all by providing a platform or small stage and transmit the speeches on plasma screens throughout the galleries for a very large event; all this can be hired. If people don't have visual contact with the speaker they will inevitably start talking to each other.

For in-house events, most museums, galleries and attractions tend to use a trusted caterer. Every now and then, think differently and ring the changes. If opening an Indian or Asian exhibition, ask yourself whether your usual caterer is up to complementing the theme with appropriate canapés. For a boardroom lunch aimed at potential sponsors, give it style by using a more up-market caterer. Whoever you decide to use, agree the brief and the budget with them well in advance, based on the particular circumstances of the event. Most curators have come to accept (white) wine and some canapés in galleries, but for some exhibitions this may not be possible. So entertain your guests in a separate area and make sure there are tables where they can leave their glasses as they enter the exhibition.

Music or other entertainment may be appropriate as background. For a special performance – a re-enactment, short playlet or special musical performance – guests should really sit down. If they are standing, with a glass in their hand, they will inevitably start to chat as they cannot see from the back. This can be very upsetting for the performers.

For formal dinners, discuss the proposed seating plan with your director on the day of the event. Ensure that tables are laid correctly, with place-names set out. It is a good idea to walk the route with your director shortly before the event to ensure that he or she is happy with arrangements and familiar with the route. If you, as head of PR are to be seated, make sure that you are within sight of your director so that you can be summoned if needed.

The best way to get people to leave an evening reception is to stop serving wine and food (15 minutes or more before the official end of the event); for serving staff to start removing glasses, politely and discreetly; and for you and your colleagues to gently move people towards the exit.

BRIEFING YOUR COLLEAGUES

Don't leave this to the last moment. For a major event, make sure that everyone is involved and committed from the beginning. The last thing you want on the big night it to be let down by your own staff.

So make sure that for the big night (or lunchtime event) you have the right number of staff members on hand for the occasion. First there will be those on duty, who need to be clearly briefed as to the kind of guests attending, and what to do. For a daytime event when the museum or attraction is open to the public, front-of-house staff should be looking out for your invited guests and escort or direct them to the welcome area.

For an evening event, work out how many people will be required to provide security, cloakroom and other services, and how many – possibly from the PR and marketing team – should handle the welcome and badging. You may need extra people at the reception desk, particularly at the start of the evening to avoid queues.

In your daytime cultivation events, ensure that the heads of departments or curators are stationed along the route to be taken by your special guests. They should be ready to provide a brief introduction to their area and answer questions. Make sure that they know who the guests are and how they should gear their comments. Whether it is a formal or informal lunch, there should be senior staff members included as guests, acting as hosts, circulating, making key points and answering questions.

For a large event, you need a good representation of staff members among the guests. They are there to work, and should therefore not be accompanied by partners. They should be well briefed and clearly badged, and they should be given specific targets to find among the guests in order to perform introductions and generally look after them. Staff should limit their own consumption of alcohol. (Some organisations will not allow any drinking of alcohol by staff until after all the guests have gone.) They should be positively discouraged from talking to each other rather than to guests, and should consider themselves on duty for the duration of the event.

DOS AND DON'TS

- Check the status of your licence months ahead of planning an event in case a variation is needed.

- Be aware of the risks involved in mismanaging licence applications: reputational and business risks to the institution, and financial risks to the individual licence holder.

- Manage the PR aspects of every stage of a licence application or variation application.

- Guests arrive early and find the doors closed. This happens all the time in the museum world where a certain amount of time is needed between closing to the public and opening for a special event. On a cold or wet night, try to ensure that guests can at least get into the lobby.

- If using name badges, make the print at least 14pt – ideally 16pt – so that it can be read without peering too closely.

- Uninvited guests may turn up – there were notorious freelancers in London for many years who tried to talk their way into press and other receptions. Use common sense as to whether to turn them away, ensuring the least embarrassment for yourself and your guests.

- Children and babies sometimes arrive with hard-working and earnest parents for evening events. Again, use common sense and don't turn them away unless they disturb other guests (during speeches for example).

- Be prepared – for royal guests and politicians changing their timetable, transport strikes causing delays, speakers not turning up (or getting drunk).

- Something will go wrong – it nearly always does. Just keep calm and rely on the help of your team and the catering manager to cover the cracks. (See also the Kew Gardens case study, introduced below).

ON DEPARTURE AND THE REVIEW

Rather than burdening people with your annual report or a heavy folder on arrival, distribute it at the end, ideally in your own branded carrier bag – ethically produced of course.

It is very nice for guests to be 'seen out' on departure, so have a rota of staff members on hand for this part of the evening. There are lots of things for them to do, including encouraging people to leave a card to join your e-news list, if not already on it. They should collect badges and put them in the correct box, while asking whether guests have enjoyed a pleasant event. They can also help to get taxis or explain the way to the bus or train for those who are unfamiliar with the area. VIP guests, mayors, ambassadors and disabled guests should be escorted to their cars by the director or other senior member of staff. (Royal programmes will have separate arrangements for this, involving possibly a whole contingent and flowers on departure.)

Not later than two weeks afterwards (as memories fade) arrange your follow-up meeting with those directly involved and consider the event from beginning to end:

- Planning and organisation – did you have enough time; did it all go well?
- Guest list and invitations – any problems here? Have all amendments been fed back into the mailing lists?
- Celebrities and VIPs and other media opportunities – did these work, what was the coverage like? If not good, were there reasons for this?
- Were you and the director satisfied with reception arrangements, catering, staff welcome and interaction?
- Any comments received from the guests?
- The next step – follow up any leads or promises made – for funding, for example.
- Budgeting – was there any overspend? Why? And how could you avoid it in the future?
- Overall, did the event meet the objectives?

STAGING OR ATTENDING AN EVENT AWAY FROM YOUR OWN VENUE

When you and your colleagues go outside the museum to attend conferences or run workshops, do you make the most of the opportunity? Organisers of events at the Museums Association or similar conferences, for example, frequently forget to highlight their own institution and its activities.

This does not have to be blatant, but should be conveyed simply – by producing an effective PowerPoint presentation with the logo, and possibly handouts with more information or a contact. Make sure that all staff who take part in external events have business cards, and that they provide any feedback which might be useful for others. At some conferences and seminars, email lists of attendees are circulated in advance or after the event.

Decide whether you should send follow-up information to some or all on the list. Any business cards you received should be checked – what did you promise to send that person you spoke to for five minutes over lunch?

There is more on public events and programming in Chapter 15 (Commercial and fundraising activities).

CASE STUDIES IN THE APPENDIX

Case Study 12A: A textbook opening in Chicago: working with consultants

In May 2009, the Art Institute of Chicago opened the eighth expansion in its 130-year history, the Modern Wing. This major undertaking involved a classic publicity campaign described here by Erin Hogan, Director of Public Affairs.

Designed by Renzo Piano, the Modern Wing was built to house the museum's permanent collection of twentieth- and twenty-first-century painting, sculpture, photography, and architecture and design. At 264,000 square feet, the wing includes permanent collection galleries, special exhibition galleries, a state-of-the-art education facility, a dedicated black box gallery for new media, a restaurant and outdoor sculpture terrace, and a pedestrian bridge into Millennium Park, in the heart of downtown Chicago. With the addition of the Modern Wing, the Art Institute became the second largest art museum in the United States.

Case Study 12B: Saving Planet Earth live broadcast and party: a fabulous opportunity – and an absolute nightmare

When the BBC announced new initiatives on green issues, Sue Runyard, at that time Head of PR at the Royal Botanic Gardens, Kew, was quick to beat a path to their door The unexpected response was a request to hold a fundraising concert for wildlife conservation in an outside broadcast from the gardens. It seemed a fairly straightforward proposition to begin with.

Figure 12.2
HM The Queen's
80th birthday
fireworks
(courtesy of
Trustees of the
Royal Botanic
Gardens, Kew)

CHAPTER 13

INTERNAL COMMUNICATIONS WITH STAFF, BOARDS AND VOLUNTEERS

Building and communicating brand values within the organisation

Creating an understanding of marketing and PR objectives

Communicating with the board and patrons

Day-to-day internal communications

Communicating with volunteers

BUILDING AND COMMUNICATING BRAND VALUES WITHIN THE ORGANISATION

Building and sustaining the commitment of staff in the frontline and behind the scenes is essential in creating a visitor-services-friendly organisation and keeping it true to its brand values. This is an ongoing process and part of the day-to-day communications discussed below. The real challenge for management, supported by the communications team, occurs when developing a new brand or reassessing the values of an established institution, or when a change in culture is required to bring in new and different audiences as part of a sustained audience development programme or a new marketing approach.

An external consultant may bring the necessary skill and detachment to work with staff through this change but it can also be managed internally. The closure of the museum or attraction for refurbishment is an opportunity to update the brand and its values and, if appropriate, bring in some new staff reflecting the new brand. The redeveloped

Ulster Museum which won the Art Fund Prize for 2010 shed its traditional, more formal approach to visitors and is now staffed by young gallery assistants who interact with visitors, suggesting things they might do and things they might look at.

At the Museum of World Cultures, Gothenburg (see Chapter 8) the focus – from its opening – was on young adults. This is reflected throughout the building. The 'cool' entrance may look stark to some visitors; the casually dressed staff at the desk are not typical of museums; the-day-to-day activities and the café with background music and an ethnic menu are designed to appeal to teenagers and young adults, while the well-designed exhibitions deal with serious issues, encouraging debate and participation.

Changing the culture at an established attraction to encourage more of one particular group of visitors has to start internally with the staff, as at Alton Towers (see Chapter 6). Here the problem was too many young adults dominating the attraction, putting family audiences off. New brand values were adopted throughout, involving staff at every stage and reflected in new facilities and new promotional material. The transition to become a more family-friendly attraction was a success.

The step-by-step approach to developing a new brand or rebranding outlined in Chapter 6 starts with staff workshops. As well as gathering information and ideas from the participants, the workshops are designed to build consensus so that, by the time the new brand or redeveloped brand is adopted, the staff are committed to its values. When the Ashmolean Museum in Oxford closed for redevelopment in 2008 the process of change began, as outlined in the extract below (read the full case study in the Appendix):

> The Change Management Team was a small team set up from a representative group of staff to act as a voice and an agent for change within the Museum. A new Museum building and a new display strategy would require our staff to think differently and to work differently. Whilst the building work got underway, most staff moved out of the old building and in to temporary accommodation a mile away from the Museum.
>
> This brought a whole new set of challenges, and communication became key to getting things done. The team had the remit of acting both as a voice for staff and of being empowered to make positive changes to improve the working life. One of the early initiatives was to create a regular all-staff meeting that would bring staff together from different sites and from different disciplines to ensure that all staff were sharing the same vision. The meetings focused on the progress of the project whilst helping everyone to visualize the new building and what it would be like to work there.
>
> Our rebranding project built on the success of the Change Management Team and allowed all staff to have a say in the future brand and identity of the Museum. A number of workshops allowed mixed groups of staff to come together and to really shape and plan what it would be like to work in and for the Ashmolean Museum.
>
> (Gillian Morris, Head of Human Resources,
> Ashmolean Museum of Art and Archaeology)

Figure 13.1 Main staircase, Ashmolean Museum, Oxford (Photo: Greg Smolonski/Photovibe)

There are additional challenges when several different institutions, spread over several sites, are managed from the centre. Vanessa Trevelyan, Head of Norfolk Museums & Archaeology Service, outlined this in Chapter 6.

CREATING AN UNDERSTANDING OF MARKETING AND PR OBJECTIVES

In some institutions, the marketing and PR department is not fully integrated with the other departments. It is even regarded with suspicion or as a nuisance – always looking for more information. It is up to marketing and PR people within the organisation to communicate what they do, not just upwards to the chief executive and the board, but to all their colleagues. The communications team should keep everyone informed of new promotional initiatives and successes (more below) but also involve other staff in major projects, make them part of social media activities and listen to those who have direct contact with the public. Inductions for new staff should include familiarisation with the marketing and PR teams and with the organisation's brand values.

This applies to any PR consultants brought on board as part of the communications team, whether for a one-off project or for a longer-term relationship. Not only is it important that they reflect the organisation's brand values in all that they do but also that they are perceived by the staff as being part of the team.

COMMUNICATING WITH THE BOARD AND PATRONS

Museums, galleries and cultural attractions are governed in a variety of ways. In the UK, nationally funded museums are led by boards of trustees, with control of some board appointments by the Department for Culture, Media and Sport. Local authority-funded museums and galleries are overseen by a council committee which may change at each election. Some council-funded museums are now run by 'arm's-length' independent trusts, such as the York Museum Trust. Independent museums and attractions operating as charitable trusts appoint their own trustees in accordance with their own governance, but are overseen by the Charity Commission (in the UK). Private companies appoint their own directors, and although they have to abide by appropriate legislation, they can have a greater degree of flexibility and freedom to make changes than public bodies:

> **York Museums Trust (YMT) is a charitable trust and was set up by the City of York Council in 2002 to manage York Castle Museum, Yorkshire Museum and Gardens, York Art Gallery and York St Mary's, a fifteenth-century deconsecrated church. One of the first decisions made by YMT was to remove the entrance charge for York Art Gallery which resulted in an immediate increase in visitors. However, we have maintained entrance charges at both the Castle Museum and Yorkshire Museum,**

with local residents admitted free. Particularly effective has been the 'kids go free' offer which is an incentive for families to visit. The tickets are also valid for a year, encouraging return visits. Over the last eight years we have seen an increase in visitor numbers from 435,000 to 625,000; our turnover has increased from £3.1 million to £5.01 million, and admissions income has risen from £1.08 million to £2.05 million. The success of YMT over the last eight years is explained by our relatively small investment in the public offer (between £250K and £500K), which we have exploited via publicity and marketing to bring people into our venues. Our most recent project is a £2 million refurbishment of Yorkshire Museum which has more than doubled the visitor numbers.

(Janet Barnes, Chief Executive, York Museums Trust)

Most board members in the public sector are not paid, but may receive expenses. This has tended to limit participation on boards to those who can afford to give of their time. There is a drive to make boards more representative of the surrounding local community. This may or may not always succeed – see comments overleaf from the Director of the National Museum Liverpool – but should certainly be an objective.

Communication with board members and local authority committee members is generally in the hands of the director or his or her policy assistant, if such a role exists. It is good practice to involve the public relations team in this process so that board members receive updates between meetings as well as papers for meetings. Important news, media coverage and major achievements should be communicated to the board as quickly as possible or at set intervals – a weekly email update, for example. However, individual board members should be asked to choose whether and how much information they want to receive.

Frequently, new board members or local authority committee members are given the briefest of introductions to the organisation. In well-run organisations there will be a set induction programme, including a tour and conversations with the Chair, CEO and senior management – including the communications team. New board members need to get to know the organisation and the role that they are expected to play, using the skills and insights which they bring. So many board members walk into their first full board meeting with little idea of why they have been appointed or how they can contribute.

Every board member should feel individually valued. A quick telephone call from the CEO when something good happens is an inclusive gesture which helps everyone to feel a share in the success. It also paves the way when a call has to be made about a problem. Board members and councillors are usually very busy people. They will only read documents shortly before or en route to meetings. The role of the chair in deciding how much information to provide is crucial. There should be full disclosure of information to the chair, and a free exchange of concerns and possibilities between chair and CEO. In the best relationships, the CEO and chair should be able to identify and agree mutual objectives, working together on how to present information in order to gain the support of the board.

Some organisations find it useful to have occasional retreats for their board and senior management, usually lasting a day or so, in a location where no one will be distracted by day-to-day work commitments. This can be helpful when a major reappraisal of policy is needed, giving everyone a chance to focus on complex issues. Such meetings need careful planning and management, and a degree of detachment, so it can be helpful to have an outside facilitator involved.

Ways in which you can achieve effective communications with the board include:

- Assist your CEO to build a positive relationship with chair and board, and do the same on behalf of yourself and your team.

- Provide copies of printed material for meetings, including press releases, significant press cuttings, new publications, any promotional print and any significant customer comments.

- With your director, set up a regular one-page email update – weekly or bi-weekly, for those who want it.

- Whenever a board member expresses interest in your area, offer further information or a familiarisation tour, and make sure your director knows about it beforehand.

- Remember each board member is a separately valued individual.

Finally, don't forget to make sure that your staff know who the board members are – that they know their names, and can recognise them when they arrive for a meeting, special event or just call in on an informal visit.

Recruiting new trustees or directors is an ongoing process for most boards, aimed at finding people who represent a cross-section of the local community and/or visitor groups or those who bring specialist skills or knowledge to the board. Can boards be more representative? David Fleming, Director of National Museums Liverpool, is aware of how non-profit organisations struggle with this issue, and has some outspoken advice on the question:

> The short answer to this is 'no'. Forget it. Can't be done. The slightly longer answer is that museums are constructs of the society in which we live and are, in theory, mirrors of society. It shouldn't, therefore, be difficult to ensure that their governing bodies are themselves representative of society – whether that be local, regional, national, or even international.
>
> To make our own board more representative has taken a huge amount of research, and recommendations have been subject to veto by the Culture Minister! But basically we research possible candidates and approach them. Do not rely on the advertisements that DCMS do on your behalf.
>
> Therefore what you are trying to do is to get people with the right skills (rather than age, gender, skin colour or shoe size – though these will also be factors, all other things being equal). Personally, what I want are sensible people who align with

NML values and are courageous. After that, for me, it's less important who they are and what they have done, though I do try to get people who are well connected/ have money/have access to money/have certain skills, e.g. financial administration, construction industry experience, etc.

This all makes it sound as though it's easy to do – and it's not, and I wish people would stop pretending that it is. There are more governance problems in museums than we know about, because, for obvious reasons, people are unable to speak out. The problems that can arise take a lot of time and energy to resolve.

In some senses, achieving representativeness does actually happen, and virtually every museum I can think of is indeed governed by people who represent the variety of human life, in that some of them are good, and some of them are truly awful. It is, of course, worth adding that all sorts of social groups are, nonetheless, under-represented on museum boards – such as women, young people, and people from diverse backgrounds, etc.

Sometimes this ad hoc 'system' works well; sometimes it leads to not much more than a web of vested interests, interference, prejudice, incompetence and worse. Anyone who knows anything about museums knows this. This is an important subject that never really gets the attention it deserves in museum studies. I do not have space here to explore the subject in detail, so I will give a few headline thoughts.

There seems to be in our national psyche a worry that managing a public service like a museum will go awry unless it is policed by a governing body. We need the checks and balances that governance can provide, not least to ensure that management does not go rogue; that money is not spent improperly; and that the museum has a viable sense of purpose, policies and a strategy. Indeed, great store is often set by the make-up of a museum governing body in order to try to achieve these things.

The trouble is, we do not have a particularly reliable system for ensuring that governance actually does its job – that it is good governance that provides scrutiny, but also support. The nearest we have to a reliable system is local government, wherein people are elected to discharge public duties on behalf of the rest of us, and they are accountable at the ballot box. On behalf of their local community (the electorate) they hire professional managers, and they govern the museum through a committee system. Lord knows this isn't always brilliant, but it is the nearest we have ever got to making museum boards representative of the society that pays for them.

Outside the local government arena, we have private/commercial museums (where anything goes), university museums (ditto), independent museums (that strive to create boards that are more than a motley collection of enthusiasts, but that don't always succeed), and national museums (where governance ranges from sensible and creative, to nightmares of Orwellian proportions, not always helped by the control of appointments exercised by government ministers).

The truth is that while it is a sound enough aspiration to have museums governed by a representative cross-section of the community (however we may wish to define this term), this often doesn't happen, because of time and availability, experience, education, motivation, opportunity and other factors that militate against proper representation. All sorts of people are discriminated against and consequently excluded in various ways. While it is a positive principle that all museum boards should be made representative, it is a pipedream that they can be.

(Dr David Fleming OBE, Director, National Museums Liverpool)

DAY-TO-DAY INTERNAL COMMUNICATIONS

Setting up an efficient internal communications system can be a challenge in both large and small organisations. In the smaller organisation, internal communications tend to be ad hoc, taking place in informal meetings over a cup of coffee. As many staff and volunteers probably work part-time, this can leave several in the dark when there are major changes under way.

In the larger museum or attraction, where staff are spread throughout a big building or estate (or sometimes many buildings in different parts of the country), the challenges are the same, but greater. Poorly informed staff may resort to rumour and gossip, particularly when the media are running stories about cutbacks. Therefore, in every organisation, whatever its size, it is important to handle internal communications well.

The communications team may be charged with undertaking an audit of existing channels of internal communications and draw up a new strategy to improve the flow of communications throughout the organisation (see Chapter 2 for ways of going about this). The day-to-day communications function based on this strategy may be based in Human Resources, but more likely the PR team will be implementing it. Everyone, at every level, likes to feel that they are being kept in touch and consulted.

Face-to-face communication in formal or informal meetings is the core of good communications. It is not easy to get all staff and volunteers together at the same time, but the attempt should be made at least once a year and for very important announcements. Large organisations usually have to repeat such meetings so that everyone has an opportunity to attend. (See comments below from the Director of The Lightbox, a medium-sized gallery in Surrey.) In the normal course of events, information is disseminated from management meetings to individual departmental meetings and so on.

Today, new and refurbished museums and galleries bring staff together in something resembling normal office accommodation – but the real change has been brought about by technology. Communication via intranet or email may not seem ideal but it is certainly better than what preceded it. Intranet has led the revolution in internal communications in larger organisations, providing a safe and secure system for communicating with staff.

Update the system when possible to introduce new features such as discussion forums. When staff log on to their terminals, the menu page should list the latest news bulletins. Keep items short and lively and add information pop-up during the day, such as sudden gallery closures, or transport strikes. The editor, who may part of the PR team, can accept or reject bulletins from any member of staff, and keep inconsequential matters, such as items for sale, or club notices on a separate, accessible page. Reserve messages from the director for really important occasions, so that they are treated with special respect and immediacy. Ensure that summaries of board meetings and other important meetings appear promptly, before formal minutes appear on the public website (where required).

For smaller organisations with a handful of staff but many volunteers a simple email network can work well, although intranet software is now available for smaller numbers of users. E-news has almost replaced printed staff newsletters, but may still need to be printed out for those who have no access to the intranet or web. You will need to take a decision as to whether Friends and volunteers are included on your intranet.

In communicating any controversial discussions and decisions to staff, bear in mind that some will want to share it with the outside world in a way or at a time not chosen by the organisation. Similarly, any accidents or thefts not generally known about, but reported internally may be shared by staff with others. Unfortunately, spontaneity and inclusiveness have to be tempered by discretion and caution, and the PR department should be geared up to deal with the consequences of any unfortunate 'leaks' (see Chapter 16 on Communicating in a crisis).

As mentioned above, staff should be kept up-to-date on advertising and PR campaigns as they are implemented, so that they can respond appropriately to public enquiries. Topical bulletins should be posted about special PR achievements, such as major press articles or TV programmes, so that everyone can share in the success. Staff should also be tipped off about media appearances, so that they can tune in to hear one of their colleagues being interviewed, or watch a review of the latest exhibition. Such items can give a real boost to team spirit, and help to explain what the press team does all day. Appropriate commercial information on visitor figures, and revenues from the shop and café should also be given.

Museums and cultural attractions are ideally suited for 'MBWA' (management by walking around). This popular management technique advocated by the management guru Tom Peters (among others) provides an unstructured approach to hands-on, direct participation by the managers in the work-related affairs of their subordinates. You will probably do this as part of the communications team, but it could be the director or head of a large department who spends some of their time making informal visits to the front-of-house areas in order to keep in touch. The purpose is to collect qualitative information, listen to suggestions and complaints, and keep a finger on the pulse of the organisation.

Spending time at the information desk is always a salutary experience for the behind-the-scenes staff. It gives them an opportunity to meet the public, and to become aware of the important work done by information staff, who are often volunteers, and who need the support and understanding of curatorial colleagues. It is very easy for academic or administrative staff to lose touch with the great mix of public visitors to museums and attractions. HR can sometimes take the lead in organising short 'job swaps' to help staff development and understanding.

So in summary, good staff communications depend on:

▓ Commitment by senior management

▓ Efficient organisation of the flow of information

▓ Selection of the relevant information to be communicated

▓ Using appropriate ways of communicating, including 'walking about'

▓ Involvement of staff in new projects and developments.

The importance of taking a public relations approach to your internal communications is demonstrated in this comment from The Lightbox, a new art gallery in Woking that has received an unusual amount of accolades in a short space of time: Museum of the Year; winner of the Art Fund Prize 2008; Small Business Award Winner and Leisure and Tourism Award Winner. The Director, Marilyn Scott identifies her staff as stake-holders – in good times and bad:

> **It is easy to assume that your PR effort should always be focused on external stakeholders. We spend a great deal of time ensuring that the messages we send out externally show our organisations in a positive light. We also include as part of our PR strategy actions to be taken to manage crises – who will be our spokesperson, how much will we reveal outside the organisation. Best practice dictates that we should be as open and honest as possible in the event of that occasional disaster. I wonder how much we actually think about our own internal PR – how much do we take our staff into our confidence, how do we manage bad news with the people we should care about the most and without whose goodwill our organisations could not function.**

> **Sadly I think the message is that sometimes they are the last to know, with resulting bad feeling and, even worse, a feeling that they really are not very important to the organisation. It can be handled differently and in my experience can have quite positive results. Some time ago I was faced with a situation which involved the inevitable redundancies of some staff. However much you try to conceal bad news it races through an organisation at an alarming rate. I chose to employ the kind of PR practice one is taught in explaining a crisis or disaster to**

Figure 13.2
Interior of
The Lightbox,
Woking (Photo:
Peter Cook)

the outside world: call a press conference straight away, give no sign of conceal-ment or cover-up, decide very clearly on who is saying what and make sure the story is consistent, and be prepared to answer questions – be honest above all.

But of course in our case it wasn't a press conference – it was calling all the staff together as soon as we had something definite to say, explaining everything as clearly as possible – timescales, who would be affected and why. We then took questions, making sure that there was one clear response, and tried to give reassurance that we were doing all we could to minimise the effects of the actions we had to take. The response, rather than being hostile was almost positive, in that we had been honest and straightforward and had asked for input from everyone. There was a great feeling of support for me personally as I was able to explain all the things we had looked at to try and avoid the current situation. I was able to convey a very positive message – we were taking action before things got even worse – and this message was well received.

Bad news in the PR world is always difficult to handle – we are great at handing out the glowing reviews and the news of the big gifts of money or the award-winning exhibitions, but crises are harder to manage. This was however a really good lesson in internal PR – remember that your stakeholders are those people inside your organisation as well as outside. I now remember to share good news internally as well – share the accolades, make sure your staff know you have had a record-breaking admissions day or a particularly nice review. Good PR begins at home!

(Marilyn Scott, Director, The Lightbox)

COMMUNICATING WITH VOLUNTEERS

The moment a volunteer becomes of most value to us – when they assume full responsibility for their duties and turn up like clockwork – is when we are most likely to take them for granted. Every museum, historic house and art gallery seems to have a core of unpaid people who make contributions to success and public service. It does not take a lot to show appreciation to such well-motivated people, but it is all too easy to forget to share information with them.

Volunteers usually have a lot of contact with the public, so it is vital that they should be 'in the picture' on plans, objectives, and major events affecting the museum. Written information and newsletters have an important role to play, but in-person briefings are very much appreciated. Choose your words with care because you may find them being quoted to the public. Keep complex issues as clear and simple as possible. The phrases you use will be adopted by volunteers who answer questions from the public, so make sure that they are phrases which serve the institutional aims. Volunteers do not have a right to know everything about the organisation, but they should be kept bang up-to-date on issues in which the public have an interest. They are often the 'frontline' of the museum, so they need to be in a position to give accurate information with confidence.

Ways to communicate with volunteers include:

- Hold regular training programmes and briefing meetings
- Encourage production of an e-news network, co-edited by a volunteer and a member of staff
- Get all your volunteers up to speed on the internet and its possibilities
- Be clear and brief in all communications
- Give real-life examples wherever possible to illustrate your points

▓ Have a dedicated bulletin board in the place where volunteers meet

▓ Encourage curators to have a positive, helpful attitude towards volunteers.

The management of volunteers is a time-consuming and increasingly professional task. Consider an appropriate training course for those staff members involved in volunteer management.

CASE STUDY IN THE APPENDIX

Case Study 13A: Ashmolean Museum of Art and Archaeology: a new building and a new approach

The Ashmolean Museum in Oxford is one of the oldest museums in the world, with a collection of international importance. It was always regarded as a deeply traditional museum, but when a major building redevelopment took place, management decided to bring about change internally as well as externally. Achieving effective communications among staff was one objective, while another was to improve visitor services. Gillian Morris, Head of Human Resources tells the story.

CHAPTER 14

COMMUNICATING WITH STAKEHOLDERS AND PARTNERS – RELATIONSHIP MARKETING

Who are your stakeholders? The stakeholder audit

Setting up and maintaining communications

Local and regional politics and advocacy

Developing partnerships

Friends and members

Corporate social responsibility – sustainability

WHO ARE YOUR STAKEHOLDERS? THE STAKEHOLDER AUDIT

Queen Victoria once asked Disraeli who Britain's friends were. Disraeli replied that 'we have no friends, only interests'. Museums are in a happier position, we do have real friends, and we must keep them, but we should never forget our interests.

(Mark Suggitt, Consultant)

Good stakeholder relationships are vital to the organisation but they are also fluid, changing with time. The communications audit in Chapter 5 will have identified the key players who can influence your organisation's future. The preparation of the annual business plan, a major event, a relaunch, or an upcoming development proposal, licence or planning application are all good reasons for re-examining your relationship strategy and your stakeholder contacts. You may also want to use the publication of your Annual Report or your Annual General Meeting (where appropriate) as an opportunity to invite key stakeholders. They include some or all of the following:

- Visitors and potential visitors
- Friends and members
- Regulatory and political authorities
- Funders and shareholders (if a company)
- Sponsors and potential sponsors
- Suppliers of various kinds
- Institutions, associations and business networks
- Neighbours and the wider community.

In this chapter we are mainly going to consider authorities, funders, institutions, friends and the wider community. Visitors and potential visitors are covered in earlier chapters and sponsors and funders will be covered in Chapter 15.

If we expect society to support cultural attractions then we must be prepared to promote our values and the contribution that we make to people's well-being and education. It is now one of the expectations of cultural institutions that they aim to improve the quality of life within the communities they serve. To do this, museums and galleries have to engage with everyday life outside their walls. If we hope to educate and entertain people then we must be responsive to changes in society. In short, we need to make friends and influence people.

Analysing existing and potential stakeholders is an important part of the forward planning process. It gives the organisation a sense of perspective and helps it to position itself within local, regional and national frameworks. It also identifies institutions, groups and individuals who may be approached for advice, market research or fundraising. The audit can be carried out by an outside consultant as part of a rebranding project for example, or it can be assigned to the public relations manager with input from all those involved, including the director, chairman and members of the board.

In each group outlined above, check who you are currently in touch with regularly, and who else should be added. The longest and most challenging list may well be the wider community. Some local authorities have up-to-date information on local societies and community organisations listed on their websites. The local library is one source of information, and the events page of the local newspaper another. Examine each group and see how far your interests overlap now, and how they may interact in the future. Set up your database for each group separately.

Working with your education department, consider institutional and academic stakeholders in your area, including colleges, schools, university departments, and

Figure 14.1 Children examining the art, Walker Art Gallery, National Museums Liverpool

professional associations that touch on subjects in your collections. Finding the right person in each of these will be important – it is not the person who books school visits but often the head teacher or policy adviser or a designated person who is responsible for community relations.

The list of commercial organisations with whom you may want to stay in touch is potentially very long – from your main suppliers to the local chamber of commerce and tourist board, and business networking organisations such as Rotary Clubs. Don't forget your national stakeholders, including larger institutions such as heritage bodies and lottery distributors, professional associations, and national regulatory bodies and funders. In each of these groups there will be key individuals or organisations that carry more influence than others, are more relevant to your organisation, or more important for your future plans. Make sure that these can be easily identified and invited separately when it matters.

Here are some useful comments from Jennifer Francis, Head of Press and Marketing at the Royal Academy of Arts (RA) – an independent institution which does not receive public funding:

> **The organisation understands that building trust is key and this is achieved through nurturing and enhancing relationships. We are required to know enough about each**

different segment or group and develop an emotional connection with them. This is at the forefront of our communications and development programmes, as is the organisation's USP, raison d'être, mission and objective.

Ultimately, good stakeholder relations is about key messages for key people. Quality communications can significantly influence our positioning and strengthen relationships with our key asset – RA stakeholders.

Enablers for good communication include: a thorough identification and under-standing of issues and expectations, along with strategies that deliver clear messages via the most effective channels. Our experience in working with stakeholders, backed by proven communication methods is continuously reviewed, ensuring that our messages are conveyed to the right people at the right time.

SETTING UP AND MAINTAINING COMMUNICATIONS

Having established your contact list, decide what it is that you want to communicate – when, and with whom .This plan does not have to be extensive but should be updated regularly to include new organisations, your changing vision and upcoming projects. There are a number of ways of reaching your stakeholders:

- E-news and printed news to selected individuals
- Invitations to private views as well as open meetings, informal lunches and PR launches
- Informal meetings and events outside the institutions
- Conferences, seminars and networking events where politicians and influencers are speaking
- Contributing to 'hot' issues – sustainability for example – through the local newspaper or public event.

Local organisations and societies may appreciate receiving your e-news every month. This might be the same e-news that you send to your visitor mailing list if it is suitable. Professional institutions and organisations might need something more tailored. Include a limited number of politicians with a direct interest in your organisation in the distribution of your e-news.

Invitations to private views and receptions are a good way of bringing your stakeholders into the museum or gallery to enjoy hospitality and an opportunity to see your attraction out-of-hours. An open morning with a presentation on a particular topic or a boardroom lunch may be relevant when you are introducing a new product or planning a develop-ment. Stakeholder relations is also about you and your colleagues going out and joining in society and community events (as a speaker perhaps), attending business networking lunches from time to time, and becoming a member of some of the local groups.

In redeveloping the National Museum of Scotland in Edinburgh (reopening 2011) and targeting a growing tourist market, the museum identified a long list of local membership and business organisations with tourism interests. All were contacted, events identified and attended. The marketing manager joined a number of steering groups to get closer to the commercial sector and invited them to the museum to see the progress of the redevelopment.

It may be easy to get stakeholder relations up and running, but more difficult to sustain communications in a positive way, particularly with a small team. Contacts will constantly change and it can be difficult to keep up to date. In a larger organisation, each group of stakeholders can be made the primary responsibility of one or more on the staff, who can make sure that contacts are maintained and up to date. It is important to log contacts, whether formal or informal, with the director's office or the PR department, so that future approaches can be effectively maintained.

LOCAL AND REGIONAL POLITICS AND ADVOCACY

You need to be aware of the key corporate priorities and aspirations of your council. They can often be summarised as aspiring to a richer, greener, healthier, cleaner district with support for education and old people, provided by a leaner, efficient council. You also need to be aware of any cultural, regeneration, health, or education strategies that exist. Whether inside or outside of local government, the museum needs to map its work against these and evaluate how it helps to deliver them. Once this has been done the next step is to promote your value. This means getting out and about.

(Mark Suggitt, former museum director and now a freelance consultant – see full comments in the case study introduced below)

Most of the organisation's stakeholder activities will probably relate to funders and planners in local, regional and national government. At a time across the US and Europe when public and private funding is under pressure, these relations are more important than ever. Advocacy is the cornerstone of relations with this group. Every opportunity must be taken to make the case for any organisation that is dependent on public funding for all or part of its revenue.

In Chapter 5 we considered advocacy and lobbying at the national level in response to a crisis or particular campaign. Your ongoing relationships in the UK should include your Member of Parliament, Member of the European Parliament, and/or as appropriate, Member of the Scottish Parliament, or Member of the Welsh Assembly, as well as some key members of the House of Lords. In other European countries, identify your local members of parliament as well as MEPs, including those who have a special interest in culture such as members of the European Union Culture and Education Committee. In the United States, it means being in touch with local, State and Federal government representatives. We must never assume that politicians understand the role and value of the arts:

> **Most museums want to show they make a difference to their communities. To sustain public support they must be effective advocates, reporting both what has been achieved and how the museum's core mission distinguishes it from other public services.**
>
> **These messages require care and attention. Sometimes, while notionally targeted at stakeholders, funders and opinion formers, their content suggests that professional peers, the media or vested interests within the museum may be the real audience. The reputation of individuals may appear to be promoted more than that of the museum itself. Or claims made may be exaggerated and/or based on assertion rather than evidence.**
>
> **In such circumstances short-term advantage can turn to long-term detriment. Strong relationships – and all successful museums need these – demand openness and trust. Messages that compromise these values because they are unreliable or self-serving can weaken a museum's reputation and status. Any communications strategy should reflect the same integrity practised in managing and using the collections.**
>
> **(Adrian Babbidge, Egeria)**

It would not be possible for a small museum or gallery to implement a comprehensive programme of public affairs activities, nor would it be relevant. But you can include public affairs as part of your PR programme, as follows:

- Make sure you know who your key elected representatives are
- Include key officers at local authority level in your database
- Include them in your e-news mailings
- Invite them to special events.

It pays to become familiar with the process by which decisions are made and to keep up to date with topical local issues, including attending local authority planning meetings, for example, before submitting your own for a new development. With a specific problem that relates to your museum alone, you might find, when you have gone as far as you think you can with the local authority, that a letter or invitation to visit to your MP can be effective in breaking a deadlock. If the problem is not yours alone, get together with others in regional partnerships – as a group you may be able to use a political lobbyist to develop and present your cause. In the UK, the Museums Association offers a useful advocacy programme on its website.

DEVELOPING PARTNERSHIPS

If you think that you have more to gain by working collaboratively with others – whether tourism organisations, local businesses, cultural organisations or competitors – make a plan to achieve something bigger than you can achieve on your own. . . . Remember this is your idea, designed to celebrate your organisation – and keep in your heart the absolute essential of this proposal – that this new partnership can only work for you if based on a quality idea/academic excellence and something that you actually want to do.

(Dr Delma Tomlin, Director of the National Centre for Early Music –
see full comments in the case study introduced below)

Partnerships can be long-term and develop over time, or have a short-term focus, set up for a specific purpose to deliver a joint public event or celebrate an anniversary. In Chapter 8 (Tactical marketing) we considered long-term marketing collaborations, such as the Yorkshire 'Museums Alive' partnership. Others are set up for a specific anniversary, such as the highly successful 200th anniversary of the birth of Charles Darwin. Here is the final comment on this important partnership which has continued into the Year of Biodiversity (the full case study is introduced below and in the Appendix):

The Darwin200 partnership grew to include some 70 organisations in the UK who used the brand in their communications, and a further similar number who also created Darwin events, activities and publications, which, while they did not use the brand, in one way or another engaged with the Darwin200 partners and benefited from the network of exchange. One of the important consequences of the visibility of the network is that it made it easy for organisations interested in engaging to have relatively easy access to expertise from the many disciplines interested in Darwin and his legacy. Darwin200 as a brand also allowed organisations to be more confident and brave in their programme outputs. As a result, the mainstream BBC coverage was, for example, far richer than many had anticipated, and they were able to turn to their critics and say, 'yes, we did deal with the controversy between evolution and creation – we did it here, but look, we were also able to do so much more'.

(Bob Bloomfield, Head of Innovation and Special
Projects, Natural History Museum)

Museums in the East of England have developed a different kind of partnership – SHARE: Support, Help and Advice from Renaissance East. This innovative partnership was set up in 2009 to match the skills that already exist in some institutions with the needs in others. Over one year, a thousand working days were logged as available in a variety of skills from mentoring to marketing. Participating museums and organisations apply to the SHARE 'timebank' for individual visits, training sessions or participation in seminars.

The success of this scheme, which has potential for regional groups everywhere, was the availability of start-up funding (in this case from Renaissance) that enabled the appointment of a small team of coordinators guided by a steering group of regional museum representatives. SHARE has also been strongly branded and promoted throughout the region, now reaching 78% of all museums in the area. The value of the skills shared probably exceeds the original funding of £100,000 many times.

> SHARE is an inspiring example of museums working together to provide mutual support, sharing their experience in order to raise the quality of the whole museum sector in the East of England. It's important to note that this is not all one-way traffic. Specialists donating their time have the opportunity to increase their own knowledge, as well as building up closer working relationships with museum colleagues.
> (Vanessa Trevelyan, Head of Norfolk Museums & Archaeology Service)

FRIENDS AND MEMBERS

Museums and galleries across Europe and the US are frequently supported by Friends' or members' groups. These voluntary organisations often started life as an informal get-together led by one or more enthusiastic individuals. They have become increasingly important, because they raise finance for purchases of objects and other one-off costs, as well as stimulating interest and support for the organisation as a whole. Friends also play a part in communicating to others the values and visions of the institution they support. The British Association of Friends of Museums (BAFM), established in 1973, has over 200 member organisations. They in turn are members of the World Federation of Friends of Museums who have published a code of ethics for 'Friends'. Here is a short extract:

> Friends and volunteers carry out their activities in an open manner and in a spirit of co-operation with the institution of which they are partners.

> Friends and volunteers of a museum institution undertake to support it and its activities with generosity and enthusiasm.

> Respect for the museum's mandate: the goals they set, the sphere within which they operate and the programmes they adopt should be developed with the participation and agreement of the museum authorities and in accordance with the museum's mission.

> Friends and volunteers expect no benefit, financial, or other, save the satisfaction of contributing to the maintenance and development of the institution to which they belong and to the satisfaction of the public which it serves.

Friends' groups are sometimes independent of the museum or the gallery and sometimes run by the museum itself. Occasionally in their enthusiasm and dedication, Friends may overstep the line between their role and that of the museum's management, leading to friction. Help to avoid this by ensuring that Friends are part of the museum's communications strategy as key stakeholders. The PR team should have the Friends firmly in focus and ensure that they are kept up to date, and that key members are invited to PR events in addition to the Friends' own private views, and events at the museum or gallery. The director or nominated colleague should attend Friends' committee meetings and other gatherings to share the latest news and activities.

A potential source of friction may arise in the fundraising area (see more in Chapter 15). The Friends' fundraising objectives should be discussed and approved not only by the director, but by the museum's own fundraising team to ensure that there is no duplication or overlap of effort.

Demographically, Friends should reflect the museum's target audiences as far as possible in order to reinforce the brand and spread the word among new visitors. Encouraging an established (and possibly entrenched) Friends' group to seek new, younger and different types of members can be a challenge. One way is to follow the example of MoMA in New York, which has a number of affiliate groups, including Junior Associates, aimed at younger patrons. They also have a Friends of Education group created to foster a greater appreciation of art created by African-American artists, and to encourage African-American participation and membership at MoMA.

Friends' and members' benefits may be another area of conflict. Where an organisation has a very large membership (such as the Tate, the National Trust, or the Royal Academy in the UK, or the Smithsonian Institution in the US), the members can exercise considerable influence and enjoy benefits such as free entry to exhibitions – which could undermine the pricing strategy of the organisation. See the 'Gardens of Glass' marketing evaluation in the Appendix for an example of where free entry for Friends greatly increased the pressure on the organisation to attract additional visitors in order to cover costs. In the event, volunteer Friends were trained as special guides, the Friends also shopped enthusiastically and brought along paying friends and family, proving an enhancement rather than a liability, and contributing towards financial success. This is a case for PR and marketing being included in early planning and then helping to communicate with Friends to give a sense of inclusion.

US museums are masters at making the best use of Friends' organisations. Some of the more high-profile museums, such as the Huntington Library, Art Collections, and Botanical Gardens, or the Autry National Center, can raise a million dollars in one evening at a Friends' event. But it is not just a matter of cash, because Friends can also give direct help in a number of ways. They can muster moral and political support when needed, run events, and provide visitor services.

In summary:

- Friends and members are invaluable when the relationship works to the benefit of the museum or organisation.

- Communicate regularly through formal meetings and informal updates.

- Invite key Friends to presentations, board and management meetings, as appropriate.

- Attend Friends' and members' events to build relationships and share news.

- Set clear fundraising objectives and parameters to avoid conflicts.

- Examine Friends' benefits as part of the marketing strategy to ensure that they are cost-effective.

- Encourage 'new' Friends (to widen audiences) through younger friends and special areas' support groups.

CORPORATE SOCIAL RESPONSIBILITY – SUSTAINABILITY

Modern society is facing a number of challenges, including delivery of the 'green' agenda. Corporations are expected to contribute towards such goals, and cultural organisations need to be seen to contribute too:

> **Corporate social responsibility (CSR) is about how businesses align their values and behaviour with the expectations and needs of stakeholders – not just customers and investors, but also employees, suppliers, communities, regulators, special interest groups and society as a whole. CSR describes a company's commitment to be accountable to its stakeholders.**
>
> **(www.crsnetwork.com)**

Sustainability is one of the major issues of the decade, and museums and cultural attractions need to show their commitment to this in words and actions. Stakeholders such as funders, as well as the wider community, will increasingly expect the cultural organisation to have adopted a strategy which limits its carbon footprint.

Chapter 5 showed the importance of an ongoing PR strategy to communicate the organisation's commitment to sustainability. It could easily become a public relations issue as it has for some heritage sites in the countryside where the only access is by car – how do you promote a green agenda in such a situation? However, it must be based on facts and action, as the National Maritime Museum case study shows, where a 'Sustainability Development Group' was set up to lead the implementation of the museum's policy:

> **The resounding success of the environmental ethos that has permeated the National Maritime Museum in recent years has been solely due to dedication to the cause by the staff who work within the Museum and the cooperation of visitors. Cultural change towards a more sustainable future is not only happening at the NMM but also welcomed and, therefore, it appears that the most significant and**

yet difficult task necessary for future progression has already been achieved. [Read the full case study in the Appendix.]

Arts and cultural organisations are frequently the recipients of a CSR programme initiated by a commercial organisation (see more under funding in Chapter 15). This may involve their members of staff committing themselves to some voluntary activity in support of the museum or gallery. There is no reason why a cultural organisation within its own resources should not commit itself to a programme in its local community. Taking staff out of the museum environment for CSR work to share skills in conservation and sustainability with local schools or community organisations (not just to promote the institution or increase outreach) is invaluable experience, as well as showing the local museum's commitment to the community.

Many museums are already involved in such programmes in their neighbourhoods or alongside their funding bodies. The Royal Botanic Gardens, Kew helps a small number of local schools to manage horticultural projects, and contributes to environmental enhancement schemes, such as improvements to the local station and surrounding area. Other museums have become partners with their local authorities on youth training and young offender schemes, e.g. National Galleries of Justice. There is always some element of self-interest at work, although the public perception is one of generosity.

CASE STUDIES IN THE APPENDIX

Case Study 14A: Initiating partnerships at local level

Dr Delma Tomlin, MBE is an established authority on the promotion and marketing of early music performances. She is Director of the Beverley and York Early Music Festivals and of the National Centre for Early Music, with a background in museums and other cultural organisations. Here she encourages us to grow ambitious projects and partnerships from small beginnings.

Case Study 14B: Working with local government as a stakeholder

Mark Suggitt, now an independent consultant, has deep experience in the local authority sector. He was formerly Head of Bradford Museums, Galleries and Heritage; Director of St Albans Museums; Assistant Director at Yorkshire & Humberside Museums Council (he also held other cultural sector posts and did overseas advisory work). He is therefore well positioned to talk about managing relationships with local government. Much of this advice applies to other funding bodies as well.

Figure 14.2 York Early Music Festival, held in the nave of thirteenth-century York Minster, 2006 (courtesy of the National Centre for Early Music)

Case Study 14C: Evolving partners – celebrating 'Darwin200'

Bob Bloomfield, Head of Innovation and Special Projects at London's Natural History Museum, describes how his organisation became pro-active in order to solve a potential problem, and acted as a catalyst for a huge collaboration.

In 2006 a small group met to consider the impending celebration of the bicentenary of Charles Darwin and the 150th anniversary of the publication of *On the Origin of Species,* both of which would take place in 2009. Among them were representatives from the Natural History Museum, Charles Darwin Trust, Nature Magazine, the BBC, the Open University, the University of Cambridge (which holds important Darwin archives), the Royal Society and the British Council.

CHAPTER 15

COMMERCIAL AND FUNDRAISING ACTIVITIES – THE RELATIONSHIP WITH MARKETING AND PR

The role of marketing and public relations

Fundraising and sponsorship

The ongoing fundraising programme

Building relationships and crediting patrons, donors and sponsors

Working with Friends and members

Creating a one-off appeal

Using social media in your fundraising campaign

Commercial activities, from the shop to hiring out facilities

Retail and catering

Events and facilities

Using your assets

THE ROLE OF MARKETING AND PUBLIC RELATIONS

Never has there been a more challenging time for cultural organisations. Following on from the global recession, governments and the private sector alike are cutting budgets. Therefore, this new book is especially timely to help cultural professionals sharpen their skills in marketing and public relations. Often it is said that the USA is the best place to be for arts marketing and fundraising. However, the mixed economy model of the UK, with money coming from both the public and private sector, appears now to be the best of both worlds, but only time will tell who is right.

(Colin Tweedy, Chief Executive, Arts & Business)

Museums, galleries and historic attractions may raise some income from admission charges, but in most cases their major income streams come in two ways: first from public funding, trusts, foundations, sponsorship and patronage, and secondly from commercial activities. The role of marketing and public relations is to support the continuing programme of maintaining and increasing all forms of revenue and capital income by promoting the museum or attraction to visitors, and by raising its profile through the media and directly with decision-makers. At a time of increased pressure on public funding, and on corporate sponsors and individual donors, institutions are encouraged to explore new income-generating activities and sources. These should be in harmony with the overall vision and mission as expressed in your brand values and in the public relations strategy, as outlined below:

- Income generation should strengthen and not detract from the core function of the museum or historic attraction.

- The income-generating activity or sponsorship must be appropriate to the role and function of the institution in providing a public service.

- Income generation should be profitable and contribute to the development of the collection, museum or attraction and provide improved services to the public.

- The process must be efficient and cost-effective.

Marketing and public relations set the scene for fundraising activities. However, fundraising, or development work, should ideally be the responsibility of dedicated fundraising staff or a consultant, led by the director. This may not be possible in smaller and medium-sized museums and galleries where board members/trustees and the director share the fundraising task, from building relationships to closing the deal. For smaller attractions, with fewer visitors and less well-known brands, this is a challenge but joining with others in major fundraising drives, sharing skills and expertise could be one way forward.

Organisations such as the Association of Cultural Enterprises (ACE), the Historic Houses Association (HHA) and the Association of Independent Museums (AIM) in the

Figure 15.1 Café on the Pavilion Terraces, Alnwick Garden (Photo: Peter Atkinson)

UK – and similar organisations elsewhere – provide assistance and support to those seeking to raise their game in this area (see Resources).

FUNDRAISING AND SPONSORSHIP

Some general advice about publicising your successes from the Heritage Lottery Fund:

> Make the most of your success at fundraising by actively publicising grants, awards and donations. Think of acknowledging donors and highlighting their support as wearing a badge of pride and quality. Letting people know about your success works for your organisation as well as the grant giver – support from a high profile-funder validates your work and will encourage others to support you too. As well as the traditional things like donor plaques or rolls of honour, you should consider working with grant-makers to announce their award and develop other oppor-tunities for publicity as the project unfolds – milestones, previews, joint events – and remember to include them in openings and speeches. Delivering a scheme is complex and it's easy to forget the source of your funds once things are underway, but positive joint working will be appreciated by funders, and can deliver positive reputational benefits for everyone involved.
>
> (Louise Lane, Director of Communications, Heritage Lottery Fund)

The ongoing fundraising programme

Most organisations in the cultural sector now realise that fundraising and sponsorship are ongoing activities which involve building relationships as well as making direct approaches. Brand recognition is a strong motivational force in both marketing and fundraising. The better known your museum or attraction becomes, the easier it becomes to get sponsors and donors to listen to your needs.

The main thrust of fundraising may be towards gaining support from trusts and foundations, charitable donations, membership income, and sponsorship in cash and goods or services – but the most important funding source should never be overlooked. If the cultural institution receives its core support from a city council, local authority or national/regional government, that source should always be the number one priority (see Chapter 14 Communicating with stakeholders). It is relatively easier – and more important – to secure a regular revenue grant, than it is constantly to shop around for fresh sources of income. The same applies to previous sponsors – maintain contacts from the past and approach them again as new opportunities arise.

Building a strong case for your fundraising will involve everyone in the team taking key points into account:

- The vision for the organisation and/or project should be clearly stated.

- The financial case should be soundly based (this includes transparency and the ability to produce audited accounts if asked).

- Strong leadership from the director, the board and senior staff.

- Access to start-up funding – fundraising itself costs money.

Research in this area was until recently disregarded or just 'bolted on', but is now becoming a systematic part of the fundraising function. Finding out what donors want and need is crucial to keeping them involved and active supporters. Whether selling memberships, asking for donations, or bidding for sponsorship, look for partners with the same goals or a similar agenda to yours. For example, if an attraction is mainly family-oriented, it will need to seek funding partners who are in that market or wish to be aligned with that cause. Corporate sponsors may be looking for client hospitality opportunities. Consider whether your gallery or attraction can offer these at a standard that matches their expectations.

The pricing and benefits packages of individual and corporate membership schemes should be updated to take account of a competitive market place. Sponsored projects should be evaluated so that the relationship is clearly demonstrated to the sponsor in business terms. A good experience, well promoted, will pay dividends for the future, paving the way for future marketing partnerships and sponsorship programmes.

Ad hoc grants for events and marketing activities are sometimes available. The Scottish Mining Museum case study (introduced below and in the Appendix) shows how the museum financed a number of projects in this way, as this extract shows:

> **The only way forward was to apply for every grant we were eligible for, which proved extremely time-consuming but worth all the hours (sometimes days!) of effort completing forms and supplying figures and plans. We applied for small grants from around £500 to main grants of up to £40,000 for various projects, most of which were successful (thankfully) and enabled us to run special events targeted at both new and existing audiences and to upgrade our external and internal signage which raised the profile of the museum to passing traffic on the busy A7 Edinburgh to the Borders road.**
>
> **(Gillian Rankin, Marketing and Events Officer, Scottish Mining Museum)**

Building relationships and crediting patrons, donors and sponsors

Maintaining and building relationships with patrons, donors and sponsors is a continuous process which could be the responsibility of the fundraising manager, the director, or possibly the PR manager. There are database systems and software for fundraisers on the market to help with the task. Once you have been successful and brought a new contributor on board, involve them in the outcome of any particular project they have supported, keep them informed of the success, and maintain contact to ensure their continued support and possible further injections of funds in the future. Sometimes marketing and PR contacts will create unexpected opportunities for fundraising. Every contact, and every parent company of every contact, should be noted and treated as shared information.

Send short updates and topical news as reminders of your relationship without overloading your existing or potential sponsors. Sometimes the human factors are forgotten, as we concentrate on the business case. But corporate sponsors and private donors are often influenced by their own tastes and experiences. Make sure that they have an opportunity to see the museum and attraction 'at work' not just during special events. A $60-million gift for a West Coast US museum was 'clinched' by the donors seeing a group of schoolchildren engaged in an activity relevant to their own area of interest. The social interaction that the museum or cultural attraction can provide is so different from the corporate sector. Involving your sponsors in some CSR (Corporate Social Responsibility) activity (see Chapter 14) is another way of cementing their commitment to your museum or historic attraction. Here are ways of communicating effectively with patrons and sponsors:

- Send regular updates (such as your e-news).
- Tell them the human stories as well as the facts and figures.

- Keep them 'in the family' after particular projects end.
- Continue to invite them to events.
- Take an interest in their activities.
- Involve them in a CSR programme.

In Chapter 6 (Brands and branding), the question of crediting sponsors in a way which benefits both parties was discussed. Corporate sponsors, trusts and foundations and (increasingly) public bodies expect acknowledgements for their contribution to a project or your ongoing programmes, as a condition of the grant or sponsorship. This may include 'naming' the particular programme or new wing or even position, which is more common in the United States but quickly spreading to other countries. It may not be the ideal solution for an organisation anxious to maintain its own identity – after all, your name is one of your most valuable assets. Any branding agreement on funding or sponsorship should involve the marketing and PR team and should be checked out for negative implications. Be very clear about logos and other credits on all means of communications, including websites, press releases and print. Here are some useful comments from a London design agency:

> When accommodating funders' logos, the first rule is to avoid 'logo soup', that dreadful combination of 5, 10 sometimes 15 logos, so densely presented that they all seem to disappear.
>
> The best funding relationships offer mutual benefit for both the sponsor and the arts organisation. Therefore, identifying contributions does more than just say thank you, it can add credibility to a brand when associated with a major funding organisation or public body. Equally, the support of a large corporate brand allows the arts brand to benefit from the positive reputation of the corporate organisation. This brand benefit is not just one-way, and more and more sponsors are recognising the positive benefits that can be gained through association with arts brands. More than just CSR, association with an arts brand that has an established reputation for quality, innovation or creativity can deliver a 'halo' effect for the sponsoring brand. Therefore, this symbiotic relationship should be considered when recognising funders on publicity material.
>
> Be proud of your brand and the benefits that a well-designed, well-presented brand mark can offer. Don't be bullied by the funders. Understand that they have brand guidelines – but so do you, and while everyone should stick to their own guidelines, sometimes compromises have to be made. But, these compromises should be done to benefit all of the organisations involved – the arts organisation, at centre stage, and the funders and sponsors aligning themselves to the arts brand.
>
> (Laura Haynes, Chairman, Appetite)

Working with Friends and members

For many museums and galleries, Friends and members are worth their weight in gold, delivering the major part of sponsorship funding and substantial donations from individuals. The director and fundraising team should meet regularly with the Friends to encourage and nurture their fundraising approaches and to ensure that they are in line with your vision as well as the overall fundraising strategy. Their support will also add strength to approaches to trusts and foundations (see also Chapter 14).

Independent museums are very good at raising what may seem like small amounts of money and sponsorship-in-kind for everything from printing to cleaning. The National Galleries of Justice in Nottingham have a dedicated commercial officer developing partnerships and in-kind sponsorship from a range of organisations in the region. This is a two-way process – the museum offers discounts on admissions, room hire, training sessions and skills, in return for free services and discounts from suppliers. They maintain a busy network involving schools, universities, tourist information centres, recruitment agencies, pubs, restaurants, banks, hotels and other museums. 'Offer something before asking' is their motto. And don't forget Gift Aid. In the UK, this can add a substantial amount to your income from donations and admission charges (see Resources).

Creating a one-off appeal

Every now and then an opportunity to acquire an outstanding object for your collection comes along. For a small organisation, building a one-off appeal can be daunting. It can be made easier by working in conjunction with others. This is a time when a strong PR campaign as well as marketing support is required. In the UK, the Art Fund (National Art Collections Fund) not only provides cash but will also take the lead alongside the museum or gallery to secure the funding by using its expertise to get the public and other funders involved. When the Staffordshire Hoard, a major Anglo-Saxon treasure was discovered in a field in 2009, the Art Fund joined a partnership including museums in the West Midlands and the British Museum to raise £3.3m. This successful campaign illustrates the effective use of public relations and marketing. Here are two quotes from the Staffordshire Hoard case study, which is introduced below and in the Appendix:

> The campaign was launched at a press conference on 13 January 2010. David Starkey (TV historian) gave a rousing speech and coined the term 'gangland bling' to describe the Hoard's dazzling beauty and links to bloody warfare. The media coverage that followed was widespread, and helped to launch the campaign microsite with an online giving function. Branded donation boxes were placed in key sites, including the British Museum, and Birmingham Museum secured free

billboard space across the city during February, which boosted regional donations. Almost £650,000 was banked in the first four weeks. . . .

PR moments were planned and seized upon throughout the campaign. HRH Prince Charles and Camilla, Duchess of Cornwall, visited the Potteries Museum display in February, giving a significant PR boost. Events in Parliament gave MPs and Peers the opportunity to donate and be photographed with objects from the Hoard, and the three main party leaders (including David Cameron and Gordon Brown) issued supportive quotes. Late in February the Art Fund brought together some of the leading experts to discuss the emerging theories about what the Hoard could be and who buried it, which led to a Tony Robinson-penned article and spread, exclusively in the *Sunday Times*.

(Sally Wrampling, Head of Policy and Strategy, the Art Fund)

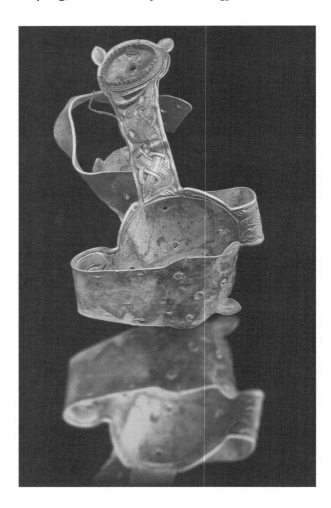

Figure 15.2 Staffordshire Hoard folded cross, Birmingham Museum and Art Gallery

It may seem a good idea to create a fundraising event for a one-off appeal. These events have become an art form in the United States where millions can be raised from those who attend. There is less of a tradition elsewhere, and events of this kind should only be embarked upon with an experienced and well-connected fundraiser, perhaps in conjunction with a major charity. While the climate in the US is more conducive to this kind of fundraising than it is in other parts of the world, the attention to detail applied to planning them is astonishing and painstaking. Enormous effort will be made to research beforehand: preparing biographies of key donor targets, getting to know their interests, likes and dislikes, and ensuring that the event aims at nothing short of perfection in its execution. So when the Metropolitan Museum of Art secures donations running into millions from one fashion extravaganza, in PR terms, it can truly be described as a class act.

Using social media in your fundraising campaign

An increasing range of tools is available to the fundraising team, including websites and social media to support and initiate fundraising contacts. Facebook and other social platforms such as Twitter provide a forum for engaging in dialogue with niche communities of potential donors – some of whom may already be among your audience – sharing causes and maybe turning participants into active donors. So using your network to support an appeal makes sense, particularly if you do not have much time in which to raise funds. Make sure your website can handle donations and then provide an online visual and audio experience about your project for YouTube and other networks, with a link back to your website – this will be more convincing than just text. The mobile internet is accessed by a growing number of mobile phone users and lends itself to spur-of-the-moment donations.

For smaller organisations and newcomers to fundraising, 'giving markets' is another possibility. They offer a readymade online mechanism for giving, developed initially for charities and voluntary organisations, but also for individuals with creative ideas. They provide easy accessibility to an existing platform which collects a host of small donations, saving your resources and administration costs. But make sure that the giving market you choose (which will take a percentage of your donations) has a track record, bank credentials, and preferably a personal recommendation (see Resources).

COMMERCIAL ACTIVITIES, FROM THE SHOP TO HIRING OUT FACILITIES

Many museums and galleries expend a considerable amount of time, energy and money undertaking market research. Sharing this information with the commercial team, and indeed planning in some research about visitor behaviours on site and their spending patterns, can make a significant difference to the thinking and to

Figure 15.3 Café exterior, Ulster Museum (courtesy of National Museums Northern Ireland)

the strategic commercial and retail planning. Too often, especially in small- and medium-sized enterprises, retail is an afterthought for the marketing team, when actually it is an integral element of the visitor's perception of the museum.

(Selina Fellows, Independent Retail and Commercial Adviser)

Retail and catering

The marketing strategy in the business plan will have set targets for commercial income generation. For smaller museums, galleries and historic houses, this usually means just the shop and the café, which are also an important part of the visitor experience. The trick is to make them both visitor-friendly *and* profitable. In a smaller museum or attraction, with lower visitor numbers, it is possible that neither will make much of a contribution to the bottom line. However, this should not stop the management team from striving towards profitability, using professional services when required to sharpen up both the catering and retail offers. Nor should it stop the PR and marketing team from driving new business from visitors as well as from passers-by, where appropriate. Finding out what visitors want (and what they may want in the future) is integral to this.

PR and marketing plans for a special exhibition or major event should take into account the commercial opportunities for merchandising and for creating special menus in the café. This means working together and working well ahead. Smaller attractions might find that the investment in bespoke merchandise is too expensive, but in the case of a touring exhibition there are opportunities to join with other venues in creating more than just mugs. Well-designed items will make special exhibitions memorable for the visitor and earn extra income for each of the participants. This is where the website comes in – are you able to take on the challenging task of setting up an online shopping facility, or could you make your merchandise available through others, CultureLabel, for example? (See Resources.)

Many free museums and galleries have a very high repeat visitor rate. Those visitors want to see something new and exciting in your shop and café. At the Tate they use mobile display units to change the shops around. Here are some more tips from Selina Fellows:

> **With free admission, at least for the foreseeable future, the visit patterns of 'little and often' to many museums are likely to continue. The way the shop trades should reflect this opportunity by keeping the entire retail offer looking fresh and new to encourage those repeat visitors to buy on every visit.**

Figure 15.4 Security guard in the Prado shop (Photo: Barry Barnett)

The refresh rate of the merchandise should be considered (how often existing lines and ranges make way for new lines and ranges) as well as the frequency at which the shop is re-merchandised. Visual merchandising (which encompasses everything from the static window or above-unit displays to the way the show is laid out and how the product is put on the shelf) is often an undervalued skill in many museum shops. It is sometimes referred to as the 'silent salesperson'.

The PR team should include merchandising in their thinking too, and support the shop throughout the year, but particularly in the period leading up to Christmas, when online guides such as Culture24, magazines and newspapers are looking for unusual Christmas shopping ideas. Put a link to your Christmas offers, including cards, on the home page of your website from October onwards and use Facebook and Twitter to stimulate interest.

Outsourcing the retail and catering operations may be an attractive solution, provided that your bottom line benefits in the long run from any additional investment required. The café and shop should still reflect your branding rather than the operators' and should be part of your marketing and PR activities. The standardised heritage café and shop familiar from many National Trust houses is changing, as each property 'goes local', sourcing food and merchandise locally, reflecting the identity of each individual house, as well as that of the National Trust.

Events and facilities

Your events programme may be part of your audience development strategy designed to highlight aspects of your collection. Here is a comment from The Huntington in California:

In considering every new program, we ask ourselves the same question: How does it relate directly to our collections and our mission? If we don't have an immediate response, and can't show the obvious connection, then we don't do the program, or we tweak it accordingly. We view ourselves as a collections-based, research and educational institution. Our programming reflects that – from our small hands-on botanical workshops to our packed-house lectures by Pulitzer-prize-winning historians. People affiliated with The Huntington have come to expect a certain high standard of quality – and that's what we aim to deliver – in both an aesthetic and intellectual sense. So, in the end, it's about working at a level of specificity and detail, so that every program – or event – is thought through individually, applying the highest standards we can, and connecting it to what is uniquely The Huntington.
(Susan Turner-Lowe, Vice President for Communications, The Huntington Library, Art Collections, and Botanical Gardens, San Marino, California)

Hiring out your facilities to others may be part of PR and stakeholder relations – making lecture theatres or education rooms available at a nominal rate which covers staff overtime. This is a good way of building links with local community groups, associations and others, and conveys a welcoming message about the museum or gallery to people who may not come as visitors. All the rules on providing a friendly welcome and a favourable appearance apply, as well as making information about the museum available as people leave.

However, your events can also be part of your income-generating strategy, or at least be designed to cover their cost. In creating a programme of charging events, marketing considerations are paramount. Who is it for? What's the competition? How much can we charge? What's the break-even point? How are we going to promote it? Some events may be promoted mainly through the Friends. For others – an adult education programme, for example – you will need a wider target audience (see Chapter 8 for information on how to put together your marketing and PR campaign for your commercial events).

Room hire can also become an important part of your income stream. However, museums and attractions that start competing for business with commercial venues must raise their delivery accordingly. They will also be subject to additional local authority and health and safety regulations. Newcomers in this field who believe that their facilities are suitable should take professional advice from a specialist consultant, or initially from one of the big caterers.

Preparing for this kind of business will probably require capital investment to upgrade basic facilities such as the kitchen area with new equipment, and a budget for marketing the venue, and staff training. You have to set conditions and restrictions relating to the objects, security, and environmental control. Many museums and galleries have entered this field successfully, particularly in metropolitan cities where there is a ready demand. Historic houses and museums in remoter locations have also done well, focusing on conferences, weddings and receptions, working in partnership with a hotel or conference organiser. There are a number of commercial venue finders online who will promote your venue (for a commission) – see Resources.

Having created some general guidelines for the types of events that you would welcome, go through a risk assessment for every booking, starting with licensing, and include the following PR considerations:

- Is the event in tune with your brand and vision?
- Are the people involved going to be respectful of the collections, the furniture, and your staff?
- Will regular visitors be inconvenienced or denied access – and, if so, what are you going to do about it?
- Will it impact adversely on your neighbours?
- Are there others involved – commercial sponsors for example, who may be unacceptable to the trustees, the local community, or cause negative press comments?

Some major historic houses have made a successful business from large-scale commercial events, sometimes staged inside but mostly in the grounds of their property. At Goodwood House in Sussex, annual outdoor events include horse-racing, motor racing, golf and aviation, adding new ingredients to the mix with a Vintage Fashion Festival in 2010. Weddings are big business here, helped by the location of a hotel on the estate. Setting up events on that scale involves a commercial risk as well as large start-up costs to cover equipment, licensing, health and safety, promotion, etc. At Goodwood a dedicated PR and marketing team support the year-round events programme. Learn from others if you are going down this route and consult with HHA and ACE.

At the other end of the scale, in contrast, is the experience of a much smaller venue, Muncaster Castle in the Lake District. Iona Frost-Pennington, a member of the Pennington family who have lived at Muncaster for over 800 years, runs Muncaster with help from her husband Peter, who coordinates and runs the special events and PR. Peter says:

> The special events really bring the place alive and generate great PR opportunities which consistently get noticed by the media, both locally and further afield. These activities significantly enhance the bottom line and also the economic effects deliver benefits much further afield, as Muncaster employs performers both locally and from all over the world as well as buying more goods and services from local suppliers. Our main aim, however, is to keep the public happy – and they seem to enjoy our gently anarchic approach to presenting our historic assets in as entertaining a way as possible. [There is more in the case study introduced below and in the Appendix.]

At Pitt Rivers Museum,' Museums at Night' became a hugely successful event run in May as part of 'Museums and Galleries Month' (see the Chapter 7 case study). Kate White identified a developing trend which other cities have experienced – Berlin, Amsterdam and London ('The Sultan's Elephant' in 2006).

> There seems to be a growing demand for mass gatherings and for theatrical events (from flashmobs to festivals) where audiences come together in a shared experience, a large part of which is their own combined goodwill and participation in making it happen. Through these events, the Museums have shown that their galleries and displays can become an ideal focus for generating this sense of community.
> (Kate White, Marketing and Visitor Services Officer, Pitt Rivers Museum)

Serious money can be made from filming, whether for a commercial or for a feature film or television series. Historic houses around the UK have benefited from such collaborations, even if in the final product a number of elements from different properties have been merged to create an entirely fictional place, as happened in *Shakespeare in Love*. Others such as Castle Howard continue to benefit from the original television version of *Brideshead Revisited*, while Alnwick Castle prospers from

Figure 15.5 Mr Spin performs at the Festival of Fools, Muncaster Castle (Photo: Steve Bishop)

its inclusion in the Harry Potter films. Films of this kind can be a fantastic stimulus for overseas tourists, as well as home-grown visitors. Your tourist board or regional film council can help in promoting your facilities and there are also several online locations directories that accept free listings (see Resources).

It is important to consider the impact that filming might have on normal operations, and how to handle the arrangements. Here, Harvey Edgington, Broadcast and Media Manager of the National Trust gives some advice, based on considerable experience:

> First, make sure your whole organisation is on board. Then nominate a single point of contact for the industry. This person should have the responsibility to say yes or no, but also sufficient seniority for the internal organisation to treat it as a priority.

> If you have to say no – and don't be afraid to do so – always give a reason. Be flexible, because they might be able to achieve what they want by doing it a different way – a way that you can suggest. Be quick. Film crews' timescales tend to be today and yesterday.

> Once you have agreed a shoot it is important to issue a contract that safeguards what you want to happen and offers protection and legal redress. We have our own

and we don't sign anyone else's. Fees always vary due to the scale of the shoot and the project. Children's BBC, for instance, cannot afford the same rates as a drama production. What they pay the actors is no reflection on what the location manager has to spend. Staff costs should be in addition to the fee, unless you are prepared to absorb some of them for the publicity benefits of the film. Film days are usually 12 hours long. So make sure that you can cope with staff time on the shoot and the days afterwards.

Once the shoot is over, do a wash-up analysis. You are never too experienced to learn what went right or wrong. Share the results with relevant colleagues, especially conservation staff if you have them.

If you plan to cash-in on the publicity, be careful. The scenes shot at your site might be edited out of the final version, or your location made to look like a fictional place. Your interior may feature within another property's exterior, causing confusion to future visitors. If you're in the final film but look radically different, then your interpretation for publicity purposes must reflect that.

USING YOUR ASSETS

The collections held in museums, galleries and historic houses can be capitalised upon in a number of ways. The PR team will have an interest in this from the perspective of brand protection, appropriateness, politics, and public perceptions, and the marketing team from the point of view of promotion and income. There is a school of thought which holds that images of artefacts from public collections should be freely available to all, regardless of the costs involved. However, in a climate where publicly funded cultural organisations are expected to generate at least 30% of their own income, making money from the wealth on display or in stores has become big business.

Commercial organisations have taken advantage of the intellectual property rights of museums and galleries for years, exploiting images of objects from collections. Most cultural organisations are more knowledgeable now and in a better position to negotiate beneficial contracts with picture agencies and others to use and market their photographs worldwide. The digital environment makes it difficult to control any exploitation of copyrighted images, so a picture agency's experience can be useful in dealing with the marketplace.

It is important for the management team involving marketing, PR and sales to develop a policy for the use of images (and other intellectual property in the archives or collections) and then deal with opportunities as they arise. Photographs and rights to reproduce can become a useful profit centre even for a small gallery, such as the Freud Museum in North London who enjoy continuing demand for images from their collection – and not just of Sigmund Freud. Imaginative merchandise based on the collection is now the staple of many gallery shops. At the London Transport Museum shop in Covent Garden you see the famous underground logo everywhere. You can even buy cushions in the same (or similar material) to that used on seats on the trains. ACE (quoted earlier) provides excellent support and back-up for their members seeking advice in this field.

It is important that staff are made aware of intellectual property rights. Manipulating images or photocopying images from the collection may have copyright implications (the photographer or the living artists may still have rights). Pictures from the web or even newspaper cuttings may enjoy copyright restrictions. For more questions on copyright, see Resources, with useful web links.

Here are some useful tips from Tom Morgan, Head of Rights and Reproductions at the National Portrait Gallery:

- **Training and awareness** – make sure everyone knows that you can't reproduce things without permission.

- **Control** – make sure that the rights/permissions element as well as the tradeable asset value of 'intellectual property rights' (IPR), is appropriately addressed in all operations.

- **Integration** – make sure the information required to exploit/acquire/buy IPR (or IPR permissions) is coordinated, with the information required to license/grant similar rights, into the most obvious and accessible place.

- Make sure that IPR issues are an active part of the institution's thinking.

- **Facilitation** – help colleagues and clients to do what they want to do, by providing the permissions they need, through integrated resources, helpful, dynamic relationships, and joined-up thinking.

CASE STUDIES IN THE APPENDIX

Case Study 15A: The fundraising campaign to save the Staffordshire Hoard

This shows how an unprecedented degree of local cooperation – and fast PR reaction – saved the day for a treasure trove. The campaign to save the Staffordshire Hoard in 2010 was a triumph – £3.3 million raised in just 14 weeks, including £900,000 from public donations. But it was a logistical challenge – a secret location, five local authorities, three museums and a national fundraising appeal. How did it all come together?

Case Study 15B: Muncaster Castle, thriving on events

Muncaster Castle is a medium-sized 'stately home' situated an hour-and-a-half off the M6 motorway, in an isolated location on the west coast of the Lake District National Park in northern England. The castle is owned and managed by Iona and Peter Frost-Pennington. Here they describe how building their events programme has met with success.

Case Study 15C: Financing markets through grants at the Scottish Mining Museum

Gillian Rankin, Marketing and Events Officer, writes 'When I first started working as Marketing Officer at the Scottish Mining Museum, in January 2005, I wondered how I would ever adapt to having such restricted marketing budgets to work with. Having come from a financial services institution, running high-profile events and advertising campaigns where money seemed to be no object, I was sure I would struggle to grow the visitor numbers and increase the profile of this wonderful place. But it quickly became a passion for me and I enjoyed finding new ways to reach new and existing markets without breaking the bank.'

CHAPTER 16

COMMUNICATING IN A CRISIS

IDENTIFYING CRISES

> Reports that say that something hasn't happened are always interesting to me, because as we know, there are known knowns; there are things we know we know. We also know there are known unknowns; that is to say we know there are some things we do not know. But there are also unknown unknowns – the ones we don't know we don't know.
>
> **(Donald Rumsfeld, former US Defence Secretary)**

Some crises can be foreseen and prepared for. Others cannot, as they are, by definition, 'unknowns'. The 'black swan' is another term for the unknown, the event for which we are unable to prepare because it is an 'outlier' – something out of the normal – described by Nassim Nicholas Taleb in his book *The Black Swan: The Impact of the Highly Improbable*.

So any crisis communications plan has to prepare for the events that are possible, likely and probable, as well as for those that are totally unforeseen. Many small crises occur all the time in small and large organisations dealing with the public, in sometimes old and fragile buildings. These are dealt with by staff without necessarily involving senior management or the PR team. Such minor crises might include damage to an object, a visitor complaining about the toilets, an exhibition build falling behind schedule, or the lift out of order (again). These are not likely to impact on the outside world. Nevertheless, senior management should be aware of a build-up of problems in any one area – it could be a future crisis in the making.

A crisis which needs senior management and PR attention is:

- out of the ordinary – an unexpected and serious situation
- of potential interest to the media in a negative way
- any situation where the public interest demands a response
- when the reputation of the organisation is at stake.

The 24-hour media world is now a reality around the globe. Today, everybody can contribute to the news as a quasi-journalist with a blog or a mobile phone, photographing and videoing events as they happen. At the same time, the media's own editorial controls have slipped as the number of newsroom journalists is reduced. A survey by Cardiff University for Nick Davies's book *Flat Earth News* (see Resources) showed that only 12% of stories in UK newspapers had been checked before going to print. Not surprisingly, the public now consider journalists as the second most untrustworthy group of professionals, after politicians (YouGovStone, October 2010). However, the damage to reputation has already been done when public bodies, commercial organisations and individuals are put in the dock by the media, whether rightly or wrongly. Finding someone to blame for every accident or incident is essential. 'Acts of God' no longer exist!

The media and the public are also demanding more information, and now have access to Freedom of Information legislation in many countries. However, the increasingly litigious environment has forced organisations into a tight corner, anxious to show appropriate sympathy for those involved in an accident but advised by their lawyers to say as little as possible. Richard Bagnall, Metrica, writing about new media in his Chapter 11 case study, made this point:

> Case studies abound of organisations like United Airlines, Gap and Kit-Kat that have been caught out by the rise of social media and its ability to fan the flames of a crisis. In the past, when crises engulfed an organisation, they were far easier for the communications team to respond to by implementing a crisis communication plan. The old media did not offer easy methods for the target audience to connect with each other and fuel the situation. Negative stories might be discussed between friends in the pub, on the phone or at the fabled office water cooler, but there was no easy way for these conversations to link to each other and gain critical mass by feeding off each other. News travels much faster now – with the click of a Facebook 'like' button or a retweet on Twitter, news can spread across audiences, countries and continents in almost real time.

All of these factors need to be taken on board in the preparation and implementation of the crisis communications plan. It is unlikely that any museums, galleries or heritage attractions will ever face the scale of crises that an airline or a ferry operator has to be prepared for. But stop for a moment and imagine what would have happened if the fires at Windsor Castle (1992) or Hampton Court Palace (1986) had started during public opening hours. Museums in California have certainly experienced both brushfire and earthquake when the public were visiting. Museums in the UK are familiar with bomb threats. Attractions in rural England have lost thousands of trees in severe storms. The case studies introduced below and in the Appendix show a range of recent disasters, from fires to floods, and an earthquake in New Zealand.

THE CRISIS COMMUNICATIONS PLAN

> When things go wrong (and sometimes sadly they do) it is essential to have a plan which sets out clearly who will lead the work of dealing with the crisis and who will be linked in a network of support. The director's role is to be ready to speak to the press if needed, to liaise at senior level with the chair of the board, and with government departments or other authorities. The director's office must also advise as practical decisions are being made, and ensure that external as well as internal processes are being thought about.
>
> (Sandy Nairne, Director, National Portrait Gallery)

Any organisation which welcomes visitors should have a disaster plan, usually a legal requirement for operating a public attraction and obtaining public liability insurance. In the UK, as part of accreditation, museums and galleries develop detailed disaster plans. Such plans will be mainly concerned with public safety, security, the building and objects and often stop short of the communications function. The PR team, led by the director, should take responsibility for preparing the crisis communications plan, as follows:

Preparation

- Likely and unlikely crisis scenarios (from the disaster plan)
- Who is in charge?
- Communication centre and operating remotely
- Call-out trees and mobile communications
- Handy reference material.

First response

- The crisis breaks
- Issues of support, confidence and trust
- Access to information
- Confidentiality
- Awareness of the law.

Communications

- Getting briefed
- Agreeing policy on the hoof
- Feedback to management, board and staff
- Importance of the Q&A – website – social media
- Briefing staff.

What to say

- Useful forms of wording
- Keep it simple, honest and limited
- Follow up – restoring reputation.

INTERNAL COMMUNICATIONS, CONTRACTORS AND SUPPLIERS

Museums, galleries and heritage attractions have emergency procedures for evacuating the public and for minor accidents in public areas. The communications crisis plan should interlock with this. Security staff, room guides, wardens and volunteers should be well briefed on the crisis plan and arrangements for the communications centre. The key messages of care and concern (see below) must be built into the way that staff deal with every type of emergency involving the public, from a simple fall to a major evacuation.

During a crisis, efficient communications between security and the director and press office is essential. The plan will spell out who is in charge, who deals with what, and where and how communications take place. It is important to establish the PR presence at the start. Security concerns might see communications as unimportant – and when serious disaster strikes other priorities may quite correctly take precedence for the moment.

The J Paul Getty Museum in Los Angeles, a city which regularly experiences fires, floods and even earthquakes, not only has detailed plans for coping with disasters, in which every member of staff has a designated role to play, but occasionally has a full dress rehearsal. Public buildings in the UK are obliged to practise fire evacuation procedures at regular intervals.

In the case of criminal activities on your premises, the police will take charge, and the fewer mentions of where the incident took place the better, particularly if staff are involved. However, the police (and the fire brigade) have their own PR agenda and media contacts who might spread the story faster and wider than you would wish, so be prepared. Disputes with contractors over damage or ill-fitting or leaking showcases and tanks, or late-running contracts are not going to show the institution in a good light, even if it is not to blame. The less said the better. Food-poisoning incidents are likely to be perceived as the museum's fault, even if outside caterers were used. It is best not to blame each other in public but accept responsibility in as neutral a way as possible, while promising a full investigation.

Cutbacks in funding frequently lead to redundancies. It is important that you share the news with the staff before the media announces it (see Chapter 13 Internal communications). Legal issues, such as employment law, will also be involved. Good internal communications and staff relations are essential, and will hopefully forestall a crisis from becoming a public issue.

YOUR REPUTATION ON THE LINE AND ONLINE

> On the whole, honesty is the best policy. But be sure you know what you are being honest about. Above all, establish the facts before you offer any opinion on the situation.
>
> **(Ivo Dawnay, Communications Director, National Trust)**

Developing a strong brand and the promises that go with it can set the organisation up to be shot down when something goes wrong. There are plenty of examples in recent years where this has happened. Sometimes they are handled well and sometimes they are not. Consider the Perrier contamination of the famous fizzy water – it was well-handled, with a full withdrawal and therefore quick recovery of reputation. Contrast that with the fault in Maclaren's pushchair which resulted in little fingers being damaged – but no product withdrawal in the UK until media outrage ensued. A cultural brand is less likely to produce such a negative impact, even in a crisis, but museums in London that had accepted sponsorship from BP during the 2010 US oil spillage were subject to strong criticism from some quarters of the media, and experienced public demonstrations.

Damage to your reputation can come from a number of directions in the traditional media but the online world is adding a new dimension, as described above. Dissatisfied or disgruntled visitors now log their complaints or comments on websites such as TripAdvisor or Ripoff Report in the US, without your knowledge (see Resources). Very quickly something quite trivial gets taken up and becomes a news story, spreading like wildfire through the 24-hour media world and online, with little opportunity to answer back. Speed of reaction is of the essence here.

These websites invite organisations to respond to complaints online, and by doing so quickly you may be able to avoid wider consequences of the report showing up on search engines. If inaccurate and damaging comments about your services persist on the web you may need a specialist PR or reputation management company to assist you. So keep a watch on what people are saying about you online through email alerts from these consumer sites and from search engines (Google, Yahoo, etc.) – use keyword tracking and personalised RSS feeds and search website forums related to your industry (see Resources). Consider remedial measures such as blogs, press releases, and responding in discussion forums and social networks, as well as rebutting any claims through your own website.

Inviting a TV or film crew into your institution for a documentary may become a crisis of reputation, as discovered by some organisations after signing up for fly-on-the-wall documentaries. See Chapter 10 on how to make sure that any reality shows are filmed on your terms.

Reputations can also be harmed through a Freedom of Information request. Quite legitimate expenditure or activities can be misinterpreted or misrepresented and appear to show your board and senior management as wasting public money and resources. Any response to an FOI request should be carefully checked for such implications before they are released. You must not conceal potentially damaging information, but at least you can be prepared.

LOSS OF FUNDING AND SPONSORS

Funding crises can often be predicted, and plans can be developed to deal with them at a much earlier stage than usually happens. As a result of the credit crunch in 2008 and the subsequent recession there were severe cuts in public expenditure in the UK and loss of private and corporate donations in all Western economies. No cultural organisation has been spared from this, and uncertainties will continue for the foreseeable future. It is important to maintain advocacy and stakeholder relations with public funders, even after what appears to be the 'worst' has happened – see Chapter 14.

Sometimes there may a last-minute loss of funding for a specific project. In that situation it is a good thing to know who your friends are, and to whom you can appeal for immediate assistance. It was not enough for Tullie House when they lost their bid for a Roman helmet to a higher bid at auction, but they were well prepared to handle any media fallout.

Sponsors and donors can be a source of embarrassment – a sponsor may withdraw for commercial reasons, or because their finances are under threat, and you may become part of the negative coverage. It may be good practice not to put the donor's name on a new gallery until the money is in the bank.

IMPLEMENTING THE CRISIS COMMUNICATIONS PLAN

The critical points are: establishing who is in charge; the communications centre; the three Cs – care, concern and control; the speed of the statement; and staying in control.

Who is in charge?

In most organisations, the director will automatically be 'in charge' when a crisis develops. The disaster plan should spell out the alternatives. Who stands in for him or her when the director is absent or cannot get there quickly enough? In a major crisis, divide up the roles of managing the situation, that is, dealing with the emergency services on the one hand, and communicating on the other. A senior press officer or head of public relations will be well qualified to handle this latter part. The director should then be available for interviews. The *Cutty Sark* case study is a good example of managing communications through a 'tight' team.

Many organisations have a 'call-out tree' which starts with one telephone call, and fans out to create a network of staff who will contact one another. Using mobile phones and text messages speeds up the process. See the case studies from Tullie House and Birmingham Museum and Art Gallery which show how they coped with floods.

Remember that every situation is different and, by the very nature of crises, when it happens, a crisis will not follow exactly the scenario which your communications crisis plan spelt out. Think of the black swan – how many of those will you encounter in a lifetime? So make sure that the plan is flexible, that your staff are empowered to take control if no one else is available, that everyone realises the need for speed, and that first reactions really matter and will count against you if they are badly handled.

The communications centre

The communications centre could be the press office or the director's office. Ideally it should be close to the emergency centre but not necessarily in the same room – especially not for a major crisis. The basic requirements for a communications centre are landline and mobile phones; a computer and/or a laptop; and Wi-Fi access for emails, social networks and updating the website (fax is probably redundant). Some large organisations also keep hand-held radios in their emergency kit, and train staff how to use them. If mobile phone coverage goes down, radios should still work.

It may not be possible to get access to the building because of the emergency itself (a bomb-threat, for example) or because the building is damaged, alarmed, locked or otherwise inaccessible at night or weekends. So there should be an alternative plan which may involve a third party. If the mobile phone network is still working, you can set up your communications centre almost anywhere; in a local church hall, a civic centre, or even a nearby café. You may want to include some alternative potentially available locations in your plan.

If the emergency situation is likely to extend beyond just one or two days, a temporary office may have to be set up, and additional staff or a PR agency taken on or seconded just to deal with communications, including incoming calls on the landline, emails, networking and the website. Keep one or more mobile lines clear for the media. A commercial call centre is an alternative for public information and can be contracted at very short notice.

The three Cs – care, concern and control

The first statement by the organisation (to be made very quickly) sets the tone for the media and could well be the one by which the organisation is judged for ever more. So don't get it wrong. Remember: people before objects – always. Denials, 'no comment', or blaming others just do not work. So the organisation should accept responsibility for the situation and the action which needs to be taken without, at this stage, accepting blame or culpability.

The organisation needs to look prepared and effective, no matter what is going on behind the scenes. Media training for crises is invaluable for senior management who may find themselves in this situation now or in the future (see Resources).

The statement must start by showing that the organisation *cares* about the victim(s) of the incident; that you are *concerned* and therefore doing something about it – that is, carrying out an immediate investigation; and that you are in *control*, in the sense that the organisation had prepared itself for emergencies, and that you implemented the plans you had made. Even when the fire department is busy establishing the source of the fire, you have positive things to say because your organisation will be working closely with them (see the *Cutty Sark* case study).

In a funding crisis, blaming the government, the local authority, individual politicians, the lottery funds, or other distributing body may get some instant coverage. But it will not win friends among the people who matter for the future, and it will certainly not restore your funding. In any case, should you not have seen it coming? In this situation, a statement should be much more reflective. It should acknowledge any shortcomings and say what will be done to improve matters. Ulster museums have had their share of controversy and have learned to provide a considered response:

> There is no single answer for crisis management. The key is to review each situation on its own merit. What is the core issue? How will it affect your organisation's reputation in the short, medium and long term?

> You need to review the facts at hand and how they are being portrayed in the media before deciding whether you should publicly respond (be available for interview, or simply issue a statement), allow others to speak on your behalf, or maintain a dignified silence, based on the nature of the situation.
> (Gillian McLean, Director of Marketing, Communications & Trading, National Museums Northern Ireland)

The speed of the statement – website and social media

From the start of this chapter, the speed at which the media works has been stressed. So get the statement out quickly, within an hour, the same day or the same night – don't wait for trustees and lawyers to clear it and miss all the relevant deadlines. Email will enable you to send your statement simultaneously to a wide range of media on your contacts list. News agencies should be at the top of the list. It is important that everyone who matters gets the information at the same time. In a crisis situation it does not pay to do anyone any favours with an exclusive interview. Do that later when you start the rebuilding of the reputation programme.

With water gushing down the stairs, the staff at Birmingham Museum and Art Gallery had plenty to do, just getting visitors out and stemming the damage (read the full case study in the Appendix):

> We explained to awaiting press that they would get a full statement, and gave them a time. Meanwhile, our response was to say that we were looking into what had happened but were still dealing with the situation. As agreed, and when we were prepared with a full statement on 'staff rescuing artworks from flood', we held a press briefing on the front steps of the museum. The story had great immediacy,

and turned from the potential 'vandal damage at museum' story to a more positive line.

Get messages on your home page and on your answering service quickly – this should be part of your communications plan, with responsibilities allocated in advance. Once this has been done, follow up with Twitter, Facebook and other social media, as appropriate. Monitor the broadcasting and online coverage and make corrections as quickly as possible. Set up a question and answer page on your website in an ongoing crisis. (See how Canterbury Museum in New Zealand dealt with this in the case study.)

Share the statement with all staff, through email, texts, mobile messages, etc. or by bringing them together. A mass meeting can be useful for several reasons, enabling the director to speak to staff, giving information and reassurance. Make sure that everyone is 'on message'. Be prepared for individuals to go 'off piste' sending their own photos or videos to newspapers, Facebook or YouTube, and making statements without authorisation.

Showing care and concern for what has happened is not an admission of guilt, whatever your lawyers may say. It will stand you in good stead with the media in a major crisis, and in a minor incident will ensure that instead of a legal bill you have a grateful visitor who will return again and again. So when an elderly woman falls and hurts herself on your premises, send her home in a taxi and follow up with flowers to her home or hospital. Equally, you cannot rely on 'being nice'. Possibly months after an accident, people can suddenly decide to sue. So make sure that all witness statements, staff accounts and other details, including photographs of the incident are recorded and preserved.

A few tips from Historic Royal Palaces

Historic Royal Palaces is the body that looks after the Tower of London, Hampton Court Palace and Kensington Palace, among others. Here, Katrina Whenham, Media and PR Manager, gives the benefit of her advice on being prepared for drama, and how to handle it:

> The very nature of a crisis is that it is unpredictable, a certain element will always contain an on-the-spot reaction. However, what you can be certain of is that a crisis is inevitable and therefore must be planned for.

> Planning for a crisis should not be underestimated. The best way to plan is often to practise – for example, conducting a crisis stimulation exercise with your PR team. This can help to build up communications planning skills and experience working under extreme pressure to a tight deadline – as well as iron out any creases in the management of a crisis (for example, the availability of senior management at short notice). Here are some tips for dealing with a media crisis:

- Plan ahead – make sure there is always a trained PR professional to answer the phone and a pre-selected media-trained spokesperson on hand.

- When the crisis happens, keep calm but act fast.

- Gather as much information as possible, particularly from any journalists that call you. Don't be pushed into providing information you are not ready to divulge publicly.

- Make a note of all the journalists that call you and their deadlines. Ensure you get back to them promptly. The sooner you can collate an official response, the more likely you are to have some control over the story and to create a more balanced piece, as well as have an opportunity to correct any inaccuracies.

- Make sure you have immediate access to the ultimate decision-maker, be that a director or CEO, to ensure your reactive statement is clear, on message and consistent.

- Ensure you inform all staff of what is going on. Internal communication is just as important as external communication.

Staying in control

Staying in control means continuing management of the news situation until the media has run out of steam and/or something else taken their attention. Issuing regular bulletins will keep people informed – try to find new angles for those who are prepared to be positive. Make sure press office phones are manned seven days a week and that senior management and any experts are available to make statements, be interviewed and take people on tours, if appropriate.

The challenge of staying in control when the crisis may continue for several months is illustrated in the case study by Patrick Greene: 'Aboriginal barks at Melbourne Museum – the public relations challenge'. (See the full case study in the Appendix.) Here is an extract from the final, legal stage:

> After six months of deliberation, the judge found that an inspector could make one thirty-day declaration (to retain the bark objects in Australia) but after that responsibility passed to the Minister to exercise his powers. Once the ruling had been made, the Minister stated that he would not make temporary or permanent declarations in respect of the bark objects which were then returned to London at the end of May 2005.

> The Museum had successfully discharged its obligations but there was no sense of triumph – quite the reverse in fact as morale within the Museum's own Indigenous staff had suffered. As CEO, I made sure that I met with the staff throughout to explain clearly my view of the issues and to hear their concerns. It

took time for the wounds to heal, but the willingness to engage in difficult meetings and to be open and honest made recovery easier.

WHEN IT IS ALL OVER – REBUILDING THE REPUTATION

When the immediate crisis is over, the real work of rebuilding the reputation starts. The timing of this is important – you cannot wait too long – but, on the other hand, you might waste energies by going too early.

An immediate image-rebuilding campaign may start by targeting journalists not involved in the day-to-day news story, creating positive features on how the emergency has been tackled and how new funds are going to be raised. In other cases the damage may be so severe or beyond your control that you have to go with it until the emergency subsides. If there is real public hostility or fear, lying low for quite a long time is exactly the right thing to do. Test the waters and develop a public relations plan to rebuild your damaged reputation, restore your funds, and lead to the return of visitors.

Figure 16.1 The warship *Vasa* sank in Stockholm's harbour on its maiden voyage in 1628. The Vasa Museum housing the salvaged ship and its contents opened in 1990 and is now one of Sweden's most popular tourist attractions (Photo: Anneli Karlsson, Swedish National Maritime Museums)

In the case of loss of funding, the situation might really be beyond saving. The PR strategy must then be developed to support a new funding strategy or closure.

The recovery plan can take years to implement, as this quote from the Vasa Museum in Stockholm, Sweden's most popular museum, shows:

> **In the summer of 2000 our conservators noted that the *Vasa* showed tendencies of deteriorating. The PR staff on duty had to handle a media invasion caused by the image of the ship falling apart. This image became a constant media story for a long time which was bad for our marketing efforts where the *Vasa* had been a story of success.**
>
> **First we had to make sure that everybody on the staff, especially the guides, were constantly updated. Then we worked to show media and visitors how the threat to the *Vasa* was calmly and capably handled, by direct care, help from international top research and eventually also by fundraising. But in the long run we aimed to erase the image of the unfortunate and threatened ship so that the success story, the *Vasa* as a winner, could emerge again.**
>
> **(Maria B. Andersson, Information Director,**
> **Swedish National Maritime Museums)**

SO YOU HAVEN'T GOT A PLAN

The museum and gallery faced with a crisis and no communications plan should do the following:

▨ One senior person should take charge of communications.

▨ The situation should be assessed and a rapid statement issued to the media.

▨ Keep staff/trustees informed and 'on message'.

▨ A key media list is an essential – if it does not exist, call a friendly PR person or company and be prepared to pay.

▨ Deal in the same way with all media – do not give any exclusives or favours.

▨ Maintain communications – don't clam up after the first statement, but don't say more than you know or can appropriately disclose.

▨ Do not blame third parties or quote third parties.

▨ Start to rebuild your reputation with a proper PR programme – and put together a crisis communications plan.

HOW AND WHEN TO COMPLAIN TO THE MEDIA

The media coverage of a crisis may in itself generate further problems. The crisis may in fact have started with a spiteful and erroneous article in a magazine or newspaper or online. What do you do? It is important to recognise that you cannot really win against the media. They will almost always have the upper hand. Even in a libel case where they may lose – the public has enjoyed column inches of negative coverage against the complainant before the judgement is passed. And it will have cost a lot of money – only the lawyers have benefited.

Online, the damage can be even worse as search engines can repeat damaging material seemingly for ever. So the first decision is: what is there to gain by complaining? These are the situations in which you should consider complaining:

Mistakes and errors of fact in print: Email a polite letter to the relevant editor immediately and ask them to rectify the mistake. In listings and magazines, follow-up phone calls are usually required to get telephone numbers and opening hours amended.

Online errors can be more difficult to eradicate. Some sites have a mechanism for you to respond to erroneous or justified complaints from visitors but the original complaint will still stay online.

Strong opinions by journalists or in editorials with which you do not agree: Prepare a 'letter to the editor' by email, making a positive point, and making it interesting and humorous if possible. It will have a much better chance of being used.

Vicious and potentially libellous attacks on individuals or the institution: Take legal advice and then email and mail a recorded letter to the editor in person and, if a published apology is not offered, file a complaint with the Press Complaints Commission in the UK. The same applies to TV and radio – file your complaint with the broadcasting company or Ofcom (see Resources). When you are forewarned of a potentially disastrous piece of broadcast coverage or damaging article, take legal advice and if you have sufficient grounds (and it really matters), go for an injunction – but in full knowledge of the potential costs.

When to apologise: Sometimes your organisation might be in the wrong. If so, always apologise and put an explanatory statement on the media pages of your website if the issue has spread to news programmes.

When in the middle of a serious crisis, we have no time to reflect, but afterwards it really is a good idea to figure out what worked well and what did not. We learn from every disaster, and hopefully we apply the lessons learned.

CASE STUDIES IN THE APPENDIX

Case Study 16A: Aboriginal barks at Melbourne Museum – the public relations challenge

Dr J. Patrick Greene, Chief Executive Officer of Museum Victoria in Melbourne, Australia, describes an incident that put the museum into news headlines around the world, and caused shockwaves within the profession. It required careful directorial and PR handling on many different fronts simultaneously.

Case Study 16B: The *Cutty Sark* fire: a fast-moving media crisis

On 21 May 2007, the historic ship *Cutty Sark*, preserved at Greenwich, was discovered ablaze. As one of the last remaining tea clippers from the age of sail, and positioned within easy reach of the UK media, the story broke early in the morning, became huge, and followed events live throughout the day. Richard Doughty, Chief Executive of the Cutty Sark Trust, found himself under the spotlight as events unfolded.

Figure 16.2 Scotland Yard investigators on board the *Cutty Sark*, the day after the fire (Photo: Tim Keeler)

Case Study 16C: Floods and loss, Tullie House Museum and Art Gallery

Tullie House Museum is a much-loved building in historic Carlisle in the north of England. The twenty-first century has not been kind to it. First it was swept by damaging flood water. Five years later it was swept by enthusiasm for an astonishingly beautiful Roman helmet unearthed in the locality. It sprang into action to raise an enormous sum, only to find that destiny had other plans. Director Hilary Wade reports.

Case Study 16D: More flooding, Birmingham Museums and Art Gallery

The art collections in Birmingham are among the finest in the country. Carmel Girling, Deputy Head of Marketing and Communications, Birmingham Museums and Art Gallery, explains what happened when water poured through the galleries – during public opening hours.

Case Study 16E: Earthquake rocks Canterbury Museum, Christchurch

When a powerful earthquake hit Christchurch, New Zealand, Karin Stahel, Communications Manager of Canterbury Museum, found herself handling a series of actions aimed at containing and satisfying press interest.

PART 3

RESEARCH AND RESOURCES

CHAPTER 17

RESEARCH AND EVALUATION IN MARKETING AND PR

In his book, *A Social History of Museums*, Kenneth Hudson describes the early days of museum surveys, explaining how Milwaukee Museum has the proudest history of visitor research, going back to the 1950s. In the UK, in 1967, the Ulster Museum was one of the first to look at who was visiting and why. In both instances, the early surveys were focused on the type or social category of visitor, and attempted to discover something of their experience of the museum. People were beginning to reassess the role of cultural institutions and to become more knowledgeable about the way they were perceived and used. In 1967 at the Museum of the City in New York, Marshall McLuhan, speaking at a conference on the 'Media and Museum', said:

> **I have watched people in museums for many years and it is rather interesting, both in Europe and America. You find a person will walk up to an object and look at it casually, read the label, give it a cursory glance, and walk on. They have not really looked at anything, because they are data-oriented and they figure that now they've got the answer to that and they know it's tenth century this or that, so they walk away from it.**
>
> **(Museum of the City, *Exploration of the Ways, Means and Values of Museum Communication with the Viewing Public*, 1969)**

It was the start of an explosion of curiosity that continues to this day. Educationalists and some curators began to pay close attention to visitor studies. Old assumptions were rocked, installations torn out and re-interpreted. In the USA, PR professionals were quick to realise the value of accumulating statistics, and began using them to inform their work and to commission studies of their own. Europe followed a decade or so later. The visitor is looking at us, but we are most definitely looking at the visitor.

Today, there are any number of books on market research and visitor studies – and some on monitoring and evaluation techniques. Professional institutions in every country have useful information on their websites and can help with advice and guidance. This chapter is designed to introduce research and evaluation as part of the process of marketing and public relations. It is not intended to be technical but will introduce basic concepts as well as some of today's idioms.

The process of research and analysis starts with the information required for the preparation of marketing and PR strategies as well as individual promotional plans. It includes the internal audit (examining your existing visitor and other data) and the external audit (examining the marketplace and trends).

Forward planning and individual campaigns will require more information about your existing visitors: who they are and what they are like, who else might be attracted, and can they be segmented using existing information? New ideas and developments will need to be explored in brainstorms and focus groups. Evaluating an established brand and launching a new one also requires research, testing creative ideas on the potential target audience. Tactical marketing plans and PR campaigns may require some additional research, as well as aligning with the marketing and PR strategy as a whole.

The second phase of research is all about monitoring and evaluation – setting sensible targets, introducing ways of measuring and analysing results. This applies just as much in traditional marketing and media activities as to websites and social media.

The bottom line of any campaign for visitor attractions such as museums, galleries and heritage sites is going to be the increase (or otherwise) in visitor numbers and spend. The growth and diversity of the communications tools available makes it more complicated to ascertain which part of the marketing communications spend was the most effective in achieving this. The graph in Chapter 7 showed how the balance is changing as 'paid-for' media – advertising, posters, etc. becomes less effective than 'earned' media – media coverage through PR and social media.

This chapter sets out the various tools for measuring and monitoring these activities, from basic collection of data, through quantitative and qualitative research, to evaluating the results and planning for the future.

COLLECTING VISITOR AND OTHER DATA

Visitor attractions should know how many visitors come each day, each week, each month and each year. Only by collecting such basic data on a consistent and accurate basis can decisions about marketing activities be made and measured. For charging attractions this should not be a problem – each paying visitor is recorded on entry, and computerised systems can provide additional information, such as time of day, type of visitor (student, adult, family, senior), as well as details on any discount voucher used; they may also process gift aid, if relevant. More advanced systems will also handle advance and online bookings with timed tickets, if applicable, and integrate income with your financial systems, providing 'real time' information not only on admission income, but also spend in the café and shop. This information can then be shared with all relevant departments.

Cultural attractions, museums and galleries should consult their peers as well as museum/gallery/historic associations for advice and assistance on choosing the best admissions system. Adoption or change to a new system will require dedicated time for staff training and teething problems, and is best done in a quiet season.

National museums in the UK, free since 2001, have introduced a variety of means for counting visitors (which have increased substantially in the period since). Some use a turnstile or issue a 'free' ticket; these are the most accurate measurements. Others consider this a barrier to visiting and rely on pressure pads or 'clickers' (staff record by clicking a counting device to monitor the number of visitors entering). Neither of these systems is very accurate, especially pressure pads, which count members of staff and visitors to offices alongside visitors to the museum. The most you can say about them is that they might identify a trend.

Those who charge for special exhibitions have introduced sophisticated systems, facilitating advance bookings, timed ticketing and accounting for admission income. They use this and other information to provide a series of contracted performance measurements annually to the Department for Culture, Media and Sport. These statistics are published on the DCMS website and include a detailed breakdown, as well as website visits, trading income and fundraising income. This plethora of performance indicators is not always comparable across the sector as a whole or with visitor attractions.

Remember that your basic data records 'visits' rather than 'visitors' – you also need to know the average frequency of visits per visitor over the year. You can then divide the overall visit figure to arrive at your 'unique' visitor attendance, which will be lower. The balance between 'new' and 'repeat' will influence your marketing, retail and catering offer. This unique visitor figure will also enable the museum to ascertain its share of the existing local market (people who regularly visit museums – at least once a year), and to set targets for growth in different market segments including non-visitors.

Your web statistics are part of your basic data. The most used overall measurement is currently unique website visitors, followed by page impressions. More advanced profiling can be obtained through Google analytics, a free tool, described later.

Susie Fisher, Director of the Susie Fisher Group, comments:

> It's important to make your evaluation work hard for you. Many museums spend the money and don't get nearly enough out of it, probably because evaluation has come to be seen as something of a box-ticking exercise.
>
> Two things to think about. An annual visitor survey, however short, begins to show you trends after a couple of years, and lets you see how your museum is doing. Qualitative evaluation can throw light on some quite difficult questions and put you on the right track at the outset. If you can frame the question, the chances are, focus groups can lead you to a useful answer.
>
> Here are two examples of ongoing projects:
>
> - Hackney Museum is working out what role it should play in the borough's response to the 2012 Olympics. Audiences have responded, and the Museum now knows how people feel about their borough, about the Olympics and how they expect their Museum to speak for them.
>
> - The V&A has expanded heroically in the past few years in terms of public learning programmes. But what is the unique nature of learning at the V&A? Searching and sympathetic interviews have now been set up with programme participants to explore exactly this.
>
> These are not easy questions, but they *can* be taken forward and this forward thinking transfers directly to planning. The evaluator needs to be seen as an ally in the camp, not as a box to be ticked. The whole process can be exhilarating. Briefing alone forces museum and evaluator to shine a light on their own ideas. It's a good way to start dismantling the barriers which lie in wait further down the line.

THE WIDER MARKETPLACE AND BENCHMARKING

As part of the external audit, visitor data for competing attractions should be analysed. There is more information available than most people are aware of. In the UK, visitor figures of national museums and galleries are published on the DCMS website. VisitEngland (and national tourist boards) publish annual visitor figures for tourist attractions, broken down by type of attraction and region. This information is provided by the attractions themselves. Information on overseas visitors, compiled from the International Passenger Survey, is also available online. This is a continuous survey based on interviews with a sample of visitors leaving the UK.

In England, museums, galleries and cultural attractions also have access to *Taking Part*, an ongoing national survey, commissioned by the DCMS, of those living in a representative cross-section of private households in England. The survey of adults was launched in July 2005, with the survey of children introduced in January 2006. The purpose is to develop the current knowledge base of engagement and non-engagement in culture, leisure and sport by gathering data on participation, attendance and attitudes across the sectors covered by the DCMS – arts, sports, museums, broadcasting, libraries, gambling and volunteering.

Taking Part for 2009/10 showed that 46.7% of adults had visited a museum, gallery or archive in the last year, an increase from the 2008/09 result of 44.5%. The DCMS note that although this is not a statistically significant change in this one year, it represents a continuation of the upward trend since 2006/07 which recorded 41.5%. It also found that museum visits are highest in London at 55.5% and lowest in the East Midlands at 39.5%.

The survey revealed that 75.7% of adults have engaged with the arts at least once in the last year. Proportions ranged from 69.7% in the West Midlands to 84.9% in the south east, a pattern that has proved continuous since 2005/06.

(DCMS 2010)

Comparing your performance measurements with overall regional figures through this survey, and with other attractions through benchmarking, is a useful way of analysing your trends. This is a good reason for using standard demographic profile breakdowns (as used in *Taking Part*, for example). Benchmarking can provide important feedback on particular marketing initiatives or customer services. However, it is important to make sure that you are part of a similar group of attractions or museums producing the figures against which yours are compared. In the UK, ALVA (Association of Leading Visitor Attractions) set up a benchmarking scheme for members and others in 1996, boosted by a 'mystery guest scheme' involving reciprocal visits among some 190 attractions. Read more about this in the case study introduced below and in the Appendix.

Others who conduct surveys and publish data on a regular basis include: the Arts Council, the Art Fund, the Strategic Contents Alliance, and the University of Leicester – Research Centre for Museums and Galleries (see Resources).

PROFILING RESEARCH

In addition to continuous data collection, museums and visitor attractions collect information on their visitors through regular profile research, as outlined earlier by Susie Fisher. This can be carried out once or twice a year, or preferably as a rolling process to iron out seasonal fluctuations. The aim is to collect information from a representative sample of visitors which can be applied to the total visitor number, providing demographic and qualitative information for forward planning and marketing.

Whenever possible, use a professional research agency (see how to choose an agency below). The results will be more accurate, professional and consistent. Questionnaires will be designed to be unambiguous and the interviews will be unbiased. The results will be presented in a detailed and professional way. Sometimes local business colleges will undertake a survey as part of a practical project for their students. These need careful supervision and instruction.

Self-completion surveys are the only option when funds are tight. It is better to put intensive effort into a short period of time with volunteers as canvassers, inviting visitors to take part. Computer terminals can be installed for one-off surveys – visitors are invited to fill in an online form at the end of their visit. None of these methods will provide a representative sample, however, because those participating will be self-selected.

Since 2003, research has been conducted across 45 museums and galleries in England as part of 'Renaissance in the Regions'. This continuous annual survey collects representative data (that is, the composition of the samples matches the existing visitor profile) on visitors, as well as information about visitor satisfaction, propensity to recommend and general attitudes towards the museums and galleries. The survey is carried out by BDRC and based on face-to-face interviews using CAP (computer-assisted personal interviewing) with hand-held PDAs (personal digital assistant devices) and includes up to 11,000 people per year.

Those planning new visitor-profiling research will find the standardised approach used for this research useful as it allows for comparisons with others. In this context, consider the responses to the 'satisfaction' question:

> **We have found that the highest satisfaction ratings are given by those visitors who are the least knowledgeable, the least experienced, are on their first visit, spent**

the least time visiting and are least likely to return. Conversely, those who are know-ledgeable, experienced, regular visitors who spent the longest time engaging with the objects and who are most likely to return gave lower satisfaction ratings.

(*Never Mind the Width Feel the Quality*, 2005,
Morris Hargreaves McIntyre)

Website surveys are an easy and inexpensive way of finding out more about your online visitors. Using a pop-up box, visitors logging on are invited at random to fill in a questionnaire about their experience of your website. However, bear in mind that this will be a self-selected audience and not necessarily representative of all those who use the website.

Web analytics is a more advanced method for investigating the actions of users on your website. Setting this up commercially could be expensive but the tools are available free from Google Analytics. Once you are signed up (Google will embed a tracking cookie on your site) you can customise up to 80 different reports, analysing where visitors come from – other sites, as well as where they are based through GPS (global positioning system) technology – which pages they look at and for how long, and identifying keywords which you can build back into your search engine optimisation programme (see also Chapter 7).

SEGMENTING YOUR AUDIENCE

Audience segmentation approaches were discussed in Chapter 7. Your profiling research is the starting point for segmenting your current audience and identifying new segments that might match your product with the local community. Segmentation can be very simple – based on age, for example. Compare it with the local population profile in your catchment area. Are there obvious gaps? More sophisticated lifestyle segmentation is based on postcodes, so use various means to collect these from your visitors – gift aid forms, mailings, and competitions offline and online. Here is a breakdown of the most commonly used segmentation systems:

'ACORN' (Caci) is a geodemographic segmentation of the UK population which segments small neighbourhoods, postcodes, or consumer households into 5 categories, 17 groups, and 56 types from 'Wealthy achievers' to 'Moderate means'.

'Mosaic' (Experian) is available in 20 countries. In the UK it classifies consumers into 61 types, aggregated into 11 groups. Mosaic Origins can be used to profile areas and communities by name, origin, ethnicity and language. It uses an individual's first and last names to find their most likely original home country.

'Social Grade' is the 'common currency' social classification (the ABC1C2 etc. system) originally developed as the National Readership Survey. It is used by the advertising industry and common in marketing and market research. The classification assigns every household to a 'class', usually based upon the occupation and employment status of the chief income earner, but in some cases using other characteristics. Social Grade is incompatible with the UK government social classifications (see below) and can only be properly determined by trained market research interviewers backed up by expert coders.

Taking Part – the survey undertaken by DCMS in the UK, referred to above – uses the relatively new occupationally based classification scheme 'NS-SEC' (National Statistics Socio-economic Classification) managed by the Office of National Statistics (ONS). This ranges the population from 'higher managerial and professional occupations' to 'never worked and long-term unemployed'. *Taking Part* also includes a breakdown by 'personal income', 'household structure', and 'qualifications', and analyses results using the ACORN categories where the 'urban prosperity' group is shown to be the most likely to visit museums.

Since 2001, the NS-SEC has been available for use in all official statistics and surveys. More recently, as a result of an EU Sixth Framework Programme project coordinated by ONS, a similar classification to NS-SEC has been produced for comparative European research, the European Socio-economic Classification.

Arts Council England has developed an arts-based segmentation system designed to provide greater knowledge of the levels and broad patterns of arts engagement in today's society, across both arts-attendance and participation. It incorporates a better understanding of the motivations and behaviours of different audience groups, both those who are already active in the arts and those who currently have little or no engagement. The inspiring names for the 13 segments in the Arts Council system are shown below.

HIGHLY ENGAGED

- Urban arts eclectic
- Traditional culture vultures

SOME ENGAGEMENT

- Fun, fashion and friends
- Mature explorers
- Dinner and a show
- Family and community focused

- Bedroom DJs
- Mid-life hobbyists
- Retired arts and crafts

NOT CURRENTLY ENGAGED

- Time-poor dreamers
- A quiet pint with the match
- Older and home-bound
- Limited means, nothing fancy

There are some other segmentation concepts in common usage. From the 'technology adoption lifecycle' (developed at Iowa State University), we get a bell graph showing the rate at which new ideas are adopted, and a series of descriptions – from the first group of people to take up the innovation, called 'innovators', followed by 'early adopters'; then come the early and late majority, and finally the 'laggards'. The names themselves suggest what sorts of people might fall into each group.

In this decade it has become common practice to refer to 'Generations X, Y and Z'. Precise definition of these groups varies from country to country but it also refers to the rate at which new technology is being adopted by different generations. Generation X are the 'baby-boomers' born after 1945, who use technology for convenience; while for Generation Y – people born after the mid-1970s – technology is embedded in every part of their lives. Generation Z can only be further down that line. For marketing purposes these definitions are far too wide as there will be variations within each generation group, based on social class, education, income, etc.

MEASURING ATTITUDES, PERCEPTIONS AND BRAND RECOGNITION

In a perfect world, we would all survey our visitors, using consistent questions and methodology, every year, and apply the results to our marketing plans. Some organisations are able to do this, and have a superior grasp on the nature of their business as a consequence. As a result, they are less likely to embark on what could be expensive qualitative audience research without clear objectives. Marketing and research departments in the cultural sector will be all too familiar with copies of surveys stashed away in filing cabinets, or pdfs in the website archives, looked at once or twice and then forgotten. So, consider carefully the reasons for conducting a one-off survey. It could be the launch of a new product or service; an evaluation of an exhibition or programme of events; to demonstrate accountability and value for money; to assist in attracting sponsorship; to inform business planning of a new commercial service; or to help in developing a niche audience.

Some of this research could be built into your regular visitor-profiling research. In other cases you need to set up a separate survey, deciding which format to use, depending on the budget and who you want to target.

Focus groups are valuable when developing a new product or service, but only work if they are professionally organised with carefully selected groups. This means an investment in time and money, briefing the researcher/facilitator, being on hand during discussions, and ensuring that the results are in some way conclusive and informative.

Brainstorms have been referred to earlier (Chapter 5) as a way of developing your marketing strategy – through the SWOT and the PEST – as well as stimulating new ideas around your branding. They can be informal, consisting of just a few colleagues around the table, or more elaborate away-days with board members involving professional input. It works best when the conversation is led by someone not directly involved in the activity under discussion. Ideas should be recorded and summarised, and a mechanism agreed in advance for how the recommendations will be carried forward

In-depth interviews carried out among a sample of your target group should be professionally organised and take place over the phone or in person by experienced interviewers. The success of this method depends on how the questions have been framed or 'modelled' in order to obtain useful answers from members of a new audience group, or from influencers and decision-makers. This should be a way of gauging popular perceptions, misconceptions, and levels of interest in your brand, as well as visitors' engagement with your displays and programmes, and a way to measure outcomes. In their report *Never Mind the Width Feel the Quality*, Morris Hargreaves McIntyre explain the four key drivers for visits – social, intellectual, emotional and spiritual, with further breakdowns in each section. They have developed a set of norms based on their research – museums (more social) and art galleries (more spiritual) – against which we can all measure our visitors' engagement and outcomes. They have devised a useful 'Hierarchy of Visitor Engagement' displayed on their website: www.lateralthinkers.com.

Observational research can also be used to test the functionality and use of your website as part of a redesign. Research of this kind has developed sophisticated techniques for observing visitors in cultural attractions to gauge their involvement with displays and exhibitions.

An effective and reasonably cheap way of buying national or regional qualitative research is to take part in an *Omnibus survey*. These national 'polls' by Ipsos MORI and other organisations are conducted as telephone interviews of a statistically representative cross-section of the British public on a variety of subjects. You buy as many questions as you like, but yours will be one of maybe up to 20 different subjects. This can be a good way for a large museum or heritage attractions to measure awareness of its activities or of special promotions.

You can organise your own *group session* or *hall test* to gauge public views on a proposed development by inviting local residents to your venue, providing some refreshments as a bait. Recruit from existing visitors but also from others who are not regular attendees to get a more representative sample. It is a way of obtaining the views of a cross-section of people, but you need to make sure that there are plenty of staff on hand to gauge people's views, and then follow up with a meeting to gather and discuss responses.

PR surveys have developed something of a bad name. These are opinion-seeking snapshots designed to bolster a particular event or campaign. As long as they are honestly compiled and used in a light-hearted way there is no reason why this kind of survey cannot be quoted in a press release (with the proviso of the small number usually interviewed).

A new concept in this area is *crowd-sourcing*. This is more to do with problem-solving, and consists of inviting anyone, via the web, to contribute to the solution of a problem. You may get thousands of responses or none at all. The challenge is to use any of the information in a useful way.

SETTING TARGETS, MONITORING AND EVALUATION

It is important to set targets for your promotional campaigns so that you can monitor progress, intervene if they are not working, and evaluate the results. Often evaluation is an after-thought put in place once the activity has happened. It makes much more sense to build it in from the beginning. With so many different tools available to marketing and PR professionals it can be difficult without evaluation to identify which communications channels are working best for your particular campaign, and thereby to budget effectively in the future.

Marketing in the commercial sector is judged by its cost effectiveness, or return on investment (ROI). This is measured by the amount of spend generated by your customers against the cost of marketing and PR. There is no reason why cultural attractions should not apply the same discipline, as long as other measures of success are included, for example visitor numbers, satisfaction rates and propensity to return. The Kew Gardens case study introduced at the end of this chapter is about an evaluation carried out by Kew's corporate communications team, following the exhibition of the work of US sculptor Dale Chihuly. It provides a wealth of financial measures but also includes a qualitative judgement:

Qualitative outcomes

- The exhibition was judged to have attracted a new audience segment: a significantly higher percentage of young professionals (25–35-year-old couples) and that group will be more likely to visit Kew in the future.

- It was considered to have changed perceptions of Kew from 'just a garden' to something more relevant to a wider audience.

- It was recognised as having attracted a more arts-based audience, supporting future aspirations to open up Kew's art collection, including opening the new gallery of Botanic art.

By focusing on your range of targets and not just the bottom line, you are gathering useful information for future activities. It will also give management the information they need to persuade funders and to raise finance for future programmes.

Monitoring marketing and PR campaigns

In all of your marketing activity you should include a 'call to action'. This means being very clear about what you want people to do as a result of looking at your communication to them. The same will apply to your media coverage, which ideally should include dates, times and website details, as well as key messages. In paid advertising or joint editorial promotions, offline and online, it is possible to frame this 'call to action' as an incentive, special offer, vouchers or a competition, thus making it easier to track responses and add people to your database for future promotions. Specific targets for a new exhibition or a programme of events could include some or all of the following:

- Visitor numbers – to attract an additional XX% of visitors over a 6-week period; or if the entry to the special exhibition is separate, to attract XX% more visitors compared with a previous exhibition.

- Analyse your audiences by type of admission charge – groups, students, children, etc. – to see whether you are meeting basic targets in each group. For a more sophisticated breakdown, identifying new audiences, commission a visitor survey either with interviews, use of computer terminals, or self-completion questionnaires (as outlined above).

- Set targets for increased spend in shop and café, based on exhibition-related merchandise or special menus, or just general spend.

- Set targets for website visits and page impressions based on the specific pages or microsite (with its own url) related to the exhibition or event.

- Measure the returns on any special offer, e.g. 2 for 1, 'kids go free', etc. Such offers can be placed in local newspapers or be printed out from your website.

- Set targets for social media activities such as Twitter and Facebook and the rate of subsequently generated website visits.

- Media coverage – set specific targets, either for total value, or broken into different media categories. Follow through with an analysis at the end of the campaign. Consider commissioning a more sophisticated media analysis.

- Set up (or add to) your contact database through visitors to the museum and the website.

- Are your key messages being absorbed? Some informal analysis of this may be possible from visitors' comments on cards or a visitors' book. For a more professional approach, use visitor research and/or media analysis.

- Measure the overall success – this can be partly a subjective judgement based on opinions of critics, visitors and other influencers, collected at the end of the exhibition/campaign. Visitor services staff who come into direct contact with visitors might have a valuable contribution to make.

- Recommendations for the future – the final analysis should look critically at the results and suggest which communications channels should be used in similar, future campaigns.

When planning a *general awareness-raising campaign*, start with benchmark research among stakeholders and the public. At the end of the campaign, the benchmark research should be repeated and measured against the targets set at the beginning. It is tempting to carry out this part without doing the initial benchmark study, but it will not have the same relevance if the starting point is not clear.

Museums, galleries and cultural attractions are actively engaged in *developing new audiences*, including the socially excluded and others who are hard to reach (see Chapter 8). Over the year, a number of different activities may have been implemented across the organisation, whether by the education department or the special events team, or through PR and niche marketing activities. Targets should have been set for these in the audience development plan as part of the marketing strategy. Finding time and resources to collect the results and relate it to the original strategy is not always easy – but it is essential. The analysis should look critically at the various activities, the communication channels used, and the results, so that mistakes are not repeated and successful initiatives can be identified and included as part of ongoing marketing activities.

Evaluating media coverage

Media services companies have developed some useful tools and services to assist PR departments and agencies in measuring media coverage in a meaningful way. These values are changing as the printed media decline and online and social media grow.

Your media evaluation now has to include these media outlets, but the collection of press cuttings and the monitoring of the broadcast media remain important, as they are major influences on decision-makers and on other media.

A small museum or gallery, mainly concerned with achieving local media coverage, can set up an effective in-house monitoring system which ensures that all local newspapers, local websites and radio are well covered. Any additional coverage in a national magazine or newspaper will probably come as the result of a press visit – arranged by the local tourist board, for example – and again, it should be possible to keep track of it. Specialist campaigns – aimed at archaeological publications, or art or garden magazines, for example – can also be monitored in-house, allowing for the longer lead time of such publications. Use some of the following measurements:

- Target media and others, broken down by type
- Initial targets in terms of coverage set for each type, including photographs
- Actual coverage achieved against each group
- Tone/key messages – a simple evaluation of the tone or key messages achieved
- Advertising value equivalent – AVE (see below).

Any larger museum or institution initiating a major PR campaign or appointing a PR agency should invest in a media monitoring service. Some of these companies are listed in Resources. Services may include some or all of the following:

- volume and favourability of coverage
- delivery of key messages
- issues and trends
- key publications and journalist tracking
- full intelligence on competitors' media presence
- breakdown by brands/services/products/business areas
- impact achieved
- media type
- opportunities to see, regional and socio-economic profile
- reach and frequency of coverage in terms of actual number of people against tightly defined core-target audiences
- concise summary of entire report
- full qualitative analysis in easy-to-understand explanatory text.

Media monitoring serves several purposes. While it is essential for the end-research of the campaigns referred to above, it is also part of awareness and tracking research.

So read the cuttings to see if the coverage is 'on-message' and pick up any negative comments and misinformation. Respond immediately where appropriate (see also Chapter 16 on how to handle hostile media campaigns). Notify front-of-house staff about errors that may affect visitor expectations.

The AVE (advertising value equivalent) favoured by clients and PR agencies has always been suspect as a measurement because it equates editorial with advertising and, more controversially, it enhances 'editorial' coverage with a multiplier to indicate its greater 'worth' or impact on the reader. With the decline in the printed media, its days are probably numbered, as are some of the other measurements, for example OTS (opportunity to see – an advertising industry measure) which records the opportunities to see a message but gives no indication that people actually looked at the message or absorbed it.

The PR industry in Europe and the US has developed new ways of measuring the impact of public relations. A new system launched in 2011 is led by AMEC (International Association for Measurement and Evaluation of Communication) and is supported by CIPR (Chartered Institute of Public Relations) and by PRSA (Public Relations Society of America). It is based on the Barcelona principles (developed at a conference in 2010) and is designed to provide a comprehensive way of measuring PR impact. Toolkits will be available from national PR associations. The principles are set out as follows:

- **To demonstrate the value of PR and the attainment of both PR and business objectives – not only in terms of outputs but what the campaign has led to (the outcomes – for example behavioural change)**

- **To facilitate more effective audience engagement and to feed into PR planning**

- **To help build the credibility and influence of PR within organisations, and demonstrate its contribution to strategic business decision-making and organisational success**

- **To analyse key message pick-up, adoption and reproduction among publics and those who influence publics**

- **To gather intelligence about a sector, trends and issues (historic and future) and how an organisation and its peers and competitors are regarded**

- **To provide a benchmark against which to measure the effectiveness of a PR programme**

- **To provide a 'hard' measure of success to reinforce the case for PR.**

Measuring social media

Social media is having a profound impact on PR practice – how we influence, communicate and engage with our publics, internally and externally. The challenge for PR and marketing practitioners is how to identify, track and analyse the thousands of conversations, tweets, posts, comments and other content about organisations, the issues that impact on them, or their markets, competitors, products or services. But it is not just about tracking, or trying to understand how influential a particular commentator or participant is. It is about identifying what conversations the organisation should participate in (or initiate), and understanding how all of these interactions and mentions (the 'outputs') impact on the organisation. In other words, what impact do these outputs have on the organisation's goals?

A wide range of social media monitoring tools are available (sometimes called social web analytics, listening platforms, social media analytics, or social marketing analytics) via media evaluation companies or tool providers that can deliver all or some of the following:

■ Track blogs, forums, comments, tweets, online news, social networks and video for mentions of your organisation or client and your competitors

■ Analyse these mentions and produce reports which summarise the number of Twitter followers, comment counts, tweet counts, retweets, @replies, DMs, comments, ratings, YouTube comments/ratings, media type and sentiment (positive, neutral, negative)

■ Segment this data by geography, media type and language, and identify links and sources, or segment by keywords

■ Present this information in various reporting formats, including 'dashboards' that summarise key data points.

This type of analysis can help to inform the PR programme, by identifying what people are saying about your organisation or client and the key issues and trends, and by tracking active commentators, user responses, likes, comments and actions. The CIPR, AMEC and other bodies (see above) are working to identify ways in which output analysis can be linked to outcomes, because this is the real measure of the success of online marketing and PR activity.

Metrics such as the number of Twitter followers or Facebook friends do not measure influence per se (a participant with 60 Twitter followers may be more influential in terms of your audiences than a participant with 6,000 followers, for example). It is important not to confuse popularity with influence. Therefore, as with traditional public relations campaigns, it is essential to try to understand and identify those who influence your target audiences, for example:

■ Are your customers among your Twitter followers or Facebook friends?

■ Are those media contacts who have influence quoting or linking to particular bloggers or tweeters?

- Does the journalist/blogger/commentator/tweeter have an impact on decisions, for example through consumer reviews or by recommendations to family and friends?

- Does the journalist/blogger/commentator have authority? For example, a tool such as Technorati will give an influence score based on the number of blogs linking to a particular blog.

- The number of people who point to a journalist, blogger or commentator is another indicator of authority.

The growth in social media has led to a raft of products and tools claiming to measure influence. According to CIPR, we should be clear that some of these tools have opaque ways of measuring influence which may provide little or no insight into real influence. (The Tate case study introduced below and in the Appendix has some reassuring comments on this.) Similarly, a whole new language has developed around social media. Keep up with developments and language by asking people around you (especially younger members of staff). Attend seminars, check professional websites, and subscribe to e-newsletters.

Economic impact surveys

It is of increasing importance to have the ability to demonstrate the value of museums as economic generators. In 2006 the National Museum Directors' Conference (NMDC) in the UK commissioned a far-reaching economic impact study which was updated in 2010 as 'The case for museums: Museums deliver'. Both of these documents are available on the NMDC website.

Major galleries such as the Metropolitan in New York (see Chapter 8) have commissioned economic impact studies to show the value of individual exhibitions to the local economy. English Heritage carries out an annual survey, *Heritage Counts*, examining the value and economic impact of heritage. Below is a short extract from the 2010 report:

HERITAGE COUNTS

Heritage Counts is produced on behalf of the Historic Environment Forum. It provides evidence on the wider social and economic role of heritage, assesses the state of the historic environment through analysing data trends, and provides an update of the policies affecting the historic environment in the last year. The key findings from this year's report are outlined below. This year *Heritage Counts* explores the economic impact of the historic environment. Key findings from the report include:

- *Historic environment regeneration.* £1 of investment in the historic environment generates £1.6 of additional economic activity over a ten-year period.

- *Investment in the historic environment attracts businesses.* One in four businesses agree that the historic environment is an important factor in deciding where to locate, the same as for road access.

- *Investing in the historic environment brings more visitors to local areas and encourages them to spend more.* Approximately one in five visitors to areas which have had historic environment investment spend more in the local area than before and one in four businesses has seen the number of customers increase.

- *Heritage tourism is a vital economic sector,* directly generating £7.4 billion of GDP annually and supporting 195,000 jobs.

- *Heritage attracts inbound visitors.* A third of all international tourists cite heritage as the main reason why they come to the UK.

- *Historic environment attractions generate local wealth.* Half of all jobs created by historic environment attractions are in local businesses.

(English Heritage 2010)

CHOOSING A RESEARCH AGENCY

For visitor profiling, in-depth research, focus groups, and economic impact studies, you will need to work with a research agency or consultant. How do you choose one? First decide what it is you want the agency to do. Is it just advice or a full-scale research project? Work up a draft brief which includes as much information as possible, including what it is you expect from the research, the timescale and budget.

You may want to invite several agencies to put in competitive bids for your work. It is not reasonable to ask more than three or four agencies to bid. There are many different types of agencies, so take advice from others in the sector, or your professional association, and do some searching on the internet to make sure they cover your requirements, whether it is interviewing, focus groups, data processing, or benchmarking.

If you have three or four proposals to choose from, how do you decide? Ask yourself: Have they understood what it is that we want? Do they have experience in the sector? Are they offering value for money – as far as you can tell? Can they meet our timetable? And do they fit with the culture of our organisation, stakeholders and visitors?

Once appointed, make sure, as with any consultancies, that there is one person on the in-house team in overall charge; that there is an initial briefing involving all those who will be affected by the research process; that there are regular meetings; and that the timetable does not slip. The final results should be shared with all your colleagues, as set out below. (There is more information from the Market Research Society – see Resources.)

SO WHAT IS IT FOR? UTILISING YOUR DATA

The end product of any research or evaluation should be shared with all those who could benefit, excluding any market-sensitive or confidential matters. You could set up a seminar with your colleagues, perhaps including your partners in the city or region (depending on the subject), and ask the consultant to present the results, followed by a discussion. Where appropriate, a summary of the results should be disseminated to all staff throughout the organisation, to better inform their work, and to add to institutional understanding of visitors and of subsequent marketing strategy.

Bear in mind that some information could be regarded as sensitive or could easily be misinterpreted by the media whose grasp of statistics is not always good. What might look like an endorsement to you – 60% of visitors approved of your project, for example – could be re-interpreted as two in five were against it! The recommendations arising from the research should then be part of the next stage of your forward plan, marketing or PR campaigns. Do not just add another report to the dusty pile on the shelf or in your electronic archives – act!

CASE STUDIES IN THE APPENDIX

Case Study 17A: Benchmarking research in action at the Association of Leading Visitor Attractions

Alan Love, BDRC Continental, offers suggestions to help you design the research you need to build a clear idea of how visitors regard the experience of visiting the museum.

Case Study 17B: Evaluation of the Dale Chihuly exhibition 'Gardens of Glass' at Kew

It is a requirement of forward planning that reasons for past success and failure are thoroughly understood. Here is a summary of the evaluation carried out by the Corporate Communications team at the Royal Botanic Gardens, Kew, following their exhibition of the work of US sculptor Dale Chihuly entitled 'Gardens of Glass'. The evaluation was led by Tina Houlton, now Acting Director of Communications and Commercial Activities. The evaluation was made more difficult by virtue of the fact that the exhibition was not freestanding with a separate admission charge – but was scattered throughout the gardens and included in the general admission ticket to the site as a whole, which was free to children and Friends of Kew.

Case Study 17C: Measuring social media success: advice from the Tate

Pete Gomori, Marketing Manager, Tate Modern and Jesse Ringham, Digital Communications Manager, Tate, give some advice on measuring social media success.

CHAPTER 18

NOTES AND RESOURCES

Awards and prizes

Copyright

Data protection and freedom of information

Digital technology and social media

Fundraising and commercial activities

Marketing concepts and tools

Marketing and audience measurements

Media and metrics

Partnerships and promotions

Professional associations and representative organisations

Publications (books, e-news, magazines and websites)

Research (international and national societies and organisations)

Sustainability

Tourism and travel trade information

AWARDS AND PRIZES

This is a short list of UK and international awards. There are many more – check the trade press and the internet.

AAM Awards – organised by the American Association of Museums http://www.aam-us.org

Art Fund Prize – annual, organised by the Museum Prize Trust www.artfundprize.org.uk

England for Excellence – regional heats leading to national awards organised by VisitEngland www.enjoyengland.com

European Heritage Awards – annual, awarded by the European Commission and Europa Nostra www.europanostra.org

European Museum of the Year Award – annual, awarded by the European Museum Forum (Council of Europe) http://www.europeanmuseumforum.eu/

Jodi Awards for best practice including websites – organised by the Jodi Mattes Trust http://www.jodiawards.org.uk/

Museums and Heritage Awards – awarded annually by the Museums and Heritage Show www.museumsandheritage.com/awards

Royal Institute of British Architects' Stirling Prize www.architecture.com

Webby Awards – international internet award presented by the International Academy of Digital Arts and Sciences www.webby.com

COPYRIGHT

Copyright regulations vary from country to country. Consult these websites:

European Union: http://ec.europa.eu/internal_market/copyright

Museum Copyright Group: http://www.museumscopyright.org.uk

National Portrait Gallery http://www.npg.org.uk/about/creators.php

Newspaper Licensing Agency (NLA) represents 1400 titles and licenses the copying of newspaper content under the authority of the Copyright Designs and Patent Act 1988. www.nla.co.uk

Strategic Contents Alliance: http://sca.jiscinvolve.org/wp/ipr-publications/

US Copyright Office www.copyright.gov

DATA PROTECTION AND FREEDOM OF INFORMATION

Data Protection Act UK – www.ico.gov.uk

Data Protection in Europe as a whole – http://ec.europa.eu/justice/policies/privacy

UK Information Commissioners' Office ICO: Freedom of Information Act 2000 www.ico.gov.uk

United States Freedom of Information Act www.state.gov

(Similar legislation applies in Australia and many other countries.)

DIGITAL TECHNOLOGY AND SOCIAL MEDIA

A brief introduction to some of the language and services in new media.

Apps is an abbreviation for application. An app is a piece of software. It can run on the internet, on your computer, or on your phone or other electronic device. Available from Apple (for iPhones and Macs); from Google and from Android.com (for smartphones etc.)

Blogs are personal comments – journalistic features published through Wordpress.com, Blogspot (Google) or through your own website.

Culture Mondo is an international network for online cultural portals www.culture mondo.org

Facebook – social network (independent) www.facebook.com

Flickr – picture-hosting network (Yahoo) www.flickr.com

Google Analytics (free) measures your advertising ROI as well as tracking your Flash, video, and social networking sites and applications – www.google.com/analytics

GPS (global positioning system) is a US Air Force-owned service providing users with positioning, navigation, and timing; 24 satellites transmit one-way signals that give the current GPS satellite position and time, picked up by worldwide monitor and control stations. GPS receives and uses the transmitted information to calculate the user's three-dimensional position and time. http://www.gps.gov/systems/gps/

iTunes hosts thousands of downloadable music and other free podcasts www.apple.com/itunes/podcasts

Linked-In – professional network (independent) www.linkedin.com

Meta tags enable webmasters to provide search engines with information about their sites. Each system processes only the meta tags they understand and ignores the rest. Meta tags are added to the <head>section of your HTML page and generally look like this: <!DOCTYPE HTML PUBLIC '-//W3C//DTD HTML 4.01 Transitional//EN' 'http://www.w3.org/TR/html4/loose.dtd'> (Source Google.com)

Myspace – social network (News Corporation) www.myspace.com

Podcasts are digital audio or video files. Available from websites and/or iTunes and downloaded on an iPod or to a computer.

Seb Chan at Powerhouse Museum – keep up to date on the latest digital developments http://www.powerhousemuseum.com/dmsblog/

Technorati – popularity index for user-generated media www.technorati.com

Twitter – sharing network (independent) www.twitter.com

Url (Uniform Resource Locator) – website address

YouTube – video-sharing site (Google) www.youtube.com

Wi-Fi – wireless network – managed by the Wi-Fi Alliance, a global non-profit industry association. The Wi-Fi CERTIFIED™ program was launched in 2000. www.wi-fi.org

Wikipedia – a user-maintained information website www.wikipedia.org

FUNDRAISING AND COMMERCIAL ACTIVITIES

ACE (Association of Cultural Enterprises) – a membership organisation which promotes commercial enterprise in museums and galleries. www.acenterprises.org.uk

Arts and Business – provides advice, seminars and resources for fundraisers in the UK www.artsandbusiness.org.uk

Association of Fundraising Professionals US – membership organisation http://www.afpnet.org/

CultureLabel – an online shop which promotes the sale of museum and art gallery souvenirs and products www.culturelabel.com

Gift Aid – registered charities can increase their donations and admission charges from UK income-tax payers by registering for gift aid. Check current regulations with the Inland Revenue at http://www.hmrc.gov.uk/charities/gift_aid/index.htm

Giving Markets collect charitable donations online, e.g. Just Giving, Virgin Money Giving, The Big Arts Give, Kickstarter, See the Difference.

Licensing for venues/events: check with your local authority.

Locations and venue finders – agencies which assist film companies and those looking for party and conference venues – http://www.locationsindex.com; Fresh Locations at http://www.freshlocations.com

National Art Collections Fund – Art Fund – independent membership organisation which funds art in the UK www.artfund.org/

National Council of Voluntary Organisations provides advice to charitable organisations in the UK http://www.ncvo-vol.org.uk/

Volunteering England is the leading development agency and works across all sectors to increase the quality and quantity of volunteering www.volunteering.org.uk

MARKETING CONCEPTS AND TOOLS

Ansoff Matrix, first published in the 1950s by Igor Ansoff in the Harvard Business Review as a framework for expanding business activities

Barcode technology used on print and in press advertising is a unique matrix which can be scanned by a mobile device and then link to a website page, a special offer, or to respond to a message. A number of companies now offer this service. Search for 'Barcodes in Marketing'.

The Black Swan: The Impact of the Highly Improbable by Nassim Nicholas Taleb, (Penguin, 2007)

Peter Drucker (who died in 2005, aged 95) was 'the inventor of modern management' according to another management guru, Tom Peters. The Drucker Institute (of management studies) is at Claremont College, California. http://www.drucker institute.com/

Leaflet and door-to door-distribution: Find a local or national distributor through your local council, tourist board, or by searching the web.

The Leisure Pass Group provides smartcard solutions for the tourist industry www.leisurepass.com

The long tail, first identified in 2004 by Chris Anderson, editor of *Wired Magazine*. His book, *The Long Tail: Why the Future of Business is Selling Less of More* (Hyperion, 2006) has been followed by others on the same theme www.longtail.com

Marketing Transformation Leadership Forum set up by the Chartered Institute of Marketing as a group of marketing professionals to generate thought leadership and inspire transformation. http://www.marketing-transformation.com/our-findings/

MBWA (Management by Walking Around) – popular management technique advocated by the management guru Tom Peters (amongst others) is exactly what it says.

Product Life Cycle describes the stages through which individual products develop over time. The classic product life cycle has four stages: introduction, growth, maturity, and decline.

SEO (Search Engine Optimisation) – find companies offering this service through the web or your professional organisation.

The Tipping Point: How Little Things Can Make a Big Difference by Malcolm Gladwell (Abacus 2000)

USP – unique selling point

MARKETING AND AUDIENCE MEASUREMENTS

ACORN (A Classification of Residential Neighbourhoods) segmentation by postcode www.caci.co.uk

ALVA (Association of Leading Visitor Attractions) provides benchmarking survey and other services www.alva.org.uk

Arts Council England: *New Audiences* (2004) – special grant-funded programme targeting hard-to-reach audiences, and run over two years www.artscouncil.org

Arts Council England segmentation by arts use and types www.artscouncil.org.uk/aboutus/research

The Art Fund surveys trends in museum and gallery purchasing and other issues www.artfund.org.uk

BDRC Continental – research company www.bdrc.co.uk

Census (current) www.ons.gov.uk

Census (past and archived) www.nationalarchives.gov.uk/records/census-records.htm

EU Euro Barometer of cultural participation http//:epp.eurostat.ec.europa.eu

EU statistics website http//:europa.eu

European Socio-economic Classification funded through the Sixth Framework programme of the European Union, was undertaken between October 2004 and September 2006 by a consortium of nine institutions http://www.iser.essex.ac.uk/research/esec

Generations X, Y and Z – precise definition of these groups varies from country to country

International Passenger Survey samples visitors leaving UK for tourism trends on a monthly basis www.statistics.gov.uk

The London Hub (lead organisation for London's non-national museums) published *Insight: A survey of the London museums market*, in 2008 www.mla.gov.uk/renaissancelondon

Morris Hargreaves McIntyre – creative and intelligent cultural sector management consultancy www.lateralthinkers.com

Mosaic UK – social and household segmentation in 20 countries www.experian.com

NS-SEC (National Statistics Socio-economic Classification) introduced in 2001 for all official statistics and surveys in the UK www.ons.gov.uk

Office of National Statistics UK www.ons.gov.uk

Renaissance in the Regions annual visitor survey www.mla.gov.uk.

Social Grade is the ABC1C2 etc. system) developed as the National Readership Survey and maintained by the Market Research Society www.mrs.org.uk

Strategic Contents Alliance works on behalf of the public sector to encourage use and reuse of digital content www.jicsinvolve.org

Taking Part in England – annual tracking cultural and sports participation survey, Department for Culture, Media and Sport www.culture.gov.uk

Technology adoption lifecycle was developed at Iowa State University http://www.it.iastate.edu/

University of Leicester – Research Centre for Museums and Galleries http://www.le.ac.uk/museumstudies/research/rcmg.html

US Census Bureau http//:www.census.gov.

Visitor Attractions Survey – annual survey of visitor attractions including museums, galleries, historic houses and heritage sites www.enjoyengland.com

Web analytics, see Google Analytics

MEDIA AND METRICS

Audit Bureau of Circulation (ABC) (UK) is owned by the media industry and independently verifies and reports on media performances www.abc.org.uk/

Audit Bureau of Circulations (US) – a not-for-profit organisation providing media audits etc. www.accessabc.com

AVE (advertising value equivalent) is calculated by measuring cuttings in column inches or centimetres and multiplying this figure by the equivalent advertising cost. Some apply an editorial multiplier as editorial is considered more impactful than advertising

BARB (Broadcasting Audience Research Board) responsible for producing television viewing estimates, obtained from a panel of television-owning private homes representing 26 million UK households www.barb.co.uk

BBC website is a useful source of news and information, including how to set up Newsfeeds http://www.bbc.co.uk/news/10628494.

Broadcasting complaints in the UK are now handled by Ofcom – see below

Coalition for Innovative Media Measurement (CIMM) founded by 14 leading television content providers, media agencies and advertisers to promote innovation in audience measurement for television and cross-platform media www.cimm-us.org

Crowd-sourcing – outsourcing to an undefined, generally large group of people in the form of an open call through social media

Flat Earth News: An Award-winning Reporter Exposes Falsehood, Distortion and Propaganda in the Global Media by Nick Davies (Chatto & Windus 2008) – an attack on the newspaper industry, regulators and the PR industry

Institute of Practitioners in Advertising (IPA) UK is a membership organisation offering a variety of services, including TouchPoints which is a multi-media database providing insights into how people use all types of media. www.ipa.co.uk.

Intranets – created in the 1990s as private networks using Internet Protocol

Media and internet monitoring – a range of companies provide these services. Here are just three: Durrants – UK's leading media planning, monitoring and evaluation agency www.durrants.co.uk; Nielsen Media Research (see also below) http://www.mediamonitoring.com/; Cision – the leader in global media tracking solutions www.uk.cision.com

Media services – dozens of companies offer press release writing and distribution services (watch out for 'free' services – likely to add to media spam); also press cuttings, broadcast and internet monitoring and analysis. Seek advice from your professional PR association. Here are a few operating in the UK and internationally: Arts Media Contacts http://www.artsmediacontacts.co.uk; PR Newswire www.prnewswire.co.uk; Metrica (including Durrants) http://www.metrica.net, www.durrants.co.uk; Nielsen Media Research http://www.mediamonitoring.com; Cision www.uk.cision.com

Media Spamming Charter – full text at www.cipr.org.uk

Media training – consult your professional PR association for advice on training in your part of the world

Newspaper Licensing Agency (UK) (see Copyright above)

Newspaper Society UK publishes Media Portfolio database, New Society Database and JICREG (the Joint Industry Committee for Regional Media Research) www.newspapersoc.org.uk

Nielsen provides rankings and information to the advertising industry on broadcasting, online, mobile and social media across the world www.nielsen.com

Ofcom is the UK communications regulator of TV and radio sectors, fixed line telecoms and mobiles, plus the airwaves over which wireless devices operate and handles consumer complaints www.ofcom.org.uk

PPA (Periodicals Publishers Association) (UK) has nearly 200 publishing company members, representing 3,000 consumer, business and customer magazines, many now publishing online www.ppa.co.uk

Press Complaints Commission (UK) – independent body dealing with complaints about the editorial content of newspapers www.pcc.org.uk/

Ripoff Report – independent (US) consumer complaints website www.ripoffreport.com

RSS (Really Simple Syndiaction) – newsfeed from selected websites

TouchPoints – see below Institute of Practitioners in Advertising (IPA) UK

PARTNERSHIPS AND PROMOTIONS

There are thousands of partnerships and promotions. Here are few to look out for.

Black History Month in October in the UK celebrates the Afro-Caribbean heritage and culture www.black-history-month.co.uk

Corporate social responsibility (CSR) – a company's commitment to be accountable to its stakeholders www.crsnetwork.com

Museums and Galleries Month, first launched in 2000 in the UK following the successful annual Museums Week, was organised by the charity Campaign for Museums (led by Loyd Grossman, until 2008). Its activities were transferred to Culture24, see below.

Museums at Night takes place in European countries in the middle of May; it was launched by the Culture Department of the French Government in 2005, supported by the Council of Europe. In the UK it is organised by Culture24, see below. www.nuitdesmusees.culture.fr

SHARE – Museums in the East of England have developed a different kind of partnership – Support, Help and Advice from Renaissance East www.mla.gov.uk/renaissance eastofengland

PROFESSIONAL ASSOCIATIONS AND REPRESENTATIVE ORGANISATIONS

Accreditation – museum registration was established in the UK in 1988. In 2004 it became accreditation and has led the way in raising museum standards www.mla.gov.uk

ACE (Association of Cultural Enterprises) – a membership organisation promoting commercial best practice in the UK's cultural and heritage sector by providing training and networking www.acenterprises.org

Agenda – international communications agency based in Paris, organises international annual Cultural PR Marketing conference http://www.communicatingthemuseum.com/

AMEC (International Association for Measurement and Evaluation of Communication) – global trade body for media research agencies www.amecorg.com

American Association of Museums (AAM) – founded in 1906, now represents more than 15,000 museum professionals and volunteers, 3,000 institutions, and 300 corporate members http://www.aam-us.org

American Marketing Association (AMA) – professional association for individuals and organisations. Marketing Power is the AMA's information and sharing website www.marketingpower.com

Arts & Business connects companies and individuals to cultural organisations www.artsandbusiness.org.uk

Arts Council – the national development agency for the arts; England www.arts council.org.uk; Scotland www.scottisharts.org.uk; Wales www.artswales.org.uk/; Northern Ireland www.artscouncil-ni.org

Arts Marketing Association – membership organisation for arts professionals www.a-m-a.co.uk

Association of Independent Museums (AIM) provides advice and support for independent museums throughout the UK www.aim-museums.co.uk

British Association of Friends of Museums (BAFM) – established in 1973, now has over 200 member organisations www.bafm.org.uk

CERP (Confédération Européenne des Relations Publiques) represents about 22,000 PR practitioners, consultants throughout Europe www.cerp.org

Chartered Institute of Marketing (CIMG) – membership organisation promoting marketing in the UK www.cimg.co.uk

Chartered Institute of Public Relations (CIPR) membership organisation for PR professionals in the UK www.cipr.co.uk

Collections Trust is the UK organisation for collections in museums www.collections trust.org.uk

Department for Culture, Media and Sport (UK) www.culture.gov.uk

Disability Discrimination Act in the UK – has been incorporated and expanded by the Equality Act 2010 www.direct.gov.uk. See also Americans with Disability Act 1990 (US) and other countries.

Engage – the national organisation for gallery education www.engage.org.uk

English Heritage – responsible for the built and natural heritage www.english-heritage.org.uk/

European Union Culture and Education Committee http://www.europarl.europa.eu/committees/cult_home_en.htm

Heritage Lottery Fund uses money from the National Lottery to provide grants to museums, galleries and heritage attractions www.hlf.org.uk

Historic Houses Association (HHA) supports around 1,500 privately owned historic houses, stately homes, castles and gardens www.hha.org.uk/

ICOM – the international organisation for museums and professionals http://icom.museum

MLA (Museums Libraries and Archives Council) – government-funded organisation to support the sector in the UK. To be wound up by March 2012, with some functions transferred to the Arts Council (see above) www.mla.gov.uk

Museums Association – membership organisation for individuals and museums in the UK. Programmes include: 'Diversify' to assist ethnic minority candidates; guidance on restitution of cultural property, and advocacy www.museumsassociation.org

Museums at Night – Nuit des Musées organised by the French Department for Culture with support from ICOM France www.nuitdesmusees.culture.fr; promoted by Culture24 in the UK www.culture24.org.uk

National Arts Marketing Project – a programme of the Association of Americans for the Arts to assist marketers in arts organisations www.ArtsMarketing.org

National Campaign for the Arts – UK's only independent organisation campaigning for all the arts www.artscampaign.org.uk

National Museum Directors' Conference – source for reports and news about the UK's national museums www.nationalmuseums.org.uk

National Trust – (3.6 million members) – protects and opens to the public over 350 historic houses, gardens, land and ancient monuments. www.national trust.org.uk

National Union of Journalists (NUJ) represents journalists in the UK www.nuj.org.uk

Public Relations Consultants Association (PRCA) represents consultancies in the UK www.prca.org.uk

Public Relations Society of American (PRSA) – membership organisation (21,000 members) for PR professionals in the US www.prsa.org

Renaissance in the Regions – a ground-breaking programme to transform England's regional museums with central government funding www.mla.gov.uk

World Federation of Friends of Museums publishes a code of ethics for 'Friends' www.museumsfriends.com

PUBLICATIONS (BOOKS, E-NEWS, MAGAZINES AND WEBSITES)

Advertising Icons Museum, Kansas City (opening 2011) http://www.advertising iconmuseum.org/

American Journalism 1690–1940 by Frank L. Mott – a legendary history of American newspapers (Macmillan, 1942); revised edition, *American Journalism 1690–1960* (Macmillan, 1962)

ArtDaily News www.artdaily.org

Art Industry: www.artsindustry.co.uk is an online magazine for those who work in arts and culture in the UK

The Art Newspaper – definitive guide to international news in the arts, monthly and online www.theartnewspaper.com

Artists, Patrons, and the Public: Why Culture Changes by Barry Lord and Gail Dexter Lord (AltaMira Press, 2010)

Arts Professional (Arts Intelligence Ltd) www.artsprofessional.co.uk

Attractions Management (Leisure Media Company) online and monthly magazine www.leisuremedia.com

The Black Swan: The Impact of the Highly Improbable by Nassim Nicholas Taleb (Penguin, 2007)

Connected Earth – a history of telecommunications on the web by BT www.connected-earth.com

Culture24 (formerly the 24-Hour Museum) UK's online database of museums, galleries and heritage attractions with news and views www.culture24.org.uk

Debrett's Online – the authority on etiquette, taste and achievement www.debretts.com/

The Hidden Persuaders by Vance Packard, first published in 1957 (paperback edition: Ig Publishing)

The Long Tail: Why the Future of Business is Selling Less of More by Chris Anderson (Hyperion, 2006)

The Marketer (Chartered Institute of Marketing) – online magazine www.cim.co.uk

Museum Marketing & Strategy by Neil Kotler, Philip Kotler and Wendy Kotler, (2nd edition, Jossey-Bass, 2008) – thorough marketing textbook. Philip Kotler, another marketing guru, is Professor of International Marketing at the Kellogg School of Management at Northwestern University, US.

Museum of Brands, Packaging and Advertising, London www.museumofbrands.com/

Museums and Heritage magazine, M&H online (Ten Alps Publishing) www.mandh-online.com

Museums in the Digital Age by Ross Parry (Routledge, 2010)

Museums Journal; Museums Practice; MJ Update Online www.museumsassocation.org

National Arts Marketing Newsletter (Americans for the Arts) www.artsmarketing.org

News from the CIPR (Chartered Institute of Public Relations) www.cipr.co.uk

No Logo by Naomi Klein (Flamingo, 2000)

PR Week – the latest PR and public relations news and jobs www.prweek.com

PRWeek (US) www.prweekus.com/

Science Media Centre supported by the Royal Institution promotes the voices, stories and views of the UK scientific community www.sciencemediacentre.org

A Social History of Museums by Kenneth Hudson (Macmillan, 1975). Hudson founded the European Museum of Year awards, amongst other achievements

Teacher Net http://www.teachernet.gov.uk/teachingandlearning/resourcematerials/

The Tipping Point: How Little Things Can Make a Big Difference by Malcolm Gladwell (Abacus, 2000)

TripAdvisor – the world's largest travel site (part of Expedia) www.tripadvisor.co.uk

VisitBritain E-News www.visitbritain.org

RESEARCH (INTERNATIONAL AND NATIONAL SOCIETIES AND ORGANISATIONS)

See also Marketing and Audience Measurements above.)

Australian Museum Audience Research Centre (AMARC) http://australianmuseum.net.au/Audience-Research

Exploratorium Visitor Research and Evaluation Department (US) provides a range of research reports and publications http://www.exploratorium.edu/partner/evaluation.html

Market Research Society (MRS) – the world's largest professional association representing providers and users of market research www.mrs.org.uk/

Media Evaluation & Research Center (US) gathers information about parks and historic sites and their visitors http://www.nps.gov/hfc/products/evaluate.htm

Natural History Museum, London – website offers research and evaluation information /www.nhm.ac.uk/about-us/visitor-research/index.html

Research Centre for Museums and Galleries (RCMG) (UK) established in 1999, is based within the University of Leicester's Department of Museum Studies http://www.le.ac.uk/museumstudies/research/rcmg.html

Strategic Content Alliance works on behalf of the public sector to reduce the barriers to digital content www.jics.ac.uk/contentalliance

Victoria and Albert Museum publishes visitor research reports and information on its website http://www.vam.ac.uk/res_cons/research/visitor/index.html

Visitor Studies Association (VSA) (US) – a group aiming to improve the quality of visitor experiences through audience research and evaluation http://visitorstudies.org/

The Visitor Studies Group is a community of professionals from the UK and abroad whose members work in the field of visitor studies in a wide range of cultural and natural heritage organisations. www.visitors.org.uk

SUSTAINABILITY

Dana Centre – an adult-only venue run by the Science Museum which explores issues in contemporary science www.danacentre.org.uk

DCMS Sustainable Development Action Plan 2008–11 details UK current plans for implementing sustainable development www.culture.gov.uk

Museums and Art Galleries Survival Strategies – a guide to reducing operating costs and improving sustainability www.mla.gov.uk and www.arup.com

National Trust 'Going Local – Fresh tracks down old roads' www.nationaltrust.org.uk

World Commission on the Environment and Development www.un.org

TOURISM AND TRAVEL TRADE INFORMATION

Cultural Olympiad – the key creative programme for the London 2012 Olympics http://www.london2012.com/plans/culture/now-to-2012/getting-involved.php

European Capital of Culture is an EU programme www.ec.europa.eu/culture/

Guides, tourist guides' associations – there are professional guides' associations, nationally and regionally: check with your tourist board

Tourism Society – UK membership organisation for tourism professionals www.tourism society.org.uk

Trade Fairs – check with your local tourist board and the web for the most useful trade fairs in your country or region; here are a few: British Travel Trade Fair www.biz tradeshows.com/trade-events/bttf; Best of Britain and Northern Ireland Trade Fair www.britainandirelandevent.co.uk; Education Show www.education-show.com; World Travel Market www.wtmlondon.com

UK Inbound – a trade association for the inbound tourist industry www.ukinbound.org

VisitBritain www.visitbritain.org; see also www.enjoyengland.com for England; www.visitscotland.com for Scotland; www.visitwales.com for Wales; www.discover northernireland.com for Northern Ireland.

APPENDIX: CASE STUDIES

These case studies are listed by chapter. The authors are identified at the start of each case study. The contents of each case study is the responsibility and copyright of its author. This book's authors have carried out some editing and formatting to standardise the presentation.

CHAPTER 5 A PUBLIC RELATIONS STRATEGY FOR EVERY OCCASION

Case study 5A: The National Maritime Museum and sustainability

Kate Winsall, Marketing Manager, and Sheryl Twigg, Press and PR Manager, National Maritime Museum

In 2007 the National Maritime Museum received the Visit London Award for Sustainable Tourism. The Museum, which incorporates the Queen's House and Royal Observatory, Greenwich, is exceptionally proud of this accolade and strives for environmental excellence to act as an example of good practice within the leisure and heritage sector.

The NMM is part of the Maritime Greenwich UNESCO World Heritage Site and, as such, has a great deal of input into the WHS Management Plan. This aims to preserve the area's character and promote its cultural and educational resources whilst recognising Greenwich's importance as a place of international significance.

In 2005, the NMM developed a permanent exhibition entitled 'Your Ocean' that addresses issues of marine conservation. The exhibition was developed using entirely recycled or recyclable materials, whilst a 'Your Ocean' website was also designed as a learning resource for teachers and pupils and as an interesting and intriguing resource on our ocean. With accompanying environmental awareness-building events, this sustainable stance was believed to be a first for a national museum.

The Museum implemented its Sustainable Development Policy in October 2006 and a Sustainable Development Group (SDG) was created, made up of staff from across the Museum with particular interest or expertise in sustainability issues. The group created the forward plan and implemented projects.

The SDG engaged members of staff across the Museum as 'Green Champions' to help disseminate information and provide advice and support – and ensured that projects could be delivered at department level. A planning session took place with the Museum's executive and the senior management teams to foster support at the most senior levels in the organisation. This group also reported on a quarterly basis to the Museum's Trustees to mark their progress.

Today, sustainability has a place on the staff induction so that all new members of Museum staff understand about the Museum's approach and also who the key contacts are. The NMM's Sustainability Mission Statement and Policy are both available for visitors to access on the NMM website (www.nmm.ac.uk) along with the NMM's Energy Policy and Conservation Plan. These policies have resulted in a year-on-year reduction in the Museum's energy consumption, achieved through staff and public awareness programmes and facilities improvements.

A full recycling scheme was introduced to the staff areas and public spaces of the Museum. This innovative scheme, in negotiation with Greenwich Council, has resulted in a 60% reduction in waste going to landfill from the NMM. All office paper is now recycled, and marketing materials are printed by FSC-registered printers (Forest Stewardship Council) on sustainably sourced or recycled paper.

The resounding success of the environmental ethos that has permeated the NMM in recent years has been solely due to dedication to the cause by the staff that work within the Museum and the cooperation of visitors. Cultural change towards a more sustainable future is not only happening at the NMM but also welcomed and, therefore, it appears that the most significant and yet difficult task necessary for future progression has already been achieved.

Case study 5B: Taking awards seriously at Wimbledon

Ashley Jones, Commercial Manager, Wimbledon Lawn Tennis Museum

We at Wimbledon Lawn Tennis Museum have always taken awards very seriously. Our reasons are twofold: first that Wimbledon prides itself on being the best tennis tournament in the world, so it is important that the Museum is seen to be delivering to the same standard, and secondly, as a museum we have a quite small marketing budget, and the positive PR produced by awards judged by independent third parties is extremely useful.

In 2002 we applied for and won the London Tourist Board gold award as the best 'new visitor attraction' for the introduction of the behind-the-scenes tour of the grounds. The

PR generated by this helped launch the tours into the marketplace during a difficult trading period not long after the tragedy of 9/11 in New York, particularly as the Museum is about 75% dependent on overseas visitors.

The positive impact of this prompted us to apply for any awards which we thought we might credibly win. Applying for awards is a time-consuming business so, generally, if you know you have no hope your time would be better spent on other things!

With the planning of the new Museum in the period of 2004/5, and the remit from the All England Club to deliver the best sports museum in Britain, we kept our eye open for opportunities.

The first to appear on the horizon was the snappily named 'Chinese Tourism Welcoming Award' which we applied for on the basis that we were adding a Mandarin audio-guide to the Museum and had recently added both Mandarin and Cantonese as languages on the behind-the-scenes tour. Our efforts brought results and we won a Gold award in March 2006, five weeks before the Museum opened. This gave us good PR coverage in China, at a time when Britain was close to achieving 'Approved Destination' status. That year we also won the Sports Museums & Halls of Fame award for 'Best Marketing'. While this award brings little in PR, it is an indicator that we are delivering excellence at all levels.

The following year, 2007, we applied for the Visit London Best Tourism Experience Award and we won Gold, with a Bronze for 'Accessible Tourism'. We also won Gold in the Visit Britain 'Best New Product' category in the Youth Travel Awards. This combination of successes produced enormous PR, which was generated by Visit London and Visit Britain – with very little effort required by ourselves. The benefit of this is probably greater, as it is recommendation by a third party rather than something which we issued for ourselves. By this time, when I attended travel trade events I was commonly asked 'So have you won any more awards, then?' – an indication that the word about how good the product is was established in the marketplace.

2008 saw us achieve a Highly Commended award in the European Museum of the Year Award with the judgement that 'by using a well-balanced combination of the traditional and state-of-the-art methods of interpretation the Museum has created a show which holds the attention of the visitor from beginning to end.' Mention was also made of 'the way the Museum tells the story of all the people involved in the game, and of the Museum's impressive marketing strategy.

Again, such praise from an internationally recognised body adds to the appeal of the Museum to the public by increasing their sense of anticipation. Fortunately, the product delivers on that sense, and the Museum is judged to be good or excellent by some 90% of visitors, with none disappointed.

We have shamelessly exploited these awards in our PR and marketing, and our current leaflet carries the logo of both the Visit London and European Museums awards – after all if you are going to enter and win you might at least make the most of the results of your efforts.

The exact impact on the Museum's attendance from these awards is, of course, hard to quantify as they are simply part of the marketing mix, but the fact that the Museum's attendance has grown from 51,000 in 2006 to 70,000 in 2009 is probably indicative!

Of course all of these benefits come with a price – time! Most application processes give you a maximum amount of text you can use within each section, but also advise on the content each section should cover. This means that the revision process is longer than the initial writing of the application. For the Visit London award I would estimate that each form took about 10–12 hours, spread over a week, to complete. Then on top of that there was another 1–2 hours pulling together the support literature etc. into a presentation folder. The European Museum award took even longer – probably getting on for 20 hours, all told.

Personally, I think it is worth it – if your attraction is excellent then let the world know about it and, hopefully, the visitors will come.

CHAPTER 6 EVERYTHING YOU WANT TO KNOW ABOUT BRANDS AND BRANDING

Case study 6A: A new brand for the Great North Museum

In April 2006, the Hancock Museum in Newcastle upon Tyne closed its doors to embark on an exciting £27 million development, involving its merger with two university museums (the Museum of Antiquities and the Shefton Museum) and Newcastle University's Hatton Gallery. The result, the 'Great North Museum', was launched on 23 May 2009 and since opening has become the most visited attraction in north east England and one of the top 10 most visited museums in the UK. Steve McLean, Senior Manager, and Iain Watson, Acting Director of Tyne & Wear Archives & Museums describe the process of developing a new brand for these long-established organisations.

The project was led by Newcastle University, in partnership with Tyne & Wear Archives & Museums (the managers of the museum), the Natural History Society of Northumbria (NHSN) – the owners of the original Hancock Museum and its collections, the Society of Antiquaries of Newcastle upon Tyne (SANT) – the owners of most of the archaeology collections, and Newcastle City Council.

In developing the brand for the project (which could later be changed or adopted as the final product brand) a clear strategy was needed to convey one clear message which could be communicated to many audiences and the complex array of stakeholders and funders. The main physical element of the new museum was the existing Hancock Museum building, above the entrance of which is the original name, carved in large stone letters. However the SANT collection had no association with the Hancock Museum per se, other than originally being housed with the NHSN collections in the earlier part of the nineteenth century within the building of the Newcastle Literary and Philosophical Society. Likewise, the Shefton Museum, a collection of Greek and Etruscan Art and Archaeology, had traditionally been a teaching collection within the University. The challenge was to take four individual museums and promote them as one. Seven agencies were invited to generate brand name ideas which, on submission, clustered around three main themes:

Geographical – a name placing the new development in the context of its location. Examples included: The Barras (the museum's postal address is Barras Bridge), The Newcastle Museum, The Haymarket (the area adjacent to the museum).

Descriptive – a name based on the theory of bringing the four museums together to form one attraction. Examples included: The Collective, The Union, The Combined Museum, The Quadrant, The Forum.

Conceptual – a name devoid of any relationship to the theory behind the project or its location and history, a name designed to inspire excitement. Examples included: Mondo, Axis, Muse, The Ark.

Two agencies were subsequently asked to present their thoughts on three potential names: The Barras, the Great North Museum, and the retention of the original Hancock Museum name.

The 'Great North Museum' became the clear leader for the project brand, for a number of distinct reasons:

- The use of the word 'Museum' immediately encapsulated the project's objectives.

- It created a sense that something new was happening.

- The use of a new name signalled change.

- It was campaignable.

- The name engendered a sense of excitement, it was aspirational.

- The use of the word 'Great' gave the project scale and importance.

- The use of the word 'North' defined where the project was on a national level.

- The name and its association with the world-famous 'Great North Run' identified the project with the North East on a national and international level – a destination brand. On a regional level, the project was being built adjacent to the Great North Road.

- It was not registered online and the name could be used as a URL on the internet – which was a vital tool for awareness-building for the project even before building work commenced.

- Overall, and importantly, the Great North Museum name was flexible in use – Great Museum, Great Café, Great Cuppa, Great Day Out, etc.

The project's visual identity had a deliberate style reflecting historical associations, and the chosen typeface echoed the work of the North East engraver Thomas Bewick, whose story and collections featured in the Museum.

Before developing the project brand to the final product brand we commissioned qualitative research to test public and stakeholder opinion about the name of the Museum and brand values. Six hundred interviews were conducted with culturally minded members of the public, across a number of market segments – local (Newcastle), regional (rest of the North East), day trip/stay away (Leeds, Wakefield), stay away (Sheffield, Nottingham), and stay away (London).

The name 'Hancock Museum' had little or no meaning outside the region, but in the region the name was strongly recognised. Very locally, and particularly amongst people connected with the Museum, it was regarded with some affection, but often there were also negative brand values due to the tired state of the Museum and its displays. Both inside and outside the region the 'Great North Museum' signalled change and had gravitas that would work well in both the promotional campaigns and the various market segments, particularly the hard-to-reach tourist.

The Great North Museum became the over-arching brand for three sites:

- The Great North Museum: Hancock – the main Museum site

- The Hatton Gallery (Great North Museum) – remaining on its existing site within the campus.

- The Great North Museum: Resource Centre – the collection store and research centre where the bulk of the non-displayed collections are now housed.

In developing the brand for the Great North Museum, a complex set of relationships were negotiated, from building and collection owners with strong historical associations, to funders with performance-led targets including the development of new and out-of-region audiences. The new visual identity developed for launch of the project was created to reflect the new brand and to be instantly recognisable. It was designed to work on all communications material and to be suitable for a broad range of merchandise.

Given that the museum has surpassed its original target of 350,000 visits in its first year (achieving 1,000,000 visits in just 15 months), the rebrand of this iconic North East institution has been an unprecedented success. (See Figure 6.5 on p. 76.)

CHAPTER 7 CREATING THE MARKETING PLAN

Case study 7A: The National Brewery Centre – creating a marketing plan

Planning Solutions Limited (www.pslplan.co.uk), founded in 1995 by Mike Stickland, is a specialist operator of visitor attractions and other leisure businesses throughout the UK, including the 'National Brewery Centre', 'Conkers' (an award-winning visitor centre in the National Forest, Derbyshire), and an extreme adventure experience in Ebbw Vale. Below, Richard Linington, who manages marketing and research aspects, sets out a reduced version of the marketing plan for the National Brewery Centre, which drew on the experience gained from opening and managing Conkers.

The National Brewery Centre

The Bass Museum (as it was formerly known) represented a major heritage attraction in Burton upon Trent, based on the history and world-influencing techniques of brewing that were developed in the town. It was renamed the 'Coors Visitor Centre' in 2002, and subsequently closed in 2008. At its peak, the Bass Museum was generating over 100,000 visits per annum.

Planning Solutions recognised that there was a demand for a major heritage visitor experience in Burton upon Trent and, given the historic buildings and vast array of artefacts housed in the existing site, it seemed logical to explore this opportunity. Discussions with the site's owner, Molson Coors, to reopen the museum as the 'National Brewery Centre' culminated in the relaunch of the Centre in May 2010.

There are three main elements to the revitalised National Brewery Centre:

- The visitor offer – which incorporates a Red Carpet Tour, live period actors who help to bring the former brewery to life, a new holographic-style experience, vintage steam and motor vehicles, live events and shire horses. There are also supporting catering and retail functions. A micro-brewery is also planned to open shortly and will be part of the tour. (Now completed.)

- The corporate and functions offer – which combines the above elements with corporate meeting rooms and function spaces in an historic setting.

- The education offer, which includes a nationally important archive.

The marketing plan

The marketing plan sets out the key markets to engage with, the core messages and the brand to be promoted in a strategic and coordinated way. In addition to this, the business plan also sets out the visitor targets to be achieved. A number of 'tools' are used to reach the different audiences in this competitive and changing market place. These tools are used to raise the awareness of the National Brewery Centre within the core 60-minute drive-time radius of the attraction and the specialist visitor market place.

In our experience of managing visitor attractions there are three key elements which a marketing plan must include:

- Research – understanding the needs and expectations of visitors to help prioritise and define the main messages that the National Brewery Centre will present.

- Reaching the audiences – setting out the tools and communication channels which the National Brewery Centre will use to reach these audiences.

- Evaluation and monitoring – identifying the effectiveness of the marketing plan to measure responses to the campaign and to enhance it for the following year.

'The marketing plan is an essential part of the business plan and provides a map for the journey from business start-up to business success' (Mike Stickland, Managing Director, Planning Solutions Limited).

With today's economic climate there is a requirement to 'do more with less' and a budget is allocated for the marketing plan – based upon estimated visitor numbers.

One of our first steps was to examine the branding of the visitor experience. The 'National Brewery Centre' is used as the main brand and 'The Brewing Experience' as the sub-brand, with reference made to the Bass Museum because of residual brand loyalty to the former Bass Museum. This has helped to reposition the visitor experience in the minds of visitors.

UNDERSTANDING THE MARKET

Without understanding the audience and market size it is difficult to produce a robust marketing plan. A module of intensive research was carried out to identify who will visit, the market size, visitor expectations, needs and motivations.

By understanding the dynamics of the market, the National Brewery Centre can target the different market segments more effectively and identify where on the visitor journey they can engage them (pre and post visit).

Tools used to reach the audiences

The National Brewery Centre's marketing plan sets out the different tools which are used to reach and engage with potential visitors and the associated budgets for each activity. At the National Brewery Centre the tools include the following.

DEVELOPING AN ONLINE PRESENCE

Having an online presence is essential in order to reach and communicate with our visitors in a cost-effective way. A well-structured and usable website has been developed to engage with different audiences – from specialist heritage-based visitors, through to education-based visits. Importantly, visitors can sign up to receive an email newsletter, opening up another cost-effective communication channel. Our experience of managing Conkers (www.visitconkers.com) identified that there are also significant opportunities to generate revenue via the online sale of tickets.

Social media services such as Facebook and Twitter allow the National Brewery Centre to engage with visitors. They are both used to notify 'followers' about our latest activities, events, special offers and news. It is also important to respond to all comments posted on user-generated content websites such as TripAdvisor.

The National Brewery Centre's marketing plan identifies ways to increase traffic to the website – for example, link building, converting online visitors to paying visitors and ongoing improvement of the website in terms of its functionality and usability.

GENERAL PROMOTIONAL LEAFLET

At the National Brewery Centre, a targeted brochure outlining the facilities and key experiences, along with an effective distribution channel, has been essential.

The marketing plan sets out how the leaflet was going to be redesigned and subsequently updated each year. With the reopening of the attraction, a full-colour, distinctively branded leaflet was designed to give visitors a glimpse of the visitor experience at the National Brewery Centre and encourage them to visit. The leaflet, which folds out in concertina style, used strong photographic images to help get the core messages across. The leaflet emphasises the free car parking and children's play areas – which are particularly important for the general 'family days out' market.

Liaising with the distributor, we decided on the key locations where the brochure would be distributed. The leaflet has been distributed via a media company to key outlets – motorway service stations, libraries, accommodation providers, for example – and the onsite team of live interpreters have also helped to distribute the leaflet locally. The leaflet is particularly effective in reaching the tourist market.

DESTINATION MANAGEMENT ORGANISATIONS

Destination management organisations (DMOs) produce a number of tourist publications which target tourists, day visitors and group organisers. DMOs also have a good online presence which links through to the National Brewery Centre's website. To attract tourists, working in partnership with the DMO has helped to cost-effectively raise the profile of the National Brewery Centre within Staffordshire and the National Forest. Destination management organisations also manage familiarisation visits from visiting journalists and tourist information centre staff. DMOs work a year ahead, so it is important to book early to ensure that advertising space is reserved.

Press advertising

It is generally costly to advertise in local newspapers and we have often found that press adverts need to be led by a strong offer – 2 for 1 admission, for example – to generate sufficient numbers to justify the cost of advertising. However, once the visitor is onsite they are likely to generate revenue in retail and catering spend. The National Brewery Centre avoided national advertising as it is not cost-effective for the attraction at this stage.

(As the marketing manager, make sure you research and target the publications you want to be in, thereby ensuring that your budget is used carefully. Don't react to calls from all and sundry just because they offer you a discount!)

Joint ticketing

Managing two visitor experiences in the National Forest (www.nationalforest.org) has allowed Planning Solutions to cost-effectively cross-market the attractions to different audiences.

Word of mouth

Word-of-mouth recommendations still remain one of the most effective ways to generate visits from the local community. By exceeding the visitors' expectations during their visit they are more likely to make a positive recommendation to friends. The Marketing Manager works closely with each General Manager to help enhance the visitor experience.

PR

Working with a specialist PR agency has helped to generate significant coverage in the local, regional and specialist press. This has been particularly important during the pre-opening and immediate post-opening periods. Essential to a successful relationship with a PR agency is providing a clear brief, with agreed key performance indicators. A press pack containing answers to frequently asked questions, an online photo library and branding guidelines has enabled the National Brewery Centre to respond to press enquiries in a consistent and professional manner.

Group travel

The group travel market is difficult to tap into. There are a number of essential aspects ('golden rules') such as remembering to look after the coach driver with a complimentary meal and ticket.

Specialist markets

Being the 'National Brewery Centre', one of the core target markets is the traditional ale and beer enthusiasts. Working with CAMRA, the National Brewery Centre has been able to raise its profile within the traditional beer and ale enthusiast market place.

EDUCATION-BASED VISITS

An education brochure is being developed to engage with the education market, which will be available in 2011. Teachers are encouraged to come to the National Brewery Centre as part of a free familiarisation visit. The brochure will be sent out to a database of named teachers. At the National Brewery Centre we have found that a successful education visit can often lead to a family visit at a later date.

ON AND OFFSITE SIGNAGE

The National Brewery Centre is adjacent to two very busy roads in Burton upon Trent and this has presented an excellent opportunity to promote our core messages and latest events to passing motorists and pedestrians. Also, brown tourist signs within Burton upon Trent help to raise the profile of the National Brewery Centre.

SOUVENIR GUIDES

Souvenirs are often overlooked as a marketing tool. They have a long shelf life, help to generate revenue and can be handed out as complimentary gifts. Visitors often look after the guides and share them with friends. As part of the medium-term strategy, the National Brewery Centre has identified a need to produce a souvenir guide.

THE VISITOR EXPERIENCE

Until the visitor has paid their admission fee, the front-of-house team are still 'marketing' the experience. The greeting and experience that visitors receive is essential in converting a potential customer into a loyal, and hopefully a repeat, customer. The National Brewery Centre promotes service excellence and takes the opportunity to capture visitors' email addresses at the point of sale to engage with them once they leave with news and special offers to encourage repeat visits.

Monitoring and evaluation

A key, often overlooked, element of the marketing plan is to carry out an evaluation exercise each year to identify what has worked and what can be improved. Over time, it will also provide useful trend information and help with budgeting, allowing for more effective targeting. Additionally, monitoring and evaluation identifies new product and service ideas which could be introduced to increase market appeal, dwell time and secondary spend.

A visitor feedback form, which asks a number of questions (including 'Where do you live?', 'How did you hear about the National Brewery Centre?', 'Did your visit today offer value for money?') enables the National Brewery Centre to identify what elements of the marketing plan have worked and which need tweaking. It also provides information on future ticket pricing and the distance that visitors are prepared to travel to reach the National Brewery Centre. Holding face-to-face interviews with visitors has also helped the team to monitor the marketing plan and provide detailed feedback.

Google Analytics is used to monitor the website and is interrogated to provide information on number of visits, average time spent on the website, keywords and bounce rate.

Summary

In Planning Solution's experience of managing the National Brewery Centre and Conkers, one of the essential elements of a successful marketing plan is that the document needs to be regularly reviewed and flexible enough to cope with tactical marketing.

Case study 7B: Marketing and development at St Paul's Cathedral, the nation's church

Lynn Scrivener, LSM Marketing

As an iconic London visitor attraction and a landmark within the Square Mile, St Paul's consistently welcomes over 800,000 visitors a year – twice that number when including those coming to worship. To ease visitor overcrowding on the Cathedral floor and to introduce new experiences to attract and engage the ever-demanding international tourism market, plans were well underway by 2008 to extend visitor access. Even more of the Cathedral's historical and unique spaces were due to be opened in the next two to three years, namely the Triforium floor up in the Dome and an interpretation hub down in the Crypt.

A marketing strategy was commissioned at the end of 2008 to concentrate on marketing and communications for the period 2009–2011. This needed to take into account the current visitor attraction and audience profile, as well as the planned improvements to the visitor experience and opportunities for new audience development.

Research findings

An audience development strategy and an interpretation strategy were jointly commissioned in early 2008, which contributed greatly to the marketing strategy. To inform all this work, both qualitative research (focus groups and telephone interviews) and quantitative research (exit interviews) were carried out which identified a number of key issues including:

- Compared to other leading London heritage attractions, a more 'overseas weighted' visitor profile (76% v 42%), suggesting a relative lack of interest to a domestic audience.

■ A trend towards adult-only audiences – overall 84% adult visitors, with UK family groups accounting for only 6% of visitors.

■ Barriers to visiting amongst domestic audiences included: a complete lack of understanding as to why an entrance charge is necessary; considered to be a 'place for tourists' with little relevance for local audiences; not an appropriate attraction for children.

■ By contrast, faced with actual descriptions of the Cathedral, strong drivers to visit were identified, including the art, architecture, beauty, spirituality and sheer awe-inspiring size of the building, as well as the opportunity to gain a deeper understanding of its place in history as 'the nation's church'.

An overview of tourism forecasts by the tourism agencies Visit London and Visit Britain indicated a certain continuation of the traditional markets for St Paul's – namely, North America, France and Germany, but a narrowing gap, indeed replacement longer-term, with emerging markets in Eastern Europe, China, India and Brazil. Telephone research, in addition to forecasts, indicated that the UK visitor market, especially those from London and the SE on day trips from home, those staying with friends and relatives, and special interest visitors (educational and cultural tours), would also be of considerable potential. In addition, developing special projects and activities to reach minority and 'hard to reach' audiences, especially in partnership with other local organisations, would all contribute to important 'outreach' objectives.

Target audiences and marketing approach

With an already extensive portfolio of activities and products on offer at the Cathedral, the following future audience segmentation and marketing approach was identified.

OVERSEAS ADULT INDEPENDENT VISITORS
As the biggest proportion of visitors, the main source markets will remain USA, France, Germany – plus Canada and Australia. Emerging markets include Poland, Hungary, Turkey, Italy and Spain and, longer-term, India, Russia, China and Brazil. Motivated by history and heritage, for the majority of these visitors St Paul's is a 'must see' iconic London attraction.

Longer-term marketing and PR about new interpretation facilities (introductory Hub as well as new multimedia tours) and Triforium space will drive visitation, especially the varying layers of interpretation in 11 different languages.

OVERSEAS GROUP VISITORS
Source markets as above. Whilst consultation suggests that the new Triforium will not be of particular interest to commercial operators (owing to time limits on tour itineraries), the new space and improved interpretation will undoubtedly impact on all visitors and on overseas tour groups with more leisurely itineraries, especially the exclusive 'behind the scenes' tours of the Triforium.

Marketing and PR to groups and travel trade will need to start to this target segment from 2009.

UK ADULTS

Around 21% of visitors are domestic, predominately London and South East day-trip visitors – mostly *working greys* and *empty nesters* (45–65) – plus those on short breaks from further afield, often staying with friends and relatives. Motivated by history and heritage, this audience has a vast array of places of interest available to it and they will tend to choose an attraction or activity that they believe to be unique or distinct from those in their own locality. First-time visitors will look to London's iconic attractions though many repeat visitors to London will be looking for somewhere 'new'. The planned developments at the Cathedral provide a brilliant opportunity either to encourage a repeat visit or to attract first-timers by succeeding in presenting the Cathedral as either something 'new' for those who think they 'know about it already '(or came when they were a child) or as somewhere accessible and engaging for those who think 'it's not for me'.

Preparations for marketing and PR need to begin in 2009 as well as tactical offers over the coming year to catch the eye of domestic visitors looking for value for money, genuine 'history where it happened' experiences.

FAMILIES – UK AND OVERSEAS

Presently only 6% of UK adults visit the Cathedral with a child, and 10% of overseas adults. The new developments offer opportunities to concentrate on attracting this audience, such as:

- Interpretation that can be enjoyed as a family
- Storytelling and activities
- Family audio guide and trails (possibly linked to school curriculum)
- Special events in the school holidays.

Child-friendly activities will act as a positive motivator for family groups. Meantime, special price offers should also be tested now for UK families with children – including joint offers with the café and shop.

'HARD TO REACH' LOCAL COMMUNITY AUDIENCES

Boroughs surrounding St Paul's are all potential areas for special joint 'outreach' activities to be tackled by specially funded projects, working in partnership with other existing groups and organisations.

This is a low-volume but important new market with particular marketing/communication requirements, such as local print and posters and micro-websites (possibly multilingual) to be prepared in due course.

Visitors with disabilities

Part of all the audiences listed above and below. Longer-term, the new developments and interpretation facilities will allow for more confident marketing and PR to these groups.

Primary and secondary schools and teachers

Drawn primarily from neighbouring boroughs.

Special interest adult groups and individuals

History, architecture, art – drawn primarily from those living and working locally in the City and London or SE regional catchment area. Longer-term, they will be attracted by new 'exclusive' spaces/interpretation and a developing programme of specialist and/or 'behind the scenes' tours and talks.

Marketing and PR programme will be required to target this market, planned in 2009 for early launch in 2010.

Special Church interest groups

Locally and nationally and even internationally – may require marketing/PR in target media – e.g. *Church Times*, as well as local newsletters and on website.

Recommended marketing focus – domestic audiences

At the time of the strategic report, the level of marketing and communications activity for a London attraction of such significance as St Paul's was considered to be relatively modest, especially in such a fast-moving media environment and with a view to the forthcoming, once-in-a-lifetime London Olympics 2012 platform. A step change in the general level of activity and investment was recommended so that audiences could be developed to their full potential.

Focus on the domestic audience was particularly recommended, partly to temper the risk of relying too heavily on overseas visitors and partly because the research results described above showed that the new development plans offered opportunities to re-present the Cathedral as an attraction with major appeal to these audiences, both adults and families.

Case study 7C: 'In a Different Light' – a series of evening events at two Oxford museums

The Pitt Rivers Museum and the Oxford University Museum of Natural History share a single front door, one being accessed through the other. A series of evening events were held at the museums, in association with 'Museums and Galleries Month' and Nuits des Musées in 2005, 2006, 2007 and 2008. The objective for these collaborative events was to encourage visitors to re-engage with the collections by changing the context in which they are viewed, and to draw in new visitors who may find this approach more to their taste. The events were free, and marketed through email networks rather than traditional posters and leaflets, to reach a wider number of young adults and other non-traditional museum visitors. Below, Kate White, Marketing & Visitor Services Officer, Pitt Rivers Museum, explains further.

Each late night event has included a wide and perhaps unexpected choice of activities, on offer simultaneously in different areas of the galleries, so as to bombard visitors with a range of options, and a sense of urgency to grab opportunities and not miss out. The programmes, targeted as much at adults as children, have included: unusual live music performances, films, activities (such as lantern-making or mask-making) for young and old, handling of insects and minerals, and art installations; and radical changes to the usual lighting, including torchlight-only viewing of the Pitt Rivers displays; and – of course – a bar. All this leads to a complete change in atmosphere, which is all-important. The combination of the lights, sounds, and action animating the architecture and displays draws a throng of excited people who themselves generate a huge sense of occasion.

From the start, we were taken aback by the public appetite for these events (1,500 visitors to the first in 2005, 2,500 in 2006), as museums were not typical venues for a Saturday night out in Oxford. In 2007 more than 3,000 visitors came during the 3-hour event (including 1,400 on time-ticketed entry to the 'Pitt Rivers by Torchlight'). Most people came through word-of-mouth recommendation, based on the previous two events, and about 15% had not visited previously. Some queued for 45 minutes to get in, as numbers quickly reached capacity, so inevitably there were a few disappointed visitors, and the tickets for the Pitt Rivers ran out very quickly. However, the wide choice, the repeating programme, and the general ambience ensured most visitors felt they were witnessing something special.

The feedback was, on the whole, ecstatic – 'Awesome, much better than excellent' was one visitor's response on the evaluation survey. Visitors were thrilled by the performances, particularly within these unusual and very informal settings: masked dances by Tibetan monks in amongst the crowds and skeletons in the Museum of Natural History, Kora and Mbira players in the dark Pitt Rivers, a chance to take part in a Gamelan orchestra, drummers outside on the lawn. The torchlight experience on the ground floor of the Pitt Rivers is an extraordinary experience (few other museums have risked turning their lights off), both to take part in, and to view from the gallery above, and has become a vital part of each subsequent event. Handling the millipede also proved extremely popular, and many adults continued to wear the elaborate masks they had made when they left the building. The screening of relatively obscure short films attracted an entirely different group of devotees. Perhaps, being Oxford, the remarkably high percentage of young adults could have been anticipated (the indication being that around 38% of the 'adult' visitors were aged between 16 and 34).

The positive feedback has encouraged us to put rather more resources into these higher-profile and all-encompassing joint events, once or twice a year, as opposed to the more focused and targeted events we were used to running. Although the outlay, both financial and in staff time, is greater, it has achieved far more in rapidly expanding public awareness and putting us on the County's cultural and community maps. It has helped bridge the town/gown divide and fed into the City's planning for major public events. In professional circles it has also drawn attention to the University's museums, since we were one of the first to link up with Nuits des Musées European-wide event, and we also won the Museums and Galleries Month commendation award in 2007, sparking interest from other museums in the formula we were using. On a different level, it generated a sense of pride amongst staff (these events relied on a big team of volunteers, including many members of staff), changing the way we saw ourselves and the impact we were capable of making.

There seems to be a growing demand for mass gatherings and for theatrical events (from flashmobs to festivals) where audiences come together in a shared experience, a large part of which is their own combined goodwill and participation in making it happen. Through these events the Museums have shown that their galleries and displays can become an ideal focus for generating this sense of community.

'Perhaps the most wonderful aspect of the event was the sense of community – from toddlers to teenagers, adolescents to adults, we were all united in our exploration of an inviting and intriguing world that can teach us so much about our own less soothing environment' (written comment, visitor from Banbury).

CHAPTER 8 TACTICAL MARKETING AND AUDIENCE DEVELOPMENT

Case study 8A: Visitor-centred transformation of the Detroit Institute of Arts

Under the directorship of Graham W.J. Beal, the Detroit Institute of Arts has undergone a major overhaul of the way in which the collections are displayed, guided at every stage by knowledge of the visitors' reactions. Beal describes it as the DIA's contribution to a global debate about the role of museums in a democratic society. 'Our big decision was to abandon the specialist-based framework (art history and connoisseurship) of the past hundred years or so and present works of art in the context of shared human experience. We attempted to build on the knowledge that general visitors brought with them, rather than trying to equip them with the terminology of a particular intellectual discipline.' The results have been acknowledged internationally as a huge success. The re-think of the presentation enabled a re-think of marketing and PR. Here Graham Beal tells more of this major transformation.

The complete renovation and expansion of the 55,000 m^2 facility that was the Detroit Institute of Arts necessitated all the galleries being demounted, and a motivating factor for me in accepting the position of director in 1999 was the opportunity to rethink the way art was presented to the general public. Doing so with one of the US's greatest universal collections would stress the project as a deliberate choice and not a tactic designed to obscure 'weaknesses.' I was fortunate to inherit a small group of DIA staff who shared this ambition, brought specific strengths to the table and who had, under interim leadership, been experimenting with special exhibition presentations as well as in several areas of the permanent collection. An in-depth 'archetyping' study had been carried out to establish the underlying motivations that drove people's desire to connect to cultural institutions. An extensive survey had delivered the chastening news that the DIA was not regarded as relevant to an unexpectedly wide range of people in Southeast Michigan. As the DIA is emphatically not in a tourist area, regional patronage and the return visitor are crucial. Many sessions with curatorial, educational, PR and marketing staff, and a number of consultants led to several interrelated determinations: the DIA was going to be visitor-focused; was going to *engage* the visitor and, to that end, was going to abandon art history in favor of story-telling.

In order to counter tendencies to fall back on traditional specialist interest, three teams drawn from across the staff were established, each one dedicated to different areas of the collection. Over the next 18 months, these teams worked with specialist curators and educators to learn about 'their' collections and draw from the objects themselves the stories that brought them to life. 'Always ask,' I charged them, 'two questions: why does this object exist and why is it in the DIA?' At the same time three 'Visitor Panels' were formed to parallel the reinstallation teams and, over several meetings, were asked to critique our themes (Are they interesting to you? Are we being effective in getting them across?); asked about terminology, definitions, and way-finding issues – but *not*, contrary to rumour, asked for thematic ideas. All along, evaluation was being carried out in the galleries where permanent collection installations designed to further our research in visitor behaviour were in place. All of this data was fed into the design and appearance of the galleries, the development of panels and labels and the creation of interactive stations, both high- and low-tech. The overarching idea was to make the visitor feel in control of the whole experience.

In 2001, we embarked upon a PR campaign aimed at dispelling the notion of the DIA as elitist. At the core of the campaign were 30-second TV spots that featured a young African-American male called Art, who lived in the DIA and invited the viewer to visit for special exhibitions, late Friday evenings, music and 'fun' workshops. The tone was light-hearted and slightly self-mocking. A major Michelangelo exhibition spot featured pizza being delivered (think Teenage Mutant Ninja Turtles). Whistler's mother was shown being helped up the museum steps (the painting was here on loan). It was very successful; surprising, and appealing to a wide audience. And, although Art's race was not cited as a factor in our surveys, a leading African-American who I'd earlier failed to convince that we were building a truly 'New DIA,' commented 'I didn't think you were serious until I saw those ads.' Designed to last for two or three years, Art lasted almost five.

Ongoing marketing and advertising continued to stress the DIA as a lively place until, with the opening of the New DIA, we launched a major rebranding and advertising campaign. The DIA's restrained and erudite 'Minerva Head' symbol was replaced by a vibrant blue graphic logo. The same blue was employed throughout all media and DIA ephemera – a blue that was continued in the way-finding outside and within the institution.

The lynchpin of the rebranding campaign was a series of 30-second, mainly black and white, animated spots based around the theme, 'The New DIA: Let Yourself Go' and rooted in the notion of transformation. One featured a woman who wanders through the museum until, inspired by a painting (based on a Miró), leaps into the work to emerge on the other side transformed by the colour of the painting. The second featured a behatted man who morphs into a version of whatever work of art he's viewing, until, confronted by the Egyptian hawk-god Horus, he flies off into the sky accompanied by a soft-spoken 'The New DIA: Let Yourself Go.' As Cole Porter's song of the catch-phrase proved prohibitively expensive for our campaign, we used a jaunty number by a local band that plays a Django Reinhardt/Stephane Grappelli style of Jazz.

The transformation of the DIA itself is complete and has been successful beyond our expectations. Earlier this year we engaged a company to carry out focus groups and formal polling. To the question 'Who do you think goes to the DIA?' the answer was invariably a version of 'Oh *everyone* goes to the DIA!'

Case study 8B: A journey to diversify audiences for the National Trust

Ruth Clarke, Community Projects Manager London, gives a personal account of three consecutive projects that she was involved with over a ten-year period that helped the National Trust in London to extend its audiences. (www.nationaltrust.org.uk/sutton house; www.londonvoicesproject.org.uk)

Set up in 1895, the founding principles of the National Trust were very much those of nourishment for the masses through the preservation of and access to beautiful places and spaces. When the organisation reached its Centenary in 1995 there was an awareness that the access 'for the masses' aspect of these principles needed to be reinvigorated and as such the original intention of being 'for ever for everyone' was re-launched.

On the ground, the impetus created through the build-up to the Centenary could be said to have impacted on the Trust's decision to renovate its Tudor property, Sutton House in Hackney, London and respond to a local campaign to see the house used as a cultural centre for the local area. This decision provided the Trust with an opportunity to develop programmes that connected the organisation with its local and urban audiences. The specific context of Hackney, whose population is culturally and socially diverse, placed a real focus on the development of new audiences.

The next stop on this journey is in 2000, and the 'for ever for everyone' slogan has become a cornerstone of the work taking place in the National Trust's Learning Department. Sutton House reflects this shift with a refocus of its techniques for local engagement, moving from a broad-based cultural programme to one that puts community learning at the property's centre. The community learning work had three aims, to:

- Work with new audiences

- Support the property in finding its local relevance

- Democratise interpretation.

These aims were supported by an ethos that foregrounded discovery, participation, creativity and partnership.

The work at Sutton House was valued in the National Trust for its success in engaging a local, new and diverse audience, and the organisation was keen to share the practice developed throughout the London (urban) area. The route chosen to enable this was to extend the remit of the Community Learning Manager post, making it London-wide. In turn, this change provided an opportunity to create a pan-London project 'London Voices' that addressed the needs of a key (but at this time often overlooked) Trust audience: local families. The 'London Voices' project was funded by the Heritage Lottery Fund and spanned three years, 2006–2009, and echoed the principles of engagement at Sutton House, valuing: local partnerships, participation, discovery and creativity. London Voices was an extremely successful body of work that had the following outcomes:

- Barriers to access and motivations for visiting were identified, and actions relevant to these were put in place, e.g. affordable membership.

- Properties in the London area adopted a family-friendly ethos enabling them to be welcoming to a diverse audience.

- The development of new models of consultation/participation.

- Identification and demonstration of key principles that promote family learning.

- Development and sharing of tools for effective family engagement and participation.

The momentum created through the work at Sutton House and the high profile and more broadly impactful work of London Voices can be said to be supporting factors in the next, final stage of this journey. In 2006 Khadambi Asalache, the Kenyan-born poet, architect and mathematician left his house to the National Trust. A modest property on the Wandsworth Road in Lambeth, Khadambi's house is a testimony to his creativity.

Each room is decorated with wooden fretwork friezes that he carved over a twenty-year period, interspersed with collections of objects and ceramics from all over the world, chosen for their decorative physical form and for their cultural associations.

When gifted the house, the National Trust process of acquisition required the organisation to assess its significance and to look at the practicalities of protecting it inalienably. This was especially challenging because: there was little to compare the house with – that is, no single authority to assess its significance; the size of house would limit access and income; and there was uncertainty about which audiences the house would attract.

A process of consultation with heritage and arts experts provided the information, from which an assessment of 'significance' could be made, but the audiences had still not been identified and it was unknown whether their interest was great enough to secure additional and much-needed external funds.

As a result, a pilot engagement programme was undertaken in 2009 that consisted of creative workshops, guided tours, arts projects and outreach talks. The programme was targeted at London, South East regional, and local audiences. The results demonstrated very clearly that the house provided an extremely intimate and often moving experience for people and that the themes of creativity, journey, home, and human endeavour were dominant. Perhaps though, for the National Trust the most significant aspect of the pilot work was the very strong connection made by Londoners, especially those living locally to the house, and that almost immediately the house engendered a fierce and often extremely personal sense of ownership. For National Trust members from the South East this 'fierce' connection was equally strong but broader in its flavour, with a very real desire to connect with the people behind the spaces and places cared for by the Trust. Consistent throughout were the extremely high numbers of people who wanted to access the house. For example, one weekend 3000 people applied for 48 pilot tour places!

In 2010 the Trust accepted the home of Khadambi Asalache into its portfolio and it was clear in this acceptance that the pilot programme had been helpful in the decision-making process. Simultaneously, the new organisational strategy was launched. It was a strategy that echoed the findings of the pilot engagement programme and the work undertaken at Sutton House and through London Voices. This new strategy stresses that engagement should focus on local audiences and that pivotally, when most effective, it is about spiritual and physical refreshment. In this and other ways, the Trust enjoys the opportunity for a new level of engagement with its supporters and audiences and really gets to grips with the potential it has to enrich the lives of a contemporary, diverse population.

The home of Khadambi Asalache is due to be open to the public in 2012. Prior to this an extensive conservation programme will be taking place, working with the local community. The house will also be participating in the Stories of the World Cultural Olympiad project. (See Figure 8.2 on p. 122.)

Case study 8C: Museums Alive! A long-term regional marketing initiative in Yorkshire

Great partnerships can last for years. Barbara Woroncow, past President of the Museums Association, and Deputy Chair of the Leeds Cultural Partnership, describes a collaboration that brought in new visitors and proved the enduring power of print.

In 1988, the then regional development agency for museums, the Yorkshire & Humberside Museums Council (YHMC), initiated a joint marketing project on behalf of its 200 or so diverse member museums. There was a specific hook on which to hang this new activity as 1989 was designated 'Museums Year' in the UK in celebration of the centenary of the national Museums Association.

External funding was obtained from the then national advisory body for museums, the Museums & Galleries Commission, to kick-start the three elements of the scheme: training in basic marketing skills for museum staff, six free marketing consultancies for individual museums to act as demonstration projects, and a regional print-led marketing initiative called Museums Alive! The last consisted of a first print-run of 50,000 copies of a handy A5-sized guide booklet with a glossy full-colour cover which listed all the museums in the region, together with a brief description of their collections, plus visitor information such as opening times and onsite facilities. The booklet also received funding from national and regional tourism bodies in its first year which provided useful endorsement and assisted in distribution through Tourist Information Centres (TICs). A series of press releases was used to promote the new publication which was free of charge for the general public. Entries in the booklet were free of charge for the museums too, as it was a new activity and its value had to be proved.

The popularity and demand for the booklet was such that its print run was doubled to 100,000 for the second edition in the following year. Its handy size and comprehensive regional coverage made it a favourite with tourists and residents alike. Having proved its worth in the first year, individual museums were subsequently asked to contribute modest amounts for their entries, with half of the total cost being covered by YHMC. The regional tourist board continued to help with distribution to TICs, retail centres and other outlets.

Over time, this model continued, with extended print runs and further enhancements such as paid advertising (but only by museums within the region), translation of the introduction highlighting new developments into French and German, an expanded key to visitor facilities and colour photography throughout. Strong demand continued for the booklet from TICs, accommodation providers and museums themselves. The model of joint regional production continued for nearly 15 years, until structural changes to the remit of YHMC curtailed resources and rapidly growing internet access increasingly became the norm for seeking such visitor information.

Although all museums gained something from participation, very small institutions particularly benefited from the joint activity. For tiny sums of money, they were able to reach large potential audiences via a high-quality piece of print. It was important, at that time, to demonstrate the benefit of joint marketing without seeking financial contributions from the museums in the first year. It was also very helpful to launch the booklet as part of a wider marketing initiative which involved training and professional development. After the initial publication, there was little or no resistance to contributions being paid by individual institutions. What was key, was to provide additional new staff resources to coordinate the project. In the first few years experienced arts marketing consultants carried out the work, while in later years when the format was established, the compilation of information and liaison with designers was taken on by YHMC's administration staff. Bringing in all the information from so many sources proved to be very time-consuming and required tenacity in order to meet the publication deadlines. Partnership activity always demands clearly defined additional staff time resources.

The long-term nature of the project over so many years helped to keep awareness of marketing issues high among smaller museums and it also built a loyal following among visitors who eagerly collected each new annual edition. Evaluation showed that a small but significant minority of the region's 8 million visitors per annum had attended as a result of seeing information in the booklet.

Inevitably, the time comes when any long-term project has to be critically reviewed and then altered significantly or even ceased altogether. Visitors now want even basic information to be presented in many different ways and websites can easily respond to tailoring for individual needs, as well as being capable of frequent change and updating. Nevertheless, there remains a role for print marketing material of an appropriate scale and nature, especially for the time-pressed visitor or traveller. Not many back-packs or car glove compartments can accommodate lap-tops, and mobile phone reception is still poor or non-existent in some of our finest landscape areas.

CHAPTER 9 MAKING THE MOST OF YOUR TOURISM POTENTIAL

Case study 9A: Notes from the Gulf; marketing in a different dimension

Throughout this book we have been describing how to operate in a Western cultural tradition, using its behaviour patterns and attitudes. Marketing and PR need to work within different environments. Here, Sue Underwood and Pamela Erskine-Loftus who work for the Qatar Museums Authority, describe what they have learned from their experiences.

Over the last five years the face of Persian Gulf museums has changed dramatically. For many in the West, the arrival of the Gulf States in the museum world has been caused by the announcements of international agreements with existing Western museums, such as the UAE's Louvre and Guggenheim projects. What all this belies is the existence since the 1970s of museums in the Gulf. From the formation of several of the smaller Gulf States in 1971 a large number of public and private museums appeared – from historic houses and forts to purpose-built museums. Part of the lack of knowledge of the existence of museums in the Gulf has been a lack of marketing. This case study aims to highlight one of the several ways this is changing in the Gulf through a review of Arab women and social media.

Several research projects in the first half of 2010 have addressed the use of social media and the internet by women within the Arab world. What has been shown is that innovative social media use by women in the Gulf is extensive and growing. One report states that, across the Arab world, 71% of women who use the internet are members of at least one social media network, Facebook being the most popular. In the UAE, 83% of Emiratis have internet access; of that 71% of women use Facebook, and 55% of women spend more than seven non-work hours a week online. Of the women online in Kuwait, 53% spend more than seven hours a week online and in Qatar 47%. In both countries, 68% of online women have a Facebook account.

Arabic is the largest growing language online; Arabic-speaking internet users increased by 2,064% between 2000 and 2008, yet less than 1% of online content is in Arabic. Interest in the online Arabic language market by established Western internet companies is not restricted to social media; Yahoo plans to offer their Messenger and Mail in Arabic. Social medias that do not support Arabic have given rise to conduits, for example Artwitter.

Female visitorship to museums has huge growth possibilities throughout the Gulf. By nature of the temperature in the summer (which can reach 50°C/130°F) indoor activities are sought. Western studies have shown that interest in museums and their visitorship is greater for those with a Bachelor's degree or higher. In the Gulf, women heavily outnumber men at universities – in Qatar, Bahrain and the UAE, approximately 70% of university graduates are women. However, the number of national women who enter the work force is considerably lower. In Qatar it was reported in 2008 that 49% of national women were in the workforce, in the UAE 59%, Kuwait 43%, and Bahrain 34%. Therefore there is a large non-working educated female population. What this means for museums in the Gulf is that extensive marketing through social media may be a far-reaching, inexpensive and quick way to reach a primary – though currently underserved – audience.

Related to this aspect of reaching audiences is the use of text messages as museum marketing, particularly for information concerning public programmes and exhibition openings. As of the beginning of 2010 the number of mobile phones per person in the UAE stood at 2.4, the highest mobile phone penetration in the world, with Bahrain coming a close second. One of the reasons that text messages may be so popular and work well for museums in the Gulf is the cross-cultural communication research area of chronemics – the understanding of time – which has been shown to be culturally specific. Unlike Western cultures, which are *monochromic* (time is linear and segmented), Arab cultures are seen as *polychromic*, where time may be seen as more cyclical and fluid. One of the impacts of this is that decisions on leisure activities are not necessarily decided far ahead of time. A Western museum may send out an exhibition opening invitation three or four weeks before the event, most often an invitation for an exhibition in the Gulf is received two to three days prior. Therefore monthly/quarterly programme calendars, or similar marketing materials, may not have the desired action unless an event is imminent.

For Gulf museums this means that marketing through social media is a prime area for expansion and one that works in tandem with more 'traditional' methods. It also suggests that to maximise visitorship, some form of reminder is beneficial, whether by Facebook posting or text message. There is a large, untapped potential museum visitor base within the Gulf. The difficulty is attracting audiences in the first place. Although some museums and organisations have made inroads into reaching the multitude of communities within the region there is much more that can be done in order for people to place a museum visit on their list of places to spend leisure time. Reaching these audiences is not a matter of simply more marketing, but a strategic use of marketing avenues specific to the region and audiences.

Case study 9B: Making the most of Liverpool, European Capital of Culture

Tracey McGeagh, Director of Marketing and Communications, National Museums Liverpool

In 2005 when I joined National Museums Liverpool (NML), the buzz about 2008 Capital of Culture was already audible – and growing day by day. It gave us an unprecedented opportunity to showcase Liverpool's museums and galleries, and a chance not just to grow our audience numbers but to attract new visitors who would come back time and again. With various false starts and negative media coverage about the Capital of Culture in the run-up to 2008 we were also acutely aware that the pride of Liverpool was at stake. To overturn long-held misconceptions we had to do our bit to showcase the city at its best.

Preparations began long in advance. We actively promoted 2008 exhibitions and events to partners such as Visit Britain at least a year ahead of the launch. We made sure that our key events were featured prominently in tourist agency promotions, hosted familiarisation visits and prepared a lot of groundwork, such as producing the first set of foreign-language guides for the museums. Along with other Liverpool arts organisations, the Capital of Culture gave us a reason to work more collaboratively. Various consortia were formed, including a group of arts marketers, enabling us to jointly schedule events and even plan joint launches. This was a long-overdue development which would not have happened without the focus of 2008.

Six months ahead of the launch, we released our 2008 programme to the press. This ensured our events were featured heavily in the December and January round-ups of the year to come. An annual highlights leaflet, which brought together the top ten must-sees at NML, was mailed to an extensive contacts list and distributed in all our venues. This publication supplemented our usual quarterly guides, but such was the demand that by May we had to reprint the leaflet. Based on a significant body of evidence about the visitor profile at each of our museums, we worked up campaign plans for the year's exhibitions programme. We were already aware of the varying catchment areas for the museums, and their potential to attract overseas and domestic tourists. Five years of profile data meant that we were able to segment audiences for each of the main campaigns.

Due to limited budgets, our strategy was to devote advertising spend largely within the region, but to include within this extensive outdoor advertising and print distribution in Liverpool. We relied on tourism agencies and other high-profile city events to attract people from outside our usual catchment area. Once they were in town, there was no way that they would miss messages about our museums and galleries.

The choice of exhibitions was crucial to the success of the year. At NML, audience considerations and potential marketability are always important criteria when it comes to choosing the elements of the programme. Even within resource constraints we were able to put together a set of temporary exhibitions which were likely to appeal to our core audiences locally and from further afield.

At the Walker Art Gallery, for example, where audiences had previously been waning, we were lucky to have two star art shows which complemented each other very well. The first, 'Ben Johnson's Liverpool Cityscape', was a photo-realist panorama of the city which proved extremely popular with crowds gathering to watch the artist complete the work in the gallery itself. Then in the summer season we launched 'Art in the Age of Steam' with a region-wide marketing campaign and extensive PR promotion. This included a press trip from London, partnerships with steam train operators, advertising at Liverpool Lime Street station, and interviews with Michael Palin who attended the launch. The marketing campaign won us the Mersey Partnership's Tourism Marketing Award and the Marketing Society's Northern Award for 'Best Tourism and Leisure Campaign'.

As part of our strategy to 'wallpaper' the city with NML messages, we interspersed exhibition advertising with a campaign about the Walker's collection which we had previously prepared. Together with other initiatives such as securing partnerships with hotels such as Radisson to promote our venues to guests, it ensured that visitors to Liverpool were never far from a reminder to visit us.

During 2008/9, our visitor numbers grew from 2.2m to 2.7m. At the Walker Art Gallery, numbers grew 32% to 353,000, with 56% of visitors coming from outside Merseyside. What we planned and hoped for – a long-term effect with audiences – seems to have been achieved. We didn't expect 2009 visit numbers to exceed 2008, but we were encouraged to find they were 5% higher than in 2007. In 2009, Liverpool was named in the top three UK city break destinations by readers of Condé Nast Traveller. In our own profiling survey, 58% told us that one of our venues was their main reason for visiting the city that day. And even more amazing, we welcomed more visitors from overseas to our museums and galleries during 2009/10 than we did in 2008/9.

Case study 9C: Manchester Museums Consortium's Creative Tourist – a new collaborative model for museums marketing?

Susie Stubbs, consultant, with thanks to Alex Saint, Kate Farmery and Helen Palmer. Manchester Museums Consortium is: Cornerhouse, Imperial War Museum North, The Lowry, Manchester Art Gallery, Manchester Museum, MOSI (Museum of Science & Industry), People's History Museum and Whitworth Art Gallery. (www.creative tourist.com)

Two years ago, Manchester Museums Consortium faced a dilemma. It had secured funding – from the Northwest Regional Development Agency and Renaissance in the Regions – to stage an ambitious programme of international exhibitions and events. Part of this funding was to be used to promote the programme to 'cultural tourists', those national and international visitors who may be persuaded to visit Manchester on the strength of its cultural offer. The dilemma the Consortium faced was this: how could it make marketing work for the Consortium as a whole, for the eight very different museums and galleries that formed its membership, and for a programme that was both disparate and lengthy (it would run for two years and include everything from performance art to historic collections displays)? How, in other words, could it keep its members happy while satisfying the needs of a highly discerning and dispersed audience?

The answer was surprisingly simple. The Consortium adopted a new, digital way of working. It looked to the tourism sector for inspiration. And, most importantly, it made a genuine attempt at collaboration, favouring a 'one for all, and all for one' approach that prioritised the collective over the individual. The answer, then, was 'Creative Tourist', a weekly online arts magazine and series of seasonal city guides that promoted Manchester to national and international audiences. Creative Tourist made perfect sense. After all, the most effective way to reach such audiences is via digital media – and Creative Tourist is almost entirely digital, a website built on Wordpress that is supported by social media and high-quality digital content and marketing campaigns.

But Creative Tourist is more than just a website. It is part of an overarching com-munications strategy for museums and galleries marketing in Manchester, a strategy that remained entirely focused on its bottom line: to drive cultural tourism. So rather than focusing on separate venues and individual events (as in traditional arts marketing), Creative Tourist has instead attempted to create a new credible, cultural brand for Manchester – not just for the museums and galleries that are a part of the Consortium, but for the city as a whole. It is an approach that recognises that cultural marketing is closely related to tourism marketing – that what the Consortium wanted potential visitors to do was not simply visit one exhibition or gallery but in fact take a city break. With this in mind, Creative Tourist developed its series of seasonal city guides that feature not only exhibitions and events but the wider cultural offer of the city – the bars and cafés, the parks and hotels, the nightlife, shopping and more.

The strategy was also based on what the Consortium coined its 'editorial approach'. The argument for this market-driven approach runs thus: if Manchester's museums and galleries wish to appear credible to highly discerning cultural tourists, they should promote only the very best to that market – the edited highlights, if you like. So Creative Tourist picks from the overall cultural programme, choosing only what will appeal to its markets.

Although the argument is perfectly logical, it is by no means easy to implement, not for eight Consortium members who in the past would expect to be featured equally in return for their individual marketing investment. But without this focus Creative Tourist wouldn't have worked and, to their credit, the Consortium members wholeheartedly embraced the idea. For the Consortium, the benefits of creating a bigger picture outweighed individual venue concerns. When the city benefits, it reasoned, we all benefit.

There is something else that is crucial to the success of this project. Manchester was and remains the Consortium's core brand. Creative Tourist sells the city and its history, its culture and radical political past and its recent social, cultural and economic renaissance. With Manchester as its brand, Creative Tourist differentiates itself from an extremely competitive cultural marketplace by ditching bland marketing truisms ('world-class', '21st-century city', and so on) and instead creates a compelling editorial voice for Manchester. Creative Tourist has a little Mancunian personality, if you like.

So does Creative Tourist work? As an online magazine, it is editorially independent and attracts around 22,000 unique users every month, with high dwell times on the site and low bounce rates. 80% of readers are from outside the North West – exactly its target audience. The site has won two digital awards, and publishes original features, news, podcasts and audio from some of the UK's best-known writers and artists. Running alongside, and timed to coincide with the three peak tourism seasons in the city, are its city guides. Pegged to these guides are parallel marketing campaigns that use a combination of online and offline media to boost web traffic and encourage downloads of the city guides (and thus visits to Manchester).

The city guides support the weekly magazine, and the magazine supports the city guides, two elements that dovetail to create a sense that, year-round, there is always something interesting to do in Manchester – crucial if the Consortium is to change perceptions of the city as a cultural destination. Research suggests that Creative Tourist is succeeding here, too: at the last site review, for example, 40% of those surveyed said that the site changed their perceptions of Manchester for the better. Elsewhere, the Consortium has begun coordinating individual venue programmes so that they coincide with peak tourism periods. The February 2010 city guide, for example, drew together a string of major exhibition openings and delivered a joined-up PR and tourism campaign that generated media coverage worth around £5 million. The 'Manchester Weekender', meanwhile, in October 2010, both commissioned and presented a joined-up, city-wide cultural programme for the first time, and created the kind of buzz normally only seen during major events such as Manchester International Festival.

Two years ago, however, the world of museums and galleries marketing was very different. There were fewer financial constraints and greater opportunities for funding. Cultural marketing now is something of an unknown – cuts have begun and how deeply they penetrate is yet to be discovered. But the plans put in place in Manchester in 2008 may yet yield results. Manchester Museums Consortium has pioneered a new, collaborative way of working. It has moved towards market- and tourism-led communications. It has demonstrated that culture is a vital part of a city's national and international profile. It is hoped, then, that the lessons Manchester Museums Consortium has learned over the past few years may yet be ones that develop and expand in the years ahead, no matter how drastically the political and funding landscape changes.

CHAPTER 10 THE MEDIA OVERVIEW – THE FUTURE IS . . . ?

Case study 10A: Banksy at Bristol – the unexpected impact of social media

In June 2009 an exhibition called 'Banksy versus Bristol Museum' hit world headlines. Banksy – a graffiti artist from Bristol – had 'taken over' Bristol Museum and Art Gallery in secret to curate his first ever museum exhibition. After this stunning success, the museum had to consider how to prolong the effect and maintain their profile. Rebecca Burton, Deputy Head of Commercial and Customer Services talks about the exhibition and its aftermath.

With over 100 pieces of Banksy art, many created for the show and referencing Bristol's collections, the exhibition was a huge popular success. Over 300,000 people visited in 12 weeks, making 'Banksy versus Bristol Museum' one the year's most visited exhibitions globally.

Spend on marketing was minimal. There was no advertising or print to promote the exhibition. Word spread through social networking sites such as YouTube and Twitter – demonstrating the potential power of social media marketing – and international PR.

Banksy created a short film posted on YouTube the night before the exhibition opened. Within days this had had several hundred thousand hits from across the world. To date this video has had nearly a million hits and people are still posting comments. The exhibition was covered in the international news – radio, television and printed media.

The audience were active in promoting the show. Banksy is protective of his images being used by companies for commercial purposes, but allows the public to freely photograph and distribute images of his artwork. A noticeable trait of visitors to the exhibition was the way they viewed the art, often through the lens of a camera or their mobile phones. Thus images of the exhibition multiplied through its duration, as visitors photographed the artworks, posted images and reviews on to the web, and texted images around the world to friends and relations.

From the opening day there were queues. As the reputation of the exhibition spread through social networks and media, the queues built to a point where people were waiting for up to 7 hours to see the exhibition. In fact the queues became part of the visit experience, with people coming prepared to wait. There are accounts of people making friends, taking part in sing-alongs, and settling down with chairs, coffees, newspapers and books whilst they waited to see the Banksy exhibition.

The audience reflected the national and international appeal of the artist and the publicity. People travelled from across the world to see the exhibition. 60% of the visitors came from outside of Bristol, specifically to see the show.

When it closed at the end of August 2009, 'Banksy versus Bristol Museum' had generated over £14m in economic benefit for Bristol. It gave Bristol Museum and Art Gallery and the city an international profile. From autumn 2009, the challenge for Bristol Museums was how to build on that success.

'Banksy versus Bristol Museum' was a reasonably high-risk enterprise for Bristol museums – museum staff never knowingly met the artist and the exhibition was developed in secret, with very few people involved. In fact the decision to do the exhibition was informed by strategic work that had already taken place on the Bristol Museums, Galleries and Archives (BMGA) brand. The brand model features words like 'provocative' and 'edgy'.

This thinking meant that when approached by Banksy's agents the BMGA management was open to the opportunity of working with the artist. The exhibition was something that fitted with the values and ambitions of the museum service identified through the brand project. The service aspired to be provocative and edgy, to do things in new ways and to work in collaboration, to actively empower and engage visitors. The brand model is still used actively and regularly to challenge what BMGA does and how it does it.

There is a comfortable fit between these ideas and social marketing. In social media marketing, visitors can take ownership of marketing and promotion, reviewing and even extending museum activity and displays/exhibitions by using websites such as Flickr and Myspace to add their own contributions.

BMGA is now actively using sites such as Facebook and Twitter to promote the museums and exhibitions and to share latest news, enabling comment and feedback from visitors. In addition, curators and marketing staff are blogging on social networking sites. Twelve months on from Banksy, an exhibition called 'Art from the New World' displayed works from new American contemporary and street artists in a new *'low-brow'* art movement. In this case the artists again promoted the exhibition, blogging on their own and other websites about the works they had created and about the exhibition. Dita Von Teese performed at the exhibition opening and within a few hours had tweeted on her Twitter site about the museum and her favourite objects in the museum collections.

BMGA is applying what it has learnt about social media in the creation and marketing of a new £27m city history museum for Bristol, called M Shed. M Shed will be a new kind of museum where visitors will be able to add their own stories and perspectives in the galleries and online, and to debate issues that affect the city today and in the future. The interim promotional website interfaces with Flickr, YouTube and Myspace, and an RSS feed enables interested parties to pull information from the website. The updated website will become an extension of the visit experience, not just a marketing tool. It will enable visitors to upload their own images and stories, debate and vote online, as part of a community of users.

Cultural organisations using social media no longer seems 'cutting edge' – it is an essential in terms of meeting the expectations of many visitors. The challenge is to keep up with visitors – particularly younger visitors – and make the right decisions about where to invest limited marketing resources. Since 'Bansky versus Bristol Museum', BMGA has significantly reduced its promotional print and advertising spend for the museums – and yet visit numbers are up on previous years. As yet BMGA does not have the market research to understand to what extent this is due to the impact of social media marketing.

CHAPTER 11 ENGAGING WITH THE MEDIA THROUGH PR

Case study 11A: Marketing and PR at a small, underfunded gallery

Today, Dulwich Picture Gallery enjoys an international reputation. This has not always been the case. Kate Knowles, now retired Head of Communications, was only able to be employed for two days a week when she first started at the Gallery, and everything had to be done on small resources.

Dulwich Picture Gallery receives no government funding and therefore all its budgets are tight. There is an admission charge for everyone except children, students, the unemployed and the registered disabled. It runs an award-winning education department and three critically acclaimed exhibitions a year. It is an old master collection of outstanding quality. Despite all these strengths it has to battle with its location, which is off the beaten track. When I arrived at the beginning of the 1990s, there were 20,000 visitors a year, and now it's nearer 140,000.

The first thing I did when I arrived, and realised that whatever action I took would need to be done as cheaply as possible, was to telephone the press. Press coverage is a form of free marketing. By focusing my limited time in this way we soon gained press coverage, and within three months the visitor figures had risen by 25%.

When the Gallery was faced with bankruptcy, we held a press conference at Christie's auction house in central London, knowing that the press would be more likely to go there than to Dulwich. I also contacted ten important journalists, including leader writers, and told them the story, embargoed until the morning of the press conference. This gave them time to research long and interesting stories about the Gallery. The plight of the Gallery made headlines. It was covered on BBC news programmes, and the story became international, reaching America and Japan. We were sent a huge cheque that very day by a generous donor.

On discovering that the managing director of Ipsos MORI lived nearby, I asked him whether his organisation would conduct a visitors' survey free of charge. To our delight they did so. From the survey we learned a great deal about our visitors and were able to target the type of person who clearly liked the gallery. We learned that they were, on the whole, middle-aged women who liked art , which provided us with a rationale for our marketing and for any modest advertising that we were able to do.

I then tried to do some joint ventures with other more popular galleries. We did a leaflet called 'Soane's London' (the Gallery is one of a number of London buildings designed by Sir John Soane). This attracted visitors interested in architecture. Another successful leaflet was called 'Alternative Old Masters'. The unwritten message was that there were places apart from the National Gallery and well-known central London locations where you could see old master paintings. We teamed up with the Wallace Collection, Apsley House and Kenwood – all of whom had great old master collections and were trying to appeal to the same audiences as us. At that time, all of them had more visitors than we did. I asked a reprographic machinery company to print our literature during their open days for free – and they did. Every time I went abroad I checked the overseas 'Guides to Britain' – none of which ever mentioned Dulwich, so I would note the name of the publishers and send them details of the Gallery with the aim of getting us into every guidebook in the world!

Our visitors tended to come at weekends so we targeted groups who were at leisure during the week to get them to come midweek. We begged, borrowed and stole lists of group organisers from, among others, NADFAS (National Association of Decorative & Fine Art Societies), the University of the Third Age, art history societies, the National Trust, and the NACF. Three times a year we sent them information about all our forthcoming exhibitions, together with a form telling them how to book in. From an average of one group a week, we found ourselves at capacity and having to turn them away.

We did promotions with newspapers, with local railway lines, with local cinemas, with the events listing magazine *Time Out*, and with other magazines. These promotions allowed us to monitor who was coming, and told us something about their reading habits.

We asked the British Tourist Authority (as it was then) to bring foreign journalists to see the Gallery. From among our foreign volunteers we found people to translate our press releases. We also got them to contact arts journalists from their country of origin to invite them to visit England to see the Gallery – with some success.

We targeted destination travel companies. For example, when we had our Beatrix Potter exhibition, we asked a Japanese volunteer to get in touch with Japanese travel agents because we had been told that Beatrix Potter is extremely popular in that country. We also contacted all the Japanese newspapers and magazines in the UK, and wrote to Japanese companies based in London telling them about the exhibition and how they could hire the gallery for parties. This made a significant contribution to our visitor figures from among London's Japanese communities and by visitors from Japan.

Every now and then we have journalists' lunches or breakfast conferences and keep them up to date on things that are happening. We try to make news stories all the time. If a tree is being chopped down in the garden we get the local press to cover it. When the descendant of the King of Poland claimed that our pictures were rightly his (in the 1790s the collection now at Dulwich was destined to be the Polish royal collection, but history intervened and it was never delivered) – we turned it into an attractive press story. (One newspaper even sent a reporter to Poland to interview him.)

Since reopening the Gallery after refurbishment, we have, with the assistance of a grant, been able to develop a very good website, designed by Reading Room. We hire the Gallery out for weddings and parties – and the corporate hire income has doubled in the last year. We also keep an email list for anyone who wants to be kept up to date with monthly information. The Friends organisation is now over 50 years old. They put on musical events, lectures, parties, walks, visits and films, so the Gallery isn't just a gallery – it's a way of life. In 2011, the Gallery celebrated its 200th anniversary.

Case study 11B: Reaching an ethnic mix from an electronic press office at LACMA, Los Angeles

Barbara Pflaumer, Associate Vice-President for Communications and Marketing , Los Angeles County Museum of Art, describes how a great Los Angeles collection moved its press office into the electronic age, and now reaches out across language barriers to its local communities with inventiveness and a sense of immediacy.

The Los Angeles County Museum of Art (LACMA) is located in one of the most culturally diverse cities in the world. It is said that over a hundred languages are spoken in the public schools here. Connecting with the various ethnicities and diverse cultures that populate this megalopolis is a challenge for anyone, but for the non-profit environment with its limited resources this is especially true.

In 2008 LACMA opened the Broad Contemporary Art Museum – BCAM as it became known – and the Communications and Marketing Department learned a variety of techniques which were put to use for the 2010 opening of the Lynda and Stewart Resnick Pavilion. The most valuable of the new approaches has been the expanded use of the museum's homepage.

Historically, when preparing to inform the media of upcoming events, many hours would be spent assembling photographic images (black and white photos, colour slides and colour transparencies), assembling press kits, writing cover letters, etc. Not only would this take enormous human resources but the mailing costs were staggering (we won't even touch on the vagaries of the US postal service!). After these materials were mailed, the press professional would have to follow up by constantly confirming with the recipient that these lovingly assembled press materials had been received. Since most of the addressees received hundreds, if not thousands, of similar packets from others, it was inevitably an ongoing struggle to get LACMA's kits to the top of the heap. During the opening of BCAM a press page was introduced on the web, complete with an image bank. The image bank was replete with both high- and low-resolution, pre-screened, rights-cleared images that the outlet could download and use immediately. In addition, we placed the entire contents of the press kit online, thus simplifying access to key information. This revolutionized how we proceeded – it saved money and literally hundreds of hours of staff time. The department hasn't mailed a CD in two years!

This saved time allowed the staff to further concentrate on the media segments most important to LACMA. Although, as mentioned earlier, Los Angeles has a highly diverse population there are primarily two market shares that the museum particularly wanted to connect with: the Spanish speakers and the Korean audience. (Los Angeles has the largest Korean population outside of Seoul!) The Spanish-speaking audience does not speak with a single voice, since there are many countries of origin represented within this category. The largest segment is originally from Mexico, followed by the substantial number of Angelenos from Central American countries, each with their own cultures and Spanish dialect.

LACMA has an ongoing Latin America initiative which combines exhibitions, permanent and temporary; an education component, which includes film and music; and, in addition, programmes that focus specifically on the art in the permanent collection. The Communications and Marketing Department has added a Spanish Twitter account, a bilingual visitor information page on the web, and has extended its scope by forming partnerships with all the substantial Spanish-speaking media outlets in the region. Press releases have been translated into Spanish whenever possible, and strategic alliances have been formed with publications such as the hugely influential Spanish-language newspaper *La Opinion*, and with the electronic media such as Telemundo and Univision (with hundreds of millions of viewers/users throughout the Latin American world). Although advertising budgets continue to be modest, the museum has been able to create trades with the primary communicators to the Spanish-speaking audience.

LACMA has been able to reach the Korean public more effectively by working more closely with the two big Korean newspapers in the city. Since they are competitors, the museum has had to create separate but equal relationships with each – sometimes proving a bigger challenge than working collaboratively with the *New York Times* and *LA Times*! A Korean-speaking member of the department has stewarded this process, with the necessary understanding of the sensitivities of both, and managing to find unique materials for each. This is an audience where LACMA has seen real growth in the past year, partially because of the reopening of the Korean galleries and the presentation of a contemporary Korean exhibition, but also as a result of carefully orchestrated media work. For the contemporary Korean show, each of the young artists in the exhibition was profiled by one of the key newspapers, while to the other the museum offered special access to a Korean national treasure on loan to the museum. All this was timed to coincide with the opening of the newly reinstalled galleries. Both were given access to the curator, a native Korean.

The opening of the Resnick Pavilion offered the LACMA team a chance to use all the techniques above as well as to further utilize the blog, podcasts, Flickr, iTunes, Twitter, etc. These options have made it possible for the museum to reach out quickly; to constantly update the public on exhibitions, events, and news; and to do so in a time-effective and cost-effective manner that is dramatically different from the way it was done, even as recently as three years ago. The museum blog has also resulted in coverage beyond expectation. Time and again, small blog entries have become stories in major outlets. The museum continues its efforts to connect with a variety of audiences by making sure that the voices on the blog are not solely academic in tone – in fact the opposite has been the goal. Hence everyone across all disciplines and all levels of staff has contributed, from guards to the museum staff photographer.

Accessibility has been the call to arms, and 'Unframed' – the award-winning blog – has achieved its goal. When LACMA opened a mini-exhibition which coincided with the 6-month long 'Eat LACMA' project, many of the paintings of fruit in the permanent collection were brought together, including a particular painting of a pear. During a routine preparatory inspection, the Conservation Department discovered the stem of the pear glued to the back of the canvas, together with an explanation of why the pear had been considered important enough to have its portrait painted – it was a four-pound prize-winner from 1864, dubbed 'The Great California Pear'. The conservator who made the discovery told the story in the official blog, causing enormous public interest.

The museum has a large outdoor sculpture titled 'Urban Light' by Chris Burden which was installed when BCAM was completed. It is a work made up of 202 municipal lampposts from all over LA County which have been renovated, painted and installed on the campus facing the street. This solar-powered work has become an iconic landmark, and there is virtually no time when there isn't someone there photographing a friend or making a video. There have even been wedding reception photographs taken there. On the one-year anniversary of Urban Light, the museum held a contest inviting the public to send their photos of the sculpture, and was immediately inundated with entries, to such an extent that LACMA ended up offering a print-on-demand book of the best entries. Obviously, this exercise had the unintended consequence of offering an insight into who was following the blog – something which is always of interest to the research department.

The museum's homepage had almost four million unique visitors for the fiscal year 2009–2010, and is the number-one way that people prepare for their visit to LACMA. It is no coincidence that the museum's attendance in the past four years grew from the mid-600,000s to 904,000 for the 2009–2010 fiscal year.

While promoting the gala to launch the week of celebrations surrounding the opening of the Resnick Pavilion, the museum sent out a release via AP (Associated Press news agency) from which we garnered over 119 million impressions. The ability to calculate the impact of such releases is also crucial to assessing how we expend our resources. More and more, LACMA employs web banner advertising, not only for its cost-effectiveness, but more importantly for the impact on broader audiences. We can geo-target our advertising dollars in very strategic ways to ensure a particular audience is seeing our messages. Measuring agencies such as Vocus and Cision can give back very detailed information about who is seeing and hearing the museum's messages, and when dollars are limited, this is an invaluable tool.

There is no replacing the bread and butter of press relations: the building of relationships with members of the media. Despite all the innovations of the web, the fundamental tools cannot be abandoned. The one-on-one outreach done by the staff is central to the department's efforts. The team continues to develop media plans for each exhibition, studying the primary and secondary markets and then making a plan of action. We collaborate with the marketing team to highlight the messages for each show and to make certain there is an alliance between those messages and the LACMA brand. We underscore the museum's literal and figurative location as 'the town square'; that we are the county museum, which means we are the people's museum, and through our programming we offer something for everyone. This reflects the encyclopaedic nature of the collections and we have an obligation to do so.

Ultimately it is persistence that wins the day – we continue to use the time-tested strategies of crafting specific messages and pitches that are in sync with the brief of the outlet we are pitching to. Over time, the PR professional comes to know what will and will not work for any given medium, and works within that guideline.

Case study 11C: Twitter campaign for National Poetry Day

Truda Spruyt, Associate Director, Colman Getty

National Poetry Day was established sixteen years ago to celebrate the reading, writing and performing of poetry. It takes place on the first Thursday of October each year. An umbrella campaign with lots of grassroots involvement from poets and educators,

National Poetry Day has always relied on PR to communicate and maximise its impact. Colman Getty has worked on the PR campaign for National Poetry Day since its inception.

As part of an ongoing strategy to grow National Poetry Day's visibility in the digital sphere, it was decided in 2009 to establish a presence on the social networking website Twitter, which, with its emphasis on writing with economy and wit, was already becoming a firm favourite in the poetic community.

Our planning was informed by the following strategy:

1   Define aims and decide on relevant platforms

2   Research other organisations and campaigns

3   Set measurable targets (relevant to aims)

4   Set up a branded pages/accounts

5   Participate and monitor conversation

6   Evaluate with analytic tools.

The aim was to establish a presence for National Poetry Day (NPD) on Twitter in order to:

   find new audiences and to engage traditional audiences

   drive traffic to the NPD website

   create a buzz around NPD

   promote NPD events

   share e-poems

   generate conversation about the 2009 theme, 'Heroes and Heroines'

   work with other organisations to cross promote NPD events to their audience.

We researched the Twitter pages of other awareness days such as Red Nose Day and International Women's Day, and other literary organisations, including the *Bookseller*, Bookslam and the Poetry Society.

We decided that National Poetry Day should aim to have at least as much reach as the Reading Agency or Apples & Snakes. Bookslam and Red Nose Day are good examples of organisations that use Twitter around events and the media, so would be good upper-range targets to aim for.

Targets:

   to attract 150–500 followers

   to have journalists, poets, publishers and poetry organisations as followers

- to encourage use of @nat_poetry_day and #poetryheroes

- to boost traffic to the NPD website.

We set up the Twitter page in August 2009 with branding and profile to match the National Poetry Day website, and asked friendly organisations to notify members. We then began following relevant must-read tweeters, from poets to bookshops to literature organisations.

Monitoring:

- following threads of conversation in *Tweetdeck*, using *hashtags* such as *#national poetryday*

- mentions of @poetrydayuk monitored in *Tweetdeck*

- *Tweet Beeps* (like Google Alerts for Twitter) set up for National Poetry Day.

Our participation was a mixture of planned and responsive. The Colman Getty team planned two tweets a day at the beginning, then three to four times a day in the two weeks leading up to National Poetry Day. The tweets, polite and informal in tone, consisted of NPD updates and interesting poetry stories, including re-tweeting relevant information. We took care to respond to any direct tweets and shared insights into National Poetry Day.

Evaluation – we used a number of Twitter tools to evaluate our success including:

- Twitter searches for @nat_poetry_day, #nationalpoetryday and National Poetry Day to see what people were saying about NPD

- Trendistic to monitor the level of conversation relative to other topics

- TwInfluence to measure the reach of @poetrydayuk

- Google Analytics to measure traffic to the NPD website.

By November 2009, National Poetry Day had 412 followers on Twitter, including journalists, poets, magazines, newspapers, publishers, poetry organisations and individuals. This compares with Free Word Centre: 226 followers, Apples & Snakes: 262, the Reading Agency: 521, Red Nose Day (Comic Relief): 552, Bookslam: 648 and Poetry Society: 1,748.

National Poetry Day tweeted 304 times in September and October 2009. Our followers (see above) passed on our messages to their own networks 286 times. If all of our followers re-tweeted just one message from National Poetry Day we would reach a readership of 315,206 on Twitter. Further highlights included:

- For a few hours on 8 October, National Poetry Day was second most talked about subject on Twitter worldwide. It remained in the top ten Twitter trending topics for about 12 hours.

- The buzz about NPD on Twitter was so big that it spread around the world, with tweeters from as far as Australia, Korea and America applauding the idea of a national day for poetry in the UK.

- TED, an influential US video site, blogged about the phenomenon.

- 231 people followed links to the NPD website from Twitter, making it the fifth biggest source of traffic behind search engines, the BBC, Facebook and the Children's Poetry Bookshelf.

Case study 11D: Measuring social media in PR – a professional approach

Trying to measure the results of a social media campaign might be a fool's errand, but here, Richard Bagnall, Managing Director of Metrica, comments on the role of such campaigns and gives sensible advice. Metrica is one of the world's largest specialist PR measurement consultancies, established in 1993. In 2009 Metrica became a part of the Discovery Group of companies, joining forces with media monitoring firm Durrants and PR planning and journalist database specialists Gorkana.

Metrica and Richard are both active in social media themselves and invite you to join the conversation with them via their blog www.metrica.net/measurementmatters on Twitter (@richardbagnall and @metricameasures) and on their Facebook page.

The rise of online and social media has created great challenges for modern PR professionals and their media relations strategies. Not long ago journalists were the gatekeepers of access to – and influence over – an organisation's target audiences. Well-connected PR professionals could leverage their relationships with journalists to seek to achieve positive coverage in the publications that their target audiences read.

Web 2.0 and the advent of social media have changed all of that. The old world of media is caught in a perfect storm. Hurt from the advertising recession that started with the economic downturn, the pain has escalated as advertising revenues have moved away from regional and print publications to online outlets instead. This, coupled with advances in technology that make it easy for anyone to create content and effectively become a publisher, has meant that the media is fragmenting, audiences are diversifying and most journalists are consequently less influential than before. Today's modern PR professional ignores the new media at their peril.

Case studies abound of organisations like United Airlines, Gap and Kit-Kat that have been caught out by the rise of social media and its ability to fan the flames of a crisis. In the past, when crises engulfed an organisation, they were far easier for the communications team to respond to by implementing a crisis communication plan. The old media did not offer easy methods for the target audience to connect with each other and fuel the situation. Negative stories might be discussed between friends in the pub, on the phone or at the fabled office water cooler, but there was no easy way for these conversations to link to each other and gain critical mass by feeding off each other. News travels much faster now – with the click of a Facebook 'like' button or a re-tweet on Twitter, news can spread across audiences, countries and continents in almost real time.

The knock-on effect has been total upheaval in the communications industry, with Rupert Murdoch commenting as far back as 2006: 'It is difficult, indeed dangerous, to under-estimate the huge changes this revolution will bring or the power of developing technologies to build and destroy – not just companies but whole countries.'

As we accept the importance of social media the challenge of how best to measure it is more pertinent than ever. The first thing to do is to make sure that you are monitoring the millions of conversations relevant to your organisation that are going on. There are a number of ways to do this, from setting up your own free feeds, using tools like Google reader and blog search, to paying for one of the social media monitoring tools to do this for you. It is important to remember that these tools are not all as good as each other – recent research undertaken by Metrica found an alarming conflict in total numbers of posts reported by competing platforms.

Monitoring social media will only tell you so much, however. The next step is to measure it and understand what it all means. Here the tools are limited in use and should come with a health warning. Many of them include indices and scores which attempt to identify influencers and trends. The problem with this approach is that they are basing their metrics around what is easy to find, but not necessarily what matters to you – and your organisation. Just because someone has over a million followers on Twitter – Jonathon Ross for example – does not make them necessarily relevant to the conversations that affect you and your target audiences.

The best practice approach to measuring social media is to start at the beginning by asking yourself at the outset of your programme some basic questions. What are you looking to achieve with this campaign? What is the goal of your social media activity? Who do you want to communicate with? What are your objectives? What would success look like to the organisation and the department? Ask yourself these questions and you should rapidly find that you have a tailored list of objectives around which you can wrap your metrics. This approach will ensure that your metrics will also speak to your organisation, rather than running the risk of being a number that doesn't have any true meaning or reflect your endeavours correctly.

When we started out at Metrica 17 years ago, we found that the PR world faced similar challenges then as now. Companies were starting out on the journey to measure PR, and different suppliers were offering different approaches to fulfil this need. There was a clamour for an industry standard number to measure PR but it never occurred because communications can't be measured with single numbers and indices.

PR has always been about establishing goals, setting measurable objectives and then looking at appropriate metrics to reflect the messaging and target audience exposure to the content. Taking this further, organisations look at what the effect of the communications programme was on the target audience – did it raise awareness or drive footfall, sales or similar. Measuring social media successfully should be approached with the same mind-set. Sometimes the more things seem to change, the more they stay the same.

CHAPTER 12 EVENTS AS PART OF PUBLIC RELATIONS

Case study 12A: A textbook opening in Chicago – working with consultants

In May 2009, the Art Institute of Chicago opened the eighth expansion in its 130-year history, the Modern Wing. This major undertaking involved a classic publicity campaign described here by Erin Hogan, Director of Public Affairs.

Designed by Renzo Piano, the Modern Wing was built to house the museum's permanent collection of twentieth- and twenty-first-century painting, sculpture, photography, and architecture and design. At 264,000 square feet, the wing includes permanent collection galleries, special exhibition galleries, a state-of-the-art education facility, a dedicated black box gallery for new media, a restaurant and outdoor sculpture terrace, and a pedestrian bridge into Millennium Park, in the heart of downtown Chicago. With the addition of the Modern Wing, the Art Institute became the second largest art museum in the United States.

The first critical step in putting together the publicity campaign for the Modern Wing was engaging an outside firm to assist the staff at the museum. The public affairs staff consists of three people, and, throughout the Modern Wing project, all of the ongoing activities of the museum – 40 exhibitions per year across ten curatorial departments, acquisitions, gifts and donations to the museum and to the capital campaign, staff additions, and related reinstallation projects – required consistent attention. The Art Institute selected Ruder Finn Arts and Communications Counselors as independent consultants for the project, in part because of their excellent history with high-profile museum building projects.

The campaign began with an audit of the museum conducted two years before opening. In this audit, staff from Ruder Finn assessed the perceptions among professionals both inside and outside of the Art Institute to identify areas of both strength and weakness. From this audit emerged several central ideas and opportunities around which the publicity campaign was based. For example, while the Renzo Piano Building Workshop was extremely well known and a considerable asset, findings from the audit indicated that little was known about the Art Institute's vast contemporary collection that the building was constructed in part to house. Additionally, the connection to Millennium Park was identified as an important platform to increase the awareness of the museum's role in the civic life of Chicago.

The publicity campaign, shaped by Ruder Finn and the Art Institute, concentrated on the messages informed by the audit, worked on a specific timeline laid out in a work plan, and hinged on events in both Chicago and other cities. Starting two years in advance of the opening of the building, the focus of the publicity efforts of the museum centred on acquisitions and exhibitions of contemporary art, milestones in the building process and capital campaign, and enhancing the perception of the museum internationally.

Beginning in early 2008, multiple events were held in Chicago, New York, and selected European cities to introduce the museum and the Modern Wing to as wide an audience as possible. Locally, tours of the unfinished building were held over the course of several months for a number of different constituencies: elected officials at the local, state, and national levels; downtown 'neighbours' such as professional and cultural organizations; leaders of large religious organizations; educators from all categories of Chicagoland institutions; donors; and of course art and architecture critics.

Thus, in New York, about 18 months before the Modern Wing opened, the Art Institute hosted a luncheon event for art, architecture, and cultural critics. In late 2008, approximately 6 months before the opening of the Modern Wing, the museum hosted further similar events in Berlin, Frankfurt, London, and Paris for international art and architecture critics, as well as travel writers and industry professionals. These events were designed not only to introduce attendees to the museum but to Chicago in general as well. Appearing at each of the events in other cities were: the director of the museum, Jim Cuno; curators representing the departments that would be housed in the new building; and representatives from the Renzo Piano Building Workshop. Each presentation included: an introduction to Chicago and to the Art Institute; specific information about the museum's collections in modern European art, contemporary art, modern photography, and architecture and design; and a detailed explanation of the goals and design of the Modern Wing.

Additionally, in late 2008, Ruder Finn and the Art Institute brought a select group of art and architecture critics, both national and international, to Chicago for two days to hear more from the curators and director, physically tour the building before art installation, and become familiar with the city and the museum.

Printed press materials began to be distributed two years prior to opening, with an online press room going live about a year prior to opening. The materials included slideshows of significant works in the collection, timelines of construction progress, and a general introduction to the museum. These materials were translated into French and German for the European events.

The timing of the campaign ensured that many different audiences would get an 'early look' at the building, either in person or through presentations. After the press trip to Chicago in late 2008, access to the building was severely restricted, both to ensure that the final process of art installation would not be disrupted and to be able to 'reveal' the building (and its collections) when it was all fully installed and complete.

In the week before opening week, select local and national critics visited the building to ensure coverage for the opening weekend. The opening week of the Modern Wing, from Saturday, May 9 until the public opening day on Saturday, May 16, was highly scheduled, with 23 events in those eight days. The opening week began with a fundraising gala, proceeds of which were used to support the opening week and the week following, in which free admission was offered to the whole museum. From May 11 to May 16, preview events were held for a number of different groups, including Chicago educators and students, members, donors and collectors, two separate press events (one local and oriented toward broadcast media, the other oriented to national and international critics courted over the previous two years), an opening party for art-world leaders and professionals, a late-night party for younger audiences, and events for the four curatorial departments whose collections were installed in the building.

The building officially opened on May 16, 2009 with a public civic dedication and ribbon-cutting ceremony featuring the mayor of Chicago Richard M. Daley, White House Chief of Staff Rahm Emanuel, Renzo Piano, President of the Board of Trustees Tom Pritzker, Jim Cuno, and leaders of four boards of the museum. At the conclusion of that ceremony, the building opened to the public and hosted 44,000 visitors in the opening weekend alone.

Case study 12B: Saving Planet Earth live broadcast and party: a fabulous opportunity – and an absolute nightmare

When the BBC announced new initiatives on green issues, Sue Runyard, at that time Head of PR at the Royal Botanic Gardens, Kew, was quick to beat a path to their door. The unexpected response was a request to hold a fundraising concert for wildlife conservation in an outside broadcast from the gardens. It seemed a fairly straightforward proposition to begin with.

Kew holds a licence for about 50 weddings each year; a series of summer picnic concerts; public festivals all year round; and much more. When the BBC said that they wanted to do a live broadcast from the gardens with rock band performances and a grand opera finale, we thought we were the luckiest PR people in the world. It would position Kew with a young audience, and showcase our wonderful gardens and venues.

With just five weeks to plan it, we hastily called a meeting with our commercial events team, security chief, caterer, and estate manager, and established that the brief could be met. However, we had reckoned without the fluidity of TV production. The BBC looked around and saw many potential backdrops, becoming more ambitious in their plans. The Kew team looked around and saw a fragile UNESCO World Heritage Site that needed careful management. During the first two weeks of planning, the guest list changed from 400 to 2,000. Three locations turned into six, requiring the erection of two sound stages, installation of generators and a complex power network, and access for 40 large trucks. And, finally, someone was needed to row the opera star across to an island on a lake.

As we got into the final details, it became obvious that we could not contain guests within the areas for which we had a licence. Kew is situated in the middle of a residential area, and every licensed area we had was hard-fought-for. The relationship between myself, as PR champion of Kew's licensing applications, and the local council's licensing officer, was not a smooth one, but I had to call him in. We were now two weeks from the already publicised concert, when the licensing officer declared the event illegal.

Aside from any penalties, it was obvious that our licence for all those weddings and festivals would be at risk. What would the licensing officer do in our situation? Mindful of the charitable nature of the event, he pointed me to the small print of the 2003 Licensing Act, which has a provision for private parties. How do you make an event of this scale private? Answer: if you can supply a name and address for every person attending the party, and if they can prove their identity on arrival.

We threw ourselves into the challenge. Forewarned of requirements, our guests arrived clutching passports to have their names checked off on mighty long lists at reception points with treble the number of staff originally planned. The procedure took place under the noses of inspectors sent by the council to ensure that we did not infringe the rules.

Honour was saved. The party was great. Relationships were salvaged. What did I learn? Risk-averse organisations never venture into new territory. Where people are well-motivated and experienced – and enjoy working as a team – you can solve all problems. In addition, every experience teaches you something new. Six months earlier we had hosted the Queen's 80th birthday party, with a private dinner for 28 members of the Royal family, a firework display for the public, and security issues beyond imagination. It had presented a completely different set of challenges, but we did it, and it made us a team.

CHAPTER 13 INTERNAL COMMUNICATIONS WITH STAFF, BOARDS AND VOLUNTEERS

Case study 13A: Ashmolean Museum of Art and Archaeology: a new building and a new approach

The Ashmolean Museum in Oxford is one of the oldest museums in the world, with a collection of international importance. It was always regarded as a deeply traditional museum, but when a major building redevelopment took place, management decided to bring about change internally as well as externally. Achieving effective communications among staff was one objective, while another was to improve visitor services. Here, Gillian Morris, Head of Human Resources, tells us more.

The vision of the Ashmolean Museum is 'to be an open door to the excellence of Oxford, sparking in everyone a curiosity for the beauty, diversity and intellectual richness of our collections'. As an essential step towards achieving this, the Museum completed its Masterplan redevelopment in November 2009, delivering 39 new permanent galleries, together with new temporary exhibition galleries, study and teaching facilities, conservation studios, and significantly enhanced visitor facilities, including Oxford's first roof-top restaurant. A new brand identity was also established. The redevelopment has received huge critical and public acclaim, evidenced by the very significant number of visitors to the Museum since its reopening, exceeding one million in the first year of operation.

The gallery installation work was led by the curators, but was a task that called heavily on many others too – our designers, conservators, educators, IT specialists, and photographers – everyone in the Museum. It was a huge task, way beyond anything else in the Ashmolean's history, and it would be hard to exaggerate the pressure the staff were under to make this vision a reality. It was remarkable how much they managed to continue their normal work, whether front of house continuing to make our visitors welcome – despite the unavoidable closure of much of the museum – or behind the scenes researching, teaching, and adding to the collections.

The dream was not just to replace tired buildings with a thrilling new one but to take the opportunity to rethink fundamentally the way the Ashmolean's collections should be presented to the world and so make it once more a jewel in Oxford's crown. This was an ambitious task, consisting of a 100,000-square-foot new building of six floors intermeshed with the older structure. It was vital that the dignity of the old façade be respected, while achieving a modern presentation of the collections inside.

The project had four main components: construction of the building; installation of the gallery displays; fundraising; a change management programme involving every member of the staff; and a re-branding project that engaged and excited all who were involved. For the staff, the most demanding aspect of the project was working up the new gallery displays. Guided by our theme 'Crossing Cultures, Crossing Time', these displays make the new Ashmolean a distinctively exciting museum to visit, along with the tone of voice being adopted to explain them. This vision and approach was suggested by the Director and agreed at a very early stage of the redevelopment. It informed everything we then did to bring the project to completion. The curators were fully involved in the new interpretation techniques, with support from the project team.

Staffing levels grew throughout the period of the project in order to meet the short-term, specific needs of the project and to ensure that we had suitably skilled and qualified staff in place ready for the reopening. We knew that with the reopening we would not only be a bigger organisation but a more public-facing, open and engaging one.

A project team was established, and developed and changed throughout the course of the project in response to needs. The project team consisted of external experts, internal project staff and those with responsibility for making the vision a reality right through to the reopening.

The Change Management Team was a small team set up from a representative group of staff to act as a voice and an agent for change within the Museum. A new Museum building and a new display strategy would require our staff to think differently and to work differently. Whilst the building work got underway, most staff moved out of the old building and in to temporary accommodation a mile away. This brought a whole new set of challenges, and communication became key to getting things done. The team had the remit of acting as both a voice for staff and of being empowered to make positive changes to improve working life. One of the early initiatives was to create a regular all-staff meeting that would bring staff together from different sites and from different disciplines to ensure that all staff were sharing the same vision. The meetings focused on the progress of the project whilst helping everyone to visualise the new building and what it would be like to work there.

Our rebranding project built on the success of the Change Management Team and allowed all staff to have a say in the future brand and identity of the Museum. A number of workshops allowed mixed groups of staff to come together and to really shape and plan what it would be like to work in, and for, the Ashmolean Museum.

With so much work going on in both old and new buildings, we reluctantly took the decision to close the Museum to the public from the end of 2008 until the reopening in November 2009. This helped to ensure that the galleries were complete, ready for the reopening. Unfortunately, the impact of this decision placed a small group of our staff at risk of redundancy, and we worked closely with them to ensure that they were supported and given other opportunities within the Museum. The building work was completed in early 2009 and then the huge task of reinstalling the collections began, with 12,000 objects selected for public display in 400 showcases.

In preparation for reopening, the Museum required the appointment of a large number of Visitor Services Assistants (VSAs). The job purpose was to be part of a front-of-house team ensuring a high level of visitor care: 'they will help to ensure that the environment allows the visitor to open his/her mind to the joy of learning'. This was a very different role to that of 'Invigilator' which had been in place prior to the museum's closure, and the VSA role and recruitment to it had to be designed from scratch.

The recruitment campaign was designed to provide a diverse team, reflecting the wide range of visitors expected. We looked for transferable skills, concentrating on the desire and ability to communicate and help people. As well as placing advertisements in the usual media, we recruited through Job Centres, perhaps perceived as an unorthodox move for an academic organisation – but one that proved successful. In all, 49 VSAs were appointed, 22 men and 27 women, with an age range of 18 to 70. One quarter were from ethnic minority groups. Three appointees are known to have learning difficulties or disabilities. One had previously been long-term unemployed. One man and one woman are lone parents. We offered a mix of full-time and part-time work.

A bespoke training and induction programme was created for our new recruits (some of whom were Invigilators before the Museum closed at the end of 2008). The induction programme was intense and detailed, and covered every aspect of the Museum building, the visitor experience, the history of the Museum, and the new display strategy, as well as the key aspects of the role: visitor service, safety and security. This was completely new and the programme was developed before the building was handed back to us. Staff were recruited during the Summer of 2009 and were brought in to undertake their training before the reopening so that they would be ready and prepared to welcome the first new visitor to the Museum. One of our most exciting visitors was Her Majesty the Queen who officially opened the Museum on 2 December 2009.

The efforts of everyone in the museum have ensured that the new building was delivered on time and on budget, and is a tribute to the very hard work of our staff and of the other members of the team – architects, project managers, builders, engineers and many others – with whom we worked. (See Figure 13.1 on p. 191.)

CHAPTER 14 COMMUNICATING WITH STAKEHOLDERS AND PARTNERS – RELATIONSHIP MARKETING

Case study 14A: Initiating partnerships at local level

Dr Delma Tomlin, MBE is an established authority on the promotion and marketing of early music performances. She is Director of the Beverley and York Early Music Festivals and of the National Centre for Early Music, with a background in museums and other cultural organisations. Here she encourages us to grow ambitious projects and partnerships from small beginnings.

It's not easy being a small team – organising exhibitions and events one moment, answering inconsequential enquiries from the public the next and then dealing with the overflow from the sinks in the loo after an excitable group of youngsters have swept through the building leaving you feeling frazzled, and your beloved venue in serious need of a deep clean. Does it make you wonder whether it would be advisable to return to the 'good old days' when curators treasured objects, and the community treasured curators – and all was well with the world?

Do not be tempted! Take a strong coffee, read the local paper, walk around town and keep your eyes open. Who else is looking at the same target market as you? Who is making things happen? Can you think of a way in which you can offer added value to their idea? Whether an idea springs instantly to mind or not, talk to them, offer to help. Get their audience base through your doors and get the local press to acknowledge your support.

If you think that you have more to gain by working collaboratively with others – whether tourism organisations, local businesses, cultural organisations or competitors – make a plan to achieve something bigger than you can achieve on your own. Choose a date which is at a strategic point in your season (at least 10 months ahead – do not be tempted to rush this), think carefully of an idea which reflects your collection and then call a meeting for everyone/anyone who might be interested in learning more. Be welcoming at the meeting – offer light refreshments – be prepared to stand up for your original idea – and be even more prepared to say no to the well-meaning but uneconomic/unrealistic (or just plain dreary) ideas that might also come up. Keep the meeting short and cheerful – and take up ideas from people who you think have something really interesting to offer on another occasion. Remember this is your idea, designed to celebrate your organisation – and keep in your heart the absolute essential of this proposal – that this new partnership can only work for you if based on a quality idea/academic excellence and something that you actually want to do.

Having got your dates and ideas sorted out – continue to tell everyone. Tell the local press and tourism organisations about the dates – give them a working title, a couple of lines of copy, a website and a telephone number for further details. Tell the local schools – if history doesn't interest them, think of a business/enterprise angle. Get the students involved in selling your product and offer work placements to teenagers who are interested in marketing (in the UK all sixth-formers are given time out of school to work in the community) – don't think of your relationship with schools as 'just' teaching them about your collection – they'll learn to value/research just as well by looking at one object in depth and organising/marketing their own exhibition around it.

An added bonus is that you will become part of the community. Once started, there will be an expectation of more to come in later years – it's a bit of a roller-coaster and you'll never have time to sit still again, but working in partnership this way is extremely rewarding – for you, and for your organisation.

The National Centre for Early Music in York is the 'proof of the pudding'. The central conceit is a promotion of historically informed performance practice (aka Early Music). Based on the success of the York Early Music Festival – which was started by a group of interested, academically intelligent enthusiasts in 1977 and increasingly acknow-ledged as 'the' festival of early music in the UK – we had gained enough friends and supporters to enable us to consider applying to the Arts Council Lottery for a grant to create our own performance space.

A grant of £1.5 million, alongside partnership monies of £500,000 from a wide variety of organisations including English Heritage, the Foundation for Sport and the Arts and the Garfield Weston Foundation, enabled us to restore the previously redundant church of St Margaret's – nestling within the medieval walls on the East side of the City – and create an award-winning building which was opened in April 2000.

Ten years on, the NCEM is the bedrock of an international programme celebrating music from the medieval to the classical period, working in partnership with the five local authorities around the City of York, with the Universities of York, Huddersfield and Southampton, with BBC Radio 3, and with partner festivals across Europe. Last year we worked with nearly 2,000 young people as well as promoting three festivals of early music, a regular series of jazz, world and folk concerts and running a nationwide programme of early music concerts in partnership with venues, promoters and artists across the UK – from little acorns mighty collaborations grow!

Case study 14B: Working with local government as a stakeholder

Mark Suggitt, now an independent consultant, has deep experience in the local authority sector. He was formerly Head of Bradford Museums, Galleries and Heritage; Director of St Albans Museums; Assistant Director at Yorkshire & Humberside Museums Council (he also held other cultural sector posts and did overseas advisory work). He is therefore well positioned to talk about managing our relationships with local government. Much of this advice applies to other funding bodies as well.

Stakeholders are those people within and outside an organisation who have the potential to help it thrive. They are people who can directly help us – just as we can help them to achieve their objectives. Organisations and their stakeholders are bound together, and successful organisations map these relationships as a part of the cycle of researching, planning and delivering. Sometimes we only need to monitor and maintain our stakeholder relationships, but there are times when one group or groups become more important than others, and then we must pay them more attention. Those with considerable influence will always remain high-priority, and our relationships with them must be managed closely.

Local authorities are not just direct providers of services. They can also grant-aid independent organisations and commission work. When dealing with local authorities, the key thing to remember is that your organisation can help them achieve their objectives. If you are looking for support from the authority then you also have to realise that they will expect you to demonstrate and prove how you do this. In a world of shrinking resources this is important for those working within both independent and local government museums.

For the huge number of locally funded museums and galleries, relationships with local authorities are of prime importance. In fact, nearly all museums have to engage with them at some level, whether they are directly run by them, operate as trusts running buildings and collections owned by them, or operate as independent charities who obtain grants, support and rate relief from them. Local authorities, in whatever shape they choose to take, will remain important. It is a sector in which many changes have taken place in the past few years, and there may be more to come. If they change their operational practice – for example, to a commissioning model – museum leaders must be aware of the changes afoot and act to take advantage of them.

The first step in forming a positive relationship is to research your authority – which, thanks to the web, is now very easy. Local government websites are packed with information on the political and socio-economic make-up of an area, and a bit of navigation can take you to relevant reports and strategy documents. Understanding the political make-up of an authority is also important, especially when dealing with elected members. Although local authorities continue to be directed by central government and monitored by top-down targets, politics does influence how they act.

Local authorities may appear to be similar to one another, but they are all different. It has to be recognised that, from the cultural perspective, some are better than others. Some genuinely understand the value of culture to tourism, regeneration, education, health and image and seek to develop it; others may talk the talk but fail to invest. The strategies and policies have to be set against what has actually been delivered. The central relationship is that between the senior managers and the politicians. If both understand the burning issues and work together to tackle them they are usually successful. Those where the politicians dominate weak senior officers (and vice versa) are less effective. Understanding where the power lies can be very useful.

You need to be aware of the key corporate priorities and aspirations of your Council. They can often be summarised as aspiring to a richer, greener, healthier, cleaner district with support for education and old people, provided by a leaner, efficient council. You also need to be aware of any cultural, regeneration, health, or education strategies that exist. Whether inside or outside of local government, the museum needs to map its work against these and evaluate how it helps to deliver them. Once this has been done the next step is to promote your value. This means getting out and about.

Paradoxically, it is often easier for museum leaders from trusts and charities to gain access to leading officers and politicians. Often the senior museum officer within local government is at the third tier, and no longer has a committee to present reports to. The downside of this is that it is harder to meet a range of members and develop a working relationship with them. The key relationship is now with the Cabinet Member. Senior staff usually meet with their Cabinet Member every week or so. Local politicians are often quick to appreciate the spending and employment brought to an area by charitable and voluntary organisations. Your trustees will often be well connected with local opinion leaders, and can offer valuable support.

For charitable and trust museums you need to provide good news about your organisation so that when you do need a face-to-face meeting about funding or any other issue the members are already familiar with what you do. This can be done by:

- Ensuring senior officers and politicians are on your mailing list for events and openings

- Sending senior officers and politicians your annual report

- Turning up at local authority openings and events

- Engaging in any cultural/tourism forums that the Council sets up (exercising caution, because some descend into 'talking shops')

- Requesting that you give a brief presentation to a Cultural Scrutiny Committee about your work

- Inviting the Cabinet Member and senior officers to visit your organisation

- Cultivating ward members from the area in which your organisation is based in a similar way. (Many authorities are considering or operating devolved neighbourhood funding, and ward members play a key role in distributing this.)

Local authority officers know the value of providing good news all too well. They also know that a good Cabinet Member will trust good officers. Smart people do not micromanage, but neither do they like unpleasant surprises. If you think an upcoming issue needs their support – a controversial exhibition for example – then talk it over in advance.

To conclude, engage in constructive dialogue and remember that local authorities are under great pressure to deliver on areas like education, regeneration and social services. If they can offer support it is only fair that your case supports their priorities and it is quite reasonable that they ask you to prove it.

Case study 14C: Evolving partners – celebrating 'Darwin200'

Bob Bloomfield, a scientist and Head of Innovation and Special Projects at London's Natural History Museum, describes how his organisation became pro-active in order to solve a potential problem, and acted as a catalyst for a huge collaboration.

In 2006 a small group met to consider the impending celebration of the bicentenary of Charles Darwin and the 150th anniversary of the publication of *On the Origin of Species*, both of which would take place in 2009. Among them were representatives from the Natural History Museum, Charles Darwin Trust, *Nature* magazine, the BBC, the Open University, the University of Cambridge (which hosts important Darwin archives), the Royal Society and the British Council.

Interestingly, while all saw the importance of Darwin's work and its relevance to the present day, a primary concern was the risk that any public celebration might be highjacked to become a narrow, evolution-versus-creation-based argument so typified by the right-wing Christian agenda in the United States.

Everyone around the table knew this would be a travesty, were it to happen, because there were so many significant and important stories to explore: how Darwin's prescience preceded the world of molecular biology, both anticipating it, and being vindicated by it; how Darwin's ideas so questioned our sense of being human that they challenged the arts – for example, making the romanticist John Ruskin furious about its implications to the very notions of the aesthetic and of the meaning of beauty; how it was that Darwin's final paragraph describing the complexity of life within an 'entangled bank' paved the way for the emergence of ecology, a science now central to the consideration of a world dominated by biodiversity loss, climate change and sustainable development; and not least, how Darwin's science was influenced by his ethical world view, and in particular by his opposition to slavery. Here was so much that could be, indeed needed to be, explored. While half a century ago Theodore Dobzhansky had proclaimed that 'Nothing in biology makes sense except in the light of evolution', many philosophers today consider that the depth of Darwin's insight penetrates all areas of human thought and knowledge.

It seemed crucial that any celebrations would need to achieve a diverse public engagement around these many points of engagement. This would call on scientists, historians, artists and many others to share the explorations of the rich facets that Darwin's legacy underpins and to engage various sectors of society.

It was out of this early discussion that a proposal emerged which was to be led by the Natural History Museum, and it was something of an anathema to modern marketing convention. Yes, there would be a branded year with an identity mark (this finally emerged as Darwin200, www.darwin200.org.) Yes, it also had top-line messages about:

(a) how Darwin's ideas have stood the test of time

(b) how congruent they remain with the evidence of modern science

(c) how they underpin our knowledge and so are crucial to not just our understanding of both past life on Earth and our own origins, but also to the future of ourselves, our environment and our fragile planet.

What was different about the campaign was the appreciation that to achieve this we needed to encourage a diverse partnership of organisations which could both bring wide-ranging perspectives, and have the potential to reach different audiences. We needed to form a partnership which would be symbiotic.

The innovation team at the Natural History Museum which formed the secretariat to the Darwin200 partnership provided a number of key elements:

- the brand identity

- regular networking meetings for the growing number of partner organisations to share ideas, seek synergies and often to create small delivery partnerships within the wider programme

- a core website which listed and connected to the partners' websites, which also provided information and held a database of the partner's events

- a simple, monthly e-newsletter to partners.

The secretariat also produced regular events listings and press bulletins, based on the partners' collective activities, which were released to the press and media at regular intervals.

What had started as a discussion around how to address the risk of a highjacked level of public engagement emerged as a mechanism for partnership engagement which had many attractions. It was of course a partnership of convenience – the core secretariat was not giving out funds but it proved to be the case that, through association with the Darwin200 identity, some partners leveraged funding from a number of Trusts who had themselves partnered in Darwin200, including the Wellcome Trust, the Gulbenkian Foundation and the Heritage Lottery Fund. Partners did benefit in other ways from adopting the Darwin200 identity as a mark of endorsement. It meant that their work was clearly presented in the context of a recognised greater output from reputable partners. Then, because we were able to aggregate partners' outputs we could segment these, to focus for example on Darwin in the contemporary arts, or to look at partners in particular regions to support local press coverage. In this way all individual partners gained the benefit of wider engagement with the media.

So Darwin200 allowed many partners to create their own broad explorations of Darwin's legacy, within a context which gave them a larger platform for visibility while all could benefit from the added marketing potential that the aggregated efforts presented. Darwin's legacy is central to the work of the Natural History Museum, whose mission bridges both primary research and the wider communication of science to the public. Darwin200 being coordinated by a museum was important, and the Museum's position statement on evolution was a useful tool for partners who did not have scientific authority themselves, to help present and contextualise their work. Collectively, the partnership generated a wide reach – for example, the large number of arts projects gave reflections which were unexpected, and which were often picked up by the press in a way that communications from the 'usual suspect science organisations' were not.

This 'year of' had the advantage of some key dates, most notably Darwin's birthday on 12th February, and 24th November, the publication date of *Origin of Species.* These were major opportunities to aggregate partners' projects and focus mainstream interest. Meanwhile, the emerging research on how Darwin's character, social and ethical views affected his science ideas gave a more accessible and intimate approach which worked well with non-specialist media. Additionally and importantly, visibility of the year was also maintained by many partners aligning to the brand projects they did annually, such as the British Science Association and National Science Week, or the Shrewsbury Festival, and others, such as the Cambridge Darwin Festival, that were scheduled in the summer as simply the most clement and accessible time, but which attracted high-level interest and benefited from, as well as contributed to, the integrity of the Darwin200 brand.

Hosting the secretariat was important for the Natural History Museum. It occupies an important position in promoting science as part of culture, and Darwin200 allowed it to demonstrate its 'pivotal convening power' in bringing together the support for the Darwin celebrations from so many partners and sectors. This was handled with some sensitivity, regarding its role as a supportive partner that used its authority and position with integrity and trying to support the aspirations of all partners with equanimity, regardless of their size and position.

The Darwin200 partnership grew to include some 70 organisations in the UK who used the brand in their communications, and a further similar number who also created Darwin events, activities and publications which, while they did not use the brand, in one way or another engaged with the Darwin200 partners and benefited from the network of exchange. One of the important consequences of the visibility of the network is that it made it easy for organisations interested in engaging to have relatively easy access to expertise from the many disciplines interested in Darwin and his legacy. Darwin200 as a brand also allowed organisations to be more confident and brave in their programme outputs. As a result the mainstream BBC coverage was, for example, far richer than many had anticipated, and they were able to turn to their critics and say, 'yes, we did deal with the controversy between evolution and creation – we did it here, but look we were also able to do so much more'.

CHAPTER 15 COMMERCIAL AND FUNDRAISING ACTIVITIES AND THE RELATIONSHIP WITH MARKETING AND PR

Case study 15A: The fundraising campaign to save the Staffordshire Hoard

Sally Wrampling, Head of Policy and Strategy, the Art Fund

This shows how an unprecedented degree of local cooperation – and fast PR reaction – saved the day for a treasure trove. The campaign to save the Staffordshire Hoard in 2010 was a triumph – £3.3 million raised in just 14 weeks, including £900,000 from public donations. But it was a logistical challenge – a secret location, five local authorities, three museums and a national fundraising appeal. How did it all come together?

The discovery of the Anglo-Saxon treasure trove has been well-documented: uncovered by a metal detectorist on farmland near Lichfield in July 2009, and removed in secret by the British Museum 'flying squad' in order to protect the find-site. Before the Hoard was officially declared treasure, it was clear this was an unparalleled find of international importance, and one that could offer a unique opportunity to promote heritage, tourism and regeneration in the Midlands region. While the find was being valued, five local authorities from across the Midlands – Birmingham, Stoke-on-Trent, Staffordshire, Lichfield and Tamworth – gathered to discuss pooling resources, and it was agreed that the regions two largest museums, Birmingham Museum and Art Gallery and the Potteries Museum and Art Gallery, Stoke-on-Trent, would work together to jointly acquire the treasure. The museums contacted the Art Fund, the fundraising charity which has a history of leading successful campaigns to secure artworks and treasures for museums, to coordinate a public campaign. At the end of November, the Hoard was valued at £3,285,000, and a deadline of 17 April was set for raising the funds.

The campaign was planned during December. The Art Fund agreed to give a grant of £300,000 and the two museums' acquiring councils, Birmingham and Stoke-on-Trent, allocated £100,000 each, meaning the campaign could be launched with £500,000 in the pot. Dr David Starkey (TV historian) agreed to be the campaign's figurehead, and several well-known names were approached to lend their support at key moments along the way, including historian Tristram Hunt (now MP for Stoke-on-Trent Central), *Time Team*'s Tony Robinson, Rolling Stone Bill Wyman (a metal detector enthusiast) and 'national treasures' Michael Palin and Dame Judi Dench.

The campaign was launched at a press conference on 13 January 2010. David Starkey gave a rousing speech and coined the term 'gangland bling' to describe the Hoard's dazzling beauty and links to bloody warfare. The media coverage that followed was widespread, and helped to launch the campaign microsite (www.artfund.org/hoard), with an online giving function. Branded donation boxes were placed in key sites, including the British Museum, and Birmingham Museum secured free billboard space across the city during February, which boosted regional donations. Almost £650,000 was banked in the first four weeks.

Items from the Hoard went on display at the Potteries Museum for 23 days in February and March: 52,500 people visited, and over £150,000 was donated locally. Three weeks after the main campaign launch the Art Fund mailed its 80,000 members to encourage donations, and organised a door-drop to selected postcodes in the Midlands area.

PR moments were planned and seized upon throughout the campaign. HRH Prince Charles and Camilla, Duchess of Cornwall, visited the Potteries Museum display in February, giving a significant PR boost. Events in Parliament gave MPs and Peers the opportunity to donate and be photographed with objects from the Hoard, and the three main party leaders (including David Cameron and Gordon Brown) issued supportive quotes. Late in February the Art Fund brought together some of the leading experts to discuss the emerging theories about what the Hoard could be and who buried it, which led to a Tony Robinson-penned article and spread, exclusively in the *Sunday Times*.

In total, £900,000 was donated by members of the public (£640,000 from Art Fund members and supporters) – the highest sum ever donated by ordinary people to a museum acquisition campaign. Over £600,000 was raised from charitable trusts and foundations, including £200,000 from the Garfield Weston Foundation and £200,000 from the Sir Siegmund Warburg Settlement. The single largest application was made to the National Heritage Memorial Fund (NHMF), the government's 'fund of last resort' for heritage items at risk. On 24 March the NHMF awarded £1,285,000 – the amount needed to close the gap, three weeks before the final deadline.

The Hoard is now jointly owned by the two museums, and items are being displayed on rotation at both sites while the Hoard is systematically catalogued and conserved. The museums and the five local authorities are now working on Phase 2 of the campaign – to raise a further £1.7 million to fund future conservation and interpretation of the

Hoard, including the creation of a 'Mercian Trail' across the region to highlight the history of Mercia. (See Figure 15.2 on p. 222.)

Case study 15B: Muncaster Castle, thriving on events

Muncaster Castle is a medium-sized 'stately home' situated an hour-and-a-half off the M6 motorway, in an isolated location on the west coast of the Lake District National Park in northern England. The castle is owned and managed by Iona and Peter Frost-Pennington. Here they describe how building their events programme has met with success.

Despite this remoteness, over the last ten years Muncaster has consistently attracted over 80,000 visitors a year, far more than similar historic properties much nearer to large centres of population.

Muncaster offers a good blend of attractions, delivering an enjoyable whole-day visit. These include dramatic woodland gardens, famous for their rhododendrons and other Himalayan plants, the World Owl Centre and a MeadowVole Maze as well as shops, cafés, playgrounds and more. Muncaster makes the most of good PR and special events whenever it can. This has undoubtedly helped to increase and maintain visitor numbers at a viable level.

For example, Muncaster is known as the home of 'Tomfoolery' due to the original 'Tom Fool' living there around 400 years ago, and some people think he still haunts the castle to the present day. This leads to lots of good PR stories, and every Whit Week holiday the Castle hosts a five-day 'Festival of Fools' in Tom's honour. Jesters gather at Muncaster from all over the world and compete to be crowned the next 'Fool of Muncaster'. The current incumbent is Mr Spin from Adelaide in Australia.

Other special events include a 'Feast of Flowers' in early May, 'Summer of Fun' every day in August and a mediaeval re-enactment weekend over the August Bank Holiday. The 'Christmas at the Castle' festivities are expanding each year, especially the popular candlelit Victorian tours with servants from 1885. Muncaster's biggest event, however, is 'Halloween Week'. Over eight days at the end of October a garden lighting scheme installed a few years ago ('Darkest Muncaster') allows thousands of visitors to enjoy spooky castle ghost tours after dark and even the Scary Maze if they dare! Muncaster makes the most of its haunted heritage, and Halloween fun has grown like Topsy, with many visitors dressing up in the spirit of the event.

Muncaster has deliberately aimed to distance itself from the traditional 'please don't touch' way of presenting historic properties to the public and has deliberately gone for a more family-friendly and entertaining approach, especially during peak school holiday periods. The intention, however, is not to 'dumb down' but still to appeal to the more discerning visitor – and this has, on the whole, been achieved. Muncaster looks to the future, while still honouring the past without living in it, and looks to harness new technology when possible to improve and enhance the visitor experience.

Iona Frost-Pennington, a member of the Pennington family who have lived at Muncaster for over 800 years, runs Muncaster with help from her husband Peter, who co-ordinates and runs the special events and PR. Peter says 'The special events really bring the place alive and generate great PR opportunities which consistently get noticed by the media, both locally and further afield. These activities significantly enhance the bottom line and also the economic effects deliver benefits much further afield as Muncaster employs performers both locally and from all over the world, as well as buying more goods and services from local suppliers. Our main aim, however, is to keep the public happy – and they seem to enjoy our gently anarchic approach to presenting our historic assets in as entertaining a way as possible.' (See Figure 15.5 on p. 229.)

Case study 15C: Financing marketing through grants at the Scottish Mining Museum

Gillian Rankin, Marketing and Events Officer

When I first started working as Marketing Officer at the Scottish Mining Museum, in January 2005, I wondered how I would ever adapt to having such restricted marketing budgets to work with. Having come from a financial services institution, running high-profile events and advertising campaigns where money seemed to be no object, I was sure I would struggle to grow the visitor numbers and increase the profile of this wonderful place. But it quickly became a passion for me and I enjoyed finding new ways to reach new and existing markets without breaking the bank.

However, less than two years later the museum lost an element of its key funding and, as is most often the case, the marketing budget was first to be cut – by a whopping 50%.

The only way forward was to apply for every grant we were eligible for, which proved extremely time-consuming but worth all the hours (sometimes days!) of effort completing forms and supplying figures and plans. We applied for small grants from around £500 to main grants of up to £40,000 for various projects, most of which were successful (thankfully) and enabled us to run special events targeted at both new and existing audiences, and to upgrade our external and internal signage which raised the profile of the museum to passing traffic on the busy A7 Edinburgh to the Borders road.

In May 2010 we were successful in our application for a grant of £15,000 to subsidise our marketing and events programme. We were able to put in place a marketing plan for the whole year which included brand new events linked to our collection, promoted through radio and press advertising campaigns targeting new and existing audiences, both local to us and throughout the coalfield communities of Scotland. Evaluation is extremely important, and we carry out face-to-face visitor surveys at each key event (and on other busy non-event days too). The information we capture tells us if the visitors came purely for the event or to visit the museum itself, how they heard about it, where they travelled from, and so on, evaluating the success of the subsidised marketing plan.

Already our visitor numbers have increased in the year to date, and with six more events still to take place over the next few months, accompanied by a further radio and press advertising campaign, we hope we will finish the year (2010) on a high note. It doesn't end there though. The funding only lasts for one year and then it's back to the grindstone, seeking out new and innovative ways to bring in visitors with little or no budget! It's a constant struggle but hopefully one day all that will change.

CHAPTER 16 COMMUNICATING IN A CRISIS

Case study 16A: Aboriginal barks at Melbourne Museum – the public relations challenge

Dr J. Patrick Greene, Chief Executive Officer of Museum Victoria in Melbourne, Australia, describes an incident that put the museum into news headlines around the world, and caused shockwaves within the profession. It required careful directorial and PR handling on many different fronts simultaneously.

Museum Victoria is the State of Victoria's museum organisation, comprising the Melbourne Museum, Scienceworks, the Immigration Museum, the Royal Exhibition Building World Heritage Site and IMAX Melbourne (museumvictoria.com.au). In 2004 it celebrated its 150th anniversary with a range of activities throughout the year taking place at all the venues. One project, the display of bark etchings produced by Aboriginal people in Victoria in the mid-nineteenth century, proved to be a contentious issue that threatened to harm the Museum's reputation and to place in jeopardy its relations with Aboriginal communities. It required considerable efforts to produce a resolution of the matter, including careful handling of public relations aspects.

There is every reason to think that the three objects in question were given willingly to John Hunter Kerr, the settler who collected them. They were loaned to Museum Victoria in 2004 by the current owners, the British Museum and the Royal Botanic Gardens, Kew. As the exhibition neared the end of its season, Emergency Declarations – to keep the objects in Australia – made under the Aboriginal and Torres Strait Islander Heritage Protection Act 1984 were issued at the request of Elders of the Dja Dja Wurrung and Jupagalk Peoples of northern Victoria. The Museum was bound to honour its obligations to return the objects to Britain as set out in the loan agreement. It was also obliged to comply with the law under which the Emergency Declarations had been made. Returning the objects would have incurred penalties that include heavy fines and imprisonment. Whatever the outcome, the Museum was faced with a necessity to communicate the issues clearly, and the public relations team was crucial to that role. Headlines quickly appeared in the local press such as 'Kooris grab museum art – Brits seek legal advice' (*Herald Sun*, 27 July 2004); 'Aboriginal group fights for rights to its "crown jewels"' (*Weekend Australian*, 31 July 2004). The Museum's response was to stick to the facts and to state clearly the essential issues: that we had to honour the legally binding loan agreements, and that the loan had been supported by an appropriate representative of the Aboriginal people.

The issue resulted in numerous requests for interviews, particularly by radio stations, and sometimes by newspapers. We decided to be sparing in our response, carefully choosing when to participate and when to decline, particularly when there was no new information to add. There would be only one spokesperson for the Museum and, as CEO, it was my responsibility. We would keep to the facts, stressing the Museum's proud record of working with indigenous communities, emphasising our obligation to return the objects, and stating our concern that future loans would be placed in jeopardy. Passions and concerns were running high, and both British and Australian governments became involved. The case began to attract worldwide media attention.

I was advised by our small PR team at every stage. Six months of discussion failed to produce a solution. Eventually Museum Victoria went to court, essentially to question the way in which legislation was being applied. The courts upheld the Museum's position and passed the decision to the government of Victoria, upon which the loans were released for return to the UK at the end of May 2005.

The Museum had successfully discharged its obligations but there was no sense of triumph – quite the reverse, in fact, as morale within the Museum's own indigenous staff had suffered. As CEO, I made sure that I met with the staff throughout to explain clearly my view of the issues and to hear their concerns. It took time for the wounds to heal, but the willingness to engage in difficult meetings and to be open and honest made recovery easier. It had been a complex episode that raised complex issues for museums internationally, and this complexity was not easy to communicate.

I am grateful for the efforts of our PR team in working very hard to limit the damage of the barks case. It required enormous efforts on the part of very many people, such as my Executive Management Team colleagues, the Museum's Board and its President, our legal advisors and the indigenous staff. We were supported throughout by the Museum's Aboriginal Cultural Heritage Committee. The amount of work needed to deal with a difficult issue such as this is prodigious.

Case study 16B: The *Cutty Sark* fire – a fast-moving media crisis

On 21 May 2007, the historic ship Cutty Sark, *preserved at Greenwich, was discovered ablaze. As one of the last remaining tea clippers from the age of sail, and positioned within easy reach of the UK media, the story broke early in the morning, became huge, and followed events live throughout the day. Richard Doughty, Chief Executive of the Cutty Sark Trust, found himself under the spotlight as events unfolded. This is his story.*

Cutty Sark's international reputation drew the media like moths to a flame. Within an hour of the fire story breaking, the public space surrounding the ship was choked with satellite vans and reporters. Richard Doughty gave his first interview to James Naughtie on the BBC Radio 4 *Today* programme from a train, a full 90 minutes before arriving in Greenwich.

Open lines of communication with the emergency services dealing with the incident meant that Richard had a good grasp of the situation. He had been told the ship was '100% alight from stem to stern'. This knowledge influenced his initial response. He deliberately used short, succinct sound-bites in all of his interviews. These included statements like:

> **Cutty Sark is one of those rare things which are truly emblematic and intrinsically inspiring. Quite simply she is a piece of history which cannot be remade.**

> **When original fabric is lost, the touch of the craftsman is lost, history itself is lost.**

> **These are the timbers and iron frames which sailed to the South China Seas. They are the very essence of this historic ship.**

The Trust used a tight team to respond to the media. Only Richard Doughty (Chief Executive and Project Champion), Chris Livett (Trustee) and Stephen Archer (Marketing Director) were authorised to give interviews.

This team consistently gave the same story, and used the media as a platform to launch a public appeal for fire recovery funds. Also all three representatives remained on site for the lifetime of the story. This approach freed up the operational team, led by Julia Parker, to deal with the practicalities of assisting the emergency services. In addition, Doughty seconded other project staff to assist his Head Office team, who fielded a huge volume of calls and enquiries over the next 48–60 hours.

The story was given greater attention because it was a quiet news day, and coverage was assisted by the fact that local residents had captured early footage of the fire on mobile phones and cameras. As a result, very dramatic images were available for all the breakfast news programmes.

The 'mystery' of what had caused the fire helped to keep the story alive – Was it arson? Who was driving the white car spotted at the scene? Interest was kept alive by high-profile visits from HRH The Duke of Edinburgh (the Founder President of 'The Cutty Sark Society') and from the Government's Secretary of State.

Richard Doughty's footnote: The response from home and abroad was phenomenal and resulted in over £2 million being donated to the Trust. Conservation began immediately and can be tracked on the website www.cuttysark.org.uk, where regular updates and photographs are on display. The conservation project is scheduled for completion late in 2011.

Case study 16C: Floods and loss, Tullie House Museum and Art Gallery

Tullie House Museum is a much-loved building in historic Carlisle in the north of England. The twenty-first century has not been kind to it. First it was swept by damaging flood water. Five years later it was swept by enthusiasm for an astonishingly beautiful Roman helmet unearthed in the locality. It sprang into action to raise an enormous sum, only to find that destiny had other plans. Director Hilary Wade reports.

On Saturday, 8 January 2005, Carlisle suffered its worst flooding in living memory. Over 1900 homes and businesses were flooded. At Tullie House Museum and Art Gallery, flooding affected one of the galleries, the Millennium Gallery. Because of the flooding there was no electricity or telephone system throughout Carlisle. Nevertheless some 18 staff came in to help with the removal of the displays from the cases and transfer the collections to a safe location. The next day they 'bailed out' the Gallery.

In the overall scale of the disaster to Carlisle, what happened at Tullie House was insignificant. 3000 people were made homeless for up to 12 months and three lost their lives. We managed to be very self-sufficient, used the skills and knowledge of the staff and coped without seeking help from the Emergency Services. We felt in this type of situation, it was important to keep a low profile.

Five years later, in 2010, a situation arose regarding the auction of the Crosby Garrett Roman Helmet, which was found in Cumbria by a metal detectorist. Tullie House ran a major fundraising campaign in the three weeks before the auction on 7 October 2010. Media and public interest in the sale of the Helmet was unprecedented. In preparation for the auction at Christie's, we had to prepare two press releases: one saying how delighted we were to acquire the Helmet and the second to say how disappointed we were to have been unsuccessful at auction.

To add to the pressure, on the day the Senior Curator was at the auction house, and the rest of the staff (including me) were at the Museum with the media, watching a live showing of the auction. So it was extremely important to coordinate the message to the media, as well as to those who had supported our fundraising campaign.

Tullie House was outbid at the auction. Despite a pre-sale estimate of 'only' £300,000, the Helmet was sold for £2million and we had to drop out of the bidding at £1.7million. There was then an hour to prepare for a press conference. Our marketing team did a fantastic job in ensuring we were well briefed and that we were prepared to deal with the media's questions and queries.

Case study 16D: More flooding, Birmingham Museums and Art Gallery

The art collections in Birmingham are among the finest in the country. Carmel Girling, Deputy Head of Marketing and Communications, Birmingham Museums and Art Gallery, explains what happened when water poured through the galleries – during public opening hours.

In terms of PR crisis management, the worst thing to do is to hide from dealing with it, with denial. It never works. Where emergency services are called in for whatever reason, this is likely to be picked up by journalists because they listen in to call-outs. They can also be alerted by members of the public – 'citizen journalists' with mobile phones and instant access to the internet, which means the story is out before you have time to respond.

My advice would be to make sure the management team understands the need to respond swiftly to press, before rumours and speculation set in. Issue an early statement, even if it's a holding one, and create time for a more detailed, considered response by telling press when your next briefing or statement will be.

Many years ago we had a flood in the gallery, sending water cascading through the building at enormous speed. Children had been seen playing around the area but we couldn't be sure this was the cause of the hose exploding from the wall. Museum assistants on the floor responded swiftly; the alarm was raised, and the building cleared. Arriving simultaneously with the fire services were the press. Thankfully, the management team had the presence of mind to call for press office support immediately, in the midst of the emergency.

I could see for myself the extent of what was happening, with staff running through the building carrying paintings and other works. The painting store and gallery were in some real danger as water cascaded down the stairs, down walls, and along electrical channels. It felt like a worst case scenario for any gallery.

We explained to waiting press that they would get a full statement, and gave them a time. Meanwhile, our response was to say that we were looking into what had happened but were still dealing with the situation. As agreed, and when we were prepared with a full statement on 'staff rescuing artworks from flood', we held a press briefing on the front steps of the museum. The story had great immediacy, and turned from the potential 'vandal damage at museum' story to a more positive line.

The press tend to run to a format in such situations:

(a) What has happened?

(b) What is the damage?

(c) How did it happen?

(d) What was your response?

(e) Who is responsible?

(f) How will you prevent it happening again?

To respond swiftly and honestly will be much more appreciated in the long run. If you can, follow up at a later date with a positive story, highlighting the results – it helps to draw a line under it.

Case study 16E: Earthquake rocks Canterbury Museum, Christchurch

When a powerful earthquake hit Christchurch, New Zealand, Karin Stahel, Communications Manager of Canterbury Museum, found herself handling a series of actions aimed at containing and satisfying press interest.

Following the magnitude 7.1 earthquake that hit Canterbury, New Zealand on 4 September 2010, it was important for us to get information out quickly about the state of the Museum building and collections, but even more important that this information be accurate. A statement as simple as 'The collections and building are being assessed for damage, and more information will be provided as soon as it is available' was enough in the hours immediately following the quake to assure the public and media that action was being taken and that they would be kept informed.

Having a designated spokesperson is essential in an emergency, along with a backup if that person cannot be contacted. In the case of Canterbury Museum, the Acting Director was in regular contact with the Museum's Communications Manager in the hours following the quake. Once the building and damage had been assessed, a short media statement was drafted and distributed to local and national press, radio and television contacts. Internet news sites, the local council website and the Museum's own website were also important channels for the distribution of up-to-date information.

Once decisions had been made on a likely reopening date for the Museum, managers spoke with each of their staff members at home to keep them briefed. In the weeks following the quake, the Museum's website was utilised as the primary channel to provide information about the situation, from reopening dates and times to changes in exhibitions and programmes.

All staff should be informed by their managers to direct any media enquiries to the organisation's communications staff or designated spokesperson in the first instance, and to do so without giving their own version of events or opinions.

On 22 February 2011, Christchurch experienced a more severe earthquake which destroyed and damaged many buildings in the city.

CHAPTER 17 RESEARCH AND EVALUATION IN MARKETING AND PR

Case study 17A: Benchmarking research in action at the Association of Leading Visitor Attractions

Alan Love, BDRC Continental

Here are a few considerations that will help you design the research you need to build a clear idea of how visitors regard the experience of visiting the museum:

◻ What issue is your organisation facing?

   ◻ *The answer determines the research objectives.*

◻ What information will help you make a better decision?

   ◻ *The answer helps you focus on essentials and exclude 'nice to knows'.*

◻ Who holds that information? Visitors to the museum? Non-visitors? Members? Café users? Current temporary exhibition visitors? Families? Enthusiasts? Staff? Stakeholders?

   ◻ *The answer helps you decide on the target audience for the research – 'Universe', or 'Population' in jargon. This allows you to focus resources on people who are most relevant to the decision.*

◻ How can a representative cross-section of this audience be reached?

   ◻ *The answer helps you focus on how to undertake sampling and data collection. A representative sample is better than a big one.*

   ◻ *Sample size has (almost) nothing to do with population size. Sample size is determined by the degree of precision needed; the need to read results within segments; and your resources.*

   ◻ *Consider where and when to sample. Consider how to reach the audience. Consider your resources.*

   ◻ *Leaving questionnaires for visitors to pick up is never representative.*

   ◻ *Staff or volunteers require training in sampling and questioning. Staff and volunteers on survey duty are there to collect information about the visitor behaviour and attitudes, not to extol the museum. They must accept even unfair criticism without argument. Do you have enough staff or volunteers to survey in the peaks when the museum is under most stress?*

   ◻ *You can involve a professional research consultancy. Half a dozen do lots of museum research in Britain and know what they are doing. Hundreds of others are very good in their chosen sectors – but not necessarily museums.*

How can information be marshalled to inform the decisions?

- *This ranges from simple answer counts to advanced statistical analysis. Think about this early. It affects question and sampling design.*

- *Who is the audience for the results? Do they need detail? Are they comfortable with numbers? Do they prefer ideas to information?*

- *How do these results compare with others?*

And this is where benchmarking comes in – how do we compare?

- Internal: Do I do *this* better than I do *that*?

- External: Do *I* do this better than *they* do this?

- Historic: Do I *do* this better than I *did* this last year?

Here are some examples based on ALVA's Quality Benchmarking Survey 2009–10. The sample size per museum is 300. The sample size across the *c.*15 museums exceeds 5,000, and the sample across the *c.*20 heritage attractions surveyed exceeds 7,000. The examples show the percentage of visitors who give a rating of excellent on specific aspects of the visit.

Internal benchmarking in one museum

43% of visitors rate the friendliness of the museum's staff as excellent.

22% of shop-users rate the friendliness of the museum's shop staff as excellent.

35% of shop-users rate the efficiency of the museum's staff as excellent.

So, visitors think the museum's staff do better on friendliness than they do on efficiency. And friendliness is not so good in the shop. But is the museum's friendliness good enough?

External benchmarking

Across all 15 or so museums, 54% of visitors rate the friendliness of the staff as excellent.

And 56% of visitors rate staff friendliness as excellent at the 20 or so heritage attractions.

So, our museum is not a pace setter in having friendly staff.

Historic benchmarking

This year 43% rate the friendliness of the museum's staff as excellent.

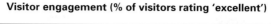

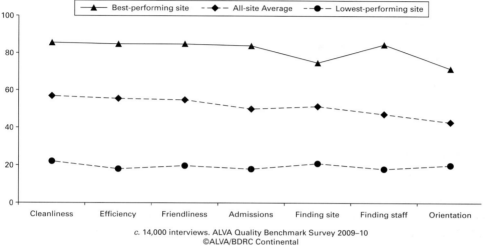

Figure A.1 Visitor services, ALVA Quality Benchmark Survey 2009–10 (courtesy of BDRC Continental)

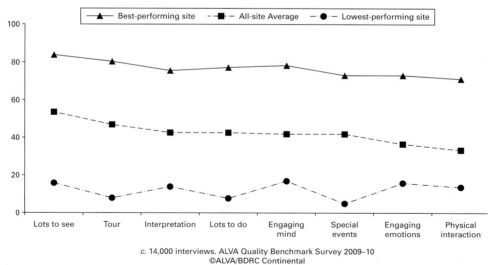

Figure A.2 Visitor engagement, ALVA Quality Benchmark Survey 2009–10 (courtesy of BDRC Continental)

Last year 40% rated the friendliness of the museum's staff as excellent.

It appears to be going in the right direction, but it would have needed a rise to 48% this year for the result to be significant.

So on this measure too there is work to be done.

One can argue that customer opinion is a soft measure and in challenging times one should focus on hard measures of business performance. But this is a matter of 'both/and' not 'either/or'.

There is a positive correlation of between staff friendliness and willingness to recommend. Other research suggests that 100 recommendations can yield *c*.25 visits.

A clear understanding of customer perceptions allows informed decision-making on the investment priorities that have highest ROI in terms of new business generated, and in terms of costs that might be controlled where there is over-performance against customer need.

Case study 17B: Evaluation of the Dale Chihuly Exhibition 'Gardens of Glass' at Kew

It is a requirement of forward planning that reasons for past success and failure are thoroughly understood. Here is a summary of the evaluation carried out by the Corporate Communications team at the Royal Botanic Gardens, Kew, following their exhibition of the work of US sculptor Dale Chihuly entitled 'Gardens of Glass'. The evaluation was led by Tina Houlton, Head of Marketing. There was a review of results in all areas, measured against expectations and previous performance, and supported by various detailed charts and tables not included here, and a final financial analysis that looked at profit and loss as well as mission objectives. The exhibition had been a costly one to present, and involved significant financial risk. The evaluation was made more difficult by virtue of the fact that the exhibition was not freestanding with a separate admission charge – but was scattered throughout the gardens and included in the general admission ticket to the site as a whole, which was free to children and Friends of Kew.

The challenge

The business plan identified a risk of a shortfall of £398,290 between the actual cost incurred by mounting the exhibition, and the income derived from the usual admission receipts. This meant that the business plan called for attracting 91,983 *extra* visitors over a period of seven months, delivering an up-weighted retail and other secondary-spend opportunities and attracting a significant sponsor in order to make the exhibition financially viable.

Visitor satisfaction

There were insufficient funds to commission a dedicated visitor survey. Evaluation was based on feedback received from visitors during the exhibition via the normal visitor satisfaction survey conducted on exit; from complaints received; from a questionnaire on the visitor map provided on entrance; and from the comments books placed at strategic points onsite. (These could be compared with similar questionnaires, comments books, and records of complaints in previous years.)

On key measures, visitor satisfaction scores for the relevant period (28 May 2005 to 15 January 2006) rose slightly in terms of enjoyment, value for money, site facilities and information. Whilst these changes were not huge, they should be placed in context of high baseline scores enjoyed by Kew and they indicate a positive perception of the overall experience.

Visitor satisfaction scores

	Chihuly period	2004	2003
Enjoyment	96%	95.6%	93.9%
Value for money	81.4%	79.7%	80.1%
Restaurants	77%	77.7%	76.4%
Shops	91.7%	92.1%	92%
Information	90.2	89.1%	86.8%

However, these figures reflected the attraction as a whole and not specifically the exhibition. A quantitative measuring device focused specifically on the Chihuly exhibition was included in the August visitor map. Of 419 responses, 87.1% were either very satisfied or satisfied compared with 12.9% not satisfied. In the comment books, 2,482 positive comments were received and 660 negative comments. The majority of negative comments were identified as coming from long-standing members of Kew who felt the exhibition was out of keeping with the role of a botanic garden. Follow-up communication with the membership base helped manage these comments down to more acceptable levels in the latter half of the exhibition.

Admissions

It was the most ambitious public programme of events and activities ever offered at Kew. 890,634 visitors attended during the Chihuly period, 14.3% up on budget, and 26.4% up on the same period the previous year.

Paying visitors were up 11.2% on budget and 24.1% on the same period in the previous year. Five special evening openings in October achieved 18,612 actual attendance against 10,000 forecast. The four 'private view' events attracted a total of 1,293 guests and generated £45,890 in sales.

Retail sales

Income from shop sales was £448,170, 22% up on budget and 139.7% up on the same period in the previous year. The average customer transaction was up 12.9%, with an average conversion rate up from 20.6% to 21.4% (i.e. conversion of browsers to actual shoppers), and average spend per visitor up 16%. A special additional shop for the period of the exhibition generated sales of £273,110, against a target of £192,000 (+42.2%). This represents 14.3% of total retail sales over the period. Sales of the commemorative book were 4,103 units (£81,506) – the best-selling product that year, and the highest ever unit sales of a book title at Kew. Total sales of Studio Glass stood at £136,405 (42 pieces), at prices from £2,500 to £6,000.

Education

A total of 56,049 students accompanied by 8,926 adults visited Kew during the period, of whom 6,184 students came especially to see the Chihuly exhibition. A family science show attracted approximately 230 people.

Approximately 15,000 'Let's Explore Chihuly' leaflets (aimed at children aged 4–10) were picked up. The education department at Kew offered an extensive arts programme to schools – more ambitious than for any previous exhibition. Following oral feedback from teachers, and a perceived success, three new arts teachers were engaged to develop future visual and performance arts programmes for schools. The linking of science and art through the education activities was commended by the Science Learning Centre, London.

Press and PR

Press coverage for the launch of the exhibition was equivalent in advertising value to an expenditure of £280,719. The total amount of exhibition-specific editorial coverage for the run of the exhibition was £1,005,090 in equivalent advertising value, with 307 press articles generated to a circulation of 52,113,231 people. Highlights included features in *The Times*, the *Independent,* and the *Sunday Telegraph*, with international coverage including a full page in the *International Herald Tribune* and in *Time Magazine*, and coverage on CNN's arts programme *360 degrees*.

Marketing communications

Total marketing spend was £340,000 against a budget provision of £397,100. (As the exhibition progressed it was realised that visitor targets were on track and the contingency amount did not need to be spent.) In the event, total spend was only £6,000 (0.2%) more than the same period the previous year.

The campaign was broken into four mini-campaigns: Summer: £244,000 (£218,000 Media plus £26,000 Design and Production); Autumn: £44,000 (£34,000 plus £10,000); Christmas: £39,500 (£31,000 plus £8,500); Last chance to see: £12,000 (£9,000 plus £3,000). This achieved a marketing spend of £0.32 per visitor.

There were five bursts of paid media activity across the four campaigns. A wide variety of mediums were used. Predominantly, the spend was on outdoor and press advertising, supported by leafleting, radio and online advertising, but a range of stand-out (more prominent, and therefore more expensive) media was used. The target audiences were identified as Art Lovers, Culture Vultures, Families with Children, and Empty Nesters (40+ people who no longer do activities with their children).

Sponsorship

Significant sponsorship was provided by GlaxoSmithKlein. A total of eight sponsor events took place during the exhibition period and a Chihuly piece was installed at the sponsor's headquarters. Feedback from the sponsor indicated that the exhibition was very popular with their staff and met their objectives of bringing Chihuly to new audiences, corporate brand exposure, image enhancement and involving their staff and partners. A full sponsorship evaluation was undertaken by the Development team.

Volunteer Guides tours and handling sessions

Volunteer Guides 'Glass handling' sessions attracted a total of 4,800 participants. A filmshow as part of the exhibition: 'Chihuly on Film' was very popular with visitors and offered a new form of visual interpretation for Kew.

Financial outcomes

1   Reminder: In order to achieve the financial target, 91,983 extra visitors were needed. The exhibition attracted 890,634 day visitors; this was an increase of 26.4% over the same period in the previous year, representing 186,042 extra visitors and making a significant profit for the exhibition.

2   An additional 10,000 visitors were forecast to attend the special evening events. Actual attendance was 18,612 visitors, giving a grand total of 909,246 visitors to the exhibition (including 47,713 group visitors). This equates to an additional 204,612 visitors on the same period in the previous year.

3   The exhibition, together with all the supplementary activities, generated over £400,000 actual profit.

4   The four 'private view' events attracted a total of 1,293 guests and generated £45,890 in sales, which broke even. Budgeted income from private view events was £10,000.

5   Retail sales contribution yielded £448,170 additional revenue, 22% up on budget and 139.7% up on same period in the previous year.

6   The special temporary shop generated sales of £273,110, against a target of £192,000 (+42.2%). This represents 14.3% of total retail sales over the period.

7   Total editorial coverage exceeded all previous performance.

Qualitative outcomes

The exhibition was judged to have attracted a new audience segment: a significantly higher percentage of young professionals (25–35 year old couples) and that group will be more likely to visit Kew in the future. It was considered to have changed perceptions of Kew from 'just a garden' to something more relevant to a wider audience. It was recognised as having attracted a more arts-based audience, supporting future aspirations to open up Kew's art collection, including opening the new Gallery of Botanical Art.

Key lessons learnt

■   The exhibition had been agreed, budgeted and forecast 24 months ahead. There was insufficient information available at that time, meaning that original forecasts for visitor admissions and installation costs had to be revised later. Initial business plans for projects on this scale should include inflation within the costs. Costs should be reviewed as more details come to light in order to enable a profitability check. More detailed research and costing was recommended for future projects.

■   Ambitious exhibitions and activities help to widen the audience and open people's perceptions of Kew as a place that is relevant for them. Once they visit there is an opportunity to reinforce other messages about Kew's work.

■   Managing the perceptions of existing members is also critical to success. Anticipating and agreeing the response to a negative reaction should be part of the plan.

- A blockbuster attraction like Gardens of Glass presents strong opportunities to attract major sponsors and to link educational, retail, events and activities within a unifying theme.

- Gardens of Glass presented the opportunity to experiment with late-night opening, which proved successful.

- Seconding staff from other duties to dedicate themselves to organising the exhibition proved successful. (There is no Exhibitions department at Kew.)

- Making a senior member of staff 'project champion' ensured that the exhibition was led effectively.

Case study 17C: Measuring social media success – advice from the Tate

Here is some advice from Pete Gomori, Marketing Manager, Tate Modern and Jesse Ringham, Digital Communications Manager, Tate.

First you should clearly define what the purpose is of using social media for your organisation. Do bear in mind that to produce a really successful and well-followed social media platform it can be resource-heavy, depending on what your aims are. Remember that, as with email, just because you have 10,000 people on your list, that doesn't mean that 10,000 people read your email every week.

There are a number of key metrics that we use to measure the success of our social media pages:

- ROI/sales
- interaction levels (e.g. comments on Facebook)
- sharing or advocacy (re-tweets, likes, trending, reposting and embedding)
- visits (people coming to your page)
- traffic generation (looking at our web traffic and seeing where it comes from)
- number of followers
- new users (e.g. looking out for any spikes)
- demographics of social media users
- actual footfall and sales.

When you have defined what your aims are, these metrics can help you to find out whether you've succeeded. In other words, if you're looking to generate customer feedback so you can improve your offer, then the level of interactions can be a useful tool, and 'revenue generated' isn't such a relevant metric. If you're looking to drive people through to your website, then measuring how much comes straight from your social media is important.

Clearly if your venue sells tickets, the ultimate scenario for a Facebook and Twitter page would be hundreds of thousands of highly engaged fans buying exhibition tickets or gift shop items. But don't forget that it's just another tool in the marketing mix – so to judge its success on sales alone would be unfair. In addition, people don't generally use Twitter for shopping in the same way that they might respond to an email.

The best way to measure success is to keep an eye on the metrics, decide which ones are most important to you, and cross-reference this with surveys asking people what marketing materials they have used. Email bulletins used to be an insignificant percentage of our audience – now they are one of our key tools that people mention when we ask how they found out about the exhibitions at Tate. The same could happen with social media in time.

Sales are important to measure, but it's important to remember the branding benefits of social media. Even if you don't make loads of sales directly out of a social media page, wouldn't you still rather have hundreds, even thousands of people signed up to your brand, getting news from you and potentially virally sharing content? One day you might have a project that you want to share with a wide audience, perhaps asking for user-generated content, and then the more people you have on channels like this the better. It makes it hard to measure return on investment, but we need to just see it as another part of the marketing mix.

Through increased activity on social media networks, Tate aims to achieve the following goals:

- Be one of the world's top cultural social media platforms
- Engage current audiences in new ways and build online communities
- Communicate through many new voices from across the organisation
- Distribute our content where audiences are active online
- Drive traffic to the Tate website
- Drive footfall to the four Tate galleries
- Integrate our social media channels seamlessly into our overall gallery marketing campaigns
- Generate sales across our income streams
- Encourage fans to act as advocates for Tate
- Build developmental audiences
- Develop partnership as a way of growing our following.

What will your objectives be?

INDEX